Beyond Monopoly

Terence C. Halliday

Beyond Monopoly

Lawyers, State Crises, and Professional Empowerment

RECEIVED
DEC - 4 1998
MSU - LIBRARY

The University of Chicago Press   Chicago and London

TERENCE C. HALLIDAY is a research fellow and chair, executive committee on academic affairs, at the American Bar Foundation. He also lectures on sociology and politics in the College at the University of Chicago.

KF
334
.C52
C544
1987

The University of Chicago Press, Chicago 60637
The University of Chicago Press, Ltd., London

© 1987 by The University of Chicago
All rights reserved. Published 1987
Printed in the United States of America

96 95 94 93 92 91 90 89 88 87   5 4 3 2 1

Library of Congress Cataloging-in-Publication Data

Halliday, Terence C. (Terence Charles)
  Beyond monopoly.

  Includes bibliographies and index.
  1. Chicago Bar Association—Political activity.   2. Bar associations—United States—Political activity.   3. Trade and professional associations—United States—Political activity.
4. Sociological jurisprudence.   I. Title.
KF334.C52C544   1987   340′.06′077311   86-30867
ISBN 0-226-31389-1

To the memory of my father, Charles William Halliday

"The establishment of a right relationship between knowledge and power is the central problem of modern democracy."

A. M. Carr-Saunders and P. A. Wilson
The Professions, 1933

Contents

Acknowledgments   ix
Introduction   xi

Part One   **Knowledge and Power**
                  1   Professions and Governability   3
                  2   Knowledge Mandates and Political Mobilization   28

Part Two   **Bases of Collective Professional Influence**
                  3   Constructing Professional Authority:
                      The Chicago Case   59
                  4   Constructing Professional Authority:
                      Portfolios of Resources   101
                  5   The Contradictions of Inclusiveness   119

Part Three   **Spheres of Influence**
                  6   The Autonomy of the Court System   145
                  7   The Normative Economy of Judicial Control   175
                  8   Crises of Rights   219
                  9   Fiscal Crisis   261
                  10 The Advance of Legal Rationalization
                      in the United States   284

Part Four   **Parameters of Professional Politics**
                  11 Transcending Inclusiveness between
                      Stalemate and Oligarchy   309
                  12 Established and Civic Professionalism   345

                  Index   377

Acknowledgments

In the course of research and writing, I have incurred many debts. First must go appreciation to John Heinz and Edward Laumann, who invited me to administer their cross-sectional survey of the Chicago bar and then allowed me a broad mandate to develop my own research program to respond in part to the findings of that project. Edward Laumann bombarded me with ideas, relentlessly pressed for systematic data sources, and urged me to explore more thoroughly the links between professions and the organizations through which they express their collective interests. Jack's congeniality and supportiveness, his constant readiness to find means and funds for more and better data, and, latterly, his provision of financial support through the American Bar Foundation to revise heavily and extend the original dissertation offered enviable circumstances in which to work. Spencer Kimball, former executive director of the American Bar Foundation, also is due considerable thanks for providing the institutional support of the foundation over several years.

A number of outstanding research assistants and colleagues, including Cathy Wildman and Catie Strong, helped collect and code the data. Charles Cappell and Mark Granfors worked on reducing the extensive quantitative files to manageable proportions and aided and advised on their subsequent statistical analysis. Much of the original data were subsequently analyzed by Cappell in his own dissertation, and we have published some of those results elsewhere.

This book grew out of graduate work in the University of Chicago Department of Sociology. Edward Shils's encouragement began from the first time I joined the stimulating seminar he taught on universities with Talcott Parsons and Joseph Ben-David. In addition to his championing of a revivified Chicago tradition of research inquiry, Morris Janowitz insisted that a case study must always reach for matters of societal or national import as the latter must be grounded in empirical realities. To other faculty who were at Chicago I also express my appreciation for their contributions in many diverse ways: Victor Lidz, Charles Bidwell, Richard Taub, Donald Levine, and Barry Schwartz. Much of what made the Chicago Sociology Department such a singular experience stemmed from fellow students who proved, at once, to be one's strongest supporters and most exacting critics. Most notable was Michael Burawoy, whose ceaseless intellectual provocation and sensitivity to research methods were constantly invigorating, and whose academic rate busting was inspiring. I also learned a great deal from and leaned a good deal on, Kathleen Schwartzmann, Bob Bogart, and Jim Robbins.

Although the American Bar Foundation provided both the research infrastructure and the underlying funding, my own research was also partially funded by additional grants from the National Science Foundation and the Russell Sage Foundation, to which I express my appreciation. The very substantial revision and restructuring that transformed the dissertation into a monograph were aided by the generous support of the Australian National University, where I was a research fellow in the Department of Sociology, Institute of Advanced Studies. Freedom from teaching allowed further thought on and reformulation of earlier drafts, and research support from the Australian National University allowed extension of my local findings to national profiles of organized bar activity. To Frank Jones, chair of the Sociology Department, I am particularly grateful.

I have also profited substantially from the comments of Richard Abel, Eliot Freidson, Carol Heimer, and Michael Powell, who read the entire version of various drafts. Valuable criticisms and suggestions were also provided on assorted chapters by Andrew Abbott, Mark Granfors, Philip Lewis, and Andrew Shapiro. To these colleagues I offer the absolution that none of them share all, and some of them share few, of my interpretations.

The Chicago Bar Association must be the paragon of an organization for its extraordinary openness and exemplary cooperation. We owe everything that arises out of this interior-scape of an important association not only to those lawyers who made the decision to keep such comprehensive records of their organization and its elite's activities at work but also to Jack McBride and Terry Murphy, executive directors of the Chicago Bar Association, for actually allowing us to mine indefinitely these rare, and sometimes very controversial, archives. I have also been very fortunate to have in Donna Hammond a secretary who typed innumerable versions speedily and efficiently, always with unflappable good cheer.

The dedication is to my father, who died shortly before this book was published, but whose intellectual curiosity and analytical mind early set a standard for emulation. Finally, and ultimately, this book owes an incalculable debt to Holly, Tyler, Richard, Kimberly, and Alastair, who risked considerably, sacrificed willingly, and nurtured unstintingly.

Introduction

When I first entered the archives of the Chicago Bar Association (CBA), one of the nation's largest and wealthiest organizations of lawyers,[1] I was greeted by row on row of filing cabinets jammed with records of association members, reports of proceedings, and outcomes of complaints against lawyers. On the shelves and in boxes were dozens of volumes of transcripts, minutes of committees, bar association publications, correspondence files, and miscellany stretching back a century. In the basement vault there was even more, partly buried in dust and once guarded by now dead mice.

Because I had no clear a priori point of entry to these materials, no well-defined substantive agenda or finely articulated set of questions, I was entirely overwhelmed. In the mid-1970s, this one organization had approximately 10,000 members, scores of committees, and dozens of administrative staff. The members represent every segment of the profession, every area of the law however obscure, and every stripe of politics and practice. Individual files on each of the current 10,000 members were accompanied by numerous pieces of information on still-living lawyers who were now "inactive" and the many thousands of earlier generations of the profession who had predeceased their latter-day brethren. There were standing committees and special committees and joint committees. Some had continued to exist since the late nineteenth century; others appeared

1. By 1983 its membership had swelled to 17,638, its staff numbered 126, and its budget of $4.4 million made it the richest and biggest of all metropolitan associations in the United States. In fact, the CBA budget in 1983 exceeded all but four of the fifty-six state bar associations. All the documentary materials cited in this book were held in the archives of the Chicago Bar Association as of 1977 unless otherwise designated. Hence committee reports, files, transcripts, and annual reports were all in the private collection of the association. For a number of years, annual reports of committees were published in the *Chicago Bar Record*; thereafter they were published separately but were available to all members. However, the Transcripts of the Board of Managers, the correspondence, and board files, together with numbers of other documents, were not in the public domain. Access to them was made possible only by kind permission of the Board of Managers and through the assistance of the executive director.

for a year or a decade and disappeared. Indeed there were so many that on one notable occasion the bar leadership lost track for fifteen years of what they later discovered had been a quite influential committee operating autonomously from the bar leadership.

Over the last one hundred years, the hundreds of committees produced innumerable reports. Some were only a paragraph or two, noting for posterity the little they had done in the preceding year; others ran to twenty or fifty or one hundred pages as they pressed the case of a committee on mostly long-forgotten issues of the moment.

Committees on the judiciary had engaged in a bewilderingly wide and variegated spectrum of activities ranging from long-term campaigns to transform the state constitution to the more trivial concerns with plaques on court buildings, the behavior of court clerks, and the drinking habits of judges. Committees on various areas of the substantive law had reviewed thousands of pieces of legislation emanating from state and federal legislatures. In turn they had drafted large numbers of suggested legislative and even constitutional amendments. House committees governed the restaurants and the library. Committees on professional regulation reviewed lawyers' ethics, lawyers' fees, and infringements on legal practice. From all of them, it seemed, had emerged a torrent of paper.

After the shock of first encounter, however, I discovered that the bar association had given me access to what may well be a unique body of data. The governing board had minutes extending back to the nineteenth century. There were comprehensive biographical files on all living leaders. There were newspaper files. There were issue files in which all matters discussed by the leadership for several decades were recorded, including all correspondence, committee reports, and newspaper clippings.

But such sources are reasonably common. What was unusual were the transcripts. All deliberations of the governing board had been transcribed by a court reporter, week by week, from 1950 to 1970. Consequently, I had a rare opportunity to "observe" the dynamics of an elite through a one-way mirror. An agenda book tells us the matters a leadership intends to discuss. A minute book provides a record of what matters were discussed and the summary record of their resolution. But transcripts open up a much richer source of information: they encapsulate a moment of elite culture, and they lay bare the usually black box of elite dynamics.[2] Because the documentary corpus is so rich from 1950 to 1970, I devote primary attention to that period.

---

2. The primary use of the transcripts in this book are qualitative and interpretative. For a more systematic quantitative analysis, see C. L. Cappell and Terence C. Halliday, "Professional Projects of Elite Chicago Lawyers, 1950–1974," *American Bar Foundation Research Journal* 1983 (Spring): 291–340.

Professional associations are one of sociology's least-researched phenomena. The reason for this neglect is puzzling. Professions have an image of prestige, wealth, and power. Even if a profession itself does not have power, it usually has access to it. And even if an individual professional has only a limited influence, large associations of professionals can wield vast influence. Each of the major professions in the United States, with the exception of the clergy and the military, has achieved a degree of collegial organization scarcely noted by sociologists or the public. Both the legal and the medical professions, for example, are organized at each level of government: there are metropolitan or county organizations; state bar associations or medical societies; and of course the national bodies, the American Medical Association and the American Bar Association. There are several hundred different professional associations alone, and they range in size from the ten or twenty-member county organizations to the 300,000–400,000-member national bodies. Crosscutting these hundreds of comprehensive associations, which incorporate practitioners of all kinds, are associations of specialists, of ethnic or religious or gender groups, of practitioners in private or public practice, of professionals in different kinds of work organizations, and of special purpose organizations that may group together a range of practitioners who have a common commitment to some defined goal such as reform of the court system or of the delivery of medical services. Each of the major professions in American society, therefore, has many hundreds of collegial associations by which to express politically the interests of its members. On the face of it, it seems entirely plausible to assume that the influence concentrated in these associations of lawyers, doctors, dentists, accountants, and teachers may be enormous.

In fact, the plausibility of that assumption has scarcely been substantiated. There are, then, collective actors on the stage of American political and economic life whose roles have seldom been identified, whose lines remain unheard, and whose entry to and exit from the proscenium pass unnoticed. We can name most of these actors. But that is all. Do professional associations attempt to influence government? If so, how often do they do so? Over how broad a range of matters? With what efficacy? Do they affect the policies and the administration of those institutions in which they have such a central role? Is their expertise deferred to by legislators and administrators? Do they effectively mold public policy—but out of the public eye? And what of the associations themselves? What kinds of resources can they bring to bear on the objects of their collective action? Can they act cohesively? Or is the internal diversity of a profession such that forceful action is all but impossible? Do professionals mobilize their clients? Can the web of associations, comprehensive and specialized, state and national, act in concert? These questions, as important for public policy as for democratic and social theory, have few answers.

It is an exaggeration to assert that the collective action of professionals in professional associations has escaped all notice—but barely so. Several recent attempts to probe the role of professions in American society have been rather tendentious in their usually incidental accounts of professions' mobilization through voluntary associations. Three recent examples suffice. Berlant exemplifies a line of inquiry that has concerned itself almost exclusively with the economic pretensions of modern professionals. To the question, What macrosocial role is played by the collegial associations of professionals? Berlant answers, Economic monopoly. In that, of course, there is truth. Professions do endeavor to establish and defend a monopoly over a given area of work. But they do much else besides. Magali Larson also underlines the monopolistic inclinations of professional bodies, but goes further. She maintains that professions play a central ideological role in monopoly capitalist societies, perpetuating a bourgeois and meritocratic ideology, ostensibly exemplified by professions, that masks the structured inequities of late capitalism. But for Larson professions have no power; they are merely its agents. Auerbach, in his discussion of the American legal profession over the last century, accuses the profession of pursuing every interest but that of justice; of enshrining formal justice to escape the mandates of substantive justice; of instituting a form of justice for one class and something inferior for another.[3]

It is also apparent, in a close examination of each of these works, that the partiality of treatment stems in considerable degree from methodological limitations: none is sufficiently proximate to the organizations from which it derives or substantiates its theories. Berlant and Larson rely on secondary literature. Auerbach gets closer, but not close enough, by using the public documents of bar associations and the private papers of numerous eminent American lawyers. Inevitably, therefore, their work suffers in two directions: with a particular thesis in hand, such as the monopolization argument, the public acts of professions attain a coherence, but only insofar as those acts pertain to that thesis. There is no attempt to grapple with all those public activities of associations that are not readily assimilated to monopolist theory. Consequently, we have no measure of the ratio of monopolistic behavior undertaken by professional associations to some total quantum of professional collegial action. Moreover, the minutes and transcripts of the CBA leadership underlined the lack of congruence between what the professional association does and what it reports it does. The disjunction is

3. See Jeffrey L. Berlant, *Profession and Monopoly: A Study of Medicine in the United States and Great Britain* (Berkeley: University of California Press, 1976); Magali Sarfatti Larson, *The Rise of Professionalism: A Sociological Analysis* (Berkeley: University of California Press, 1977); and Jerold S. Auerbach, *Unequal Justice: Lawyers and Social Change in Modern America* (New York: Oxford University Press, 1976), 63.

so radical as to distort seriously any attempt to characterize a profession's role using its major publications as a principal source. Many of the most important achievements of the professional association do not get publicized, even among members of the organization, precisely for the same reasons that much diplomacy is conducted out of the public domain. Publicity is inimical to certain kinds of influence. Secrecy is the condition of success.

The distinctive value of the CBA data set therefore lay in more than the possibilities it encouraged to explore the interiors of elite decision making. It provided a universe of professional action, a comprehensive record of professional collective activity, not as it is edited for public consumption, but as it was recorded in the careful bookkeeping of internal files. The data enabled a balanced perspective on professional associations that might serve as a corrective to the double distortion inherent in recent accounts of professional influence. The comprehensiveness of the archival material, of public declarations and private actions, allowed me to sketch the activities of a profession with a much broader brush than is usually possible.

The materials therefore commanded attention in two respects: they had substantial intrinsic interest for those concerned with the structure and change of American society since the close of World War II; and they allowed an exploration of substantive theoretical themes almost as broad as the data themselves.

For professional associations as well as individuals there was "turbulence" in the American political, economic, and legal environments over the twenty-five years from the close of the war to 1970. These were the years of the Cold War, of antisedition legislation, of Red-baiting, and of public political persecution—the heyday of McCarthyism. They were the years in which *Brown v. Board of Education* grew into street marches, when Selma, Little Rock, and Birmingham became household words, when open-housing legislation and anti-job-discrimination legislation in the states culminated in the massive civil rights acts of the Johnson administration. They were the years in which many states confronted severe fiscal crises, some tottering on the edge of bankruptcy. The years when Vietnam brought a generation out in protest on the university campuses to spill over into the streets, generating fears of widespread disorder and the breakdown of the rule of law. The years when inefficient and congested courts got to such a critical level of incapacity that civil trials would not be heard until five years after the date of first filing. In those years the political control of many state court systems came under vigorous attack. Autonomy of the legal system and the independence of the judiciary were debated in state houses and voted on in state referendums. And, in the postwar years, an impetus, dead for a century, arose again to press some uniformity into state laws growing more complex, contradictory, and inconsistent.

Those were also the years in which the major bar associations doubled, trebled, and quintupled their membership. How did these events impinge on a better-organized and stronger legal profession? Did the bar turn away from anything controversial and political to focus on arcane lawyers' law? Or did the profession endeavor to enter the public debates and national controversies at some level so it might employ its own distinctive skills in the cause of some professional conception of a more orderly world?

But the confrontation of the organized bar by these issues, together with a far greater range of less prominent judicial and legislative matters, poses more general and fundamental sociological questions. The data spoke to themes that have interpreted the role of professions in advanced capitalist societies in terms of the significance of professions for democratic politics, the social organization of modern societies, the culture of the West, and capitalist economies. Through these data could be broached the extent to which professions might affect the viability of democracy by bringing "expertise to the service of power"; the degree to which professions, including that of law, contribute to rationalization of knowledge and institutions; and the significance of burgeoning collegiality in professional associations for professional integration and political action. In short, the vast documentary corpus of the CBA provided a singular opportunity to confront a range of fundamental theoretical and policy questions posed about modern professions. They offered an indication of what might be the scope of professional influence on government and the legal system. They seemed also to yield a basis on which to establish some parameters of professional influence. My initial hesitation turned to enthusiasm as it seemed that the thousands of apparently disconnected pieces of professional action undertaken by the CBA could be pieced together into a broader mosaic that incorporated the themes of professional monopoly but went much beyond them. The vastness and disparateness of professional activity had form. It became clear that a structure of action could be discerned over many years of bar association activity, even if there did not seem to exist any conscious recognition or articulation of that structure by bar leaders.

Nonetheless, the macrosociology of professions cannot rest with the elaboration of their influence on government and the economy, on social organization and culture. It is not enough to establish the scope of professional influence; it is necessary also to discover the conditions under which professions can act at all. As I worked my way through the bar association records, I was posed a second set of questions that have been addressed by a second set of themes. The findings that emerged from Heinz and Laumann's extensive survey of the Chicago legal profession[4] have direct implications for this study. From my inspection of com-

4. See John P. Heinz and Edward O. Laumann, *Chicago Lawyers: The Social Structure of the Bar* (New York: Russell Sage; Chicago: American Bar Foundation, 1982).

mittee records, I already knew that the CBA was highly variegated, an impression reinforced by the biographies of bar leaders. But the findings of the bar survey revealed a degree of differentiation more acute than has hitherto been documented for any profession. Heinz and Laumann showed precisely and with great intricacy how much the profession was divided by specialty, type of practice, ethnicity, national politics, local politics, general values, and particular beliefs. The implications of the diversity were succinctly stated in the first report on the survey. "The price the CBA pays for its broad based, representative membership is its inability to mobilize organizational resources around specific policy initiatives and controversial areas with the profession of the larger society . . . herein lies the dilemma of every professional association. The more its membership reflects a diversity of the larger society, the more limited and non-controversial will tend to be the set of goals, however important they may be, that it can effectively pursue." A professional association with a constituency as diverse as the CBA may be prevented from "taking action on any but the least controversial, most innocuous questions." [5]

On its face, this initial judgment, which reflects a widely felt sentiment in the scholarly literature, seemed entirely plausible. There were issues so controversial that the bar association was ostensibly hamstrung. As my research progressed, however, I found that, although there were numerous examples of organizational stalemate that prevented collective action, there were also many other occasions on which the bar association acted significantly when its members must have been, or were, completely divided. The degree of professional fragmentation on a given issue was not a sufficient explanation of the incapacity of bar action. Between the views of its members and the eventual actions of its leadership there was an intervening process that determined that some controversial issues would stalemate the organization, whereas others would not. Part of the research agenda consequently became a search for the intraorganizational processes that determined which issues would have which consequences.

As a result, in addition to the macrosociological issues surrounding professions and the state, this study responds to critical problems identified in Heinz and Laumann's cross-sectional survey of the very constituency from which association members were drawn. To the degree that the survey demonstrated the internal diversity of the profession, the relatively low involvement of most lawyers in its professional association, and the relatively limited perceptions they had of its potential influence, the case study was posed the problem of showing how an association of professionals might take advantage of the resources that diversity, size, and inclusiveness gave it without at the same time falling prey to counteract-

---

5. John P. Heinz, et al., "Diversity, Representation, and Leadership in an Urban Bar," *American Bar Foundation Research Journal* 1976 (Summer): 771.

ing disintegrative forces. While the survey could provide a highly detailed profile of a profession at one point in time and of the views of its members on matters that concerned the association, it could not map change within the profession, it could not divine the processes by which the profession articulated its interests and parried its detractors, and above all it could not confront directly some central theoretical questions posed by the classic theorists of professions. In fact, an intensive case study of an organization of this size is the only means by which core issues, such as collective professional action, internal professional politics, and the mobilization of professional knowledge for political purpose, can satisfactorily be addressed—at least in the first instance.

To many, the utility of the case study is highly questionable in a time of large-scale surveys and the advances of mathematical sociology. Does it make any sense to look at just one of any given class of phenomena, whether it be of horses, icebergs, banks, or flowers? In the history of science, and certainly of sociology, the question is largely rhetorical. By looking at hundreds of horses or icebergs from the outside it is posssible to draw some conclusions, but at best they are superficial and at worst illusory. At the beginning of sciences, or even at the outset of research into a new class of phenomena, breakthroughs have emerged from careful, detailed, and exhaustive probings into one or a handful of cases. With the enormous advance of knowledge to be gained in that way it is then possible, and indeed desirable, to ask whether each of the new discoveries about the phenomena in question are to be found more generally among other phenomena of the same type. Indeed it is imperative to test the limits of just how far the findings from one case can be extended to others. In sociology, where there are many organizations like professional associations that have remained immune from investigation, there is the tendency to run before we can walk, to look superficially at hundreds of cases before we have looked intently at one. The results too often are trite and naive. A case study is not a dispensable luxury or a residue of an antiquated disciplinary past. It will be immeasurably enriched, as is my institutional study, by complementary surveys. But without the sustained and intensive analysis of the single case, the survey is breadth without depth, parsimony without intricacy, science without humanity. The case study is one mandatory foundation on which the entire edifice of the theory on professions will be constructed.

If mandatory, however, the case study cannot afford to be solitary. Either in itself or by implication, it must reach out to other cases in other places and times, informing theories and situations far beyond its own narrow constraints. The methodology of this study therefore moves between the quantitative and qualitative within the CBA; it retains the tension between local events and national occurrences wherever possible; and it allows the empirical to inform the theoretical even as the latter concomitantly organizes the ordering of the former.

Within the CBA I make extensive use of the documentary materials; but as it is impossible to grasp their complexity without some techniques of data reduction, I developed several quantitative files. These include (1) coding of 240 biographies of the CBA elite from 1950 to 1974; (2) a content analysis of all legislative items on the agenda books of the CBA Board of Managers, 1950–69; (3) a content analysis of all judicial items on the CBA board's agenda books for the same period; and (4) a very detailed content analysis of two hundred issue debates within the CBA board between 1950 and 1969.[6] In addition to the survey of the Chicago bar, some of which I reanalyze for this study, two other data sets have been developed that set the CBA in a national context: (1) a 1982 national survey of all state bar associations and the coding of information on state associations collected by the American Bar Association and (2) the coding of basic membership information on all state bar associations for ten-year periods (coinciding with the U.S. census) from the 1870s to 1980.

Consequently, I do not see this book to be limited only to a study of the Chicago Bar Association, although it is at least that. Nor is it even only a study of bar associations in general, although that is an object of the research. It is also an analysis of a generic and ubiquitous kind of professional association—associations that are (1) large, (2) comprehensive in their functions and goals (including a wide range of facilities and inducements for membership), and (3) notionally inclusive of all professionals in a given work domain. It is a study of how such associations build the resources and construct the authority on which their macrosocial role rests; it is an analysis of the potential scope of professional action, especially vis-à-vis the state; and it is an examination of the conditions under which bar associations, or any other comprehensive professional bodies, may act collectively. Ultimately, it is an exploration of the conditions under and for which arcane knowledge can be mobilized for political action in contemporary democracies.

Finally, this work represents an attempt implicitly to restate, in more contemporary sociological idiom, the enduring relevance of that style of research historically associated with the Chicago school of sociology. As such it focuses on a local institution and traces in microcosm some of its implications for like institutions elsewhere. It endeavors to meld first-hand techniques of participant observation and interviewing with historical and documentary research, whether in traditional qualitative forms or in application of quantitative techniques, such as content analysis of biographical files, agendas, and annual reports. It complements the case study with the national survey. To methodological catholicity it adds a degree of theoretical eclecticism—a readiness to begin with a concrete social institution and to trace its macrosocial implications in terms of those theo-

---

6. For analysis of this last data set, see Cappell and Halliday, "Professional Projects."

ries that are most apposite, thus at once wresting the institution away from a purely parochial significance and providing empirical grounding and discipline for a more abstract understanding of contemporary institutions.

An afterword on genre and audience: *Beyond Monopoly: Lawyers, State Crises and Professional Empowerment* does not purport to be a general organizational history or narrative portrait of the Chicago Bar Association. The latter can be found in Herman Kogan's *The First Century*.[7] Rather, this book uses the Chicago Bar Association as a case to explore important themes in our current understanding of professions and politics. In this sense, it is a selective, highly interpretative treatment of events salient only to the themes of expertise and power, professions and democracy. While it is written primarily to scholars who debate these issues, the book also presents an argument that is both an appraisal of and challenge to the organized bar in the United States. General readers who wish to follow the argument without working through the more technical sociology may wish to jump over those sections that are more theoretical and esoteric—namely, chapters 2 and 10 and some parts of chapters 4 and 6.

7. Herman Kogan, *The First Century: The Chicago Bar Association, 1874–1974* (Chicago: Rand McNally, 1974).

Part One

Knowledge and Power

1 Professions and Governability

An implicit notion of professional narcissism remains a pivotal assumption in much contemporary writing on the macrosociology of professions. In this view, professions are preoccupied with pecuniary interests, committed to protection of their economic domains, enamored of the pursuit of upward collective mobility and of the consolidation of their class position and of those whom they disproportionately represent.[1] The state becomes the benefactor of sectional privilege rather than the beneficiary of professional expertise. Notions of professional civility have been jettisoned as completely as earlier functionalist interpretations have been repudiated.

I shall maintain that the corrective pendulum of reaction against an overly benign functionalism has swung too far. A view of professional action that too readily washes away the tensions between self-interest and civility, private satisfaction and public service, autonomy and accountability, prestige and wealth and the helping function, produces a bland homogeneity—a one-dimensional image of professionalism. This book rejects that criticism that allows the professions little macrosociological role other than the legitimation of the monopoly capitalist state or the abnegation of public responsibility for private gain. It acknowledges both the tensions within professions and their ambivalent relations with the state, holding in uneasy juxtaposition the two faces of professionalism—the one monopolistic, even narcissistic, and the other benign, even altruistic.

The point of entry to this reevaluation of the macrosociology of professions may be approached by examining the convergence of two changes in advanced capitalist societies, the one a trend in the political organization of liberal democracies and the other a transformation in social structure. The former concerns the

1. See, e.g., Jeffrey L. Berlant, *Profession and Monopoly*; Noel Parry and Jose Parry, *The Rise of the Medical Profession: A Study of Collective Social Mobility* (London: Croom Helm, 1976); Magali Sarfatti Larson, *The Rise of Professionalism*. For a more extended critical discussion of these and other recent influential approaches to the macrosociology of professions, see Terence C. Halliday, "Professions, Class and Capitalism," *Archives européennes de sociologie* 24 (1983): 321–46.

thesis that current stresses on Western governments may contribute to their un-governability. The latter arises from the emergence of professions as a major oc-cupational category and collective political force.

Ungovernability and Crisis

Within the last decade, numerous scholars have suggested that, if current trends continue, Western societies will experience overload, crisis, and even ungovern-ability if they have not already done so. Changes in culture, in patterns of de-mands on government, and in the organization of government itself have led to consequences that, it is argued, could bring these governments to the point of stalemate.

The sheer volume of demands on government and the range of responsibilities for which government feels itself responsible, or is considered responsible, have increased at a rapid rate. In his seminal article, which stimulated much of the subsequent debate, King wrote that government has come to be regarded as "a sort of unlimited-liability insurance company," in which "to be held responsible for everything is to feel compelled to intervene in everything." [2] Consequently, the volume and range of demands expand, and the phenomenon feeds on itself in an inexorable upward spiral. The reasons for growth in demands can be found partly in the recent past. The rapid economic growth in the 1950s and 1960s allowed great expansion in government revenue and therefore a capacity to initi-ate dramatically a spectrum of welfare and other programs. But even with the slowdown in economic growth and reduced tax revenue, governments' "inertia commitments" remained. Programs already in place, together with the laws im-plementing them, could not be easily repealed on either moral or practical grounds. Moreover, "the inertia commitments of government are not a static force, but a force steadily pushing expenditures outwards." [3] In addition, of course, public policy expenditure continues to increase when, as in social secu-rity benefits, the numbers or cohorts of people eligible for a given benefit in-crease, when there is lobbying for more consumer benefits, and when producers of public goods, within government, become lobbyists themselves for greater expenditure.

The problem is not simply one of escalating demands. Wildavsky has argued not only that there are more demands, often emanating from powerful and strate-gically based lobbies, but also that they are frequently incompatible. There are

2. A. King, "Overload: Problems of Governing in the 1970s," *Political Studies* 23 (1975): 286, 287.

3. Richard Rose, "Ungovernability: Is There Fire behind the Smoke?" *Political Studies* 27 (1978): 357. See also Richard Rose and Guy Peters, *Can Government Go Bankrupt?* (New York: Basic, 1978).

pressures both for political parties to be democratized and for election costs to be reduced, for the government to provide pure air and at the same time to consume less energy. Similar incompatibilities can be found equally readily in the areas of welfare, employment, housing, and education.[4]

With changes in the volume and incompatibility of demands come shifts in their articulation and aggregation. McKay, in his review of changes in the American political party system, points out that parties are the principal organization for aggregating demands, giving coherence to expressions of interest and forestalling fragmentation in the approach of citizens to government.[5] Yet he documents a trend toward the rapid growth in the percentage of voters who are not aligned with a party. From 1950 to 1978, the number who registered as independents doubled, from 22 percent to 44 percent. That lack of conventional alignment has been especially strong among the youngest voters. Conversely, over the same period, the percentage of people identifying themselves as Democrats declined from 45 percent to 30 percent and as Republicans from 33 percent to 21 percent. Consequently, as the size of the swing vote has doubled, demands have become less structured and political values less coherent.

Moreover, ticket splitting has increased markedly: 80 percent of voters in 1950, but only 50 percent in 1970, cast straight party ballots. As the characteristics of candidates or their positions on particular issues have achieved a greater prominence, older allegiances have broken down. A decline in party organization has also been evident in recent presidential elections. Goldwater, McCarthy, McGovern, and Carter all were presidential candidates who conducted campaigns either as a faction within the party or from personal party organizations, thus detracting from traditional party allegiances. It is not surprising therefore that party platforms and programs should also have lost their identity and coherence, a process exacerbated by the emergence of single-issue politics and its fragmentation of issue articulation. The single-issue lobbyists can stalemate or veto the passage of legislation and divert voters' attention from the general political orientations of candidates to their positions on narrow, and ultimately less consequential, problems. Loyalty to an interest group, it is argued, has superseded commitment to a party. Parties in the United States, according to one fairly pessimistic prognosis, are in "decay," as they also struggle for funds and staff.[6]

Governments have thus been caught in a "revolution of rising expectations" coincidentally with a decline of political structures that once ordered these expectations for government. Although governments have traditionally provided

4. Aaron Wildavsky, "Government and the People," *Commentary* 56 (August 1973): 25–32.

5. David H. Mackay, "Review Article: The United States in Crisis: A Review of the American Political Literature," *Government and Opposition* 14 (1979): 373–85.

6. Daniel Bell, "The Revolution of Rising Entitlements," *Fortune*, April 1975, 98–103.

goods and services that individuals could not provide for themselves, in the last forty years, according to Bell, the American government has taken on three new sets of responsibilities: from the 1930s, the health and well-being of the economy; from the 1950s, the sponsorship of science, technology, and research and support for the universities; and from the 1960s, a social policy not just to create a welfare program but also "to address all economic and social inequalities of wealth."[7] Confronted with such a wide-ranging mandate, government's aspirations outweigh its abilities.

If the pattern of demand has been transformed, so too has the internal organization of government itself. The fragmentation of legislative bodies, it is argued, has been exemplified by the decline of the seniority criterion in committee systems, the inability to maintain strong party rule, and the difficulty of Western countries in sustaining strong single-party majority governments. In 1975 there was no single-party majority in eight European countries. More recently, the crisis within the British Labour party has contributed to what may be a significant splintering of the party system in that country.

Government itself has expanded enormously: when the Carter government produced a forty-five-page compilation of agencies and bodies of the executive branch, it had to caution that the list should not be considered exhaustive, even though each agency and body got no more than a one-line entry.[8] With growth has come a homogenization of functions across the three branches of government, a process Moynihan has coined "the Iron Law of Emulation."[9] Each branch of government, to strengthen its position vis-à-vis other branches, has formed within it elements that emulate the function of the other branches. The legislature has taken on itself certain executive and judicial functions; and the judiciary has begun to develop its own executive capacity. The executive in turn has incorporated aspects of both other branches. The effect, believes Moynihan, is that each branch of government can do less, not more, because each has an enhanced capacity to veto the initiatives of the other.

Furthermore, some scholars argue that, the more government organizations, the less efficient they will become. Coordination will become progressively more difficult, even though it is already more of a strain for government than large private associations, not only because the volume and variety of outputs are greater, but also because government lacks a common denominator like money to enable it easily to monitor its own programs. On probabilistic grounds alone, it can only be expected that, the greater the proliferation of government departments and organizations, the more likely their objectives will clash.

7. Ibid, p. 100.
8. Rose, "Ungovernability," 261.
9. Daniel P. Moynihan, "Imperial Government," *Commentary* 65 (June 1978): 25–32.

Government departments and bodies thus come to act both as inertial elements and as interest groups within government itself. Each new government finds itself endowed with the legacy of programs, departments, and agencies left by preceding governments. But while programs may have responded to problems that are no longer pressing or to political philosophies that are no longer current, each program invariably gains a consumer group ready to argue vociferously against its abolition and a bureaucratic agency whose personnel have a commitment to their own positions in government that the program guarantees. Consequently, it is not new programs instituted by a particular government that constitute the problem but rather the accumulation over successive governments of initiatives and organizations that are almost impossible to eliminate. This "inertia commitment" of government, which constitutes the principal drain on public policy expenditure, is frequently translated into action and contradiction. While program and agency staffs fight for maintenance of their positions, they effectively form interest groups within government itself. Because agencies and organizations within the executive may continue to represent the political orientations of the governments that appointed them, the clash of political values between parties becomes internalized within government. Even social policies between, for example, cheaper energy and a cleaner environment can be institutionalized as interagency rivalries. Government agencies therefore fight not just for their maintenance but also for the values that justified their formation, thus drawing within government the contradictions and demands that emerged from outside it.

If government is confronted by a broader range of often contradictory demands, it has also been made responsible for many problems that some observers believe to be insoluble. While there were massive appropriations in the 1960s for education and the elimination of crime and poverty, perfectly laudable goals, the disposition of appropriations was much more problematic. An immodest social science could not specify the cause and effect relations of complex social phenomena. Indeed, even when causes were identifiable they may well have been beyond the reach of public policy, as in the findings on the effects of family background on education achievement. Consequently, King can argue that Britain, like other advanced industrial societies, has become more difficult to govern because the sheer "number of dependency relationships in which government is involved has increased substantially." [10] Social complexity is so great that, "given some probability of the occurrence of acts of non-performance or non-compliance, the probability of a government, or anyone else, getting its way is reduced." If increased dependency and complexity make state intervention more problematic and the outcomes of its actions more indeterminate, so also does the web of national and international dependency relations defy intellectual

10. King, "Overload," 290.

comprehension. In the areas of public policy, it can therefore be asserted that "men understand less, and realise that they understand less, now than 20 years ago." On this basis, some conclude that "the government is increasingly getting a skewed distribution of problems that are insoluble precisely because people demand of government what government cannot do." [11]

The consequences of new patterns of demands and new developments in government are both economic and political. The demands on the state and its expenditure on public policy have outstripped the ability to pay for it. Public expenditure exceeds public revenue, and the rate of government spending exceeds the growth of the economy. In the 1950s and 1960s governments expanded the sphere of public policy by paying for it out of the dividends of higher economic growth, not by raising taxes. But the growth of economies has not kept pace with public policy consumption. While the costs of consumption grew by 7.1 percent per annum from 1951 to 1977 in the major Western industrial nations, including the United States, the national economies grew at a rate of only 4.2 percent. Governments have thus been forced into larger and larger deficits and the real income of taxpayers may actually be declining. In economic terms, the ultimate consequence of "the structural gap between state expenditures and revenues" may be "the fiscal crisis of the capitalist state." [12]

Economic crises can generate far-reaching political consequences. There is something of a consensus, from monetarists and neoconservatives through the neo-Marxists, "that the growth of public expenditure threatens imminent political disaster," something that unprecedented federal deficits have given a new immediacy. [13] Within government the weight of often contradictory and disaggregated demands overwhelms it, imposing demands that no government can meet and that ultimately stalemate its capacity to function effectively. This paralysis precludes the passage of comprehensive legislation that might attempt to solve some of the most pressing demands. Not only does an ineffective and stalemated government fail to do those things that only government can do, but the failure itself detracts from the future capacity of governmental action. Failure breeds mistrust and discontent.

At least two consequences may follow. One view has it that disillusionment does not imply apathy—that people are actually more disillusioned and also more interested. Those interested may be channeled either into movement politics, with its single-issue focus, or further, into civil disobedience and nonlegitimate political action. Another view fears an indifference that is as debilitating to

11. Wildavsky, "Government and the People," 32.
12. Rose, "Ungovernability," 357–58.
13. Ibid., 353.

state effectiveness as resort to organized or unorganized protest.[14] Coming full circle, then, ineffectiveness engenders indifference, which in turn ensures less effectiveness. Each feeds on the other, effecting a vicious circle of declining state efficacy. The ultimate fear, as the circle spirals downward, becomes not only a withdrawal of consent from the current regime—the present office holders—but also a crisis of legitimacy for the democratic political system itself. "No democratic political system," asserts Arthur Miller, "can survive for long without the support of a majority of its citizens."[15] Without the reversal of the cycle of mistrust, which in turn requires the reduction of government ineffectiveness, the probability of radical political disruption increases markedly.

Not surprisingly, the writings on ungovernability by political scientists and economists focus almost exclusively on the legislative and executive branches. These branches command the direct focus of the citizen and voter. But the judiciary too has suffered from stresses, some quite severe. The problems are less apparent at the federal level, but they are often insistent and even overwhelming in state and local jurisdictions. Although the Supreme Court fared better than the House and the Senate or the White House in a 1973 poll that asked for public confidence in major American institutions, even then only 33 percent indicated confidence in it.[16] Had the poll asked about state and local judicial systems, that figure would have been very much lower.

The postwar court system has encountered massive demands. Rising litigation and crime rates have led to court congestion and delay in the administration of justice. The strains on the court system have been building since the 1950s. Sheldon D. Elliott, director of the Institute of Judicial Administration, told the 1956 Conference of Attorneys-General that delay in state courts between joining of issue and the beginning of trial averaged 11.5 months across the nation. In some metropolitan courts, the figure was much higher: forty-two months elapsed in a Massachusetts and a New York court, while the Supreme Court of Kings County, New York, had a waiting period of over four years. An enormously increased case load has arisen in federal courts since World War II: the backlog of civil cases increased 134 percent in the fifteen years from 1940 to 1956. Chief Justice Burger lamented the grave shortage of judges, observing that the federal backlog in 1958 totaled some 66,000 cases. The problem was metaphorically acknowledged by the American Assembly in 1965 when it devoted its twenty-seventh session to "the law explosion."[17] Mirrored a decade later, that image re-

14. Ibid., 354.
15. Arthur H. Miller is quoted in Mackay, "The United States in Crisis," 380.
16. Ibid., 377.
17. Whether there was and is a crisis in the courts or a litigation explosion is a matter of vigorous debate, with no clear resolution in view. Although the rhetoric of "law explosion" clearly points to

curred in the apocalyptic—and, some believe, naive—judgment not only that
the United States was currently experiencing a legal explosion but that an "expo-
nential extrapolation of increases over the last decade suggests that by the early
21st century the federal appellate courts alone will decide approximately 1 million cases each year." [18] Comparable figures for the mid-1960s and 1970s were
5,000 cases and 15,000 cases, respectively. Underlining this rapid trend, it has
been shown that more than 43 percent of the appeals filed in the eighty-six year
history of the U.S. Court of Appeals for the Sixth Circuit were filed in just ten
years—from 1967 to 1977. From 1963 to 1978 the case load grew 444 percent.
Phillips was thus led to conclude that "the Federal courts are confronted with a
crisis of such unmanageable proportions that their dockets threaten to become
unmanageable." [19]

The causes of these strains have been attributed to numerous factors, some of
which arise from outside the court system itself. Some are cast in the most general terms: the effects of the technological revolution; a rising crime rate; the
increased potential for disputes that has followed from the evolution of societal
complexity such that the number of transactions among individuals and corporations has grown drastically; and even the breakdown of consensus, trust, and a
common ethos in American society. But much of the burden on the courts comes
from legislatures. Congress has been progressively conferring on the judicial
branch an ever-expanding jurisdiction. Between 1969 and 1978 Congress enacted at least forty-one new laws that expanded the jurisdiction of the federal
courts. Moreover, the general burgeoning of regulation has devolved, at many
points, an added responsibility on the courts. [20]

---

rapid increases in litigation brought before the courts, Marc Galanter ("Reading the Landscape of
Disputes: What We Know and Don't Know (and Think We Know) about Our Allegedly Contentious
and Litigious Society," *UCLA Law Review* 31 [October 1983] 4–71) strenuously contests the prevailing consensus and suggests "a reading of the landscape that differs radically from the litigation explosion reading." (69). However, whereas the current debate over litigation points to excessive legalization and disputing, Galanter has less quarrel with the institutional approach of past reformers and
their concern with delay, high costs, and overloaded courts. This debate cannot be arbitrated here: I
proceed on the assumption that there is some fire behind the smoke, although the blaze may not be the
conflagration other observers predicted (see nn. 18, 19, below).

18. John H. Barton, "Behind the Legal Explosion," *Stanford Law Review* 27 (February 1975):
567. However, Galanter ("Reading the Landscape," 62–63) sharply questions the assumptions that
produce this "naive straight-line projection" and sees it as an example of judicial and academic elite
bias toward the top of the legal system—"such elites tend to have a limited and spotty grasp of what
the bulk of the legal system is really like."

19. Harry Phillips, "The Expansion of Federal Jurisdiction and the Crisis in the Courts," *Vander-
bilt Law Review* 31 (January 1978): 17–31. Contrast, however, Galanter's critique (in "Reading the
Landscape"), which views pronouncements by such leading judges as Chief Judge Phillips and Chief
Justice Burger as the uncritical perpetuation of doubtful myths.

20. Ibid, 20.

In some of these cases, a pattern has developed for congressional and state legislatures to pass on to the courts value conflicts that government has not been able to resolve and that it hopes the courts can. Such laws are likely to be partial and ambiguous if not inconsistent. The courts are therefore expected to achieve what the legislature could not. These new responsibilities, coupled with the general volume of legislation and the increasing breadth of issues on which the government has taken responsibility, have thrown more weight on the courts than they can readily bear. The weight of responsibility is compounded by the reluctance and slowness of government to expand judicial facilities and to appoint new judges. The judiciary cannot easily act for itself as an interest group. And there is little political advantage in substantially increased expenditures on the judicial branch.[21]

Difficulties within the court system reinforce those from without. Whatever problems have confronted the federal court system, they are multiplied in state and local courts. As leaders of the movement to unify and rationalize state court systems pointed out in the years following World War II, a large proportion of states had a multiplicity of different courts at various levels of jurisdiction without any effective coordination among or across them at any given level or in any effective hierarchy of authority. In these circumstances jurisdictions were too often ambiguous and often enough in conflict. Furthermore, the lack of an integrated court system contributed to an inflexibility in the transfer of personnel, particularly judges, from one specialized court to another. Facilities, such as office space, courtrooms, and records areas, were tied to the purposes and jurisdictions of particular courts and were not available for the needs of others, even though the former might be empty and the latter full. Not surprisingly, a disunified court system also utilized a variety of procedures and a lack of any standardization of court rules. In a word, the arthritic condition into which the courts' structures had fallen placed them in no position to be able to react flexibly and swiftly to massive new demands.

If one side of the two-pronged critique by the court reform movement pointed to the inadequacies in court organization, the other pointed to the manifest inadequacies in the character of the state judiciary itself. Across the United States an inability or unwillingness of legislators to relieve the strain on the courts led to a proportionately diminishing judiciary. Even those judges who were appointed, especially to the lower courts, were not necessarily raised to the bench for their legal skill or judicial promise. In most states political loyalty to the government in power superseded legal distinction. According to the reformers of the American Judicature Society, too many judges were of too low a caliber and thus

21. Barton, "Behind the Legal Explosion," 568.

evoked little respect from the public for them or the court system.[22] The crisis of authority that confronted the legislature therefore had its parallel with the judiciary. That judges were effectively without ethical controls merely compounded the malaise into which disorganization and inferior quality cast the bench.

The possible consequences of a judicial crisis are not difficult to imagine. The aphorism, Justice delayed is justice denied, expresses one result. That an overburdened judiciary must convict individuals on criminal charges less serious than those on which they were arrested may conceivably devalue the seriousness with which that system is regarded, although whether that is true of plea bargaining is a matter of considerable contention. Excessive delay ultimately becomes a major threat to the administration of justice and brings the justice system into disrepute, engendering "public cynicism and mistrust of the legal profession, the judiciary, and the legal system." [23] In the shorter term, the standing of one branch of government and the role of law has its legitimacy eroded away. Eventually, however, the denial of expeditious justice may force disaffected individuals to resolve their disputes by extralegal means or to resign themselves to the perpetuation of injustice. "In either event," concluded former Attorney General Griffin Bell, "the inevitable result will be agitation and social unrest." [24] In the final analysis, therefore, the effects of an outmoded and rusty judicial machinery are no less serious than those to which the executive and legislative branches have been subjected.

An argument about crises requires specification in three respects. First, it must immediately be acknowledged that the concept of "crisis" itself is not unproblematic. Indeed, the word is notoriously subject to ideological manipulation. Not only may one person's crisis be another's perturbation, but crying crisis is a classic way of attracting—or distracting—attention and diverting resources. As Habermas correctly perceives, therefore, the notion of crisis in late capitalist societies has both objective and subjective components: it requires objective grounding; and it is infused with subjective and normative meaning.[25] While it *is* a social construction, it is only so in part. That such objective conditions of over-

22. "The National Conference on Judicial Selection and Court Administration," *Journal of the American Judicature Society,* vol. 43 (December 1959); Glenn M. Winters, "The National Movement to Improve the Administration of Justice," *Journal of the American Judicature Society,* vol. 48 (June 1964), and "Current Trends in Court Reform," *Judicature* vol. 50 (May 1967).

23. Leonard S. Janofsky, "ABA Attacks Delay and the High Cost of Litigation," *American Bar Association Journal* 65 (1979): 1323–24.

24. Griffin B. Bell, "Crisis in the Courts: Proposals for Change," *Vanderbilt Law Review* 31 (January 1978): 3–15.

25. Jurgen Habermas, "What Does a Crisis Mean Today? Legitimation Problems in Late Capitalism," *Social Research* 40 (1973): 643. What normative meaning it may have, however, can be far from obvious.

load, ungovernability, and crisis have recently existed in many Western societies, including the United States and its constituent governments, has some credence. And as I shall indicate in later chapters, each of the crises confronting American state governments had bases in objective circumstances that can be fairly precisely identified. However, even these objective circumstances awaited public recognition before extant conditions of overload were construed as crisis.[26]

That these conditions have also been construed as crises by theoretically divergent observers provides added verisimilitude to the claim. In the second place, therefore, it bears repetition that perceptions of crisis have been proclaimed by unlikely theoretical bedfellows, although not every theory casts the situation in identical terms and not every theorist shares the same level of optimism about transcending tendencies toward ungovernability.

Birch identifies three principal, albeit loosely defined, groups of scholars who link overload with ungovernability and crisis: the neoconservatives; the liberal economists; and the neo-Marxists.[27] Although much of the preceding discussion has been developed within contexts set by the first two groups, aspects of their position bear recapitulation and extension. The neoconservatives direct their attack on excessive liberalism which they maintain, has undermined traditional institutions, such as family and church, and has so overstimulated demands for rights that government cannot possibly vindicate the burgeoning hopes pinned on it. The rise of expectations has psychological and cultural origins. Whereas for Bell, a restraining Protestant ethic has been discarded in favor of consumerism and hedonism, for Irving Kristol, youths have repudiated capitalism without engaging in productive alternatives.[28] But the causes are also structural: the fragmentation of demands into single-issue politics compounds the failure of parties to articulate programs that command broad consensus. Accordingly, an imbalance of demands on government has proceeded in tandem with the structural incapacity of institutions, both public and private. The disjunction between popular demand and institutional capacities erodes confidence in politics and fuels the "democratic distemper," as Huntington styles contemporary politics.[29]

26. "Gradient arguments," such as those surrounding "crisis," are always problematic because they carry implications about prior states of existence. As used here, the concept suggests not that there have never been problems before in the courts, the economy, or the area of rights but that this set of events is quantitatively different than sets of events in the years and decades immediately preceding. I argue not that there have never been crises in earlier times but that these crises are significant because for the first time they converge with empowered professions.

27. Anthony H. Birch, "Overload, Ungovernability and Delegitimation: The Theories and the British Case," *British Journal of Political Science* 14 (1984): 135–60.

28. Daniel Bell, *The Cultural Contradictions of Capitalism* (New York: Basic, 1976); Irving Kristol, *Two Cheers for Capitalism* (New York: Basic, 1978).

29. Samuel P. Huntington, "The Democratic Distemper," *Public Interest* 16 (1975): 9–38.

The liberal economists build on Schumpeter's warning that the political economy of democracies will be viable only when citizens exercise democratic self-restraint and restrict the range of political decision making.[30] Protection of state enterprises, like the BBC, from factional dispute sets limits on the scope of politicization. More recent economists, however, are sharply critical of Schumpeter: in an influential article, Samuel Brittan argued that Schumpeter's conditions for governability were, in practice, naive—that the intensification of electoral competition leads to an inexorable politicization of state enterprises and an unrelieved loss of restraint in political demands. Both adequate and deliberate policymaking becomes compromised and economic inflation gets out of control as rival parties bid public expenditure ever higher in the quest for electoral advantage. Without a radical retreat from materialism and egalitarianism, Brittan predicts that the "economic contradictions of democracy" will lead it to self-destruction.[31]

The neo-Marxists, by contrast, focus more intently on the state *per se* and its facility in retaining legitimacy. Habermas provides the most powerful articulation of this approach, although it is approximated by Offe, O'Connor, and others. In his discussion of legitimation problems in late capitalism, Habermas maintains that the state confronts a double crisis, each element of which arises from state intervention in the market.[32] An enormous burden of public expenditure has grown from international competition, unproductive consumer goods (armaments, space travel), infrastructural support (transportation, communications), and social consumption related to production (housing, health, education, social security). These new functions of the state require both public financing, through the levy of taxes, and administrative efficiency, through government agencies. An "output crisis" occurs because the state is simply not efficient at planning and administering the economy. The result is considerable disorganization in social life. The "input crisis" constitutes a "legitimation crisis" because the legitimation system fails to maintain the necessary level of mass loyalty for the state to act authoritatively. If efforts at state intervention and the raising of public funds exceed the quantum of loyalty—"and the rising level of aspirations is proportionate to the growing need for legitimation"—then there is a "legitimation deficit."[33]

30. Joseph Schumpeter, *Capitalism, Socialism, and Democracy* (New York: Harper, 1942).

31. Samuel Brittan, "The Economic Contradictions of Democracy," *British Journal of Political Science* 5 (1975): 129–59.

32. Jurgen Habermas, *Legitimation Crisis* (Boston: Beacon, 1975), 36–37, 68–75; Claus Offe, "Political Authority and Class Structure—an Analysis of Late Capitalist Societies," *International Journal of Sociology* (1972): 73–108; James O'Connor, *The Fiscal Crisis of the State* (New York: St. Martin's Press, 1973).

33. Habermas, "What Does a Crisis Mean Today?" 662.

According to Habermas, late capitalism seeks to fend off the crisis by "structural depoliticization" so that the contentious issues are handled outside normal arenas of conflict and ostensibly class-neutral political institutions are not compromised. This insulation of the public realm from popular participation is justified either by democratic elite theories (including Weber and Schumpeter) or technocratic theories. Habermas concludes pessimistically: "Late capitalist societies are endangered by a collapse of legitimation."[34]

Although it is wise not to overstate the commonalities in these groups of theories, certain themes recur. First, all agree that the range and volume of citizen demands on the state have grown substantially. Second, there is a general awareness that the state has been given new responsibilities about which consensus is particularly difficult to obtain. Examples include education, social legislation, abortion, family law, homosexuality, and the like. Third, it is widely believed that government agencies and state structures simply do not now, and perhaps never can, satisfy the expectations held of them. Finally, the disjunction between expectations of the state and accomplishment by the state is quite likely to undermine the foundations of legitimacy. Where there is a legitimation crisis for Habermas, there is a "delegitimation of authority" for Crozier, Huntington, and Watanuki.[35] Here there is little dissensus—democratic states cannot stand without adequate legitimation. The case is ably encapsulated by Ralf Dahrendorf.[36] To be governable, he argues, governments must be effective and legitimate. Overload on governmental capacities leads to ineffectiveness, in substantial part through "the arteriosclerosis of government." It is a short road from loss of effectiveness to loss of legitimacy. For a democratic government, effectiveness coupled with delegitimation spells ungovernability—and that constitutes crisis.

Having maintained that concepts of crisis and ungovernability transcend ideological commitments, it must be emphasized that the degree of entailment between a prognosis and its solution is not always—perhaps is never—obvious. In some cases, it is far from clear what, if anything, would constitute a satisfactory solution. Indeed, exacerbation of stresses on the state to plunge it into deeper crisis, and ultimately collapse, seems to be the unstated corollary of certain analyses. In other cases, solutions may range from adaptations by the state or reconstruction of the institutions that articulate citizen interests through changes in the substance and volume of demands. Again, the logic of argumentation may

34. Ibid., p. 667.

35. Michael Crozier, Samuel Huntington, and Joji Watanuki, *The Crisis of Democracy* (New York: New York University Press, 1975).

36. Ralf Dahrendorf, "Effectiveness and Legitimacy: On the Governability of Democracies," *Political Quarterly* 51 (October-December, 1980): 393–410.

imply sometimes that ends be changed but at other times that those ends be pursued by expedients as divergent as fortification of government or devolution by government.

The third elaboration concerns the locus of crisis. In contemporary accounts, it varies by nation-states, by elements of the state or government, and by "historical moment." While some neo-Marxists see a deep-seated malaise throughout late capitalist societies, other observers, who have weighed the evidence more thoroughly, note considerable variation among western states.[37] While, for instance, they might acknowledge that Britain and the United States may have become more difficult to govern over the last decade, the contrary might be claimed for Germany and Italy, with France remaining an equivocal case. To add further empirical qualification to sweeping empirical claims, recent scholarship is emphatic in its insistence that autonomy and effectiveness of the state or of government may vary by policy areas and, indeed, by historical period.[38]

Each of these elaborations therefore constitutes a qualification to the general thesis of ungovernability as it also sounds a cautionary note: they effectively insist that, if the notion has any credence, it must be demonstrated objectively as well as construed subjectively; its recognition transcends ideological commitments; and its manifestations must be carefully documented and specified by nation, elements of the state or government, and historical period.

Governability and the Professions

In this context of overload and crisis, the relations between the professions and the state are ambiguous. From one point of view professions are part of the problem. The intensive striving of professions over a century or more for monopoly over areas of work has been well documented. That monopoly has been achieved principally through the co-optation of government and through governmental delegation of powers of self-regulation and licensing to professional associations. Each added increment of economic advantage for a profession and each threat of incursion on its work territory, together with changes in licensing standards, pressed a profession once more on the legislature and sometimes the judiciary for the enhancement of statutory powers given it. In this respect, therefore, professions have added, however marginally, to the burden of government. And while little evidence has been proffered to support the proposition, it also seems

37. Compare Birch, "Overload, Ungovernability and Delegitimation," 159–60.
38. See Theda Skocpol, "Bringing the State Back In: Strategies of Analysis of Current Research," in *Bringing the State Back In*, ed. Peter B. Evans et al. (Cambridge, Mass.: Cambridge University Press, 1985), 3–37. Compare Terry Johnson, "The State and the Professions: Peculiarities of the British," in *Social Class and the Division of Labor*, ed. Anthony Giddens and Gavin McKenzie, (Cambridge: Cambridge University Press, 1982).

likely that, the greater the size and inclusiveness of professions, the greater the volume and the more insistent the demands they have and will make on government. For the approach of professions to power has progressively exceeded their narrow interests in pecuniary advancement and the enhancement of status. Professions have taken it on themselves to propose legislation in a variety of spheres related to the delivery of their specialist services.

Moreover, professions may oppose as well as propose legislation. If they do not always possess the political force to have their own initiatives enacted, as in the classic mode of interest-group representation, they frequently do have sufficient strength and influence to veto proposals that might undermine their occupational advantages or implement changes in the institutions that they dominate. The opposition of the medical profession to various degrees of government intervention in the delivery of health services, whether in Britain or the United States, makes it clear that not only can a profession mobilize resources against governmental initiatives but if it cannot block passage of the legislation completely it can usually manage some substantial modifications of it. In either case, the professions can constrain governments that stray into professional domains. And in both cases, with the capacity of government to act restricted, the professions effectively contribute to the overloading of demands confronted by the state.

From another point of view, however, the professions may be viewed as an agent of adaptation to ungovernability. While the contributions professions might make to effective government are absent from much current debate, a strain of writings in macrosociology did anticipate that the professions might come to have a critical function in the capacity of industrial democracies to meet the demands modernity placed on them. A line of intellectual filiation from Durkheim in early twentieth-century France, through Carr-Saunders and Wilson in interwar England, to Parsons and Bell in postwar America, each of whom wrote in strikingly different social milieus and interpreted the crises in their respective countries in different ways, nonetheless concurs that the social organization or expertise of professions may, in certain circumstances, alleviate the crises of liberal democratic societies.

For Durkheim modern France faced moral disorganization and social "anarchy," the breakdown of institutions through rampant individualism and the decline of moral authority. Because the family and the church, traditional sources of social solidarity, had themselves shared in the social decay, he proposed that social solidarity would have to find a new center—*corps intermediaires*. Noting the ubiquity of guildlike groups in history, Durkheim surmised that, "if from the origins of the City until the height of the Empire, and from the birth of the Christian societies until the French Revolution they have been necessary, this is probably because they respond to some permanent or profound need." While Durkheim does not restrict his discussion to those organizations of work subsequently designated as professions, it is clear from his description of the functions to be performed by intermediate bodies that they would act in some respects as contemporary professions have done. *Corps intermediaires* would regulate the internal affairs of their occupation, provide welfare for their members, arbitrate internal disputes among workers, and maintain solidarity and moral discipline.[39]

At the same time, the intermediate association would be more than a source of social integration—it might become "the basis or one of the essential bases of our political organization" and even "the elementary division of the state, the fundamental political unit." Durkheim does not anticipate the expert function such organizations could satisfy. He does, however, recognize that the state could "be the liberator of the individual" only if it were restrained by other collective forces, among which he would count the corporations.[40]

Whereas in France sociologists perceived that individualism was the prime threat to social stability, a number of social observers in Britain between the world wars anticipated a political crisis—that the admission of all sectors of English society into the electorate threatened to subvert standards of political decision making, that mass political enfranchisement might unduly quicken the pace of social change replacing political evolution with revolution, and that socialist politics might produce in Britain a collectivist and omnipotent state. Standing against a dominant state, it was hoped, professional associations would provide a counterweight. With the breakdown of old centers of association, voluntary work organizations might offer a compelling alternative basis of fellowship where men could find "permanent anchorage and shelter" and from which they could proceed to shape their organizations "into instruments for the fulfilment of their purposes. The professions would become the exemplars and bulwarks of social stability."[41]

In this view, their solidarity must be committed to a more critical problem: the nexus of knowledge and power. Carr-Saunders and Wilson looked less to the moral potential of professions than their promise of expert authority, for professions above all are those occupations in which there is the "application of an

39. Emile Durkheim, preface to *The Division of Labor in Society*, 2d ed. (New York: Free Press, 1964), p. 9.

40. See ibid., p. 27, and the general discussion in pp. 1–31. However, it is clear that Durkheim had a far more embracing, hierarchical, and authoritative notion in mind than most professional associations in Western countries. Compare Steven Lukes's detailed discussion on administrative syndicalism and the future organization of society in *Emile Durkheim: His Life and Work* (New York: Peregrine, 1973).

41. See, e.g., T. H. Marshall, "The Recent History of Professionalism in Relation to Social Structure and Social Policy," *Canadian Journal of Economics and Political Science* 5 (August 1939): 128–55; A. M. Carr-Saunders and P. A. Wilson, *The Professions* (Oxford: Oxford University Press, 1933).

intellectual technique to the ordinary business of life, acquired as the result of a long and specialized training." From the "centres of initiative and vitality" provided by professional associations, professions were "to bring Knowledge to the service of Power," placing their monopoly over knowledge in the service of the state. Their articulation of the issue bears direct quotation. "The association between scientific inquiry and the art of government has become a prime necessity. Knowledge is power. Authority without knowledge is powerless. Power dissociated from knowledge is a revolutionary force. Unless the modern world works out a satisfactory relationship between expert knowledge and popular control the days of democracy are numbered." [42] Insofar as professions are the principal repositories of knowledge, their relations with government become an essential component in its capacity to rule. "Over against them [the professions] stands the democracy in need of an expert. *The establishment of a right relationship between knowledge and power is the central problem of modern democracy.* Professional associations are not the only repositories of knowledge, but they are the repositories of a very special kind of knowledge; and the problem of the establishment of proper relations between them and the democratic state is one of the urgent problems of the day" (my italics). [43]

Clearly, the implications of knowledge for power are more paradoxical than Carr-Saunders and Wilson admit. On the one hand, an expertise in decision making and administration may be a necessary condition of the effectiveness and ultimately the legitimacy of the regime and form of government that it represents. By the same token, however, the predominance of those organizations that purvey knowledge in the processes of government may gradually subvert the very institution of democratic politics they purport to serve by blocking those legitimate demands on government that emerge from sectors of society not represented by professions. The call for professional commitment to government can mean either a refinement of representative government or its circumvention.

Although Parsons does not follow the English writers or Durkheim in their emphasis on occupational or professional associations per se, he does share with them a stress on professional authority and expertise as it may be brought to bear on the problems of the day. Parsons believes that "every major innovation in the organization of societies involves a new leadership element—in structural rather than personal terms." Secularization in the modern world would not allow that authority to be vested in traditional religion for the new leadership would require an intellectual and moral authority that was religiously pluralistic. In modern societies, such a leadership is located "in the marriage between the academic pro-

---

42. Carr-Saunders and Wilson, *The Professions*, 485–86. On my interpretation of "knowledge in the service of power," see chap. 12, generally and n. 35, chap. 12.
43. Ibid.

fessionals and certain categories of practical men. These latter have taken responsibility on a basis more of specialized competence than of diffuse religious or ideological legitimation, for a variety of operative functions in society." The profession of learning takes over the mantle from the clergy to emerge as the new "secular moralists" whose function is the diagnosis of the "moral problems of the human condition." With other professions, they apply cognitive rationality to the satisfaction of "our most important social functions." [44]

Daniel Bell returns more explicitly to the relations of knowledge and power in his depiction of a post industrial society in which, he maintains, knowledge and especially theoretical knowledge form the central organizing principle. That society "strengthens the role of science and cognitive values as a basic institutional necessity of a society [and] by making decisions more technical it brings the scientist or economist more directly into the political process." Technical skill becomes the base of power and education the mode of access to it. With such resources, professional and technical classes will become preeminent in the occupational structure, a class based not on property but on knowledge. Because knowledge and planning become "the basic requisites for all organized action in a modern society," scientists are drawn increasingly into the arena of public policy. [45]

The ethos of this class will arise "from the ethos of science and out of the scientific and professional community," embodying norms of social responsiveness. The norms of the new intelligentsia—of professionalism—will be "a departure from the hitherto prevailing norms of economic self-interest." [46] Carried by a community of self-regulating peers and governing the application of knowledge to public policy, that ethos will come to infuse the society of the imminent future.

The passage of time has muted many of these fears and destroyed some of these hopes. *Corps intermediaires*, as Durkheim conceived them, did not develop in the strict form he anticipated in Anglo-Saxon countries. The pessimism of English writers about universal enfranchisement and an omnipotent state was unwarranted. And the moral and normative leadership predicted of contemporary professions may be fated to disappointment. These themes have lain fallow as the theoretical temper of the times has changed. In their place have come alternative arguments that owe more intellectual fealty to Weber and Marx. For example, the very substantial commitment to both the theory and the practice of professional economic goals has proved provocative. An interpretation of this kind had already been made by Milton Friedman in the late 1940s, although he

44. Talcott Parsons, "Professions," in *International Encyclopedia of Social Sciences* (1978).
45. Daniel Bell, *The Coming of Post-industrial Society* (New York: Basic, 1973), 362.
46. Ibid.

drew more from laissez-faire economic theory than from European social theory. More recently, Jeffrey Berlant wove together Weber's theory of monopoly with Parsons's writing on institutionalization and used the British and American medical associations to illustrate the thesis that the pursuit and institutionalization of monopoly constitutes a primary orientation of modern professional associations—and that they have succeeded remarkably well. Monopolistic thinking has come to infuse a broad body of writing on many professions. Nonetheless, although telling in part, the theory of professional economic pursuits has failed to comprehend adequately the full breadth of collective professional influence, especially as it concerns state effectiveness. The consequence is at best an incomplete characterization, and at worst a mischaracterization, of professions' contemporary significance for the state.

In many ways, a more fundamental political critique of professions comes from neo-Marxist sources. By skillfully redirecting and focusing the thought of Gramsci, Althusser, and Habermas on Anglo-Saxon professions, Magali Larson has stimulated vigorous reinterpretations of contemporary professionalism. In the process, she absorbs into her argument the economic monopoly thesis and, drawing on Gramsci, broadens it into claims of ideological monopoly and hegemony.

Larson maintains that in addition to the nineteenth- and early twentieth-century professional projects of market control and collective social mobility, late twentieth-century Anglo-American professions legitimate the technocracy and meritocracy of the "new structures of domination and inequality" that characterize monopoly capitalism. For example, in order to obscure class bases of recruitment to state structures, the professions espouse an ideology of meritocracy that their educational institutions, ostensibly constructed to effect meritocratic bases of admission, effectively deny because admission policies inevitably favor applicants whose class background has afforded them better educational opportunities at every phase of their schooling. A principal contribution of the profession to the capitalist state, in Larson's terms, is to legitimate its hegemony by obscuring the real bases of state domination.

Furthermore, this argument asserts, "university-based structures of expertise . . . exert a decidedly undemocratic influence." Universities validate the knowledge claims of experts and socialize everyone into "social-epistemological deference." Not only is knowledge converted into a form of property, but the expansion of expertise shrinks the areas of "common-sense" and squeezes citizens out of decision making in areas vital to their own lives. By constituting themselves as agents of the state, professions come to define large tracts of social life.[47]

---

47. See Magali Sarfatti Larson, "The Production of Expertise and the Constitution of Expert

Consistent with Habermas, the expansion of expertise is accompanied by a contraction of politics—the "depoliticization of the public realm": decision making is diverted to the private sector and public administration becomes "effectively insulated from public debate and political conflict"; decisions become so complex that "the average person is also disenfranchised by his lack of expert knowledge." [48]

Having adeptly applied the thinking of Gramsci and Althusser, on the one hand, and Habermas, on the other, Larson more recently draws in a non-Marxist thinker, Michel Foucault. Although Foucault posits his central problem as that of knowledge/power and traces the "micro-systems of power" in great intricacy, where knowledge and power are diffused through and are constitutive of every social interaction no matter how mundane, he does not explicitly treat professions per se. [49] But where Arney has sought to interpret the techniques of control within the profession of obstetrics in Foucauldian terms, [50] Larson appropriates Foucault's thought more generally to characterize the operation of the "silent, non-personal, non-physical coercion" that professions exercise through their monopoly over a given arena of discourse, whether it be legal, medical, or theological. To the extent that professions are given "the task of defining needs and services" they develop a "penetrating technology of power" that creates a new form of discipline and social control that is barely perceived by those subject to it. [51]

These perspectives have numerous points of contact with the general problem being broached here. They acknowledge the significance of the university for legitimation of the profession; they recognize and elaborate the extraordinary permeability of institutions and society by professional modes of discourse; and they point to antidemocratic potentialities of unbridled expertise. In so doing, they reaffirm by implication Carr-Saunders and Wilson's dictum that finding a "right relation" between knowledge and power constitutes the central political problem

---

Power," in *The Authority of Experts*, ed. Thomas L. Haskell (Bloomington: Indiana University Press, 1984), 28–80, esp. 45–46, 53ff.

48. Ibid, pp. 38–39.

49. On Foucault more generally, see Michel Foucault, *Power/Knowledge: Selected Interviews and Other Writings, 1972–1977*, ed. Colin Gordon (New York: Pantheon/Random House, 1980); Charles C. Lemert and Garth Gillan, *Michel Foucault: Social Theory and Transgression* (New York: Columbia University Press, 1982); and Hayden White, "Foucault Decoded: Notes from Underground," in *Tropics of Discourse: Essays in Cultural Criticism* (Baltimore: Johns Hopkins University Press, 1978), 230–60.

50. William Ray Arney, *Power and the Profession of Obstetrics* (Chicago: University of Chicago Press, 1982); William Ray Arney and Bernard J. Bergen, *Medicine and the Management of Living* (Chicago: University of Chicago Press, 1984), 3–6.

51. Larson, "Production of Expertise," pp. 34–35.

for modern democracies. At the same time, the neo-Marxist and Foucauldian approaches have many difficulties, not the least of which is their ideological commitment to a form of government quite other than liberal democracy: it is a little wry to point out the "antidemocratic use of expert knowledge" while advocating a system in which these tensions would be dissolved but whose attributes are never disclosed. That approach recognizes the problem but still begs the question of a solution within or outside liberal democratic political systems. Moreover, depoliticization in itself cannot automatically be considered to be "antidemocratic," however that may be defined: a society or government may choose to depoliticize certain issues in order to open or keep open the political arena to others, thereby using priorities to establish what *may* be moved out of political contention in order to make room for what *must* be debated and decided in the public realm. If the significance of professions for government is to be interpreted principally in terms of culture, ideology, or material interests, then an entire field of activity, related directly to state effectiveness and thus indirectly to legitimation, will remain unexplored. It is this arena of professional collective action that may be the most consequential for ungovernability and the delegitimation of authority.

In each of these theoretical traditions, classical or modern, there are strains of thought that may be loosely woven into a new conjunction. During the past century, professions in the United States have rapidly merged features of two classical conceptions of guilds. On the one hand, they have adopted some features, including self-regulation, solidarity, and intermediate association, of Durkheim's *corps intermediaires*. On the other hand, they have developed in modern guise the monopolistic inclinations Weber described in medieval guilds. In the process of both endeavors, many professions have constructed formidable vehicles for political mobilization. The mobilization of professional expertise, however, can occur not only to inform state administration and improve government decision making on particular issues, as the interwar British theorists supposed; nor is it even restricted to ideological support of the regime, as Larson contends; but it may also be directed to the rationalization of government through structural adaptation and change. If one component of ungovernability is the inability of state and government organizations to cope with different patterns and substance of demands, then one mode of adaptation may be to alter the structure of state institutions; this can occur in the processes of articulating demands, of informing deliberation and decision making, and of effecting administration. Here the mandate of empowered professionalism becomes neither cultural nor economic but structural. Of all professionals, lawyers, whose profession is state constitutive, have the greatest capabilities for structural alterations of state organs.

To posit this putative relation between professional empowerment and structural rationalization leads the argument back to an aspect of Weber's theory seldom linked to discussions of professions.

State Crisis, Professional Empowerment, and Legal Rationalization

Rationalization is the central pivot around which Weber revolves his comparative sociology of the West. The main lines of development in Western civilization are ordered in terms of their rationality in various institutional spheres, and thus both Weber's sociology and philosophy of history are permeated by the manifold configurations of reason in this distinctive, and quintessentially modern, civilization.[52] Indeed, the theoretical force of rationalization has more than antiquarian significance: for Kalberg, the contemporary mandate for a sociology informed by Weberian thought is to explore "the vicissitudes of rationalization processes in history at all levels of sociocultural process."[53]

Weber's theory of legal rationalization remains one of the most powerful theories of legal change. The theory derives its force from several attributes. First, it is parsimonious—from a relatively economical conceptual core, it can subsume a vast range of developments in the content and organization of law in advanced capitalist societies. Second, it is theoretically embedded—unlike some other influential accounts of legal change, Weber's theory of legal change constitutes one component of a macroscopic interpretation of Western sociocultural change in terms of general rationalization, a process that extends from music and religion to commerce and social organization. Third, the Weberian corpus is empirically grounded—not only in local and contemporary social settings but in the history of institutions and the comparative analysis of entire societies. Fourth, the account of legal rationalization is dynamic—neither inflexible nor unilinear, Weber's theory recognizes both the retreats and the advances that characterize any process of rationalization as it emerges from the clash of interests and classes, from the tension of tradition and charisma.[54]

Given these several merits, it is unfortunate that the theory of legal rationalization has not received sustained *empirical* attention in any Anglo-American country. There have been valuable theoretical formulations of Weber's thinking about

---

52. Guenther Roth and Wolfgang Schlucter, *Max Weber's Vision of History: Ethics and Method* (Berkeley: University of California Press, 1979); Karl Loewirth, "Weber's Interpretations of the Bourgeois-Capitalistic World in Terms of the Guiding Principle of 'Rationalization,'" in, *Max Weber*, ed. Dennis Wrong (Englewood Cliffs, N.J.: Prentice-Hall, 1970).

53. Stephen Kalberg, "Max Weber's Types of Rationality: Cornerstones of Rationalization Processes in History," *American Journal of Sociology* 85 (March 1980): 1177.

54. For a particularly lucid and balanced analysis of rationalization processes in all their multivocality, see Donald N. Levine, *The Flight From Ambiguity; Essays in Social and Cultural Theory* (Chicago: University of Chicago Press, 1985), chap. 7.

the rationality of law,[55] and as there have also been fruitful accounts of legal change that more or less explicitly draw on Weberian ideas.[56] But there are few systematic attempts to give Weber's notion an empirical content, just as there is a dearth of comprehensive efforts to map the advance or retreat of legal rationalization in American law and legal institutions.

Weber's ideas have a further advantage—in the case of law, they are linked to the organization and politics of the legal profession. They therefore converge with the questions I have broached concerning the societal and political significance of modern, politically organized, resource-wealthy professional associations.

Weber maintained that rationalization in the legal system could proceed in at least two ways—the rationalization of substantive and procedural law; and the rationalization of the administration of justice. The most notable instance of rationalization in substantive law is codification, best exemplified in the legal codes developed by the German Pandectists in the late nineteenth century. Codification can be little more than compilation of existing law or rearrangement of the prevailing law "in an orderly and systematic fashion." Even though these are instances of increasing systematization and hence progressions toward rationalization, a more authentic codification requires a systematic revision of the substantive content of law such that a given area is subsumed under a hierarchically ordered set of legal propositions, or first principles, that range from the most abstract statements to more specific provisions. This positive law comprises a " 'gapless' system of rules" that can be applied to any concrete case by means of legal logic.[57] In Continental civil law, codes are constructed deductively from higher-order first principles; while their common-law analogues share some of their formal attributes, codes in the United States emerge from an inductive process of generalizing abstract principles from a multiplicity of cases.

Rationalization of the administration of justice occurs through the interplay of two processes—structural differentiation and bureaucratization. The latter, Weber argues, has the merit of "precision, speed, consistency, availability of records, continuity, possibility of secrecy, unity, rigorous co-ordination"—in short, attributes that ensure the most efficient administration. Nevertheless, if administration is to be completely bureaucratized, it must be accompanied by

55. David M. Trubek, "Max Weber on Law and the Rise of Capitalism," *Wisconsin Law Review* 1972, no. 3: 720–53; Anthony T. Kronman, *Max Weber* (Stanford, Calif.: Stanford University Press, 1983), 72–95.

56. Philippe Nonet and Philip Selznick, *Law and Society in Transition: Towards Responsive Law* (New York: Harper & Row, 1978).

57. Max Weber, *On Law in Economy and Society*, ed. Max Rheinstein (New York: Simon & Schuster, 1954), esp. 224–83, 349–56.

structural differentiation. Weber makes it clear that greater administrative formalism in legal institutions has required a series of successive steps in which the judiciary has become structurally detached from other institutions. In the religious sphere, judicial administration had to become separated from theocratic expediency and the substantive ideals of a great religion. In the political sphere, the judiciary needed to move away from the control of patrimonial patronage and the discretionary fiat of individual rulers. As Weber observes, legal formalism, which binds political expediency and personal fiat by rules, is "repugnant to all authoritarian powers," religious or secular.

Using the cases of Germany and England, Weber maintained that, among other factors such as the character of lawyers' education, the pace and types of legal rationalization are highly contingent on lawyers and judges, the modes of organization and collective action open to them, and the ways in which they choose to deploy their collective advantages.[58] The most startling contrast, in Weber's comparison of English and German professions, was the inverse relation between degree of collective organization and the propensity of legal professions to engage in rationalizing activity. In Germany, where codification proceeded rapidly, the organizations of lawyers were relatively weak. In England, where rationalization of a Continental form, among other reasons, was retarded, the Inns of Court were particularly strong. Indeed, legal rationalization in England proceeded slowly precisely because it was actively impeded by lawyer "guilds."

It is the very essence of Weber's comparative methodology that a set of relations that hold in one historical context must be systematically examined in others. The value of that methodological imperative is vindicated by a thesis in this book: in sharp contrast to the English legal profession, which opposed rationalization, its common-law sister profession in the United States has in recent decades become a forceful agent of legal rationalization, if not exactly of the forms articulated by Weber. Its role in this respect has significance not just for a sociology of law: to the extent that law and legal systems constitute elements of the state, rationalizing propensities also have direct ramifications for state effectiveness and legitimacy.

Consequently, an advance in the macrosociology of professions requires a retreat into classical writings to pick up themes that have lain dormant and to revivify these themes in a new historical and comparative juncture. Once we proceed in this fashion, we should find that the significance of professions for modern societies may well go beyond monopoly and beyond ideology. When professions bring knowledge to power, their consequences for governability may

58. Ibid., 198–224.

also go beyond enlightenment of legislators and assistance in delivery of services. The new task is to investigate the significance of professions for the structure of the state itself.

The rapprochement of expert knowledge and political power, especially as it is manifested by the professions, represents an enduring conundrum in which excess in either direction destabilizes democratic institutions. An excess of knowledge, particularly if it is monopolized by small, elite occupations, disenfranchises effective political participation; an excess of participation, particularly if it is uninformed by technical expertise and "social intelligence," deprives the state of effectiveness. Consequently, expert authority, as it is extensively mobilized by professions, confronts representational authority, as it is lodged in the electorate. Finding the actual balance between the forms of authority, as they are exemplified by the professions and the state in different places and periods, represents the primary empirical task of the macrosociology of professions.

2 Knowledge Mandates
and Political Mobilization

Strains and crises of governability have pressed elements of states to seek alternative structural arrangements.[1] I have suggested that a new symbiosis might emerge between such overburdened states and empowered professions. Put another way, confronted with a surfeit of expectations and an incapacity to resolve them internally, the state may volunteer—or be forced to devolve—some of its responsibilities and to delegate more of its functions on professions if only to allow other areas to remain in the political arena.

The emergence of potentially powerful occupational groups like the professions and the convergence of this development with the crises of an overburdened state raise as many questions about professions as those that have been addressed to the condition of ungovernability itself. How can professions be a major contender as an auxiliary to government? How have they persuaded or enabled governments to devolve responsibilities and functions on them? How great has their influence become? What determines the variable scope of that influence? Have the professions expanded the domains in which they have become involved? These questions pose a theoretical and research agenda far beyond that which can be satisfactorily accomplished in one work. However, we can broach some of the circumstances in which answers can be found.

Two sets of conditions order profession-state relations: the attributes of professions and those of states. When the state confronts tasks in excess of its capacities, then the accompanying crisis becomes a necessary, but not sufficient, condition of intervention by professions. Yet any possibility of symbiosis depends, not just on opportunities for intervention unwittingly proffered by the state, but on the facility of professions to take advantage of them. Having addressed some state precursors to a new rapprochement, it is necessary to turn to the preconditions of activism by professions.

1. Pages 29–49 of this chapter are a revised version of Terence C. Halliday, "Knowledge Mandates: Collective Influence by Scientific, Normative, and Syncretic Professions," *British Journal of Sociology* 36 (September 1985): 421–47.

For all professions, the ability to exert collective influence depends, first, on knowledge mandates and, second, on collegial mobilization. The *knowledge mandate* of a profession is its capacity to exert influence in virtue of the substance, form, transmission, efficacy, objects, and legitimacy of its cognitive core. It is an epistemological warrant for public influence. Knowledge mandates and the state are mediated by occupational and organizational politics. Consequently, professional influence requires *political mobilization*, at least insofar as the profession speaks on its own corporate behalf. Clearly, there is also an enormous amount of influence, albeit diffuse, exercised by individual practitioners within and outside governments. That is not the focus here. Rather I am concerned almost entirely with action by professions qua professions.

The extent to which professions can bring their expertise to the state through knowledge mandates and collegial mobilization can be specified in terms of their standing on four dimensions: (1) the epistemological bases of professional knowledge; (2) the forms of professional authority; (3) the institutional loci of professional activity; and (4) the attributes of political organization. These dimensions allow similarities and differences among professions to be developed systematically. At once they provide a comparative framework for quite diverse professions and set the legal profession in a broader context.

Epistemological Bases of Professional Knowledge

The special characteristics of the knowledge possessed by professions have been a principal component of their distinctive occupational identity. Yet despite some measure of agreement on the formal properties of distinctively professional knowledge, the continued appropriation of medicine as the ideal-typical, best-researched, and most-discussed profession still points to science as the prime cognitive foundation of professionalism. Although an emphasis on knowledge as a "core generating trait" of professionalism is entirely correct, the failure to set scientific knowledge within a more comprehensive epistemological context flaws any theoretical formulation of collective relations between professions and the state.[2]

Science has undoubtedly provided a more secure foundation for some older professions as well as spawning, in conjunction with technology, entire families of new and semiprofessions. Yet the success of contemporary professions cannot be attributed primarily to science per se because two of the three longest-standing professions—law and the clergy—are not scientific in any narrow sense of the

2. Dietrich Rueschemeyer, "Doctors and Lawyers: A Comment on the Theory of the Professions," in *Medical Men and Their Work*, ed. Eliot Freidson and Judith Lorber (Chicago: Aldine-Atherton, 1972), 5–19; W. J. Goode, "The Theoretical Limits of Professionalization," in *The Semi-professions and Their Organization*, edited by Amitai Etzioni (New York: Free Press, 1969).

term. Although it is true that, since the Enlightenment, the star of religion shines less brightly, the church continues to wield considerable influence over diverse areas of contemporary culture and society. Law by contrast has enjoyed virtually the same spectacular success as leading scientific professions on most indicators of professional success, whether they be completeness of occupational monopolies, expansion of the market for professional services, or rise in monetary and status rewards. If professions' achievements are to be explained, therefore, it is appropriate that stress be laid on aspects of knowledge that include science and nonscience.

Some formal properties of knowledge may be common to several professions. Hence Larson's description of the optimal cognitive base for a monopoly of skill is as apposite for law as it is for medicine. Following Goode, she argues that this knowledge "must be specific enough to impart distinctiveness to the professional commodity, it must be formalized or codified enough to allow standardization of the product, and ultimately of the producers, and yet it must not be so clearly codified that it does not allow a principle of exclusion to exist." [3]

Nonetheless, what is *common* to established professions does not enable us to explain *differences* in collective action. To do that requires a consideration of epistemology. A useful starting point for an epistemological analysis is the well-known (and much-debated) philosophical distinction in Hume's moral philosophy between judgments of fact and judgments of value. The dichotomy has been stated in numerous ways. Judgments of fact are expressed in descriptive statements by propositions that assert what *is* the case; judgments of value are prescriptive statements that assert what *should be* the case.[4] Judgments of fact, or "is" statements, can be verified by recourse to experience or empirical inquiry, whereas judgments of value, or "ought" statements, about what is right or what is good cannot be ascertained by empirical investigation. The different logical status of the two classes of statements, or the extent of logical entailment between one class of statements and the other, is encapsulated in the assertion that "moral discourse is an autonomous mode of discourse. This means that no moral or normative claim is derivable from, or depends for its validity on, purely nonmoral or non-normative statements." [5] Furthermore, morality cannot be reduced to an empirical science. A knowledge of "nonmoral facts alone" does not provide a sufficient basis on which logically to conclude what we should do. This is

3. Larson, The Rise of Professionalism, 30–31.

4. W. K. Frankena, *Ethics* (Englewood Cliffs, N.J.: Prentice-Hall, 1963); K. Klappholz, "Economics and Ethical Neutrality," in *Encyclopedia of Philosophy*, ed. Paul Edwards (New York: Macmillan, 1967), 2: 451–54.

5. Kai Neilson, "Problems of Ethics," in *Encyclopedia of Philosophy*, ed. Paul Edwards (New York: Macmillan, 1967), 3: 117–34. On G. E. Moore's refutation of ethical naturalism, see R. M. Hare, *The Language of Morals* (Oxford: Oxford University Press, 1964); Frankena, *Ethics*.

not to say that facts are irrelevant to moral judgments. Obviously, certain facts are good reasons for a moral position, although they are not value propositions in themselves. Nevertheless, at a fundamental level, there remains a logical gap between facts and values.

At once it must be acknowledged that each of the preceding assertions has been thought controvertible by one or another school of moral philosophy or epistemology. Efforts to dissolve the distinction have taken several forms. Naturalistic theories of metaethics would relate values to facts by defining "good," and therefore perhaps what should be done, in terms of observable criteria, such as the utilitarian test in one of its positive or negative formulations. Of closer proximity to social science, attempts to reduce each side of the distinction to the other are manifold. A Marxism can reduce ethics to a historical epoch, a mode of production, or the ideological hegemony of a ruling class or one of its fractions. But if morality can be reduced to a science in one direction, the obverse can occur in the other. Myrdal and others maintain that facts are subject to, or permeated by, "value impregnation." More radically, Marcuse views science itself as ideology, while Habermas maintains that a form of knowledge, such as science, contains its own implicit values.[6] Alternatively, some metaethical philosophers espouse a "good reasons" approach to the question of justification of values. Stephen Toulmin, Kai Nielsen and John Rawls, among others, have been reluctant to discard the "is-ought" distinction out of hand, but they acknowledge that it is a muddle, that facts are often good reasons for certain moral stances, and that the division of utterances into descriptive and evaluative statements is far from neat.[7] Thus while some philosophers consider the distinction to be beside the point and others can assert that the fact-value dichotomy is "an intellectual prison," yet others still vigorously assert that "for a generation or more there has been a virtually uninterrupted succession of essays insisting that the factual and evaluative realms cannot be separated. Yet . . . no one . . . appears to doubt that you cannot derive 'ought' from 'is' except perhaps in a few special cases."[8]

6. K. Klappholz, "Value Judgements and Economics," *British Journal for the Philosophy of Science* 15 (1964): 97–114; J. Habermas, *Toward a Rational Society* (Boston: Beacon, 1970); H. Marcuse, *One-dimensional Man* (Boston: Beacon, 1964); Gunnar Myrdal, *Value in Social Theory* (London, 1958).

7. Steven Toulmin, *An Examination of the Place of Reason in Ethics* (Cambridge: Cambridge University Press, 1950); Kai Nielsen, "The 'Good Reasons Approach' and 'Ontological Justifications of Morality,'" *Philosophical Quarterly* (1959); John Rawls, "Justice as Fairness," *Philosophical Review* (1955). On muddles, note Alasdair MacIntyre's characterization: "Every modern moral philosopher is against all modern moral philosophies except himself and his immediate allies" ("Why Is the Search for the Foundations of Ethics so Frustrating?" *Hastings Center Report*, 8 [August 1979], 18).

8. K. R. Minogue, "Review Article: Relativism on the Banks of the Isis," *Government and Opposition* 18 (Summer 1983): 361–62.

These difficulties cannot be dismissed. Neither can they be resolved here. I will take the position that, attempts at controversion not withstanding, there are philosophical grounds for continuing to maintain that prescription and description are logically distinct. I want broadly to characterize scientific modes of discourse and inquiry that are derived from descriptive statements as different from normative and moral discourse and the logic by which it is produced. The distinction between different kinds of professional knowledge that is developed here rests on this fundamental philosophical divide, albeit one with jagged edges and numerous dissentients.

The logical distinction between the two areas of discourse is critical for comparisons of collective professional influence. To put it oversimply, the professions divide into classes depending on whether the cognitive base is primarily of the descriptive or the prescriptive. For scientific professions, which lie on one side of the logical divide, knowledge is empirically derived from observation and experimental inquiry in methods epitomized by the natural and biological sciences. For normative professions, which lie on the other side of the divide, the substance of their discourse and the manner in which it is derived are concerned primarily with matters of value—values in respect of how one should attain salvation, how salvation should mold individual and social ethics, and how individuals and groups should act in relation to each other and the state. On these grounds, *scientific professions*, such as engineering and medicine, can be distinguished from *normative professions*, such as the clergy and law. The former are ultimately seconded on facts and the appropriate modes of inquiry, such as Popper's well-known falsifiability criterion, to ascertain what is true or false; the latter are custodians of moral enterprises, systems of rules that prescribe how individual and social lives should be ordered. In terms of Edward Shils's essay "Charisma, Order, and Status," all these professions share a fundamental ordering power of those "very central feature[s] of man-existence and the cosmos in which he lives." But whereas one class of professions is concerned with "law or laws governing the universe" established by scientific discovery, another class of professions concerns itself with "ultimate principles of law which should govern man's conduct."[9] The common identity of established professions lies in their provision of an order in which individuals can locate themselves; differentiation among professions occurs inasmuch as one group of professions derives that ordering power from natural and scientific law whereas the other promulgates divine law or positive law.

This preliminary distinction between classes of professions makes no claim to a discovery de novo. It has either been presaged or lain implicit in scholarly work

9. Edward Shils, "Charisma, Order, and Status," *American Sociological Review* 30 (1965): 199–213.

on professions.[10] But if it is to be applied to collective action, the scientific/normative continuum must be qualified or elaborated in several respects.

Consequences for professionalism do not emanate from philosophical paring alone. Social constructions are made of underlying epistemological differences. It is not just that some professions rely on knowledge generated in an alternative way than others but also that a profession and its public layer the philosophical underpinnings with a veneer of perceptions. The philosophy is not irrelevant to perceptions; the latter are substantially contingent on the former. Indeed the epistemological foundations are mediated to the public through the profession's manipulation of the knowledge to which it stakes an exclusive claim. Gieryn persuasively maintains that, in addition to the intrinsic intellectual authority that inheres in science, its practitioners must constantly engage in *boundary work* "to promote their authority over designated domains of knowledge." They develop "repertoires" or ideologies of self-description to advance their interests. The social construction of professional knowledge therefore exerts a more proximate shape on a profession's collective influence than its epistemological bases per se.[11]

It should immediately be emphasized that the distinction is not advanced as an adequate description of practitioner-client exchanges. In everyday practice all professional work, whether scientific or not, is infused by normative elements just as normative professions rely heavily on factual information. Christian ministers and priests traditionally have grounded their theology and ethics in a historical revelation; engineers are readily embroiled in normative issues in decision making over problems as diverse as transportation systems and pollution; doctors may use laboratories for diagnoses, but so much else in their consultations is infused with normative overtones, as the term "prescriptions" connotes. A recent survey on legal work finds that the skills ranked most important by urban lawyers are fact gathering, the capacity to marshall facts and order them, "instilling others' confidence in you," and effective oral expression.[12] All professions, normative or scientific, point also to bodies of codified knowledge that stand in a factual relation to a profession. Medicine has its physiology textbooks; lawyers have the Uniform Commercial Code or the All England Law Reports; theolo-

10. Eliot Freidson, *The Profession of Medicine* (New York: Dodd & Mead, 1970); Philip Elliott, *The Sociology of Professions* (New York: Herder & Herder, 1972), 143ff.; Rueschemeyer, "Doctors and Lawyers."

11. T. F. Gieryn, "Boundary-Work and the Demarcation of Science from Non-science: Strains and Interests in Professional Ideologies of Scientists," *American Sociological Review* 48 (December 1983): 781–95.

12. C. Bosk, *Forgive and Remember: Managing Medical Failure* (Chicago: University of Chicago Press, 1979); C. Perrucci and J. Gerstl, *Profession without Community: Engineers in American Society* (New York: Random House, 1969); F. Zemans and V. Rosenblum, *The Making of a Public Profession* (Chicago: American Bar Foundation, 1981), 123–26.

gians and the clergy have Thomas Aquinas's *Summa theologiae*, Calvin's *Institutes*, or Paul Tillich's *Systematic Theology*.

The division of professions into two classes therefore rests on a more fundamental cleavage at a different level of analysis. When each profession is pressed back to the bedrock of its authority, when its legitimacy is questioned at the most generic level, at that point professions retreat ultimately to the distinctive means by which their knowledge is created and the distinctive class of statements produced by that means. At this irreducible point of legitimation engineers and doctors claim a knowledge generated by the application of the scientific method, principally experimental, to natural and biological phenomena. In their turn, lawyers point to the law finding of judges and the law making of legislatures, an activity as normative in its way as the extrapolation by clergy of ethical promulgations grounded in a systematic theology that in turn may depend on an assumption of divine revelation. Whatever the admixture of normative and scientific elements at the level of everyday practice, however, the contrast between the classes of professions is most emphatic at the epistemological foundation of a claim to professionalism.

If the dichotomy better approaches a continuum and is least apparent in ordinary practice, and if it is most pronounced at a foundational level, it falls somewhere between these poles when professions act collectively. In representations before government, the respective bases of influence become more manifest simply because the elements of a profession's advice and legitimacy are scrutinized with particular care and even cynicism by parties and interest groups that have greater information than clients or patients do. Hence professions are forced to adhere more closely to their ultimate basis of legitimacy. Consequently, in general, it may be proposed that, the more consequential its collective recommendations, the more a profession's authority will be challenged, and thus the more it will be compelled to fall back on the legitimacy of its cognitive foundations.[13]

To this point, the discussion has centered only on those professions that fall squarely on one side or the other. The military and academic professions, however, are less susceptible to such categorical distinctions. Their epistemology straddles the divide. In so doing they evince what might be designated a *syncretist* epistemological foundation.[14] Apart from historical and traditional claims to the mantle of professionalism, the core of military expertise now comprises an

13. Compare William Goode: "Even if doctors do not use the full scope of scientific knowledge in normal practical medicine, they can always fall back on it or appeal to it" ("Theoretical Limitations," 287, 289).

14. The nature of the syncretism varies; for the military, science and normative components are interwoven in doctrine; for the academy, scientific and nonscientific disciplines coexist with limited effort at systematic integration, and thus the academic profession is barely syncretic in any strict sense.

amalgam of scientific and normative elements. Science and technology are a central component of the profession of arms. Much knowledge needed by the armed forces is identical to that required in the private sector, and scientific and technological advances frequently originate in civilian society. Nevertheless, the military develop and deploy their own technology, military engineers are a core component of modern armies, and some of the earliest military academies—the French Ecole Polytechnique (1794), the Woolwich Royal Military Academy (1741), and the Dutch Military Academy (1814)—began essentially as military engineering schools.

Distinctive to the military, however, and giving them an esoteric epistemology quite apart from other occupations, is the incorporation of science and technology into military doctrine. Doctrine can incorporate national military policy and strategy, broad battlefield operational plans (whether to give primacy to offensive or to defensive operations, whether to emphasize firepower attrition to maneuver), and the tactics of integrating particular weapons systems into optimal forms of organization.[15] In Abrahamsson's terms, the doctrines of the military, in terms comparable to other professions, are "strategy, tactics, and logistics."[16] At the broadest level, battlefield doctrine is set within an embracing framework of strategic doctrine—the principles that govern the place of military power in the international relations of a country.[17]

Von Clausewitz exemplifies the way in which the profession of arms formulates strategy and tactics through the distillation and codification of the lessons provided by military history,[18] thus condensing wisdom from previous instances of armed conflict.[19] Yet, even when the data are collected "in a true spirit of unfettered scientific inquiry,"[20] the doctrinal statements that emerge do not describe the shape of the last battle but prescribe the form of the next. Doctrine is a moral philosophy of military action, an "art" as much as a "science."[21] It must be emphasized that doctrine cannot be reduced to technology. Technological advances

15. J. S. McKitrick, "A Military Look at Military Reform," *Comparative Strategy* (February 1983), 50–62.

16. B. Abrahamsson, *Military Professionalism and Political Power* (Beverly Hills, Calif.: Sage, 1972), 60.

17. Morris Janowitz, *The Professional Soldier*, (1960; reprint, Glencoe, Ill.: Free Press, 1971).

18. C. von Clausewitz, *On War*, 3 vols. (London, Routledge & Kegan Paul, 1949).

19. E. M. Earle ed., *Makers of Modern Strategy* (Princeton, N.J.: Princeton University Press, 1943); F. R. Kirkland, "Integrating Technology and Doctrine: The French Experience" (paper read at the international conference of the Inter University Seminar on Armed Forces and Society, Chicago, 1983).

20. I. B. Holley, "The Doctrinal Process: Some Suggested Steps," *Military Review* 59 (April 1979): 2–13.

21. Compare D. W. Brogan, "The United States: Civilian and Military Power," in *Soldiers and Governments*, ed. Michael Howard (Westport, Conn.: Greenwood, 1957), 184.

frequently have failed for want of an embracing doctrine. The development of the machine gun, the tank, aircraft—all point to Holley's conclusion that superiority in weapons requires a coupling of "the best ideas from advancing technology" and "a doctrine or concept of their tactical or strategic application." [22]

The academic profession spans the epistemic divide most strikingly of all. It remains "the sole profession in an increasingly specialized world which still embraces the whole gamut of knowledge and professional skills." [23] The science faculties of the university and its scientific professional schools on one side of the dichotomy balance the normative professional schools on the other side. In between lie the humanities and the social sciences, the latter approaching, in certain of its disciplinary segments, a scientific epistemology, but of a kind (it will be assumed here) that is philosophically distinct from that which prevails in the natural and biological sciences. More important are the powerful normative components of the humanities and the social sciences. Since it has developed an extensive critical apparatus, especially about values, this nonscientific center of the academy "can do society's fundamental thinking for it, not least about the nature and purpose of society itself." [24] The academic profession, with its epistemological inclusiveness consequently has a unique potential for influence.

The three classes of professions—scientific, normative, and syncretic—have varying capacities for collective action as a consequence of their cognitive differences. In general, since scientific professions, like engineering or medicine, cannot even legitimately extend over the entire field of science in an expert manner, their expertise is limited to rather well demarcated areas of scientific accomplishment. [25]

Normative professions lose the authority of science but thereby obtain a broad mandate to range extensively over moral terrain. Although English barristers and solicitors have less desire or opportunity to do so, American lawyers, and the clergy in both countries, can directly address matters of public policy, within certain bounds, and they do so legitimately despite the fact that, over long periods, the legitimacy of each profession has been severely eroded. Indeed the mandate for the clergy has been so broadly construed that some Christians have publicly bemoaned "the internal transformation of the faith itself . . . 'such that' it comes to be defined in terms of political values." [26]

22. I. B. Holley, *Ideas and Weapons*, (New Haven, Conn.: Yale University Press, 1953), 14.
23. H. J. Perkin, *Key Profession: The History of the Association of University Teachers* (London: Routledge & Kegan Paul, 1969), 227.
24. Ibid., 227–28.
25. Compare, however, Ivan Illich, *Medical Nemesis* (Pelican, 1977), on the "medicalization of life." See W. H. G. Armytage, *A Social History of Engineering* (London: Faber & Faber, 1961); Paul Starr, *The Social Transformation of American Medicine* (New York: Basic, 1981).
26. Edward Norman, *Christianity and the World Order*, 1978 B. B. C. Reith Lectures (New York: Oxford University Press, 1979), 2.

There is a considerable irony here. Those professions that are quintessentially modern, insofar as they have consolidated their claim to professionalism on *science*, thereby emphasize in effect the gap between scientific and moral bases of expertise and may thus exercise relatively less *moral* influence than less cognitively secure normative professions. Therefore the philosophical distinction between grounds of professional knowledge has significant consequences for the scope of collective professional influence: scientific professions draw on the charisma of science but are thereby circumscribed in the transparency and scope of their normative contributions to public policy; normative professions, such as law, which specialize in moral or normative discourse, are able legitimately to engage the spectrum of policy issues but with a cognitive base that is possibly less secure, and wanting more in legitimacy, than that of science. In other words, although its epistemological foundation may be somewhat insecure, the more normative the profession, the more expansive its potential collective influence.

From this line of reasoning it would follow that a profession that incorporates both epistemic bases, giving it the authority of science but the breadth of normativeness, should have most scope of action. In fact, however, the academy, and perhaps the military profession, probably do not have as much effect as the argument might presume. Furthermore, the professions that are grouped together in each class differ from each other. The epistemological dimension must therefore be specified more precisely by its interaction with three other dimensions.

Technical and Moral Forms of Professional Authority

In writings on professions and in the discussions of professionals themselves, a fundamental distinction recurs between a profession's expert or technical authority and its moral or normative authority, whatever the profession's epistemological base. At best, the distinction is blurred. Yet there is a consensus, sometimes explicit but more often implicit, among quite different theoretical traditions that the narrowly technical knowledge on which a profession establishes its authority is significantly different from the authoritative application of that technical knowledge to public policy decisions, or even to everyday practice, where moral and ethical issues assume as much importance as the technical information. The distinction receives a classic formulation in the argument by Carr-Saunders and Wilson that professions should reserve their contributions to technical matters alone.

> There are certain broad issues of public policy concerning which every citizen should be in a position to come to a decision; if there is a reasonable standard of education, these issues can be grasped by all alike because ethical judgement rather than special knowledge is involved. Professional associations should not take sides on these issues, even if all members think alike; if they do so, they are inevitably suspected of being moved by political and not by professional

motives, not only on these but on all other occasions, and their influence with the public as experts is undermined.

Taking these principles as a guide it follows that professional associations of lawyers should not concern themselves with the problem
of capital punishment or even with the treatment of the problem of
juvenile offenders, nor should doctors as a group express an opinion
on the question of whether every effort should be made to prolong
the lives of the suffering and incurable. All these matters are broad
issues of public policy.[27]

Hughes, speaking from another theoretical tradition, also recognizes that

esoteric knowledge and high skill are quite different to moral authority expressed on public issues. Lawyers not only give advice to
clients and plead their cases for them; they also develop a philosophy
of law—of its nature and functions, and of the proper way to administer justice. Physicians consider it their prerogative to define the nature of disease and to help them to determine how medical services
ought to be distributed and paid for. Every profession considers itself
the proper body to set the terms in which some aspect of society, life
or nature is to be thought of, and to define the general lines, or even
the details of public policy concerning it.[28]

Formulated somewhat differently, the distinction recurs in Eliot Freidson's influential work on medicine. Discussing the nature and limits of medical expertise, Freidson offers the example that "we can all agree that how a road is to be
built is a *technical* question best handled by engineers" but that an evaluation of
whether it *should* be built is "normative in character."[29] Decisions to act in areas
in which expert knowledge is relevant thus include both "moral or evaluative"
and "substantive" elements. Freidson elaborates the distinction further by holding in apposition what professions "know" and what they "do." Thus, he argues,
"it seems as appropriate to distinguish the body of knowledge as such from the
human activities of either creating that knowledge (research) or applying it (practice)"—a distinction, I will suggest below, that professions frequently have a
vested interest in effacing.

To define the difference between these two points of authority is more difficult
than to declare it. *Technical authority* refers to a high degree of facility in the
manipulation of professional knowledge but it is manipulation of a quite restrictive nature. Technique frequently appears as an accompanying, or even a necessary, condition of successful claims to professionalization. Some scholars go so
far as to emphasize technicality almost exclusively, an error related to the sister

27. A. M. Carr-Saunders and P. A. Wilson, *The Professions* (Oxford: Oxford University Press,
1933), 486.

28. Everett C. Hughes, *The Sociological Eye* (Chicago: Aldine, 1971), 376.

29. Freidson, *Profession of Medicine*, 121–215.

temptation of conflating the dimensions of epistemology and technique. Distinctive they are nonetheless. For scientific professions, highly developed technical expertise is readily understandable—the surgeon is perhaps the most vivid example in medicine. But normative professions also have their areas of narrow technical authority. Lawyers may develop great skill in understanding statutes, drafting contracts, and executing corporate mergers, that is, in exercising technical expertise, without taking an explicit stand on what the law should contain. Clergymen may be "technically" versatile in exegesis, biblical criticism, and languages of the ancient Near East without also being moral theologians, just as literary critics can dissect the works of D. H. Lawrence or James Joyce without endorsing the values contained in *Women in Love* or *Ulysses*. Military leaders, for instance, may concede that whether, where, and when to use force is a policy decision undertaken by political leaders; implementation of the decision "is a technical function that must be left to the tacticians." [30]

The exercise of *moral authority* occurs when a profession exceeds its narrow scientific or technical bounds and intervenes in more general ethical issues. When a profession attempts to influence public policy on the substance of law, or on the delivery of health services, or on the uses to which nuclear physics should or should not be put, the profession acts prescriptively—as a normative authority. Technical issues become political issues. Professionals become public moralists. To attribute moral authority to a profession is not to concede that professional authority is necessarily "good" or that its actions are "moral" rather than "immoral." That is a subsequent judgment that must be founded on an explicit ethical criterion and an empirical understanding of professional actions. To observe that a profession exercises moral authority therefore is merely a statement that acts prescriptively, not a moral judgment on the goodness of its action.

Again it has to be underlined that values and technique are intertwined in practice, even though they may be disentangled analytically. Historically, theologically conservative scholars have been much more reluctant to employ the methods of form and redaction criticism than their theologically liberal counterparts. Restatements of law by the American Law Institute seem more compatible with conservative lawyers than the efforts at codification undertaken by the National Conference of Commissioners on Uniform State Laws. Moreover, technical innovations can have sweeping practical ramifications, and not only in medicine and engineering. F. W. Maitland long ago demonstrated that innovations in legal technique, such as the creation of fictions, open up new substantive domains that can be "reached" by law. [31] Nevertheless, expert and moral elements in profes-

30. R. K. Betts, *Soldiers, Statesmen, and Cold War Crises* (Cambridge, Mass.: Harvard University Press, 1977), 12–13.

31. F. W. Maitland, *Equity, also the Forms of Action at Common Law* (Cambridge: Cambridge University Press, 1929).

sional action are analytically separable and frequently vary independently of each other in practice.

The distinction between the two forms of authority is of fundamental importance for the role and influence of professions. In an increasingly complex society that depends on advanced technical expertise, the scope for professional action is considerable and expanding. If professions can add moral authority to their already significant technical expertise, then they may exert enormous influence in great tracts of social life. Stated propositionally, the greater facility a profession displays in adding moral authority to its technical claims, the wider its scope of putative influence.

The capacity to attain this additional influence turns in part on the blurring between the two forms of authority, an image that frequently recurs in contemporary writings. Betts observes that "the boundaries between policy, strategy, and tactics are rarely clear for the Joint Chiefs of Staff." [32] Handler points to the "confusion of the role of scientist qua scientist with that of scientist as citizen . . . blurring the distinction between the intrinsically scientific and intrinsically political questions." [33] The boundaries are especially grey, it seems, for the clergy. David Martin's comments that clergy "feel footloose, castaways without proper moorings," or indications that the Church of England clergy are confused about the roles they should play hint at the sometimes imperceptible shading between types of authority. [34] Further, it seems consistent to expect that, the more hazy the line of demarcation between expertise and morality, the more easily a profession can convert expertise into moral influence. The legitimacy it is granted for one type of authority is transferred almost imperceptibly to the other, at least in zones of conceptual transition.

The varying capacity of professions to make such a transition rests significantly on their epistemological foundations. It can be posited that, the more normative (or syncretic) the epistemological core of professional knowledge, the more readily that profession will be able to exercise moral authority in the name of expertise and thus the greater will be its potential breadth of influence. Professions whose expertise rests on the sciences, where methods and results appear relatively distinguishable from value considerations, will find more impediments in slipping from a narrower to a broader form of authority. Simply because an experiment, for example, is such an autonomous mode of producing knowledge and appears so distant from public scrutiny, the gap is widened between hard science and soft policy. That experimentation may provide persuasive evidence on behalf of a moral position is not denied; but the more scientific the method,

---

32. Betts, *Soldiers, Statesmen, and Crisis*, 12–13.
33. Philip Handler, "Public Doubts about Science," *Science* 208 (June 1980): 1093.
34. David Martin, "Revived Dogma and New Cult," *Daedalus* 111 (Winter 1982): 53–71.

the more radically does a profession appear to divorce its expertise from pre-scription. Normative professions, by contrast, have their expertise in materials that are infused with normative elements; they are practitioners in normative dis-course, where the technical and the moral are easily melded over.

The boundary between the two forms of authority is not only blurred but flex-ible. It is constantly under a process of negotiation and redefinition.[35] Just as pro-fessions have historically negotiated expansions of limits on their monopoly over areas of work, they have also negotiated the extent to which they can influence public policy under the pretext of technical and expert insight. The extent to which the profession exercises moral authority therefore depends in part on its success in representing policy initiatives, an area in which the profession is likely to have less legitimacy, as matters of expertise, an area in which the profession generally does have substantial legitimacy.

The uniqueness of the legal profession largely inheres in the fact that it has technical authority in a normative system, namely, the law. Because the distinc-tion between what is technical and what is normative in the law becomes very opaque, the legal profession has an unusual opportunity to exercise moral au-thority in the name of technical advice. It can move with such an easy facility between one form of authority and another that even bar leaders become uncer-tain as to the bounds of their expert role.

Primary and Secondary Institutional Spheres

A third dimension determines differences in influence yet crosscuts the technical-moral distinction and elaborates the contrast between scientific and normative professions.

Each profession has primary and secondary institutional spheres of activity. The institutional sphere can be defined by two criteria—an objective criterion that concerns the principal institutional locus of professional practice and a sub-jective criterion in terms of what are considered by professionals and their public as legitimate domains of activity. Hence the *primary institutional sphere* is that institution, and the organizations that constitute it, in which most of a profes-sion's work is undertaken and in which, therefore, it is thought to have a legiti-mate and particular interest. This is the field in which, Elliott indicates, a pro-fession's "judgement may appear absolute."[36] Each profession presides over a primary institutional sphere, usually from a position of dominance over other subsidiary occupations within the institution. Doctors have a primary interest in the health system, engineers in the manufacturing sector of the economy, lawyers

35. Compare Hughes, "Sociological Eye"; and Illich's argument (in *Medical Nemesis*) that medi-cine's attempts to suppress and smother pain have displaced moral and spiritual systems of meaning.
36. Elliott, *Sociology of Professions*, 137.

in the legal system, clergy in religion, the military in defense, and academics in higher education. Each institution comprises a complex of organizations from hospitals and health clinics for doctors to army bases, West Point, or Sandhurst for the military.

Yet all professions include some specialties or segments that practice in other institutions. Just as engineers and doctors are found in the armed forces, lawyers are employed by corporations and ministers serve as chaplains in hospitals. The syncretic professions have a special status in this regard: as an almost total community in its own right, the military draws within itself professionals from every other area; and the academic profession, by virtue of its special function of education and research for other professions, finds itself incorporated into virtually all other institutions. Where the practice of professionals is limited and they have a circumscribed legitimacy vis-à-vis the principal focus of an institution, that will be defined as a *secondary institutional sphere*. All professions have such spheres; and every primary institutional sphere for one profession is a secondary institutional sphere for another. However, in their secondary spheres, the scope of professional authority is severely limited.

Professions vary in the extent of practice and the degree of legitimacy they have in secondary institutional spheres. It may be argued that, the more normative the epistemological core of a profession, the more extensive will be its breadth of influence in secondary institutional spheres. Although research support for this proposition remains to be provided, a brief contrast of engineering and medicine with law and the clergy suggests that such evidence could be adduced. Engineers, it is true, are involved in the construction of the physical sites for much professional work. Even so, it is likely that their collective contribution to policy in health, education, law, and religion is minimal; their special relation with the military provides the principal instance in which their authority is substantial in a secondary institutional sphere. The medical profession is not so circumscribed: medical associations can have an effect on limited areas of the legal system, on environmental and public health issues, and even on the psychiatric implications of combat tours of various lengths and front-line fighting. But they have little practice and even less legitimacy in religious and educational institutions, the economy, or foreign policy. Although the British Medical Association was welcomed by the state into a "partnership in the administration of a national health system," that arrangement extended little beyond the health system.

Contrast those scientific professions with law and the clergy. Law governs, with varying degrees of generality and specificity, all social relations in a given society. It extends from the primary sphere of the legal system to an almost all encompassing secondary sphere, especially in the United States. American federal and state constitutions enable the legal profession, in theory at least, through its expertise in constitutional interpretation and application, to intervene in the distribution of power within the branches of federal or state governments, between federal and state governments, and between state and local municipalities. Law defines relations between the state and the economy, as, for instance, in the kinds and levels of taxation; between the state and the individual, as in the practice of religion or free speech; and between consumers and producers, parents and children, churches and schools. All can be claimed as the province of the legal profession. In his research on the American Bar Association, Melone found that virtually no legislative area is considered to be outside the purview of that national lawyers' association, something that cannot be said, for instance, of the American Medical Association, which defines its public legislative activity in a more limited manner.[37] Compared to engineering or medicine, therefore, the legal profession has an enormous breadth of opportunity for influence in both primary and secondary spheres—as wide as society itself.

Breadth of activity, through bodies like the National Council of Churches, can also be claimed by the clergy, whose domain seems unbounded. The Fourth Assembly of the World Council of Churches (1968) reported that "no structures—ecclesiastical, industrial, governmental or international"—lie outside the churches' prophetic task, a sentiment echoed in a bold hermeneutical leap by the Anglican Consultative Counsel, which appropriated the Magnificat as a justification for "radical changes in economic, political, and social structures."[38]

The two syncretic professions also have broad capacities for legitimate action in secondary institutional spheres. The military are a special case because, as Finer convincingly argues, "modern armies are a microcosm of the state."[39] Summarizing developments in many Western armies, Abrahamsson finds that the number of areas of potential military interest has increased sharply during this century, so much so that under the rubric of foreign policy the military can advance their interests in the negotiation of alliances, foreign loans, arms support, and arms control. In domestic policy they claim valid concerns with the economic infrastructure (roads, power plants), industrial production, scientific research, public education, mass media, and labor and management organizations.[40] Although there is the clear understanding in the United States and Britain

---

37. Albert Melone, *Lawyers, Public Policy and Interest Group Politics* (Washington, D.C.: University Press of America, 1977).

38. Quoted in Norman, *Christianity and the World Order*, 22, 74.

39. S. E. Finer, *The Man on Horseback: The Role of the Military in Politics* (London: Pall Mall, 1962), 12.

40. Abrahamsson indicates that the army is a virtual "replica of civilian society" with, among others, its own legal, educational, transportation, health service and engineering systems (*Military Professionalism*, 141–42).

that civil authority is paramount, nevertheless "deference to the military in fields of foreign policy and even domestic policies is a commonplace."[41]

The primary institutional sphere for the academy is a stratum of the education system; but the academic profession, too, has extraordinary institutional reach, at least notionally. Very little of university scientific research is irrelevant, and much is germinal, to applied scientific and commercial programs wherever they occur in society; a good deal of social science appears superficially to be pertinent to social problems and institutions of all kinds. And, as Schumpeter once commented, the humanists have expanded their zones of activity into the "fields of manners, politics, religion and philosophy," such that, "from the criticism of the text to the criticism of a society, the way is shorter than it seems."

As a corporate body, the professoriate seldom acts collectively in its entirety on wider political issues; neither does the university take political stands. In two areas, however, the university faculty and the state have moved much closer to a bond of reciprocal influence. The very heavy dependence of state and even private universities in the United States on federal funding and the intrusion of the state into university budgeting and decision making point to direct incursions by the state into university domains. From the other direction has come what Nisbet has described as the "politicization of the university," a label applied not merely to the rather transient student disturbances of the 1960s and early 1970s but also to the extensive involvement of academics, as individuals and consultants, in political affairs.[42] Thus the academy and the military, albeit by entirely different organizational—or nonorganizational—means, have secondary institutional spheres almost as expansive as those of the normative professions. As distinct from the latter, however, the syncretic professions very frequently have their initiatives in secondary institutional spheres sapped by a loss of legitimacy.

It is clear that the extent of influence that a profession may wield is not fixed and immutable. A profession is not simply endowed with control over a given area of work. A domain of influence must be created by the profession itself. Degrees of influence are negotiable with other occupations and with government. Consequently, professional influence can expand and contract depending on the success of the profession in asserting its "rights" over various kinds of work and in insinuating its counsel into the policy-making of various social institutions, a process that inevitably engages it in conflict with other groups pressing contrary claims. Like other professions, therefore, the legal profession in the last century has been committed to a policy of professional expansionism, both in the areas of

41. Finer, *The Man on Horseback*, 24, 66.
42. Robert Nisbet, *The Degradation of the Academic Dogma: The University of America, 1945–1970* (New York: Basic, 1971).

work over which it claims a monopoly and, more important, in the affairs of institutions, including, but not limited to, the judiciary.

The extent and success of a profession's expansionism is contingent, therefore, in the first instance, on the ability of the profession to establish its expert credentials—to gain legitimacy for its demand that the profession confronts esoteric and complex problems and that the resolution of those problems must be limited to those persons with requisite education, training, and certification. The complexity of professional skills has been reinforced by professions that have gained statutory mandates to exclude unauthorized practitioners.

Having established the arcane and complex nature of professional knowledge and skills, an expansive profession must secure legitimacy for its contribution to policy issues. Insofar as professions are not readily granted authority to pronounce on moral or policy matters, the parameters of their influence will be a function of the skill with which they represent moral or policy matters—on which they are not likely to have great authority—as technical contributions, over which their authority is unquestioned. The legal profession, for instance, may insist on its technical contributions to constitutional reform of state taxation provisions. As I shall demonstrate later, once its legitimacy is accepted on technical grounds, the profession may find it a relatively simple matter to begin advising on aspects of state taxation policy—whether, for example, the state should allow a graduated income tax, clearly an issue in which lawyers have no more natural claim to authority than do architects.

It is not correct, however, to say that, the more technical an area in which the profession is involved, the greater its likely influence. Rather, it is to say that, the more a profession can *represent* an area or issue as technical, the more influence it is likely to have. The former proposition assumes that the degree of technicality of an issue is given for a particular profession or intrinsic to a given issue. The latter proposition argues, on the contrary, that the degree of technicality is a negotiable matter—that a profession will have influence insofar as it can cultivate the *appearance* of technicality, whatever the reality. Thus professional expansionism into areas of public policy is a direct result of a professions' accomplishments in dressing its normative contributions to change in technical clothes.

The scope of professional influence is contingent, in the second instance, on the capacity of the profession to exert control over its primary sphere of institutional activity and to extend its influence into various secondary spheres. Again, the process is one of negotiation. Professions can expand their influence in other institutions, sometimes by creating wants and needs for particularly professional services, and then by exploiting their limited contributions to those institutions.

Professional influence thus moves along two axes: the one concerned with the type of professional authority and the other with the institutional arena of action.

TABLE 2.1. Bases of Legitimacy for Collective Professional Action

	Primary Institutional Spheres	Secondary Institutional Spheres
Expert authority	Complete legitimacy (1)	Contested legitimacy (2)
Moral authority	Contingent legitimacy (3)	Marginal legitimacy (4)

The conjunction of the two axes poses several different problems of legitimacy for a profession and therefore confronts it with varying degrees of difficulty in persuading government. Table 2.1 summarizes the relations between the two aspects of influence.

Complete Legitimacy—Where a profession attempts to use its expertise in a primary institutional sphere, such as lawyers in the courts and doctors in the health system, it will usually have full legitimacy: its authority will be assumed within the profession, recognized by other occupations within an institution, and acknowledged by government and the public. As professional efforts move away from cell 1, however, legitimacy becomes progressively more attenuated and the task of collective influence more formidable.

Contested Legitimacy—In secondary institutional spheres (cell 2), a profession's claim to special knowledge will more probably be contested since a secondary sphere for one profession will be a primary sphere for another. A striking example from practice can be found in the ongoing conflicts between doctors and lawyers over expert medical testimony in trials. Lawyers have often strenuously opposed any attempts by the medical profession to allow a single expert witness to replace countermedical witnesses introduced by each of the plaintiff's and the defendant's sides. The assumption underlying the lawyer's position goes to the heart of the authority question: lawyers maintain that no single medical position can be taken as authoritative, that even in medicine diagnoses and treatments are subject to dispute. At the level of the state a struggle for legitimacy by several professions can be found over the vexing issue of abortion, which draws at least three professions—medicine, law, and the clergy—into conflict.

Contingent Legitimacy—A not dissimilar problem arises when professions attempt to affect policy, by recommending policy options, in their primary spheres (cell 3). In practice professions can be highly influential along the lines discussed above. Yet their legitimacy remains contingent: neither does the profession expect to be given, nor do legislators or the public grant a blank check to a profession so that it might explicitly implement its own conception of policy. Success in such an instance therefore depends on the erasure of the already indistinct line between cells 1 and 3, complete and contingent legitimacy, respectively.

Marginal Legitimacy—When professions venture forth to shape policy in their secondary institutions (cell 4), they face a double liability. In a vacuum of legitimacy, they appear impotent. Yet a residue of legitimacy from expertise remains, especially for normative professions. Lawyers, the clergy, and academics can and do make moral pronouncements in all manner of areas outside their own bailiwick. Moreover, the first two professions make such attempts through their collective organizations, and, the legal profession may experience some success.

The degree of success for any profession, either scientific or normative, must yet be empirically substantiated. Nevertheless, in terms of my argument and what evidence already exists, it appears that, while all professions have legitimacy and influence on expert matters in their primary spheres, the more normative a profession, the greater its probability of securing legitimacy for moral interventions in secondary spheres. Put another way, as we move from cell 1 to cell 4, normative and syncretic professions will be more efficacious in exercising collective influence on government than scientific professions.

The Organization of Collective Action

For most but not all professions, effective professional influence requires collective professional action. The realization of the full advantages of a profession's knowledge and expertise depends on organizational factors. Bar associations and medical societies, councils of churches and engineering societies, become intervening links in a logic of action extending from epistemology to power.

Although associations have been considered a precondition of influence, for the most part the conditions of association activity have been taken for granted. The assumption that collective action is unproblematic may derive from a concept of the identity of professional interests or from a belief in the pervasive permeation of an occupation by the values of professionalism. In the latter case, the distinctive ideology and culture of professionalism was expected to smooth the differences in background and interests that new entrants bring to professions. In the former case, an identity of interests was assumed to emerge from within a profession through selective recruitment, through professional socialization itself, and through the common position professions occupied in the class structure of capitalist societies. Recent research renders the position of these judgments quite precarious. But in any case the assumption that a profession acting for itself can do so without difficulty remains largely intact and untested.

Professions confront three sets of organizational problems, and they differ markedly in their capacity to solve them. In the first place, professions must attain a substantial degree of political integration. Scholars who have emphasized the monopolistic proclivities of "market" professions have correctly assumed that, apart from a very few elite associations, a profession attains political authority to convey its collective interests from a representative association. The point holds equally well for interests beyond monopoly—perhaps more so. Yet even established professions have had mixed success in securing the political integration of the profession. That is the case particularly for national peak associations in a federal country such as the United States. Even here there is remarkable variation among professions, from the military, who are tightly organized in their service branches and associations, to academics and the clergy, who have never attained highly inclusive, purely professional, political integration.

Much less is known or written about subnational political integration. Although it is recognized that several professions, including law and medicine, are legally regulated by state, not national, government, it might therefore be supposed that political integration will be at its strongest for such professions. However, that remains supposition—if plausible on its face—and must be balanced with the recognition that professions within a state are frequently organized in county and metropolitan associations that will likely make more complex the inclusion of all professionals in a statewide unified polity.

In the second place, professions must confront the problem of mobilization, something not automatically guaranteed by structural political unification. Epistemology constrains a profession's ability to mobilize. It may be proposed that, the more normative the epistemic foundation of a profession's knowledge, the less readily it can mobilize. A narrow epistemological base confines professions, such as engineering and medicine, to a narrower spectrum of issues on which to agree—issues, furthermore, that will more often be concerned with self-regulation and economic preservation where consensus can be achieved with greater ease. Normative professions encounter two impediments to mobilization: they have a wider range of issues on which they can become engaged (moral and technical authority in primary and secondary institutional spheres); and a broader focus on moral concerns and secondary spheres brings into play conflicts of religious and political values that yield less pliantly to compromise and trade-off. Beliefs of normative professionals may also be more heterogeneous than those of their scientific counterparts.

The third problem conditioning influence concerns a profession's capacity to draw organizations into coalitions. This is partly a function of the breadth of networks that exist between a profession and potential allies. Professions will have an advantage in two circumstances: when their mandate brings individual professionals into contact with a cross section of society and as the members of a profession participate in voluntary associations that may subsequently become mobilized as coalitional allies. Law and medicine, a normative and scientific profession, respectively, both have extensive personal contacts through practice, although in the case of law that practice is increasingly with corporate entities, which provide incremental advantages for the exercise of power. In the case of professionals in voluntary bodies, however, the available evidence suggests that normative professions have much in their favor. Engineers and doctors display nothing like the degree of associational involvement that characterizes lawyers and the clergy. There are both "push" and "pull" factors that help account for the prominence of normative professions. Attributes common to professionals— prestige, income, and leadership experience—will always be welcome to voluntary associations. In addition, however, normative professions have special organizational abilities. The skills of lawyers in dealing with rules, constitutions, and laws and in coping with the labyrinthine complexities of state agencies, together with their experience in negotiation, parallel in certain respects the clergy's mastery of conciliatory and interpersonal activities. If there is a pull factor to draw normative professionals within voluntary associations, there is also a push factor from within the clergy, who may see voluntary associations as another legitimate sphere in which to work out their spiritual calling or social conscience, just as lawyers who wish to attract clients or to make their way in politics are motivated by pull and push factors.

Furthermore, because the epistemology of normative professions gives them a wider-ranging license to influence policy in secondary institutional spheres, and because they are thereby attractive to other political associations as prospective allies, normative professions have a more extensive array of interorganizational linkages that can be mobilized for action. This third organizational factor, the ability to build coalitions, suggests, first, that, the greater the breadth of individual organization networks in which a profession is embedded, the more extensive the potential scope of influence outside its primary institutional sphere and, second, the more normative a profession, the greater its external networks will be and thus the better equipped it will be to exert influence through coalition formation. Consequently, it can be argued that an epistemological difference between law and medicine, for instance, probably does not affect their political integration at the subnational level. Nevertheless, there are grounds for expecting that, the more normative a profession, such as law, the less readily it may be able to mobilize its members, even if it may have more breadth in coalition formation.

These variations in organization for collective action are further complicated by differences in the membership policies of assorted groups *within* a profession. The policies that govern recruitment have far-reaching repercussions for organizational resources and their mobilization. The varieties of associational membership policies follow from a critical dilemma that has engaged the leadership of most professions during their period of collegial organization over the last century. The dilemma turns on two apparently contradictory principles of organization: breadth of representation and ease of mobilization. The former refers to the completeness of representation a body can achieve of practitioners in its area—

whether its membership represents a small segment or the overwhelming majority of relevant lawyers, doctors, or accountants. The latter concerns the facility
with which an association can mobilize its resources to achieve the kinds of ends
it wishes to pursue. The dilemma occurs precisely because each principle appears to have an inverse relation to the other; the more representative and broad
the composition of an association, the less able it is to mobilize quickly and
effectively. The dilemma appears especially vexing precisely because the maximal resources a profession has available to mobilize appear to occur at the point
at which its membership is most representative.

Historically, professions have resolved the dilemma by leaning toward one or
another pole of a continuum from either a highly inclusive, even legally mandated, membership or a highly exclusive membership. The *exclusive* mode radically restricts membership either to elite professionals or to practitioners who
share some ascriptive attribute such as common racial or ethnic origin, sex, or
practice in a given specialty. Such organizations include all special interest
bodies formed on a more selective basis of membership. Exclusive bodies do
retain an enhanced capacity to mobilize their members. That advantage, however, is counterbalanced by the more limited resources a restrictive organization
usually commands. Ultimately, any organization that falls short of complete representation of professionals in a state or a country can less convincingly persuade
a government that it should have the statutory powers of self-regulation and monopoly and less authoritatively influence government. All the same, there are important exceptions, and some relatively noninclusive bodies, such as the British
and the American medical associations, have scored notable triumphs.

The second mode of organization, that of the *inclusive* association, proceeds
on the contrary assumption—that professions will be powerless unless they
speak with unchallenged representative authority. Consequently, in jurisdictions
in which professions have statutory licensing powers, their associations are
vested in organizations that either compulsorily or voluntarily admit all practitioners of all kinds in the jurisdiction. Besides commanding a legitimacy by virtue of their representativeness, inclusive associations also tend to control substantial resources denied their more exclusive counterparts. Yet the dilemma
cannot be escaped so readily. It reasserts itself more pointedly the more resources
an occupational association commands. The authority of representativeness can
be internally subverted by the inability of the representative body to mobilize
quickly and consensually on many of the most critical questions either for the
profession or for the state. Indeed those questions that are most controversial are
likely to be those that are most far reaching, and it is precisely on these that the
representative organization will be least able to act collectively. The irony of this
analysis is inescapable. Representation of diverse interests presents in micro-

is evidence that a new symbiosis may be emerging between an overloaded state and empowered professions.

In the following chapters, through an intensive case study of the Chicago Bar Association and the findings of a national survey, I shall address each question in turn. Part 2 discusses the historical process by which legal professional associations constructed authority, the various organizational expedients that they have adopted to that end, the resources that they accumulated, and the paradox that appears to threaten the efficacious application of authority at the very point at which the acme of their influence seems assured.

Having posed the paradox that confronts collective professional action, I then examine the scope of influence that a professional association may exert. Following the analytic categories developed in this chapter, part 3 provides an account of professional influence, both expert and moral, in the primary institutional sphere and the parallel attempts at influence in secondary institutional spheres. It will focus on three contemporary crises of the state and the profession's contributions to their solution.

Part 4 returns to the processes by which a profession can solve the organizational paradox. In the final chapter I take up again the more general issues of the convergence of professions and the overburdened state, together with a more speculative reformulation of some aspects of the macrosociological role of professions in advanced capitalist societies.

Part Two

Bases of Collective Professional Influence

3 Constructing Professional Authority: The Chicago Case

The politics of expertise are contingent on an authority that can be constructed only through assiduous and persistent effort. Since the 1870s, metropolitan, state, and national bar associations in the United States have been engaged in a sustained process to construct that authority, whether through the monopoly of expertise, the mandate of elite or representative memberships, or the creation of organizational vehicles to convey professional interests to the state. The Chicago Bar Association (CBA) offers a narrow lens through which to view this century-long bid for professional empowerment. By examining in some detail the processes through which the CBA developed an organization for collective expression of lawyers' interests, it is possible to discern some key dimensions of professional influence that evidence suggests may be typical of many, perhaps most, major state and metropolitan associations.

Viewed from within bar organizations, the development of potentially influential organizations stems from the interplay of increasing size and inclusiveness; differentiating organization structure; and adaptations in the private governments of bar groups to the exigencies of greater size, inclusiveness, and differentiation, respectively. None of these developments were immune from cultural, population, and ecological influences: there are new indications that the founding period of bar associations was a particular manifestation in one sphere of a much wider social process;[1] and the attempted transformation of bar associations in the 1920s and 1930s resulted from a social movement among lawyers that radiated throughout the nation, spurred in part by the Great Depression. While external influences are still poorly understood, however, the records of the CBA allow a closer understanding of internal organizational change.

The process of collegial empowerment between the 1870s and 1950 can be encapsulated in three propositions. First, as membership went from a few score to many thousands of lawyers, the CBA underwent a transition from a relatively

1. Robert H. Wiebe, *The Search for Order: 1877–1920* (New York: Hill & Wang, 1967).

elite or noninclusive body to an open and highly inclusive voluntary association. Second, the pressure of expansion was accompanied by a transformation in organizational structure from a simple and undifferentiated to a highly complex and elaborated committee structure, which in turn offered the organization new political capacities and inducements for membership. Third, as size and structural complexity increased, the internal polity shifted from a fairly direct form of democracy, in the earliest years, to a more nearly representative government, by the mid-twentieth century. The added autonomy gained by the bar leadership in the later period served both to facilitate political mobilization and to consolidate what was viewed by some members as the intimations of oligarchy.

Institutional changes have been the cause and the consequence of perceptible shifts in the focus of collective action by Chicago lawyers. Whereas in the late nineteenth century a fairly even balance of activity was maintained between professional control and judicial reform, by the mid-twentieth century the proportion of resources committed to control of markets was drastically reduced and a much more significant investment committed to legal education, judicial reconstruction, and legislative reform. The earlier period, when professional self-defense was a matter of imminent—but, by no means, exclusive—concern, may be appropriately labeled an era of *formative* professionalism; the later period, when professional monopoly is intact and collegial resources can be directed into more expansive channels, can be designated as an epoch of *established* professionalism. The shift from one to the other signifies a major reorientation of relations between the profession and the state.

Genesis of the Organized Bar

The wave of bar association formation that began in the 1870s marked not the first but the second attempt by American lawyers to represent their common interests in professional associations. Since the mid-eighteenth century, several phases of collegial organization can be identified, although none of the earlier phases have received sustained scholarly attention by sociologists or historians.

The earliest fairly widespread evidence of law societies and bar associations can be conveniently dated from the 1758 founding of the Suffolk County Bar Association in Boston. According to Gawalt, associations in the northeast arose because lawyers wanted "formal vehicles for professional improvement" and "social centers" that would foster collegiality and solidarity.[2] Indeed, on the eve of the Revolution, the Massachusetts bar had a surprisingly "modern" notion of a profession. A bid to control entry to law coupled with efforts at occupational

---

2. Gerard W. Gawalt, *The Promise of Power: The Emergence of the Legal Profession in Massachusetts, 1760–1840* (Westport, Conn.: Greenwood, 1979).

monopoly were reinforced by attempts to improve educational standards and establish occupational prerogatives.[3] But this was not confined simply to Massachusetts: New York, New Hampshire, and Maine, together with numerous other states and counties, could all boast organizations that treated legal education, admission, grievances, courts, the judiciary, and even legislation—the core concerns that would become the first-agenda items in the resuscitated associations of the late nineteenth century.

Although the Revolution greatly disrupted the profession, it did not slow the pace of organizational foundings. If anything, the decades from 1760 to 1820 witnessed an efflorescence of voluntary associations, those of lawyers among them. While individual lawyers were rapidly seizing political opportunities in Congress and state legislatures, a strong impulse of "moral voluntarism" by professions, including law, was directed at control and reform of American society.[4]

Between the 1830s and the 1860s, bar meetings and bar associations gradually, then entirely, collapsed. This period has long been characterized as an age of professional "decadence," in the well-known periodization of Roscoe Pound.[5] Revisionist histories, however, share no such consensus. While Bloomfield denies that the antebellum period was one of "degradation" and openly doubts that the profession faced a crisis,[6] Calhoun has no compunction in characterizing lawyers, among other learned professions, as "recoiling before great Jacksonian attacks on aristocracy and privilege" and "retreating toward mediocrity."[7] For individual lawyers, Jacksonian democracy was not necessarily an unmitigated assault on their prerogatives: many in the profession welcomed its leveling tendencies and profited from the institutional shifts in governmental power that it entailed.[8]

For bar associations, however, the leveling currents were completely unmitigated. Jacksonian democracy looked askance at the idea of a profession claiming for itself a special status. "To dignify any one calling by styling it a profession seemed undemocratic and un-American. Distrust of things English, pioneer distrust of specialists . . . led to the general rejection of a common-law idea of an organized, responsible, self-governing profession." By the early 1830s, prac-

3. Stephen Botein, "The Legal Profession in Colonial North America," in *Lawyers in Early Modern Europe and America*, ed. Wilfred Prest (New York: Holmes & Meier, 1981), 129–46.

4. Gawalt, *The Promise of Power*, 93.

5. Roscoe Pound, *The Lawyer from Antiquity to Modern Times with Particular Reference to the Development of Bar Associations in the United States* (St. Paul, Minn.: West, 1953).

6. Maxwell Bloomfield, *American Lawyers in a Changing Society, 1776–1876* (Cambridge, Mass.: Harvard University Press, 1976).

7. Daniel Calhoun, *Professional Lives in America: Structure and Aspirations, 1750–1850* (Cambridge, Mass.: Harvard University Press), 180.

8. Ibid., 188.

tically all bar associations fell to the assault. Whether this was a minirevolution against an eighteenth-century English conception of a bar, or whether it came to be "so many hundred or so many thousand lawyers, each a law unto himself, accountable to God and his conscience—if any," the result for the organized bar was the same. Only the Law Association of Philadelphia, and a rare isolated exception elsewhere, survived. Neither professional improvement, nor market control, nor court reform, could depend on collectivities of lawyers from three decades before the Civil War to a decade after it.[9]

Following the Civil War—indeed more than ten years later—a bar leadership took the first steps to reclaim its lost collegial organization. New forces, economic and political, conjoined with internal professional impulses to pressure the practitioners of law to reform their inchoate status. The growth of corporations "confronted the law at every point; they were the litigants in a larger and larger share of reported cases; they hired lawyers and created whole law firms."[10] For lawyers, as for many other occupational groups, economic survival demanded that organization be met with organization. As the legal profession swelled from 64,000 lawyers in 1880 to 114,000 in 1900, it also organized. Legal education, legal work, and legal associations—in each there were attempts to counter the breakdown in professionalism of the preceding decades with a new coherence.[11] Legal education began to move to the universities.[12] Alongside business corporations rose legal firms that offered to corporate clients a new form of differentiated legal organization better adapted to the contingencies of corporate demands. A new corporate lawyer emerged, less a traditional litigator and more often an economic adviser.[13]

Corporate expansion brought business to the profession but it also threatened to take it away. Title and trust companies, banks, and other organizations touching the practice of law threatened to encroach on the professional domain with

9. Pound, *The Lawyer*, 228–29. On the historiography of the antebellum period generally, see Stephen Botein, "Professional History Reconsidered," *American Journal of Legal History* 21 (1977): 60–79.

10. Lawrence M. Friedman, *A History of American Law* (New York: Simon & Schuster, 1973), 456.

11. Ibid., 525–48, 549.

12. See Robert Stevens, *Law School: Legal Education in America from the 1850s to the 1980s* (Chapel Hill: University of North Carolina Press, 1983), 20–91.

13. Lawrence E. Sommers, "Lawyers and Progressive Reform: A Study of Attitudes and Activities in Illinois, 1890 to 1920" (Ph.D. diss., Northwestern University, 1967), 10, 26; Gerard W. Gawalt, "The Impact of Industrialization on the Legal Profession in Massachusetts, 1870–1900," in *The New High Priests: Lawyers in Post–Civil War America,* ed. Gerard W. Gawalt (Westport, Conn.: Greenwood, 1984); Wayne K. Hobson, "Symbol of the New Profession: Emergence of the Large Law Firm, 1879–1915," in *The New High Priests: Lawyers in Post–Civil War America,* ed. Gerard W. Gawalt (Westport, Conn.: Greenwood, 1984).

standardized and even cheaper services. Their incursions represented an organized threat—perhaps even more of a threat because they were organized—at the
margins of law by "lawyers" without legitimate credentials. "A notorious fringe
of unlicensed practitioners" therefore propelled the bar in the same direction as
intruding corporations. The profession organized in firms to accept the embrace
of the new economic institutions. It was incumbent on the professional association to be sure that the embrace did not choke.[14]

By the late 1860s, forces converged from several sides to impel lawyers toward
collegial organizations. From inside and outside the profession, in deference to
corporations and in defense against them, at the urging of bar leaders and against
the predatory activity of unqualified individuals, a coalescence of circumstances
set the stage for a new phase in the structure of the American profession.[15]

The Emergence of an Elite Association, 1874–1917

Looking back on one segment of bar association life in the late 1870s, CBA
chronicler George Gale recorded for subsequent generations of harried practitioners, perhaps with a touch of nostalgia, the genteel pace and culinary delights
of the bar association annual dinners. In disbelief, Gale presents a menu that
opened with oysters and green turtle soup, proceeded through boiled salmon,
filet of beef, and stuffed roast turkey to cutlets of partridge à la villeroy, saddle of
venison, and roast quail on toast, eventually coming to rest, some hours later,
with dessert, fruit, and Edam and Roquefort cheeses. "That anyone could listen
to a speech after such an orgy seems incredible," concluded Gale. Even more
startling perhaps was the fact that the first speaker was followed by four others.[16]

This repast symbolizes certain features of the early CBA and, indeed, of the
elite associations of the period, whether or not they were committed to gourmet
cuisine—the hallmarks of collegiality, exclusiveness, and an appeal to a certain

14. Friedman, *American Law*, 562–63.

15. But in addition to these manifest reasons for bar organization, Halliday, Powell, and Granfors
have also demonstrated that more diffuse economic and population factors constrained the formation
of state bar associations (Terence C. Halliday, Michael Powell, and Mark W. Granfors, "Minimalist
Organizations: Vital Events in State Bar Associations, 1870–1930," *American Sociological Review*
[in press]). In their attempt to discover the environments most conducive to foundings, they discovered that the absolute number of lawyers in a state is positively associated with foundings; the ability
of a profession to support an association requires a sufficiently large recruitment pool from which to
draw. However, urbanization and size of the work force have *negative* effects on *state* associations, a
finding that is consistent with the primacy established in many states by large city associations. Economic variables, measured in terms of employment in various labor force sectors, have no effect
except for employment in public service occupations, which depresses the rate of foundings. Although these results indicate that general environmental explanations may provide necessary conditions for bar foundings, general models that complement historical accounts are still in their infancy.

16. Albert P. Blaustein and Charles O. Porter, *The American Lawyer* (Chicago: University of Chicago Press, 1954), 307–9.

style of lawyer. Undoubtedly, the intrinsic value of collegiality had a persuasive recommendation of its own. In a call for a bar association, signed by forty-two Chicago lawyers in 1873, the signatories hoped for the "creation of more intimate relations" within the bar than hitherto had existed. When the association was formally established a year later, the cultivation of professional fraternity was encouraged by the inclusion, in the suite of rooms retained by the new association, of a dining room to be open daily from noon to 3:30 P.M., adjoined by two smaller rooms to be open from 9 A.M. to 9 P.M. for "relaxation and smoking." [17]

Collegiality, while intrinsically self-validating, was not a sufficient condition of organizational formation. The call for organization envisaged an association that could "sustain the profession in its proper position in the community," a sentiment that was formalized in the 1874 statement of bar association aim: "To maintain the honor and dignity of the profession." The clublike atmosphere and the premium on prestige left little doubt that the association was not coterminous with the legal profession at large. The professional association was formed as much to divide the bar as to bind it. Like the first members of the American Bar Association, who were "to be leading men or those of high promise," and of the Association of the Bar of the City of New York, the CBA made its call to the "decent part" of the profession. As the *Chicago Daily News* summed up the founding meeting of the CBA in March 1874, the distinction of the men present was readily apparent. [18]

Exclusiveness was not a cause for apology: "Someone was compelled to take the lead, and such an association to a certain extent, must be exclusive, or the objects to be attained would be defeated at the very outset. . . . An association must be accomplished by someone, into which the more worthy members of the profession would be invited to come—at the same time reserving the power to keep out the unworthy, and thus make it an organization of honorable gentlemen of the legal profession, having the best interests of the profession at heart." Asserting a similar judgment, the *Chicago Legal News* applauded any steps by an association of lawyers to "promote the due administration of justice . . . making our laws better, and elevating the profession"; but the lawyers' newspaper also insisted that the CBA give due attention to "discountenancing the conduct of those members who disgrace the profession." [19]

That the CBA began with an elite core of members can be seen from the tri-

17. Herman Kogan, *The First Century: The Chicago Bar Association, 1874–1974* (Chicago: Rand McNally, 1974), 16, 36–37.
18. Chicago Bar Association, *Constitution and By-Laws of the Chicago Bar Association* (hereafter cited as CBA, *By-Laws*) (1874); Jerold S. Auerbach, *Unequal Justice: Lawyers and Social Change in Modern America* (New York: Oxford University Press, 1976), 63; Friedman, *American Law*, 563.
19. Kogan, *The Chicago Bar Association*, 15–17, 18.

umphs of its most notable founders. Its first leaders were either concluding or proceeding toward careers of political and legal distinction. William Goudy, the founding president, had combined a distinguished legal career—practicing before the Illinois and the U.S. supreme courts—with political aspirations, first as an Illinois state senator and later as a candidate for the U.S. Senate. Even more eminent were the two vice presidents, Lyman Trumbull and Thomas Hoyne. Trumbull, an experienced politician, who served as a U.S. senator from Illinois during the Civil War, won a wide reputation as a strong supporter of slave rights, the Thirteenth Amendment, and the Civil Rights Act of 1866. Hoyne, on the other hand, was at the end of a long career of civic leadership; he had been president of the YMCA, an important contributor to the founding of the first University of Chicago, and had held, successively, the offices of city clerk, U.S. district attorney, and acting mayor of Chicago. Among the 167 charter members of the CBA could also be counted Melville Fuller, eventually to become chief justice of the U.S. Supreme Court; Robert Todd Lincoln, son of a revered father; and Wirt Dexter, personal attorney to Marshall Field. A number of future state and national bar leaders, such as Stephen Gregory and William Black, also linked their names with the infant organization. On the evidence available, there seems no question that the moving forces of the CBA were drawn from the same circles in Chicago as those Federal and State Street attorneys who founded the Boston Bar Association and the Wall Street lawyers who initiated the Association of the Bar of the City of New York.[20]

The exclusive character of the new association can be seen as much from the proportion of lawyers who joined it as from the accomplishments of its most distinguished first fathers. Altogether no more than a third of the Chicago bar belonged to the CBA at the end of its first decade, and that proportion dropped further to 20 percent in 1889 and to a low of 13 percent in 1899. One hundred and sixty-seven lawyers became charter members of the association; by 1885 that number had expanded to 250 and by 1900 to 635. Even by as late as 1917, forty-three years after its founding, the CBA still counted only 35 percent of the profession as members (see fig. 3.1). On the criterion of membership, it still remained a relatively elite—although slightly expanding—organization of lawyers.[21]

Nonetheless, the appellation "elite" must be applied with caution. Although a principle of selectivity governed early membership policies, the degree of exclusion cannot readily be established. If there was a "notorious fringe" of unlicensed or unethical practitioners, the association's membership might still represent no more than 20 or 30 percent of the profession. In that case, the low

20. Ibid., 37–40.

21. Edward M. Martin, *The Role of the Bar in Electing the Bench in Chicago* (Chicago: University of Chicago Press, 1936), 160.

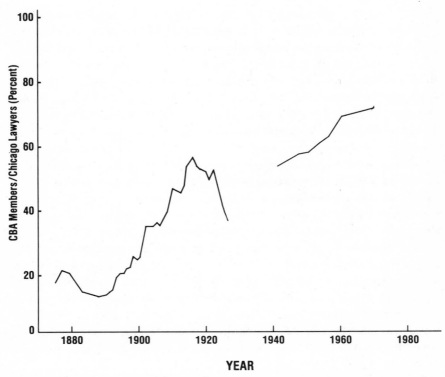

FıG. 3.1. Inclusiveness of the CBA, 1885–1980. Sources: for 1880–1936, Edward M. Martin, *The Role of the Bar in Electing the Bench in Chicago* (Chicago: University of Chicago Press, 1936), 160; and, for 1951–70, *Chicago Bar Record*, 1980; and the American Bar Association's *Directory of Bar Activities*.

degree of inclusiveness in the early years will have resulted partly from the exclusion of a small proportion of practitioners and partly from an inability to attract a high proportion of eligible lawyers. Young organizations are highly fragile; they learn slowly and sometimes fail in the process, as did close to a third of state bar associations.[22] In other words, the intent of bar leaders may have been to be quite inclusive, within limits; the ability of bar leaders to effect that intent, however, was less than successful in the early decades. Whatever the case in fact, the inevitable smallness of new organizations must be kept analytically distinct from an effective intent of keeping them restrictively exclusive.

Collegiality and standing aside, formation of the CBA was precipitated by secondary impulses, both national and local, that lent a degree of urgency to reformation that the relaxed proceedings of the annual dinners might seem to belie.

22. Halliday et al., "Minimalist Organizations."

The administration of justice in Chicago could boast little more integrity than the worst elements of the bar.[23] In both Chicago and New York, the election of judges—another bequest of the Jacksonian era—wed the bench to political purpose. Careers of judges were molded more at caucuses than at law libraries. The uncertain legal qualities of lower court judges in the great metropolitan centers, when mixed with machine politics and corporate unscrupulousness, could produce the judiciary alleged of the lower New York bench: "The stench of our state judiciary is growing too strongly ammoniac and hippenic for endurance." Yet New York had no monopoly on "stench from a courtroom." The *Chicago Legal News*—under the vigorous editorship of the redoubtable Myra Bradwell— flailed, from its inception in 1868, against "filthy and noisy" courtrooms, incompetent judges, and sluggish procedures. The impeachment of justice in the institutions designed to deliver it contributed to the formation of the Association of the Bar of the City of New York in February 1870.[24] With a similar backdrop of judicial laxity in Chicago, the CBA had followed the New York association, a trend that then quickly included the Illinois State Bar Association in 1877 and the American Bar Association in 1878.[25]

Foundings grew rapidly. By the end of 1878, sixteen city and state associations had arisen in twelve states. Altogether, ten state associations were founded for the first time in the 1870s, twenty in the 1880s, and seventeen more in the 1890s. Indeed, by 1899 all but four states had made a first attempt to form a bar association.[26]

Symbolically, therefore, the menu of the CBA annual dinner reveals much more about early elite associational life than the dietary preferences of its leaders. It suggests their principal intentions. Conviviality and an opportunity to form stronger collegial bonds outside the strictures of work have their intrinsic appeal. More critical, however, was the ostensible and overriding purpose of bar leaders to form associations with restricted memberships precisely because the principal impetus of elite action had more to do with conditions within the profession, and lawyers' primary sphere of the legal system, than problems outside it. Bar leaders might have felt their lack of standing in the public eye. That could be raised only by a concerted effort to improve educational requirements, tighten standards of admission to the profession, and implement enforceable codes of professional ethics. Expertise and probity were two, though not all, of the pillars of professional prestige. Those ideals could be best realized only if the segments

23. Kogan, *The Chicago Bar Association*, 29–30.

24. George Martin, *Causes and Conflicts: The Centennial History of the Association of the Bar of the City of New York, 1870–1970* (Boston: Houghton Mifflin, 1970).

25. Friedman, *American Law*, 325, 562–64.

26. Halliday et al., "Minimalist Organizations."

of the profession that were not judged to have the requisite education or morality were excluded from imposing their "inferior" standards on it. The organizational condition of heightened professional reputation, it appeared, could only be a fairly exclusive, perhaps elite, association. If an organization composed of leading members of the profession could also improve the quality of the court system, then the complementary goal of early collegial activity might be accomplished concomitantly.

PROLIFERATING STRUCTURES OF CONTROL

The constitutional history and committee structure of the CBA provide both an index to the aims of the organization and a mechanism to realize them.[27] It is notable that, of five founding committees, no less than three were directly concerned with professional standing. The Grievance Committee was to concern itself with malpractice by those already admitted to practice; the Legal Education Committee was designed to improve the educational preparation for admission to the profession; and the Admissions Committee enabled the association to pursue both ends with a homogeneity of membership. In addition, the CBA also established the committee on the Judiciary and an Amendment of the Law Committee that would assist with whatever legislative instruments were needed to effect the other purposes as well as contribute to statutory amendment. Presiding over the affairs of the association was a nine-member Executive Board. It was probably not coincidental that four of the five founding committees of the CBA paralleled exactly the founding committees of the Association of the Bar of New York. The latter, founded before the CBA, undoubtedly offered a model to emulate. But more than that, the similarity in initial committee structure suggests a commonality of interests—professional standards balanced by judicial and legislative reform.[28]

Successes of the reforming committees depended in turn on the capacity of the Admissions Committee to maintain a select membership. The bylaws of the association seemed to offer few impediments to admission: any member of the bar in Chicago in good standing could apply. But in practice there were barriers. All candidates were screened by the Admissions Committee, which then forwarded its recommendations to the membership of the entire association for a vote. Any-

---

27. My treatment of organizational structure is informed by D. S. Pugh et al., "A Conceptual Scheme for Organizational Analysis," *Administrative Science Quarterly* 8 (1963): 289–312; D. Pugh et al., "Dimensions of Organizational Structure," *Administrative Science Quarterly* 13 (1968): 65–104; J. Hage, "An Axiomatic Theory of Organizations," *Administrative Science Quarterly* (10 (1965): 289–320; Peter Blau and Richard A. Schoenherr, *The Structure of Organizations* (New York: Basic, 1971); and Peter Blau, "Interdependence and Hierarchy in Organizations," *Social Science Research* 1 (1972): 1–24.

28. CBA, *By-Laws* (1874).

thing less than unanimity in the Admissions committee would strike down an application; even the judgment of a unanimous committee might be reversed by the negative vote of 20 percent of the membership.[29]

In the beginning an admission fee of twenty-five dollars was a sufficient financial hurdle to turn away otherwise prospective applicants. But in the first ten years of the CBA, numbers and participation dropped drastically. By 1898, the high barriers to admission had been lowered marginally: admission fees were down to ten dollars; and it required two negative votes from the Admissions Committee and two negative votes by the Executive Board to exclude a candidate. On the other hand, the 1907 bylaws required that members have at least one year of experience at the bar before applying for membership. Other than those limited constitutional relaxations, the elite association maintained tight formal control over its composition.

The main lines of committee development indicate the major priorities of the CBA from 1874–1917. Between 1874 and World War I, the professional association extended and consolidated its structural commitment to *self-regulation,* putting in place the standard mechanisms for securing monopoly. Table 3.1 shows that by 1917 virtually all the main areas of professional control had been established. The Grievance Commtitee was initially appointed and "charged with the hearing of complaints which may be made in matters affecting the interest of the legal profession, and the practice of the law and the administration of justice." It was to monitor all unprofessional conduct by Chicago lawyers, whether or not they were CBA members, and it welcomed the cooperation of the courts in identifying such lawyers. Unprofessional CBA members would be disciplined by the CBA itself; unprofessional lawyers not affiliated with the organized bar would be prosecuted, where necessary, before the Illinois Supreme Court.[30]

In the early 1900s the bar discovered that the law and its practitioners could be dragged into disrepute as much by laymen masquerading as lawyers as by those lawyers whose conduct was less than exemplary. Moreover, laymen presented an additional economic threat to monopoly over legal services. The CBA formed its Committee on Persons Assuming to Practice Law without a License (later to be renamed the Unauthorized Practice Committee) and gave it a twofold mandate— to investigate and hear complaints about lawyers or corporations purporting to do lawyers' work and to investigate practices or methods of procuring law work by individuals or organizations not licensed as legal practitioners.

The CBA followed its Unauthorized Practice Committee with a Special Committee on Solicitation of Business by Attorneys, so that by 1917 the initial re-

29. CBA, *By-Laws* (1898, 1907).
30. *The Chicago Bar Association Annual Report* (hereafter cited as *CBA Annual Report*) (1917).

TABLE 3.1. Formation of Major CBA Committees, 1874–1974

	1874–1918	1919–45	1946–74
Professional standing	Grievance (1874) Legal Education (1874) Unauthorized Practice (1905) Inquiry (1917) Professional Ethics (1917)	Professional Fees (1930)	
Legislative	Amendment of Law (1874)	Federal Legislation (1931) State Legislation (1943) Development of Law (1942)	
Judicial	Judiciary (1874) Municipal Courts (1905) Public Service (1902) Rules of Court (1913) Relations of Press to Judiciary (1918)	Candidates (1920) Prosecutions (1922) Administration of Criminal Justice (1922) Civil Practice (1934) Judicial Selection (1934) Municipal Court Rules (1935) Federal Court Rules (1936)	Circuit Court Rules (1964) Traffic Court (1966)

Substantive

Admissions (1874)
Entertainment
Memorial (1900)

Industrial Board (1923)
Administration of Banking (1924)
Corporation (1930)
Civil Practice (1934)
Tax (1934)
Insurance (1935)
Administrative (1938)
Civil Rights (1938)
Public Utility (1938)
Juvenile (1939)
Labor (1939)
Personal Injury (1939)
Patents (1940)
Real Property, Probate, Trust (1940)
Matrimonial (1942)
Criminal (1943)
Securities (1937)
Adoption (1944)
Aviation (1944

Constitutional Revision (1946)
Anti-Trust
Federal Civil Procedure (1954)
Admiralty (1958)
Commercial Code (1956)
Consumer Credit (1962)
Mental Health (1966)
Food and Drug (1969)
Environmental (1971)
Narcotics (1971)
Science, Technology (1969)

House

Membership (1919)
Editorial (1922)
Programs and Lectures (1924)
Public Relations (1927)
Dining Room (1930)
House (1937)
Rental
Library (1924)

Association Meetings
Past Presidents (1968)
Committees (1971)

sponsibilities of the Grievance Committee were subdivided among three more specialized committees: the Grievance Committee, the Committee on Inquiry, and the Committee on Professional Ethics. The second of these was formed to extend the review of unprofessional conduct to those cases in which no specific complaint against a lawyer was filed with the CBA and to concentrate on publicity about lawyers, drawing from other sources of information such as newspapers in order to proceed to investigation without the warrant of a specific complaint. Cases that justified a more careful examination would be laid before the Grievance Committee for a hearing.[31]

In 1910 the CBA adopted the American Bar Association Code of Ethics explicitly to codify the normative standards of legal practice. The code provided a set of principles against which the practice of a lawyer might be compared, presumably as a formal criterion for the Grievance Committee. As more lawyers came to the board for rulings on the ethics of proposed courses of action, the bar leadership added the Committee on Professional Ethics, first, to undertake investigation of general practices by lawyers that could be "prejudicial to the welfare of the community or contrary to the ethics of the profession" and, second, to act as a board of advisers to whom questions about the propriety of actions could be addressed by lawyers themselves.

By 1917, therefore, the CBA had extended the regulatory reach of the profession over the entire area of legal work: it tightened controls over the practice of law within the profession; and it demarcated more precisely the boundaries of legal practice for those individuals and organizations tempted to do lawyers' work without proper authorization.

A comparable extention of functions, again reflected in structural differentiation through committee growth, also occurred in the sphere of *judicial control*. Initially, the Judiciary Committee handled all matters to do with the bench. After 1900, specialization occurred in two directions. A set of committees was created to focus on the affairs of particular courts, such as a special committee on the federal judiciary, the permanent committee on the municipal court, and a short-term committee on the juvenile court. Another set of specialized committees, formed to deal with issues that cut across those restricted to particular courts, dealt with such matters as court personnel (the Committee on Pubic Service), court rules, judicial selection, and the relations between the courts and the press. By 1918, the functions of the once omnibus Judiciary Committee were confined to the handful of matters each year concerning the misbehavior of judges.[32]

With committee and membership growth, the financial condition of the organization became more robust. The major sources of income were dues and admis-

31. *CBA Annual Report* (1911, 1913, 1917).
32. *CBA Annual Report* (1900–1918).

sion fees. Balance sheets are not available before the turn of the century, although it is known that in the late 1870s and early 1880s the financial position of the association had become so critical, presumably because of falling membership, that the CBA was forced to move its quarters to a number of successively less expensive locations until it was reduced to one room in the County Courthouse. By the beginning of the twentieth century its fortunes had changed. Between 1900 and 1913, a surplus of income over expenditure allowed the CBA to build up assets in bonds and certificates of deposit, and by late 1913 the association had assets in certificates of deposit and bonds to the extent of $9,000, approximately equal to 33 percent of the total association budget. The organization would subsequently use these reserves for collateral on bank loans in years such as 1920–21, when the CBA had to borrow $9,000, using bonds as security to meet excessive expenditure.[33]

Major lines of expenditure also provide evidence on CBA priorities. Principal expenses in the early period included the library, grievance and professional control activities, and administrative costs. Because budget lines change from year to year, it is not possible to compute exactly the shifts in proportional expenditures. Books, for instance, accounted for 28 percent of the 1900 budget, which figure dropped sharply to 8 percent in 1905 and then climbed from 12 percent to 16 percent in the next decade. In comparison, the money spent on professional control in the early years of the century rose dramatically from 15 percent of the budget in 1900 to 53 percent in 1905; but from 1905, expenditure on grievance dropped to 25 percent in 1910 and to 22 percent in 1915 and then steadily declined, falling sharply to 6 percent and 1 percent in the mid- and late 1920s. Salaries, and the general cost of the administrative component, climbed steadily from 11 percent of the budget in 1900 to 25 percent in 1915 and stabilized at about approximately one-quarter to one-third of the CBA budget for the remainder of the 1920s. The CBA began the century with one salaried assistant librarian. Twenty years later the assistant librarian had been joined by an assistant secretary, two stenographers, an attorney for grievance work, two clerks, a telephone operator, and an office boy. What is clear from the budget over the early years of the twentieth century, however, is that the CBA followed a conservative fiscal policy. The small surplus that it did manage to accumulate was not available for major reform efforts but was channeled into reserve accounts. Expenditure, almost entirely devoted to organizational maintenance, gave the CBA few fluid monetary assets, thereby restricting its capacity to engage in public campaigns for one reform goal or another.[34]

33. Kogan, *The Chicago Bar Association,* 47; reports of the treasurer in the *CBA Annual Report* (1900–1921).

34. Reports of the treasurer in the *CBA Annual Report* (1900–1921).

RETIRING FROM DIRECT DEMOCRACY

The increasing size and differentiation of the association were accompanied by a slow shift in the form of organizational government that can be discerned from an analysis of the constitution. Until 1907 the nine-man Executive Board, which was renamed the Board of Managers, was nominated and elected at the general meeting. Thereafter the association appointed a Nominating Committee to propose an official slate of candidates that would be voted on at the general meeting. The movement away from direct election continued with the 1917 amendment to the bylaws that provided that there would be no election for CBA leaders at all if there were no other nominees in addition to the official slate produced by the Nominating Committee. The ease with which the bylaws could be changed remained basically the same throughout the period, with adjustments only to keep pace with the changing size of the organization. Dues and admission fees were fixed at the annual meetings by direct vote of the members.

The Executive Board did extend centralized control over its committees: the 1874 bylaws specifically set the names and the numbers of standing committees; but they allowed the Executive Board or the president to fill vacancies or, from time to time, to create special committees. No mention was made of the degree of autonomy accorded committees to act at their own discretion. But in 1898 and then again in 1907, bylaw amendments tied the actions of individual committees closer to the control of the board. The 1898 amendment held that committees must report to the board on referred matters at least once every three months; the 1907 provision went even further by demanding that committees must report to the board on all matters pending at least once every three months. Committees had no authority to incur expenses without prior approval from the board.[35]

Before 1900 it appears that all policy decisions of any significance were decided by the complete membership at general meetings called for that purpose. Between 1874 and 1907, for instance, all legislative proposals were voted on in the general meeting. In 1907, the bylaws were amended so that all legislation that was not considered and voted on in the general meeting would be considered and voted on subsequently at a special meeting to be held at least thirty days before the opening of the legislature. In the following years, the era of direct democracy began to falter. A 1909 change occurred on membership control over legislative activities of the CBA. Legislative proposals were to be sent directly from the Amendment of the Law Committee to the board. Only if the board approved the proposal would notification of its decision be mailed to all members; and only if ten members called a special meeting would there be a vote on the

35. CBA, *By-Laws* (1898, 1970).

proposal. In effect, therefore, the board was delegated the right to veto a proposal from the Amendment of the Law Committee before the membership at large had a chance to pass on it. Nevertheless, even this relatively open provision allowed the voters to pass on the major policy issues that regularly occurred in subsequent years.[36]

It is clear therefore that an association that itself was a relatively elite segment of the bar could for that very reason function in a highly democratic manner. Indeed, until great size made direct democracy too ungainly, it appears that all major decisions were made in the presence of the membership. It is only toward the first decade of the twentieth century that a subtle shift begins to occur away from direct plebiscitary democracy to the first signs of a more nearly representative form of democratic government.

THE YIELDS OF EXCLUSIVITY

An expanding membership, coupled with a more specialized committee structure and mobilized through intimate collegial politics, offers a distinctive mode of bar organization. How successful was this rather small, noninclusive body of lawyers? To stay in existence was a feat in itself. Yet beyond that, the CBA did achieve modest advances in both self-regulation and judicial reform, its two primary areas of political activism.

From within the CBA materialized a division that may well have impeded the direction and scope of its activities. Sommers argues that the bar in Illinois split over the relation of law to commerce in the years leading up to the turn of the century. Traditionalists believed that the new corporation lawyers lowered the standing of the professions; modernists welcomed the opportunities that business provided for law. The former resented the alliance of lawyers with business because it downplayed the idea of lawyers as court counselors, encouraged loyalty to "tainted associations," and threatened the independence of the profession. The latter saw that an alliance between law and commerce would bring specialization to the bar. It would allow the lawyer to advise as well as litigate, indeed, to advise in order to forestall litigation.

But the split went more deeply: it registered the fundamental cleavage between the small-firm lawyers and general practitioners, who were usually older lawyers without formal legal education and born before 1850, and the younger, college-educated, and more ethnically and religiously diverse middle-class attorneys who saw the practice of law not in terms of the continuity of the past but in terms of the promise of the future. The division between the two wings of the profession had occurred within a decade of the CBA's formation when, in 1883, a

36. Ibid.

group of younger lawyers broke away from the CBA to form the Law Club of Chicago and protest against the stuffiness of the CBA and its control "by the old fellows." Those younger lawyers who remained in the association contributed to the stalemate that neutralized any significant attempts at reform. Only after 1900, when a new generation of lawyers came to ascendancy within the organized bar, was the growing authority of the association committed at all successfully to legal and professional reform.[37]

Strong attacks on the profession from outside occurred between 1890 and 1920. The business community was upset about inefficiency in the practice of law. Intellectuals like Veblen, Henry Demerest Lloyd, and Henry George attacked conservatives, calling them a parasitical minority in society "exclusively occupied with the details of predatory fraud." The profession was accused of being too closely aligned with the great corporations, and corporate lawyers were said to be tainted by their "interests." The courtroom lawyer was at best a pettifogger and at worst scheming and corrupt.[38]

Not surprisingly, an organization attacked from several sides, fractured internally, and having some difficulties in retaining a vigorous membership could not expect to achieve the success its first leaders had ambitiously anticipated. Nevertheless, its efforts were not entirely fruitless. From 1841 admission to the bar had been granted after oral examination by a judge in court. The CBA Committee on Legal Education strongly disapproved of this lax admission procedure and proposed instead that boards of examiners be instituted in each judicial district to test applicants on general and legal studies after they had spent three years' apprenticeship in a law office or law school. The committee modified its demands in 1889 by reducing its proposal from three years to two, although it continued to press for the longer period. But finally it did succeed in persuading the Illinois Supreme Court, in 1897, to establish a State Board of Law Examiners that would hold regular examinations of applicants who had completed not two but three years as apprentices or in a law school. That provision, adopted as Supreme Court Rule 39, remained largely unchanged until 1923.[39]

It is known that the CBA achieved a disbarment within a year of its formation, but for the next twenty-five years its successes in pursuing lawyers against whom grievances had been lodged are unknown. In his report of 1902, however, the president noted that "the Grievance Committee is still doing the most important and effective work of our Association." That year, having received a very substantial proportion of CBA revenues for its work, the committee had heard one

37. Sommers, "Lawyers and Progressive Reform," 46–47; Kogan, *The Chicago Bar Association,* 51–53.

38. Sommers, "Lawyers and Progressive Reform," 22–23.

39. Kogan, *The Chicago Bar Association,* 82–86, 167–68.

hundred complaints, disbarred eight lawyers, and filed for the disbarment of twelve others. In the following years, from 1903 through 1909, the number of complaints averaged between eighty and one hundred, rising to 215 in 1911, 214 in 1912, and 245 in 1914. In fact, after receiving 235 complaints in writing and another one hundred orally in the preceding year, a committee spokesman wrote in the 1916 *CBA Annual Report* that "your committee has been deeply impressed . . . by the apparent lack of ethical standards among a large portion of the Bar." [40] Yet the apparent lack of responsiveness of the profession to professional standards could not be attributed to the CBA's lack of industry. The rate of disbarments had been steady—eighteen in 1906, seven in 1908, and six in 1909—reaching a high of thirty-five disbarments or resignations in 1911. Moreover, the committee consistently pressed for greater funds and added authority to further its campaign. It called for a staff investigator and a stenographer in 1903 because its voluntary labor was overwhelmed with work.

From 1900 to 1917, the Grievance Committee pressured the Supreme Court—not always with immediate success—to take several steps: to allow a graduated series of penalties for legal misdemeanors ranging from private and public admonishments by the CBA through suspension of practice and disbarments; to enable the CBA to bring proceedings against lawyers in its own name rather than that of the state's attorney; and to form a state board to pass on the moral fitness of applicants. In view of its limited financial resources to follow up complaints more thoroughly, the committee requested that the association request legislative funding to defray expenses. Throughout the period, the succession of cases brought to the Supreme Court by the CBA had the effect of slowly building a case law to clarify emerging professional ethics. Supreme Court opinions "served to establish rules defining more clearly the duties and obligations of the lawyer to his client and to the community, and make it clear that the moral standard of professional conduct is higher than the criminal code." [41]

The campaign against unlicensed practitioners gathered momentum at the turn of the century. When the Grievance Committee built up a complete list of all lawyers licensed to practice in Illinois and compared that list to *Sullivan's Law Directory,* it found 196 persons listed in the directory who were unlicensed practitioners. But proceeding on a piecemeal basis of discouraging unauthorized individuals was only a stopgap measure. In 1904 the CBA drew up a bill, subsequently passed by the legislature, that made the unlicensed practice of law a misdemeanor. Even so, the rate of formal complaints sent to the CBA was not high. Eighteen complaints were received in 1908, two in 1909, and nine in 1913.

40. Ibid., 42; *CBA Annual Report* (1916).
41. *CBA Annual Report* (1899–1917).

Alarmed at this trickle of formal complaints, the committee suggested that the CBA set up a specialist body to pursue the violators practicing in the courts and that the association gain the right to take "original" action "without waiting for complaints to be filed against individuals charged with violation of the criminal code." In an effort to deter unlicensed corporate as well as individual practice, the CBA supported legislation in 1917 to prohibit corporations from practicing law, whether for pecuniary return or not.[42]

Like the Association of the Bar of the City of New York, the CBA had been as much concerned with the state of the judiciary and the courts as with professional upgrading and market control. Indeed, insofar as the fate of the legal profession and the reputation of the courts were intertwined—and a tainted court system could detract from professional stature—there were clearly extrinsic and intrinsic pressures on the profession to reform the administration of justice. Some of the CBA's earliest efforts had little effect, such as its attempt to propose a new U.S. Supreme Court justice or to convince local authorities that their methods of appointing juries might be modified to prevent the widespread bribery of jurors. Moreover, its first efforts at control of the judiciary embroiled the association in internal dissension when a scandal erupted over the improprieties of a registrar in Bankruptcy and the gross favoritism that a federal court judge was alleged to have shown corporate and big business enterprise.[43]

Yet from the late nineteenth century through 1917 the association could point to a series of achievements. Together with several other organizations it had helped establish a separate Probate Court in Cook County and had pressed for the formation of an appellate court system in Illinois. The CBA played a major role in the establishment of the first juvenile court in the United States. In 1898, the reformist Chicago Women's Club, aided by the Illinois State Board of Charities and other reforming groups, had asked the CBA to prepare legislation to remedy the situation in which children, arrested for minor crimes, were treated as adult offenders, often being thrown into prison with habitual adult offenders. The legislation establishing a juvenile court, in which a circuit judge would hear cases of children under sixteen years of age and without adversarial proceedings, was passed and signed into law in April 1899. The CBA set a precedent for its future upgrading of the judiciary with a twenty-five-year-long cause directed against unqualified justices of the peace and police magistrates who heard minor civil and criminal cases in the lower courts. Because the system was based on political patronage and provided innumerable opportunities for corruption, the CBA proposed in the late 1880s that this system be replaced by courts staffed with a judge who was a lawyer and did not depend on fines levied by the court for income.

42. Ibid.
43. Kogan, *The Chicago Bar Association*, 43–45, 47–51.

Although its legislative resolution was defeated in 1899, a committee of CBA and lay members met to draft legislation, after a 1904 constitutional amendment, to create a municipal court system. The resulting compromise bill implemented in 1905 established a court and abolished justices of the peace, replacing them with a large number of associate judges who would deal with minor infractions.[44]

After 1900 the association took a series of further initiatives, supporting higher judicial salaries, censuring a judge guilty of a misdemeanor, and unsuccessfully pressing for special judges to be assigned solely to chancery cases. Furthermore, from its inception the CBA endeavored to exercise some influence over the quality of judges elected to the bench in Chicago. A general referendum of lawyers in Chicago to establish which judicial candidates should receive nomination and backing from the profession had already occurred in 1870. By 1887, however, the CBA had become the organizational pivot around which bar efforts to influence the bench revolved: all members of the profession could bring their ballots to CBA headquarters for preferential referenda held by the association on the adequacy of nominees for judicial posts. In the 1890s the bar leaders instituted a policy in favor of a relatively balanced judicial ticket that would give more or less equal representation to Democrats and Republicans. Throughout the period, the CBA operated a variety of polling procedures to in one way or another attain a bench of high professional quality.[45]

The Bar Integration Movement

Most bar associations expanded after 1900, but at quite different rates. From the second decade of the new century, a national organization of lawyers began to urge that bar associations change even more radically than they were doing under the gradualist policies of expansion then occurring. The call for integrated bar associations—a nomenclature that referred to compulsory membership in state associations, together with extensive powers of self-regulation—presented a new and appealing image of what professional influence might achieve if the earlier forms of bar organization were totally abandoned.

The integrated bar was a child of progressivism. Herbert Harley, a Michigan lawyer, had visited Ontario in 1912 and had been highly impressed by the powers of the Law Society of Upper Canada. The Canadian association built its influence on compulsory membership and dues for all lawyers practicing in Ontario. It controlled admission to the Osgoode Hall Law School and admission to the bar. With such extensive powers, Harley believed that the loosely organized, financially limited, and poorly attended American bar associations could become

---

44. Ibid., 45–47, 99–103, 110–14.
45. E. M. Martin, *The Role of the Bar*, 33–58; Kogan, *The Chicago Bar Association*, 79–82, 116–19.

moving forces for legislative and court reform. "If the lawyer is to fulfill his role to the utmost he will develop class consciousness; he will acquire solidity of organization."[46]

Assured of the monetary support of a wealthy Michigan businessman and the moral support of Roscoe Pound and John Wigmore, Harley incorporated the American Judicature Society under Illinois law in 1913. Wigmore found Harley a place at Northwestern University, and from this seat of legal progressivism Harley employed his ample funds to circulate the newly founded *American Judicature Society Journal* to over thirty-five thousand lawyers. From its first days the fledgling society recognized that its ambitions for court and statutory reform could be achieved only through organizations of lawyers. But except for one or two large city bar associations, the voluntary bar movement did not appear to be a promising vehicle for legal change. The latter, to be effective, must proceed hand in hand with the "Redeeming of the Profession," as Harley colorfully entitled a 1918 outline of his plan for the comprehensive organization of the bar.[47]

According to Harley, the organized bar at the end of World War I suffered from numerous debilitating complaints. All the ailments stemmed from one overwhelming impediment—the bar had no power. The American Judicature Society program for an integrated bar, Harley promised, would transform these weak voluntary organizations into powerful collegial corporations. First, the American Judicature Society proposed "that what is needed is a legally incorporated society which shall include all lawyers by the simple process of fixing the fees to be paid and the requiring of every lawyer, as a condition of continuance in practice, to keep up his membership in the society."[48] Second, the incorporated state bar associations would be given powers, through state or Supreme Court rule, to govern admissions to the bar, to oversee legal education, and to prosecute unauthorized and devious practitioners with court powers of subpoena and contempt. They could then control who could practice, what would be defined as legal work, and how such work should be practiced. In addition, the integrated bar would be governed as a representative democracy, with an elected representative leadership and majority rule. With these extensive—and unprecedented—powers for an occupational group, the bar would then enter a golden age "in the future far outshining that other supposedly golden age of the pre–civil war years."[49]

46. Dayton McKean, *The Integrated Bar* (Boston: Houghton Mifflin, 1963), 35.

47. Herbert Harley, "Redeeming of the Profession," *Journal of the American Judicature Society* 2 (December 1918): 105.

48. Ibid., 105.

49. Herbert Harley, "An American Bar in the Making," *Journal of the American Judicature Society* 10 (December 1926): 103.

From the adoption of incorporation as an ideal, opinion within the already organized bar diverged sharply. Historically, bar organization was nurtured in major metropolitan centers and states with large lawyer populations. Urban bar associations usually preceded state organizations and by 1920 several city organizations were already well entrenched. The CBA, the Association of the Bar of the City of New York, the New York County Lawyers' Association, and the Philadelphia Bar Association all had memberships as large, and often larger, than most state associations. The CBA, for instance, compared its 2,900 members in Chicago alone to the 2,451 members of the Illinois State Bar Association drawn from the entire state. Moreover, the major city bar associations formed a relatively exclusive bar elite. As established leaders of the organized bar they welcomed neither a diminution of their powers to infant state organizations nor the "squandering" of their laboriously constructed facilities.[50]

For struggling state associations, however, integration was a boon. It offered the instant success of "increased energy, increased revenue, larger attendance at meetings, and larger public influence."[51] Lawyers would be propelled into the forefront of state political decision making. The government itself would legislate lawyers into positions of unparalleled power. Captured by this vision, seven states had passed a bar integration statute between 1920 and 1930, California being by far the most notable (see table 3.2).

The Illinois bar did not remain immune from the national controversy. Rural-urban tensions in New York State were reproduced in a conflict between the CBA and Illinois State Bar Association (ISBA). While Chicago lawyers were not able to share the enthusiasm of the ISBA members for integration, they did share an interest in increased powers of control and discipline over the profession. In 1933, by court rule, the Illinois Supreme Court gave the CBA and the ISBA powers commensurate with integrated bars to control admission and to discipline lawyers. The court's ruling puzzled the leaders of the integration movement, who were uncertain whether Illinois without compulsory bar membership could now be counted as a full member of their ranks. Yet the Chicago bar had gained the best of both worlds. It gained governmental and judicial powers without losing its voluntary autonomy. By 1940, the integration movement had swept across most western, midwestern, and southern rural states, even claiming Michigan and Texas. But it left Illinois intact as a voluntary stronghold.

Why did so many state and metropolitan associations refuse to take the route of complete inclusiveness? It seemed to offer, after all, the very foundations of

50. "Compulsory Incorporation of the Bar," *Chicago Bar Association Record* 10 (November 1926): 34.

51. "Cost of Running State Bar," *Journal of the American Judicature Society* 13 (April 1930): 185.

TABLE 3.2. Progress toward State Bar Integration, 1921–49[a]

Year of Integration	State	Basis of Integration			
		Statute	Court Rule	Statute and Court Rule	Other
1921	North Dakota	×			
1922					
1923	Alabama	×			
	Idaho	×			
1924					
1925	New Mexico	×			
1926					
1927	California	×			
1928					
1929	Nevada	×			
1930	Mississippi	×			
1931	South Dakota	×			
	Utah	×			
1932					
1933	Arizona	×			
	North Carolina	×			
	Washington	×			
1934	Kentucky			×	
1935	Michigan			×	
	Oregon	×			
1936					
1937	Nebraska				×
1938	Virginia			×	
1939	Oklahoma				×
	Texas			×	
	Wyoming			×	
1940	Louisiana			×	
1941					
1942					
1943					
1944	Missouri		×		
1945	West Virginia			×	
1946					
1947					
1948					
1949	Florida		×		

SOURCE.—"State Bar Integration Data and Citations," *Journal of the American Judicature Society* 33 (June 1949):25.

[a] States to unify after 1949 are: Alaska (1955, statute), Wisconsin (1956, court rule and statute), Georgia (1963, court rule), South Carolina (1967, court rule), New Hampshire (1968, court rule), Rhode Island (1973), Montana and Washington, D.C., (1975). Source: Jeffrey A. Parness, *Citations and Bibliography on the Unified Bar in the United States* (Chicago, American Judicative Society, 1973).

influence that more elite associations had been missing. The associations that rejected the universal alternative did not see the compelling need for it. It was not as if they had achieved nothing; it was rather that they had not achieved their own more exacting aspirations and ideals. In short, the bar elite did not perceive itself to be impotent or so weak as to have to take the radical step that mandatory incorporation implied. Already the long-standing northeastern associations had memberships of substantial size, they represented the elites of legal practice, they were prestigious, and they commanded reasonably sized budgets and attractive facilities. Moreover, they had traditions of their own, some inherited from the families and firms of their members, some of which had come with thirty and forty years of organizational life. Elite bodies had already traveled a good distance toward the goals the bar integrationists set for the profession.

Nevertheless there were other and perhaps more persuasive reasons for resistance. Adoption of the universal form would have had far-reaching implications for the internal politics of the profession. The integrationist ideal demanded more than the accumulation of resources and more than the exercise of power; it implied a radical transformation of professional polities by wresting political control from elites and handing it, at least ostensibly, to those very segments of the profession whom the elites had historically excluded. For established collegial organizations, the fully inclusive association meant the displacement of the traditional ruling professional elites. It inverted the pyramid of internal professional stratification and it dissociated the bar association leadership from the elites of legal practice itself. Where a ruling elite was neither historically ensconced nor sufficiently powerful to resist the democratization of progressivism, as in the frontier states and those outside the Northeast, the local elites had to capitulate to Harley and his disciples, although it is entirely possible that they fought a rearguard action within the new associations to retain their original power. But where elites were well established, where there was an interpenetration of the corporate legal elites and those of the organized bar, and where the collegial elite was large and cohesive enough to present a strong bloc within the profession, it could repel both national and local attacks on its traditional prerequisites. Furthermore, while the bar integration movement had a national reform apparatus and approached its task with the fervor of an evangelistic campaign, the elite voluntary associations made mutual alliance and the exchange of information in opposition a virtue out of necessity.

Ultimately, therefore, although a brief debate again took place in the pages of the 1937 *Chicago Bar Record* over integration, Illinois and most other industrial and northeastern states, where metropolitan organizations had dominated, remained outside the movement. Nevertheless, they were not immune from it. The waves of reform, emphasizing professional power, professional activism, and democratic values, left their residue on the exclusive associations. The stress on professional power fueled the CBA's drive for legal powers, the stress on activism reinforced its commitment to judicial change, and the stress on democratic values undergirded its commitment to greater representativeness. With other of the elite associations, the CBA emerged from the buffeting of the integrationists with added purpose and expanded influence.[52] After all, the organizations that had chosen not to follow this aspect of progressivism's endowments on the legal profession did so not because they disagreed with the conception of powerful and solidary bodies that Harley had envisioned but rather because they did not accept his assumptions. There were other routes to professional influence that would not require traditional and consensual elites to surrender their power within the profession.

The Open Association, 1917–45

The bar integration movement did not take the CBA by surprise. Pressure for organizational adaptation had been building from within the profession, as the CBA recognized some of the limits exclusiveness imposed on it; but it is also conceivable that the democratizing currents of progressivism exerted a diffuse pressure toward organizational change. In the two decades from 1900, membership in the association had doubled twice. Even then it appeared that the expansion was not sufficient.

A professional association has numerous means available to expand its membership voluntarily. First, a prestigious body is attractive for that very reason, and a call for members will immediately invoke a response from those professionals who covet the status a selected membership confers and the social contacts that elites provide.

Second, an association can broaden criteria of admission and remove disincentives such as admission fees, high dues for new members, and rigorous screening procedures. Third, it may offer a selection of incentives for prospective members.[53] A comprehensive reference library offers a facility not available to practitioners in small organizations; if the library is centrally located in the "profes-

52. Charles E. Lewis, "Illinois and the Integrated Bar," *Chicago Bar Record* 18 (January 1937): 81–83, 97–101; Donald B. Hatmaker, "A Modified Form of Bar Integration," *Chicago Bar Record* 18 (February 1937): 117–18.

53. For an elaborate theory of selective incentives in organizational membership, see Mancur Olson, *The Logic of Collective Action* (Cambridge, Mass.: Harvard University Press, 1965), although Olson's theory has important shortcomings. A more rounded discussion of incentives for joining and remaining in voluntary organizations (including solidary, material, and purposive incentives) is provided by Eric L. Hirsch, "The Creation of Political Solidarity in Social Movement Organizations," *The Sociological Quarterly* 27 (No. 3, 1986): 373–87.

sional district," it may also be more convenient than larger libraries elsewhere in the city. A restaurant allows lunchtime meetings of association committees as well as a central location for professionals to meet informally. Other selective incentives, such as insurance schemes and travel benefits, may be irrelevant to the organization's primary objectives but nonetheless provide the selective incentives for membership that a practitioner cannot get so readily elsewhere. Moreover, larger associations can offer services, such as lawyer referral programs, that direct work to attorneys on the bar association approved list. The scope of incentives is limited only by imagination and entrepreneurial vigor.

Fourth, there are incentives for membership that can be generated from the diversification and differentiation of organizational functions. Association committees, for example, can be proliferated indefinitely to meet a variety of needs and interests, both educational and reform, so much as space permits. Indeed, the very substantial capacities for internal organizational development available to professional associations remain one of their principal resources for attracting membership.

Fifth, collegial bodies can make various sorts of moral claims. Commonly, they endeavor to persuade practitioners of their moral responsibility to add support to an organization committed to improvement of the legal or health system, to the advance of professional knowledge, and to other public interest goals. Or the call may be cast in terms of personal advantage—that to be associated with the professional association both allows it better to further the interests of all professionals as well as to give the member some added standing in his or her practice.

From 1917, like other voluntary associations across the United States, the CBA greatly expanded its membership using a combination of these devices to accumulate some of the resources claimed of integrated state bar associations. The compromise approach—adopting an open form—allowed the advantages of partial inclusiveness without risking the deleterious consequences that compulsory membership, achieved by state intervention, might have involved.

ORGANIZATIONAL EXPANSION

The membership data on the CBA between 1917 and 1950 can be summed simply by two trends: a sharply rising membership curve from 1917 until 1931 and a constant membership for the following fourteen years until 1950. The 1917 membership of 2,329 became one of 4,026 by 1926 and reached a peak of 4,427 by 1931. The sharpest rise—from three to four thousand members—came in the four years from 1922 to 1926. But by 1932, in the midst of the depression, the membership of the association reached a level that it maintained, and then slightly lost, for the rest of the 1930s. Numbers only began to rise again toward the end of World War II.[54] Figure 3.1 demonstrates that the inclusiveness of the association rose rapidly from 14 percent to 37 percent between 1900 and 1917 and reached 56 percent of the Chicago bar just eight years later. From that 1926 height, the CBA dropped back to its 1917 level by the late 1930s and did not recover its 1926 level until the mid-1950s.

In part, the great increase in members was a result of deliberate membership drives. At the end of World War I, the CBA was under severe financial strain brought on by the economic hardships of the war: some members had resigned, and in addition the CBA had remitted the dues of members in active service, thus having to subsist on a constricted economic base. An editorial in the *Record,* noting the correlation between the generous (and patriotic) policy of remissions and financial strain, pleaded with members not to resign. With the end of the war, the association leaders began a concerted drive for new members. A Special Committee on New Membership, numbering forty-seven by 1919, began an intensive campaign in which they recruited a committee member from each major building in the Loop (the central business district of Chicago), which housed a subtantial quantity of law offices. Each building was completely canvassed. Advantages of membership for individual lawyers were heavily emphasized. The halls of the association, it was said, provided a milieu in which the younger lawyer could get to know judges and older practitioners, contacts that would "broaden his view and will impress upon him the value of devotion to public and professional good." The library, containing all the reference works needed in normal legal practice, was alone worth the price of membership. Moreover, not to belong to the CBA, asserted an editorial, where the standard of membership was so high, might well raise doubts about the standing of a lawyer.[55]

However, the call for membership did not rest entirely on individual advantage. Lawyers were told they should stand with the CBA as "a moral force in the community," a force directly proportional to the extent the organization is "fully representative" of the Chicago legal profession. This moral force would be directed to the public good: to selection of the best men for the bench, to legislative reform, and to court practice. It would also be employed to raise professional standards. Membership advantages accruing initially to the individual would ultimately rebound on the profession as a whole.[56]

54. E. M. Martin, *The Role of the Bar,* 160.

55. Editorial, *Chicago Bar Association Record* 3 (October 1918): 4; "Campaign for New Members," *Chicago Bar Association Record* 3 (November 1918): 1; "Campaign for New Members Has Started," *Chicago Bar Association Record* 3 (March 1919): 1; "Advantages of Membership," *Chicago Bar Association Record* 3 (April 1919): 15.

56. "Advantages of Membership."

The membership drives were complemented with bylaw revisions that eased entry into the organization, the modification of dues schedules, and the extension of incentives to participants in organizational affairs. From 1917 the conditions of admission to the CBA were gradually relaxed. Practicing judges were given automatic memberships, out-of-town members were encouraged to join, and law professors not admitted to the bar in Illinois were also granted admission. In the immediate postwar years, the CBA also began to experiment with changes in the structure of admission fees and dues. Until 1917 the admission fee had been $10; in 1917 the CBA initiated a graduated fee; and during the membership decline of the 1930s, fees were abolished altogether. Similarly, until 1906 all members paid the same dues. But a referendum in 1921 gave the leadership authority to introduce a graduated scale of dues calibrated by years of membership in the bar.[57]

The post–World War I role of the CBA was therefore viewed by its leadership as directly related to size, representativeness, and income. To broaden its base of membership the association had appealed to a broader spectrum of lawyers; gradually removed financial impediments to membership by shifting a greater burden of the organizational economy onto the shoulders of those already committed to the organization (and presumably better able to afford it); and offered a wider range of inducements, including substantive law committees and a larger role for younger lawyers, to encourage prospective members to join the ranks of the association.

STRUCTURAL ADAPTATIONS

The cycle of financial depression, war, and progressive reform acting on CBA membership drives, the bylaw changes, and the expansion of the organization placed considerable strains on the internal structure of the CBA. Nevertheless, the CBA was not a passive recipient of external pressures; several of the changes in internal structure seem explicitly designed to increase inducements for bar association membership. Internal transformations therefore reflected reactions to social change in the wider society as much as new conceptions of the CBA role in that society. In the interwar period there were four significant developments within the organization: the formal inclusion of younger members in organizational affairs; the development of substantive law committees; an expansion of internal house committees, developed to enhance organizational maintenance, the most significant of which was the new Public Relations Committee; and further differentiation of committees on the judiciary.

---

57. CBA, *By-Laws* (1906, 1917).

The CBA had drastically altered its attitude to younger members by lowering admission fees and dues to a nominal sum. Coupled with the abolition of disincentives, the Board provided new incentives for greater organizational involvement by junior lawyers. In 1932, at the beginning of the depression for the legal profession and at the same time as a new membership drive, the CBA created a junior organization that was a structural microcosm of the CBA as a whole. This "associate organization" consisted of committees parallel to all but two committees of the CBA. Each junior committee chairman was to maintain a close liaison with his senior counterpart so as to avoid duplication of effort, and the younger lawyers' organization as a whole was to be supervised by a Managing Committee of young lawyers, each member of which was assigned to one association committee. In turn the Managing Committee provided liaison between the younger members and the board.[58]

Such an ingenious absorption of younger members into active bar participation received national acclaim within the organized bar. The American Judicature Society was particularly elated because once again it saw bright prospects "for a united, enthusiastic, vigorous and integrated bar." In 1936, a year after the 1935 membership campaign, the younger members' role broadened even further. In response to consistent pressure, the revised association bylaws provided that 20 percent of all places on standing and special committees, except the Candidates Committee, should be held for members under thirty-six years of age. In six years, therefore, junior members of the bar had moved from the periphery to being a well-represented, if carefully controlled, segment of the association. The CBA's leadership heeded well the spirit of an American Judicature Society editorialist who observed that: "If the state and local bar associations could enlist as members every student at the time of his admission to practice they would have solved a great problem. . . . It appears likely that intelligent effort directed towards the beginners would yield more than repeated solicitation among older lawyers who have long declined to take any part in organized professional activities."[59] Nonetheless, creation of a new "internal organization" might also have represented an artful preemptive maneuver to forestall any likelihood of secession by a segment of the profession prone to do so, as the CBA leadership had discovered in the 1880s and would discover again in the 1970s. The 1930s were years of great transformation in the practice of law and the composition of the

58. "Law Students and Youthful Practitioners Learn Public Duties of the Bar," *Journal of the American Judicature Society* 16 (February 1933): 157.

59. "Junior Bar Movement in Chicago," *Journal of the American Judicature Society* 18 (June 1934): 31.

profession. Comprehensive associations could maintain their primacy only by expanding opportunities for participation and responsibility within the association in step with the new horizons being opened to groups of lawyers—Jews, Catholics, and immigrants—by government and corporate practice more generally. Elaboration of bar association structure might therefore be considered an act of self-preservation—to anticipate collegial segmentation—as much as an incentive to new members.

SUBSTANTIVE LAW COMMITTEES

The development of substantive law committees, almost entirely a phenomenon of the 1930s, both reflected similar concerns and signified a fundamental change in the character of the CBA. Until 1917 committees were problem oriented: they were directed to control, to discipline, to professional standards and legal monopolies; they monitored legislation and the courts. In contrast to this external concern, the substantive law committees permitted and indeed encouraged an inner focus on education and collegial solidarity. The legal "specialty" committees were not precluded from an activist stance; many committees, chafing at the imperfections of legislation, instituted an active legislative program. But lawmaking remained an option, not an obligation. Diversification of internal CBA activities greatly expanded the organizational incentives for lawyers to join: a promise of continuing education, of keeping abreast of new developments in the law, and of meeting informally peers whom one might otherwise meet only in the adversarial context of the courtroom. A new sphere of activity thus emerged to accommodate those lawyers interested in more—or less—reform. The collective instrumentality of the earlier reformist bar was matched by opportunities for individual gratification. From the standpoint of organizational analysis, substantive committees allowed subunit cohesion to complement the advance of size and structural differentiation.

PUBLIC RELATIONS

Along with the CBA's new departure into the field of specialized law, it formed several committees to take control of internal administration: dining room and rental library committees and a general house committee. By far the most significant innovation, however, was the formation of a committee on publicity and public relations.

The establishment of a public relations consciousness was one of the most far-reaching decisions made by the CBA in the interwar period because it signified a new phase in the association's program to construct resources sufficient to sustain its reform programs. Until the end of World War I there seems to have been the presumption that the successes of the CBA would speak for themselves to the press and the public. Influence stemmed from public respect for professional authority, from public recognition of the worthwhile deeds of the bar, and from the credibility of the CBA in recommending judges or initiating reform. It was not until 1927 that the profession recognized that reputation had to be cultivated. Consequently, "realizing the desirability of increasing the influence of the CBA upon the general public especially in the matter of electing judges and retaining in office judges of demonstrated fitness, and also in the promotion of other measures tending to improve the administration of justice," the Board created the Special Committee on Publicity and Public Relations.[60]

The need for this innovation was repeated endlessly in the following years. As the organization of the legal profession in Chicago, the CBA suffered a loss of credibility—or so the bar believed. Public images and stereotypes barely concealed a deep animus against lawyers in general. The bar, wrote a chairman of the Public Relations Committee, was besieged by destructive forces and had to rebut that traditional lay hostility that held that

> Lawyers are expensive, inefficient, dishonest and obstructive;
>
> Lawyers are looters in the liquidation of banks and other enterprises;
>
> Defense lawyers in criminal cases are all shysters who help criminals escape justice;
>
> All lawyers who handle personal injury claims are ambulance chasers;
>
> Lawyers as legislators are corrupt and responsible for all stupid legislation;
>
> They are for hire by anyone who has the price;
>
> They defend privilege; and
>
> They perpetuate legal jargon and technicalities, and are a drag on progress.

And if the character of the law was impugned, so too were professional associations. "They represent a purely selfish professional and business clique; they are trying to extend the monopoly of law practice beyond its reasonable scope; they are reactionary, politically partisan, and against all proposals for social and economic reform; and they are identified with interests inimical to the rights and aspirations of the Forgotten Man."[61] Much of this public cynicism, argued law leaders, stemmed from poor information. Following a radio program on its activities in the early 1940s, the CBA discovered "that many intelligent listeners have told us how surprised they were to discover that the CBA was not just a social club for lawyers but a civic organization, with definite public functions."[62]

---

60. "A New Committee," *Chicago Bar Association Record* 11 (November 1927): 81.
61. Ibid., 254–55.
62. "Report of Committee on Public Relations," *Chicago Bar Record* 23 (March 1942): 231.

The effects of the stereotypes could be disastrous. "Misinformation, distortion, and exaggeration left unchallenged may be devastating. The actual truth about lawyers seldom reaches the public mind, while misstatements and deliberate lies are commonly current. Unfortunately, lies have a life and vicious persistency."[63]

Mitchell Dawson, a longtime chairman of the CBA Committee on Public Relations, suggested that the end results of public misinformation might be as costly for the individual lawyer as they were for the organized bar. If the public became convinced that legal services were as expensive as they were inefficient, the legal profession would become highly vulnerable to the "invasion of the field of law practice by law agencies" whose service and cost would be a good deal more attractive to the average person. And if the public had reason to accept that the machinery of justice was out of date, slow, costly, and uncertain, then the profession might have functions removed from the courts, where lawyers are indispensable, to administrative agencies, where lawyers would be redundant. Ultimately, this combination of attitudes would be deleterious to the economic position of lawyers—a matter of great concern in the 1930s—and would have less tangible but no less grave effects on the social standing, prestige, and influence of lawyers and their organizations. Inevitably, the cumulative effect of such dissatisfaction with the profession sapped associational strength, debilitating its capacity to attract members and implement projects. The end result, according to the public relations spokesman, would be detrimental to the public welfare, for whatever impaired the effective execution of bar programs would undermine the public good.[64]

The formation of the new committee, therefore, indicated professional recognition that good works were good only when they were seen to be good. The editorial announcement of the new committee in the *Record* stated that the Public Relations Committee should "increase public trust in the Association . . . create in the public mind a confidence in the Bar Association, its sincere public spirit and its trustworthiness . . . and [show] that our endeavors are not personal or selfish." Some of the same themes were reiterated eight years later in the expectations that the public relations program must "enlighten the layman as to its objectives and activities . . . creating a more favorable attitude on the part of the public toward the bar," "convince the public that we are genuinely concerned in improving the administration of justice," and eventually "change the public attitude toward our profession." The CBA president echoed these sentiments in his 1941 definition of public relations objectives: "First, to win the understanding,

---

63. Mitchell Dawson, "Education by Radio," *Chicago Bar Record* 18 (November 1936): 11.
64. Mitchell Dawson, "Lawyer-Client-Public," *Chicago Bar Record* 22 (March 1941): 255.

good will, and support of the public for the legal profession generally; second, to win the understanding, good will, and support of the bar and the public for the CBA, its activities and projects." [65]

In 1937, with the former chairman appointed as public relations counsel and the new chairmanship held by Dean Clark of DePaul University, the association unveiled a comprehensive three-part public relations program to intensify its endeavors to polish the CBA's image. Since no systematic effort had ever been mounted by the CBA to inform the newspapers and other media of its affairs, the CBA committed itself to work more diligently in the cultivation of ties with the press. While the association had formed a Committee on the Relation of the Press to Judicial Proceedings in the early 1920s, this effort was directed principally to abuse by the press of its access to the courts. To the distress of the CBA, the "ancient bromide" of the press on delays in the courts failed, among other things, to acknowledge the significant advances made by the pathbreaking 1933 Illinois Civil Practice Act in which CBA and ISBA lawyers had played a prominent part. To remove the perpetuation of unfounded myths about the bar, the Public Relations Committee began to issue regular news bulletins and stories to the press. In the first year alone, forty-four releases appeared in over 218 items about the association in the newspapers; committee members built stronger personal relations with local newsmen; and the amount of press coverage expanded considerably. By 1941 the public relations counsel expressed satisfaction that "there had been a definite improvement in the tone, emphasis and type of editorial comment about the CBA and the legal profession." [66]

A second aspect of the public relations program called for a reorientation of the CBA *Record*. Although the *Record* had been published since 1910 as a means of communicating with a growing membership, it was not until the early 1930s that bar leaders recognized that it could also be a very effective medium for convincing laymen of the vitality of CBA programs. The CBA identified key civic, business, and labor leaders and placed them on an automatic mailing list; it liberally dispersed additional copies to organizations interested in a particular article; and it made the press a prime target, sending copies regularly to editorial writers, departmental editors, and columnists. City editors of the main newspapers were sent advance copies with news releases that might capture public imagination. [67]

With its increasingly diverse audience, *Record* content was carefully scru-

65. "The President Says," *Chicago Bar Record* 22 (February 1941): 191; Mitchell Dawson, "Lawyer-Client-Public," *Chicago Bar Record* 18 (January 1936): 96; "A New Committee."

66. Mitchell Dawson, "Lawyer-Client-Public," *Chicago Bar Record* 22 (March 1941): 260.

67. Mitchell Dawson, "Lawyer-Client-Public," *Chicago Bar Record* 22 (April 1941): 308.

tinized for ease of reading, while the range of articles was extended to embrace its new readership within and outside the bar. As Dawson himself put it:

> But more than that, we thought that through the magazine we might to some extent increase the prestige of the CBA not only among lawyers in Chicago and Illinois, but throughout the United States. *Prestige is probably the most valuable intangible asset an organization can have. It gives it authority and power* and attracts and holds members. Prestige even in remote parts of the United States and in other countries helps to build and reinforce prestige at home. Month by month, the CBA, through its magazine, is winning the respectful attention of lawyers in every corner of the nation as well as in Great Britain and its dominions. Articles appearing in the *Record* have been reprinted far and wide. . . . The Association is in fact, acquiring a reputation as the most vigorous and effective local bar association in the country. [My italics] [68]

As a salutary additional result, concluded this article, lawyers in Chicago would be more readily attracted to the CBA because such publicity would stimulate local pride in it.

The third basis of the public relations approach brought back to life the Speakers Service. The organization of a permanent speakers service, first broached in the early 1930s, had limped along for many years without much success. In 1941 the Public Relations Committee placed the sponsorship of the service in the hands of a subcommittee, which proceeded to implement a general program in October 1941. [69]

DIFFERENTIATION OF JUDICIAL COMMITTEES

While the Public Relations and substantive law committees were innovations, committee developments on the judiciary represented refinements and extensions of a policy whose foundations had been laid in earlier decades. By the end of World War I, forty-four years after the founding of the CBA, the original Judiciary Committee had been supplemented by occasional special committees on specific issues: the Federal Judiciary Committee, the Juvenile Courts Committee, the Selection of Judges Committee, and the Committee on Court Rules. While none of these additional units was intended to be permanent, they did anticipate several areas of future committee specialization and expanded lawyer interest in the condition of the courts (see table 3.1).

There were a number of trends away from the single comprehensive Judiciary

68. Ibid.
69. Mitchell Dawson, "Lawyer-Client-Public," *Chicago Bar Record* 22 (May 1941): 362.

Committee that arose between 1917 and 1945. Several committees were formed to monitor the operations of particular courts, such as the appointment of the Special Committee on the Administration of Justice in 1922. In addition, "thematic" committees were founded to deal with problems common to most courts: committees on judges, court personnel, and court organization and procedure inexorably expanded bar influence in the administration of justice. Finally, two committees were set up to deal with relations between the courts and other institutions. In recognition of the "great influence" newspapers had on the "dignity and efficiency of the courts," the CBA appointed a Committee on the Relation of the Press to Judicial Proceedings. That gesture of goodwill on the part of the bar toward the bench may have facilitated the 1929 appointment of a consultative Committee on the Bench and the Bar. Composed of ten judges and twelve lawyers, the committee was "designed to furnish a convenient instrument for the free exchange of opinions and observations between the bench and the bar." [70]

Consequently, in the thirty years from the turn of the century, the organized bar had moved from an earlier oppositional stance to a much warmer détente with the judiciary, an alliance of mutual benefit to both parties. The fruits of this liaison would be harvested in the four succeeding decades of wide-ranging administrative change.

AUTONOMY OF THE LEADERSHIP

With growth in size, heterogeneity in composition, and complexity in structure, the leadership tightened its grip on association activities. Representative democracy displaced direct democracy, and both were stalked by oligarchy—or so it was alleged. The subtle shifts that effected the modifications in the form of government were apparent in several areas.

Changes in the provisions on leadership continuity had been set in progress before 1917. The late nineteenth-century procedures of open nominations and immediate elections at annual meetings posed some difficulties for the leaders as the association expanded. Apart from the logistics of accommodation, incumbent leaders could not be sure that direct elections of officers would not catch them unawares. Open plebiscitary elections are especially prone to the swaying votes of an organized bloc—even more so when member turnout is low. Whether this possible threat was ever realized is not known. But the 1907 bylaws considerably reduced the likelihood that it could be by the introduction of the official

70. "The Press and the Courts," *Chicago Bar Association Record* 7 (December 1923): 2; "An Opportunity for Real Service," *Chicago Bar Association Record* 5 (January 1922): 1–2; E. M. Martin, *The Role of the Bar,* 100, 336–59; "The Selection of Judges," *Chicago Bar Association Record* 4 (November 1920): 1; *CBA Annual Report* (1913); "Committee on Bench and Bar," *Chicago Bar Association Record* 12 (February–March 1929): 249.

slate, a change that allowed the leadership to designate whomever it thought the more worthy successors and, concomitantly, to control leadership succession. The transfer of electoral debate from a meeting to the impersonality of a mail ballot greatly diminished opportunity for nonofficial candidates to present effectively their credentials to members.

Conditions that could facilitate a movement toward a self-perpetuating leadership received further impetus with a 1917 bylaw revision that held that if there were no nominees in addition to those on the official ticket then there would be no election. Only by slating a rival could members register a vote of no confidence in a nominee. Members who contemplated a rival slate knew that doing so would put the CBA to considerable expense. A fiscally responsible citizenship weighed against internal multiparty politics.

Yet the 1907 and 1917 modifications of the bylaws did not completely stifle contested elections. Periodically, one or more nonofficial nominees were presented and, with rare exceptions, rejected by the membership. The failures, of course, were due as much to structural as to personal factors, a recognition reflected in a resolution put before the 1925 annual meeting that stated: "It is the sense of the members of the CBA in annual meeting assembled, that two complete candidate tickets should be nominated hereafter, to be voted upon at annual elections." The resolution was defeated. In 1931 the position of secretary and one Board position were unsuccessfully contested. Indeed, by the mid-1930s, the single slate was so well institutionalized that it took either a very weak official nominee or an especially prominent challenger to upset the plans of the Nominating Committee. The June 1936 election illustrates just how difficult an upset could be. That year, the seats of the president, the second vice president, the secretary, the treasurer, four board members, and two members of the Admissions Committee were contested. Of the 1,529 ballots cast, the rival slate members got between 250 and five hundred votes. The members of the official slate who got the least votes received more than one thousand. So difficult was it to uspet the Nominating Committee's slate that one disgruntled and anonymous reviewer wrote to the *Record* in 1935 that "it is as impossible for an outsider, regardless of his standing or ability, to break into the bar association as it would be for the devil to secure an audience with the Pope." [71]

While the leaders more effectively assured their successors, they also extended control over committees. The formation of standing committees began as the prerogative of the annual meeting through bylaw amendment, and while the bylaws did designate the number of members in a committee, the president was

71. "The Moaning of the Bar," *Chicago Bar Record* 16 (June 1935): 263; "Report of Election Committee," *Chicago Bar Association Record* 14 (May–June 1931): 186; "Result of Annual Election," *Chicago Bar Record* 17 (June 1936): 256.

given the authority to appoint those members. The 1907 bylaws extended Board discretion by enabling it to appoint special committees without a separate bylaw amendment and to exert more board control over all committees. From 1874, committees reported on their activities once a year in their annual reports; in 1898 the board requested that committees present quarterly reports; and by 1907 committees were informed that they could not incur expenses without board approval. Except for the expansion of the number of committees to nine in 1917 and seventeen in 1935, formal authority relations between committees and the board did not change until 1943, when board powers of control were widened further and limits of committee autonomy were narrowed. The formation of new standing committees, once a matter of a membership vote, now rested entirely on the board, as did several other powers. "The Board of Managers shall have power to create committees of the Association in Addition to the committees designated in these by-laws; to define, limit, or enlarge their functions; and to discharge or terminate any such committee. The Board of Mangers may refer or assign any matter to any committee of the Association and may make rules with respect to their government not inconsistent with their by-laws."

The board might now decide the numbers on a committee as well as its members. The only restriction on composition came with the provision that approximately 20 percent of each committee must consist of younger members. Independence of committees was circumscribed further with the section of the bylaws that stated: "All reports of committees shall be made to the Board and no committee report shall be published or circulated without the consent of the Board." These formal provisions, coupled with the board practice of placing one of its members on each committee as a liaison, placed the committee in a decision-making straitjacket. Even more rigorous were the restraints on independent action.

Hence the balance of power between the board and committees shifted dramatically between 1907 and 1943. Organizational initiative, programs, policies, all became centralized in the association leadership.

Accusations of cliqueness were now made not only about the board but also about the Committee on Candidates. Because the committee bore the major burden of judging CBA approval of judges, its composition and decisions attracted careful scrutiny from several segments of the bar. Some members of the CBA questioned the representativeness of committee judgments. A letter to the *Record* editor stated, "I have often heard the complaint that the CBA is governed by a clique, but I have always contended that this is not the case. However, the fact that, of the present membership of seventeen of the Committee on Candidates, made up of former presidents, ten are members of five prominent law firms, two from each firm, perhaps gives some ground for such a complaint." Others asserted that this distinguished group was a "self-perpetuating committee," that it was inaccessible to the ordinary member, and that it was hardly representative of the association membership. Practitioners in the city courts questioned the competence of a committee whose members spent most of their time on civil and corporate matters rather than in city courts.[72]

Sensitive to such criticism because it diminished professional authority in judicial elections, the president announced in 1937 that the Committee on Candidates would be reorganized. The committee, which previously had included nine former presidents and eight former board members, would expand to twenty-two members and add to the presidents and board members the chairmen of the Judiciary, Municipal Court, and Younger Members committees and two members at large from the CBA.[73]

But despite the unassailable position of control over its own organization into which the CBA leadership had moved, democratic impulses were not completely stifled, either in decisions over house matters or in the field of association policy. The same questions of house management recurred with dulling regularity. Dues, locations, and facilities arose again and again throughout the CBA's history; indeed, because they in turn reflected general economic changes and the constant expansion of the organization, they would continue to be unavoidable. And perhaps because such questions directly affected every member, the leadership continued to consult its constituency on proposed changes. Initially, dues had been set at annual meetings; later, after 1917, the board held a number of referenda on dues to advise the annual meeting. It also consulted the membership on its idea for graduated dues applied to classes of members. The 1935 bylaw revision gave the leadership a hint of greater discretion; it could lower, but not increase, dues. This depression action, widely used to waive dues in cases of hardship, anticipated the 1943 bylaw changes, by which the board gained powers to fix dues at its discretion—to a maximum of fifty dollars—and subdivide members into classes should it wish.

The decision to move the CBA premises to new quarters affected the membership as much as a raise in dues; the change in location would affect access to CBA facilities, and an upgrading of facilities would undoubtedly require a greater income. The issue arose twice during the 1920s and 1930s. In late 1923, the board decided that with its current facilities congested by the influx of members it should move to a suite in the new Burnham Building. Both the vote and the double-barreled wording of the referendum question are instructive. The

72. Stephen Love, "Anent the Committee on Candidates," *Chicago Bar Record* 23 (February 1942): 185–86; E. M. Martin, *The Role of the Bar,* 145–46; "Letter on Committee on Candidates," *Chicago Bar Association Record* 15 (April 1932): 63.
73. "The President Says," *Chicago Bar Record* 18 (June–July 1937): 220–21.

question read: "Do you favor the plan recommended by the Board of Managers, and will you vote for the necessary increase in dues?" The members cast 1,250 votes for the costly change and seventy-six votes against it. Yet even the new and relatively luxurious appointments of the Burnham location could not accommodate the thousand members who joined the association between 1923 and 1935. When faced with another membership drive in the mid-1930s, the board again looked elsewhere for expanded facilities. But this time the mode of procedure changed. The president announced in the December 1936 *Record* that the board was in the process of deciding whether to move. It had considered having a referendum on the issue. On further consideration, however, it had concluded that the various ramifications of moving would be too complicated to submit to a referendum. Since, strictly speaking, the matter of management was entirely the jurisdiction of the board, it had therefore decided to proceed as it thought best.[74]

For many members, however, processes of leadership recruitment, issues of committee control, and matters of dues and location—the machinery of organizational structure and management—were secondary considerations. If lawyers were to be responsible for legal change and modernization of courts and laws, then it was in those areas that members' opinions should be heard—and heeded. In fact, until the 1940s, the CBA leadership was very responsive to its members' direct evaluations on matters of organizational policy.

The state constitutional convention of 1921 and 1922 was the occasion of at least two separate referenda within the CBA on various aspects of the constitution, namely, those to do with legislative apportionment and the issue of whether the CBA should support the new constitution as a whole. The location of the new criminal court building was voted on by the membership in 1915. In 1931, 550 signatories presented a petition to the Board that the CBA conduct a referendum on its attitude toward prohibition. The board sent out two ballots: the first asked whether there should be a referendum—a question answered resoundingly in the affirmative; and the second gave five alternatives for CBA action on whether to repeal the Eighteenth Amendment—which it approved. Drafts of a joint CBA-ISBA revision of the Illinois Civil Practice Act were circulated to members of the Bar. In 1934, they had the opportunity to vote on whether to call a constitutional convention. In 1936, they voted on congressional resolutions calculated to limit the power of the Supreme Court.[75]

74. "A Birthday Present," *Chicago Bar Association Record* 7 (December 1923): 1; "Our New Home," *Chicago Bar Record* 7 (January 1924): 1; "The President Says—a New Home for the Bar Association," *Chicago Bar Record* 18 (December 1936): 44–45.
75. See, e.g., "A Sensible Compromise," *Chicago Bar Association Record* 5 (November 1921): 1–2; and "Prohibition Referendum," *Chicago Bar Association Record* 15 (December 1931): 18–19; "Shall We Have a Constitutional Convention," *Chicago Bar Record* 16 (October 1934): 9–10.

Occasional votes on major policy issues aside, however, the shift from plebiscitary to representative democracy and hints of a further transition toward oligarchy did not go uncontested. Matters came to a head with the proposed bylaw changes of 1943 when a committee on bylaws proposed the first general revision since 1907. Accompanying the official explanation of the changes in the May 1943 *Record* was a detailed criticism alleging that certain suggested changes "carry centralization of control to an extreme not justified by administrative convenience and contrary to the spirit of a democratic institution." The new bylaws, it was said, would not allow adequate time for the slating of rival candidates to the Nominating Committee's choice; members would have no opportunity to vote on any action of the board to do with the internal management of the association; the new bylaws contained no provisions for a special meeting of the association to reconsider the board position on revision of the law. Dickson concluded his article-by-article critique of the proposed bylaws with the statement:

> Rightly or wrongly, there has been considerable criticism of the management of the Association in the past on the ground that it has tended to be operated by a relatively small self-perpetuating group. Instead of disposing of this criticism by affording to the membership wider participation in the management of the Association, the proposed by-laws concentrate all power in the hands of the Board of Managers and leave the members without even the control which they have previously enjoyed. Unless the amendments suggested in this article or others designed to accomplish the same purpose are adopted, I believe it would be a serious error to approve the proposed by-laws.[76]

If Dickson's sentiments reflected those of a minority, it remained silent. Only forty members attended the special meeting on 5 May 1943 to consider the proposed bylaws. A series of amendments, each calculated to democratize the bylaws, was offered and defeated.

Organizational Transitions

By the end of World War II, therefore, the CBA had undergone a fundamental organizational transition. The exclusive voluntary association of the later nineteenth century, with its simple structure and direct government, had developed into an inclusive organization with a highly differentiated structure and a representative government in which the leadership was mostly self-reproducing. The structural transformation reflected and stimulated a significant shift in activities:

76. Whitney Campbell, "The Proposed By-Laws," *Chicago Bar Record* 24 (May 1943): 320; David L. Dickson, "The Proposed By-Laws, a Criticism," *Chicago Bar Record* 24 (May 1932): 321, 348–50; "Here and There," *Chicago Bar Record* 24 (June 1943): 366.

in the early decades, a fairly even balance between professional upgrading, whether seen as a public good or as a private monopoly, and judicial and legislative reform eventually gave way to a diminution of efforts directed at the foundations of professionalism per se and a pronounced expansion of committees and expenditure of resources on continuing education and reform efforts. The decline of monopoly, as a primary goal of the young professional association, can be characterized more broadly as one mark of the development from a *formative* to an *established* phase of professional collective action in which corporate self-defense no longer absorbed any significant fraction of resources—a thesis that I shall develop and document below. The Chicago case strongly suggests that the changes can also be interpreted as the construction of professional authority. In addition to the resources of size and the authority of representativeness, the profession had also established state recognition of lawyer expertise through controls over education, admission, and unauthorized practice. All these in turn were structured for political mobilization by the creation of a sophisticated, flexible, and increasingly assertive professional organization.

The macrosociological questions, however, demand a broader canvas. Is the CBA a paradigmatic case? How widely can its historical development be held as an exemplar of subnational associations more generally? What resources do bar associations at large have to deploy in the bid for expert and moral authority? I address these questions more conceptually and cross-sectionally in the following chapter.

4 Constructing Professional Authority: Portfolios of Resources

Each of the recent studies of professional associations acknowledges their centrality to the quest for professional monopoly and upward collective mobility. Beyond those, I have proposed that professions' empowerment may have reached levels at which they have the potential for deployment to alleviate state crises. But what attributes give associations collective influence?

In the case of the Chicago Bar Association (CBA), the growth of size, inclusiveness, structural capacities, and income suggest some elements of progressive empowerment. In the case of the legal profession, special access to the state offers further advantages. In the case of all professions, knowledge mandates variably enlarge or constrict professional quests of any kind. The parameters of influence in the last two cases have already been examined. It remains to go beyond the narrow lens of the CBA and reflect systematically on organizational elements of collective professional influence. If the organizational bases of a macrosociology of professions are not to be taken for granted, and if macrosociological theories of professions are to be made organizationally contingent, as they must become, then the theory of professions must also be informed by thinking about "political" organizations.

A fresh point of departure comes from a linkage between the organizational contingencies of active professions and recent developments in theories of social movements and organizations. The social movement literature has traditionally been associated with "outsiders," "insurgents," "challengers," and the powerless.[1] I shall appropriate aspects of resource mobilization approaches to "insurgency" and apply them in a radically different context at the other end of society—to associations composed of insiders and the powerful. Such a gener-

1. Doug McAdam, *Political Process and the Development of Black Insurgency* (Chicago: University of Chicago Press, 1982); Frances Fox Piven and Richard A. Cloward, *Poor People's Movements* (New York: Vintage, 1979); Michael Schwartz, *Radical Protest and Social Structure* (New York: Academic Press, 1976).

alization of resource theory has already been extended to many organizations, in substantial measure by studies of organizational environments.[2] Nevertheless, I shall argue that an explication of professions' organizational contingencies in terms of resources can be highly suggestive for a number of reasons.

The varied capacities of professions to mobilize in organizations and their quite different abilities to develop and command resources remain largely unknown. There is a substantial heuristic utility in disaggregating that complex of characteristics that a profession deploys when it engages in collective action. Disaggregation has several merits: it presses scholars and leaders of professions to identify precisely what it is that might facilitate empowerment; it provides a conceptual apparatus for rising above the particularities of specific organizations; and, in so doing, it offers means of comparative analysis—across associations, across time, and even across professions. A systematic analysis of the breadth and depth of a profession's collective resources will also underline more forcibly why they must be taken seriously as political actors.

Nevertheless, these justifications must be balanced by several caveats. From a conceptual point of view, obtaining consensus on what shall count as resources is not easily attainable. This chapter promises no more than a first approximation. From an empirical point of view, extrapolating from a handful of cases and some limited survey data, necessarily becomes speculative. This tentative extrapolation will demand much more extensive elaboration and qualification from extended programs of inquiry. From an expository point of view, a list of resources can become a conceptual straitjacket. For the most part, therefore, the role of resources in collective action by the CBA will be explored in later chapters.

Resources of Professional Associations

Contemporary research on social movements has already demonstrated the value of a resource analysis for situations as diverse as the Boston Tea Party, European popular violence in the eighteenth and nineteenth centuries, and the American civil rights movements of the 1950s and 1960s.[3] Resources have been defined as "any means or facilities potentially controllable by an organization that can be

2. Howard Aldrich, *Organizations and Environments* (Englewood Cliffs, N.J.: Prentice-Hall, 1979).

3. Charles Tilly, L. Tilly, and R. Tilly, *The Rebellious Century: 1830–60* (Cambridge, Mass.: Harvard University Press, 1975); D. Snyder and C. Tilly, "Hardship and Collective Violence in France, 1830–1860," *American Sociological Review* 37 (October 1972): 502–32; Charles Tilly, "Repertoires of Contention in America and Britain, 1750–1830," in *The Dynamics of Social Movements*, ed. Mayer N. Zald and J. D. McCarthy (Cambridge: Winthrop, 1979), 126–55; David Snyder and William R. Kelly, "Strategies for Investigating Violence and Social Change: Illustrations from Analyses of Racial Disorders and Implications for Mobilization Research," in *The Dynamics of Social Movements*, ed. Mayer N. Zald and J. D. McCarthy (Cambridge: Winthrop, 1979).

used in adaptation between the organization and the environment."[4] As they are the means by which movements and organizations attain their goals, resource acquisition and expenditure are primary components in organizational growth, adaptation, and influence. Yet despite the introduction of the concept in order to increase precision about what makes movements effective, it has been roundly criticized. Resources often remain undefined and vacuous, or they can be proliferated indefinitely to embrace almost any organizational attribute. In either respect, they can become "untestable" and "simplistic."

One reaction to this indeterminacy is to reject the idea altogether; but that approach is premature and extreme. Another reaction is to insist on exacting tests such as "countability" (resources must be able to be measured in specifiable units) and "fungibility" (control must be transferrable from one group to another).[5] But "countability" fosters the common sociological vice of substituting something important for something measurable. Many sociological concepts and variables resist commensuration precisely because they are enormously influential; their significance cannot be easily measured and fitted for size. My application of resource theory to the study of professions endeavors to avoid either excessive vacuity or extreme calibration. The analysis of resources provided is directed only toward professional associations. Where possible, they are measurable; but where that goal is not readily realized, primary resources such as knowledge are included nonetheless.

The resources that professional associations can command may be ordered along two dimensions (table 4.1).[6] The first distinguishes between those resources that are *tangible*, that is, are clearly perceptible, identifiable, and commensurable, and those that are *intangible*, namely, resources that are significant but elusive, difficult to define, and whose commensurability is imprecise. The second dimension concerns the degree of flexibility available for the conversion and commitment of resources. Some resources are *convertible* and can readily be transformed into other resources and put to a variety of uses, and some are *non-*

4. David Knoke and James R. Wood, *Organized for Action: Commitment in Voluntary Associations* (New Brunswick, N.J.: Rutgers University Press, 1981), 15.

5. William A. Gamson, Bruce Fireman, and Steven Rytina, *Encounters with Unjust Authority* (Homewood, Ill.: Dorsey, 1982), 82ff.

6. For discussions of the resource mobilization perspective more generally, see John D. McCarthy and Mayer N. Zald, *The Trend of Social Movements in America: Professionalization and Resource Mobilization* (Morristown, N.J.: General Learning Corp., 1973); A. Oberschall, *Social Conflict and Social Movements* (Englewood Cliffs, N.J.: Prentice-Hall, 1973); J. D. McCarthy and M. N. Zald, "Resource Mobilization and Social Movements: A Partial Theory," *American Journal of Sociology* 82 (May 1977): 1212–39; Charles Perrow, "The Sixties Observed," in *The Dynamics of Social Movements*, ed. Mayer N. Zald and J. D. McCarthy (Cambridge: Winthrop, 1979), 192–211; Eric L. Hirsch, "The Creation of Political Solidarity in Social Movement Organizations," *The Sociological Quarterly* 27 (No. 3, 1986): 373–387.

TABLE 4.1. Potential Resources of Professional Associations

	Resources That Are:	
	Tangible	Intangible
Resources that are convertible	Money Meeting rooms Staff Internal media Time Members	Knowledge Organizational structure Prestige Social networks Representativeness
Resources that are nonconvertible	Buildings Libraries Restaurants	Geographic density of professionals

convertible, having a fixed and limited use. For any organization, the extent of convertibility is critical for the range of possible courses of action it can take. An organization that depends primarily on nonconvertible factors is confined to action on a narrow spectrum of issues and has limited capacities of adaptation to changing circumstances and unanticipated crises.

Professional associations combine a rare control over both tangible and intangible assets. Among their highly consequential intangible assets, the centrality of knowledge requires no underlining: it is the sine qua non of the professional category and a unique component of professional associations. It is not that other organizations are without information but that professions can claim to control it exclusively. Its content and form have already been extensively canvassed in chapter 2. Professions have the added leverage of high prestige; that in turn is related, in circular fashion, to high occupational income, not to mention the special access professionals have to other individuals and organizations that can give them added prestige and fiscal advantage. An outstanding social resource of professional associations is the range and quality of their personal and organizational networks. Because professionals are disproportionately recruited from the middle and upper classes, and because their skills and training are disproportionately committed to members of those classes, they have exceptional access to elites, political circles, commercial and financial sectors, and the media. In short, they are likely to have broad and dense networks around centers of power in modern societies. Furthermore, the representativeness of a highly inclusive organization contributes powerfully to the authority of organizational pronouncements and action.

Although not commonly viewed as a resource, the geographical density of professionals exerts a strong influence on collective action because it affects the ease of meeting. A more densely concentrated profession will be more readily mobilized. For the most part, however, density itself cannot be converted by associations; it may, however, be "manipulated" by the choice of location for an association's facilities.

Professional associations also can control, or have access to, enormous tangible assets. In contrast to most voluntary associations, professional bodies are highly affluent; they can afford the large staffs that provide organizational infrastructures for collective action. Moreover, the autonomy of much professional work allows professionals great flexibility in the discretionary use of their labor and time. To the extent that professionals also have access to the facilities of the organizations in which they work, they can add their own resources, in times of crisis or critical action, to those of the associations, thus providing what Halliday, Powell, and Granfors have called "reserve infrastructures."[7] Buildings, libraries, and restaurants are tangible and usually cannot be converted. All the same, they can facilitate collective action in numerous, less direct, ways: libraries provide one of many selective incentives for professionals to join collegial bodies; and restaurants have a solidary function that may not be satisfied in any other occupational setting.

The analytic lines between tangible and intangible resources and those that are convertible or nonconvertible are less rigid than the dichotomies suggest. In fact, the dichotomy more properly could be seen as a continuum. Money, for example, is among the most fluid of resources and easily convertible into others. Yet to the extent that the income of an association is directed to building maintenance and acquisition, staff salaries, and other fixed budget lines, there may actually be very few discretionary funds available for any collective action. Membership size can be nonconvertible. When the state makes membership mandatory, that resource becomes quite rigid. No account is given here of the considerable variations among and within professions or the relative weights each association can assign to factors in one cell or another. Neither does table 4.1 attempt to include all those selective incentives that may indirectly contribute to collective action by attracting members on by-product grounds. Nevertheless, even such a simplified analysis provides a conceptual edge for cutting through the variety and complexity of professional collegial organizations and activities. That edge has both classificatory and historical implications.

Three Portfolios

It is readily apparent that all associations cannot equally command all resources. Many are incompatible. The highest prestige associations cannot at the same time be those of the greatest inclusiveness. In other cases it is simply too difficult

7. See Halliday et al., "Minimalist Organizations."

to maximize the control of those resources that are not compatible. Consequently, comprehensive professional associations cluster into groups that control distinctive *portfolios of resources*. In turn, the latter are loosely tailored to the goals of organizational action. One portfolio may be appropriate for one "repertoire of contention,"[8] whereas other portfolios are better committed to alternative repertoires of contention and their respective outcomes. Part of the task of developing a theory of collective professional influence requires the matching of resource portfolios with repertoires of contention for given causes.

Comprehensive professional associations in the United States can be classified into three categories: elite, open, and universal. *Elite* associations are those with exclusive and closed membership policies. Only certain classes of professionals are eligible for membership, and applicants are usually carefully screened by admissions committees which may also demand proper sponsorship of candidates.[9] *Open* associations are those that enunciate a membership policy that is ostensibly inclusive of all practitioners in a given area, irrespective of their ascribed or professional attributes. That openness of course can be more apparent than real: at various times, the profession has been open to men and not women, whites and not blacks. Whereas open associations are voluntary, *universal* associations demand, as a condition of practice, that all professionals in a given region or state belong to a collegial body. Hence the three types of organizations vary in the proportion of practitioners in an area who can belong: elite associations are the least and universal associations the most inclusive.

Although membership provides a ready criterion on which to categorize these organizations, the distinctive attributes of professional bodies go considerably beyond recruitment. Each membership policy characteristically is correlated with particular clusters of resources.

Table 4.2 compares each type of organization on several of the most salient of a professional association's resources. The variations among the types by membership and representativeness are clear. But with variations on those resources come a series of correlative differences extending from prestige through funds.

---

8. See Tilly, "Repertoires of Contention."

9. Once again, however, the label "elite" requires qualification. An association will be elite when its avowed purposes imply elite organization (e.g., "cleaning up the bar"), when its membership policy is deliberately restrictive, and when its membership is highly noninclusive. A professional organization might appear elite because it is small and noninclusive; yet that will often be a function not of intent or discriminatory membership policies but of newness (most organizations start small), inexperience (organizations may not know how to attain inclusiveness), and cohort (early bar organizations pursued voluntary strategies that attracted limited numbers, while later bar associations moved more quickly to have the state legislate membership). A more elaborate treatment of size, newness, cohort, and period effects, as they influenced the formative period of bar foundings in the late nineteenth century, can be found in Halliday, Powell, and Granfors, "Minimalist Organizations."

TABLE 4.2. Resource Profiles of Elite, Open, and Universal Associations

| | Types of Association | | |
Resources	Elite	Open	Universal
Membership	Exclusive	Partially inclusive	Completely inclusive
Representativeness	Unrepresentative	Moderately representative	Fully representative
Prestige	High	Moderate	Nominal
Expertise	Specialized	General	Complete
Networks	Concentrated	Dispersed	Dispersed
Organizational capacities	Restricted	Expanded	Extensive
Funds	Limited	Substantial	Extensive

Thus it is because elite associations are so exclusive that they also have the highest prestige; the prestige commanded by open associations moves toward that of average professional standing; and universal associations by definition attain a reputation virtually identical to that of the professional at large. Organizations also differ in the type and degree of expertise they command: elite associations will have a great deal of expertise but only in more prestigious areas of the law, principally those concerning finance and the corporate sector; open associations tend to incorporate most specialties within the profession, although they too may initially be biased toward large firm specialties early in their development; and universal associations, by definition, incorporate the complete range of specialization.

A similar principle applies for networks. Whereas an elite association will have very strong ties to certain segments of the profession and to centers of power outside it, the open and universal associations will have much more comprehensive and diverse networks. The difference in ties can be seen by a contrast of the Association of the Bar of the City of New York with the CBA: the former, a highly prestigious organization, appears to have very close links with federal government but much more attenuated ties with state and even metropolitan politicians; the latter exhibits just the obverse pattern. Partly as a function of size, universal and open associations have much greater capacities for internal structural differentiation, diversification of functions, proliferation of committees, and a range of organizational facilities for responding to the spectrum of pressures and concerns that confront a profession.

The issue of funds is more difficult. Proponents of the bar integration movement strongly believed that compulsory inclusivism was the only way to solve the fiscal weakness of state associations. Yet in retrospect it appears that the long-established prestigious metropolitan associations, such as the Association of the Bar of the City of New York and the CBA, were able to maintain an elite status for long periods and, particularly in the case of the former, sustain a healthy budget. At the same time it is likely that compulsory membership and fees for state associations solve the difficulties of earning both a substantial and a stable annual income. For the majority of American associations therefore, the bar integrationists were undoubtedly correct.

However, the typological representation of these differences—and the magnitude of the contrasts among them—can be deceptive. Although the historical trend has been away from elite to open and universal bar groups, a trend that would indicate the latter have much more to offer than the former, in retrospect it appears that many nominal advantages of inclusiveness are less real than apparent. While a universal association may ostensibly incorporate all specialist lawyers in a state, thereby giving it a monopoly of legal expertise, some legal specialties, often those of higher prestige, will be less active in state universal associations than in open metropolitan or national specialty organizations. Furthermore, the quasi-public status of an integrated bar association can severely limit "political" action. Correlatively, a universal association may nominally have the broadest range of networks available to any type of organization and yet find that those networks to which the most prestigious lawyers have access are denied it simply because the most prestigious lawyers themselves maintain a marginal involvement. And while a universal association has extensive organizational capacities in virtue of its size, the geographic dispersion of members in statewide universal bodies may deny them the capacities attained by open or even elite associations whose less inclusive membership is concentrated in a few city blocks. Obviously, then, while there are marginal advantages to inclusiveness and certainly ideological advantages to representativeness, the manifest benefits of the movement to open and universal associations may not be as great in retrospect as in prospect.

Resource Portfolios: Historical Transitions

Elite, open, and universal associations bear not only an analytic and contemporaneous but also a historical and developmental relation to each other. The very little history available on collegial associations of professions will not allow any definitive judgments. Nonetheless, it is possible to discern some broad historical patterns of transition from one type of organization to another. For the legal profession, for example, the three types of associations represent, in a highly idealized interpretation, three phases of collegial organization over the last century. At each stage, the respective associations seemed to be maximizing somewhat different goals, and each adapted its resources, including membership policies, accordingly. Each stage can therefore be typified by its unique portfolio of resources.

TABLE 4.3. Dimensions of Comprehensive State and Metropolitan Bar Associations in the United States

	Forms of Professional Association		
	Elite	Open	Universal
Composition	Exclusive	Inclusive, voluntary	Inclusive, compulsory
Historical emergence	Late nineteenth century	Late nineteenth and early twentieth century	1920–50
Geographic concentration	Cities (e.g., New York, Chicago, Philadelphia, San Francisco)	Northeast and Midwest states. Metropolitan centers	South and West states.

The elite association was the characteristic form of organization from 1870 until the first and second decades of the twentieth century. From the turn of the century, most elite associations that survived—and many did not—gradually broadened their membership policies and organizational aims to take on a more open form. A very few elite organizations, such as the Association of the Bar of the City of New York, maintained that form until after World War II and even into the 1960s. But as early as 1920, the open association had clearly become the dominant form. At the moment its dominance emerged, however, it was challenged by the bar integration movement, and in the thirty years from 1920 to 1950 more than half of the state bar associations, almost all of which had previously had a voluntary but open membership, adopted inclusive and mandatory membership policies. Residues of each of these three forms of organization have continued to the present. Nevertheless, on balance, the comprehensive elite association has virtually become an anachronism. Open and universal associations more or less equally partition American collegial bodies of lawyers between them.

Further, if state bar associations are divided into their open (nonunified) and universal (unified) forms, their historical evolution has not been evenly distributed geographically throughout the United States (table 4.3). For the legal profession at least, the typology of associations has a regional, as well as a historical, dimension. Open associations are disproportionately found in the Northeast, in industrial and highly populous states, especially those in which bar associations were founded between 1874 and 1899. Universal associations are disproportionately concentrated in rural states, the Midwest, West, and South. Those elite associations that remained after World War II are all in older and large metropolitan areas. Indeed, there is often an additional upstate-downstate or metropolitan-hinterland division: open and universal state associations are concentrated in particular regions, but there is a frequent combination of universal state associations with open or partly elite metropolitan associations within the state. Similarly, a combination often occurs of open metropolitan and open state associations. Indeed, many state associations were founded well after metropolitan associations were securely established.

Resource Portfolios: Theoretical Dynamics

These trends are not disembodied developments, bearing nothing but a historically coincidental relation to each other. They form aspects of a dynamic within the emergence of professionalism itself: professions come to employ differing organizational capacities and clusters of resources to implement best the strategies relevant to given phases of professionalism in particular historical situations. In Alfred Chandler's terms, organizational composition and structure may be interpreted as a deliberate *strategy* undertaken by bar elites.[10] The phases of professional emergence are divided, as we have seen, into a *formative* phase, in which a prominent, though not exclusive or even dominant, objective of the profession is to effect occupational closure and standing through control of entry, education, ethics, and encroachments; and an *established* phase, in which a self-regulating and autonomous profession, having attained the minimum conditions of self-preservation and self-maintenance, can venture to exercise more assertively its influence both to control the wider environment of professional practice and to affect public policy.

Although analytically distinct, the two phases are not entirely historically discrete. Features of the established phase will already exist in embryonic form during the formative period and may even have some prominence. Yet they cannot become the dominant component of professional action until the problems facing a profession in its formative stage have been largely resolved. The resolution of such fundamental necessities as closure and standing are necessary conditions if professions are to attain the breadth of collective action possible in the established phase. By the same token, a profession that endeavors to exert general influence on public policy in its established phase cannot afford to take for granted the preconditions of that action established in an earlier period. Those elements of professional monopoly critical to the defense of its occupational domain must be consistently maintained and reproduced even though that effort may account for a progressively diminishing proportion of association effort.

It does not follow that occupations necessarily realize their formative goals— the sizable proportion of bar associations that failed attest to the difficulties of goal attainment. Nor do professions inevitably progress from a formative to an established form—indeed the problem for many semiprofessions is that they ap-

10. Alfred D. Chandler, Jr., *Strategy and Structure: Chapters in the History of the American Industrial Enterprise* (Cambridge, Mass.: MIT Press, 1962), 13–14.

pear to be locked into a phase of existence that older professions passed through fifty years earlier. On the other hand, when professions come under severe public scrutiny, as has the legal profession in the last decade, it may be necessary for associations to modify their activities in order to consolidate or adapt earlier solutions to the problems of autonomy and self-regulation that are no longer acceptable.[11] Of all the ancient professions, perhaps only the clergy has had to retreat from the ubiquitous influence they once had in order to resecure the foundations of their professionalism, such as metaphysical knowledge, which seem in danger of being swept away.

Of those professions that do manage the shift from the formative to the established phase, they will do so at what might be called a variable developmental velocity. Some professions, and indeed a class of professional associations within a national profession, may make the transition rapidly, especially if the groundwork of problems to be solved in the formative period is already laid by the efforts of pioneering bodies that preceded them. Conversely, it may have been the case that those organizations originally established in the 1870s and 1880s took relatively longer to make the transition precisely because they could not benefit from the experience of predecessors.

Just as there is an inner logic of change that has marked some professions, so too there is a dynamic within professional associations that presses them toward change. The form taken by a professional association consists of a match between given goals, generically expressed in constitutions, and the organizational resources necessary to reach them.

We can speculate that the three forms of association therefore represent distinctive complexes of goals, relevant to a given historical period or region and the resources the bar leaders consider will maximize those goals. If, for example, professional leaders aim primarily to heighten the standing and prestige of the profession, to improve the quality of professional education and training, and to assure the profession's moral probity, then the association will be more likely to take an elite form, under which those professionals who are more prestigious, are better educated, and feel themselves to be ethical practitioners will endeavor to impose their own standards on the profession as a whole. On the other hand, if this goal of professional standing has been substantially attained and a profession wishes to widen its sphere of influence by reforming the institutions in which it works as well as affecting government policy, then the breadth of resources that are commanded by open and universal associations would appear to be more effective.

The recent history of the American legal profession may be cast in these

---

11. Compare Michael J. Powell, "Developments in the Regulation of Lawyers: Competing Segments and Market, Client, and Government Controls," *Social Forces* 64 (December 1985): 281–305.

terms—by a considerable emphasis of elite associations, in the last years of the nineteenth century, on professional standing, and by a subsequent shift of emphasis across the United States, from 1900 to 1940, to the attributes of the legal system and the creation of statutory law. A difference in emphasis occurred from the integrity and autonomy of the profession to the autonomy of the legal system itself. From the beginning to the end of its first century of organized collegial activity, the legal profession accordingly moved from a greater preoccupation with itself to a broader concern with the legal system and the crises facing government in the formation of public policy. The movement was neither sudden nor radical. It did not represent a swing from one extreme to another. On the contrary, the general aims of the professional associations were balanced between upgrading the profession and the control of markets, on the one hand, and reforming the judicial system, on the other. The changes are less from one set of goals to another than from one set of relative priorities to another.

If each form of legal association has a characteristic portfolio of resources, and if each portfolio maximizes different objectives, there will likely be a press toward a consonance between resources and anticipated accomplishments. Organizational consonance obtains in those situations in which resources are appropriate to the objectives sought by an organizational elite. For example, in the history of the American legal profession, elite associations have adopted as a primary goal the control of nonelite lawyers and, in the elite's terms, the improvement of the quality of the profession. But while an elite form may be appropriate, or at least efficacious, for these formative tasks, it appears that the aims of an established profession can be realized only through a shift from the elite form to the other forms of collegial bodies.

By the same token, we can conceive of resource inconsonance. If a particular portfolio of resources is inappropriate to a given set of ends, then there will be a press toward the reestablishment of consonancy. That of course may be effected by changing either the ends or the means to reach them. A typical pattern might well follow the model that has been applied to the CBA: that is, resource inconsonance occurs when professional leaders develop a set of objectives well beyond the resource capacity of their organizations; they must therefore undertake a process of adaptation to bring their resource bases more into line with the new demands. But the reverse pattern can also occur: an association with broad aims may suddenly find itself stripped of assets, because of war and the loss of active members and income, the withdrawal of automatic licensing fees from government, or a general fall in professional standing because of public assaults on the profession's integrity and organization. In such cases, a profession that suffers severe reverses can achieve consonance only by constricting its operative goals. Indeed situations can arise in which the new goals themselves alienate members who withdraw and thereby force the organization to find an alternative pattern of consonance. Whatever the particular change, however, the transformation of associations from one form to another can be seen as an adaptation from a pattern of consonancy to a new resolution of the relations between ends and means.

The preceding discussion has far exceeded the evidence provided by the CBA, but that license may be justified by the utility of a formulation that allows all comprehensive professional associations to be viewed in more abstract and comparable terms. Nevertheless, typologies inevitably distort. Even on these terms, therefore, it is necessary to retreat partially from the arguments I have made with two sets of correctives.

First, some important qualifications must be added to the elementary model of goals and resources I have proposed. For the purposes of exposition, I have presented not only a highly schematic representation of the historical development of legal associations but also an excessively rationalistic image of the relation between means and ends. The records of the CBA, and especially the transcripts of the Board of Managers' deliberations, do not support such an overly purposive and calculative conception of professional action. While it is certainly true that during the founding period some aims were articulated and formally codified, for the most part it appears that bar leaders very seldom clearly enunciate either their goals or alternatives to reach them. That is not to say that particular problems or programs are not considered in detail and that extensive campaigns of action are not explicitly formulated. Neither is it to say that there may not be several such programs being considered at any one time. It is to assert that very, very seldom do professional leaders ever attempt to view the relation between ends and means with the detachment and percipience that is sometimes projected onto them by concepts such as "professional projects."

It can be said that bar leaders did recognize that certain kinds of resources and organizational factors would contribute to particular sorts of professional influence. The radical new strategies of the bar integration movement are the most striking case in point. But more usually the matching of resources with strategies to deploy them for given ends appeared not after an explicit consideration of all the possibilities but after periods of trial and error sometimes stretching over decades. Thus the shift from an elite to an open association by the CBA occurred over half a century. Particular adaptations that are treated simultaneously in typological accounts, such as the abolition of entrance fees and the formation of substantive law committees, occurred up to twenty or more years apart. To the extent that there was a strong purposive element in the bar, the changing forms of organizations evolved slowly and in response to the cumulative wisdom of successive generations of bar leaders. The only outstanding exception was the bar integration movement. Even then, however, many professional associations picked and chose among the features of the integrated bar suggested by the American Judicature Society, and they implemented their assorted choices over ten or twenty years. Only occasionally did a leader with unusual vision, such as the first chairman of the CBA's Public Relations Committee, grasp something of the contingent relation between prestige, standing, membership, and the roles an association might play.

Furthermore, whereas I have suggested that the form of organization logically follows the choice of given objectives, that process is sometimes reversed. For instance, the goals identified with the original elite associations emerged from a noninstitutionalized elite of practicing lawyers who generated goals consistent with their proto-organization and standing in the profession. Moreover, some of the changes in organization occurred less because of any explicit changes of policy about the relations of means and end than because of external forces—wars, social movements, a depression—that forced associations to change in order to maintain the organization they already had. Far from being immune to broader societal changes, the form, structure, and strategies of bar associations are subject to population density and size; economic circumstances, including not only national depressions and booms but also the composition of a state's economy; political climate, as in the proclivities of state governments to mandate legislatively or judicially the membership in bar associations as a condition of practice; and cultural movements, whether of progressivism or the women's movement. With the alleviation of the stresses that had forced organizations to make changes, many associations suddenly find themselves with resources sufficient to set new horizons. Thus while it may be argued that there had been a teleological component in the development of organizations, that perspective must be held in tension with the recognition that the link between the two has more often than not been diffuse and attenuated, more haphazard and discontinuous than planned and smooth.

The second corrective concerns the historical context of professional associations and their development. The view of bar associations presented here is essentially an interior scape. Where formative phases of professionalism coincide with quite different historical situations, Stinchcombe's influential theory would lead us to expect that associations will take on perceptibly varying forms that reflect their context of emergence. It is not accidental that associations established in the last half of the nineteenth century, at a time when there was a strong reaction against democratization of the profession and when the upper echelons were faced with an influx of immigrant and lower-class lawyers, became exclusive in membership and elite in form. Neither is it surprising that associations becoming established during the height of progressivism came to reflect the reactions against elite control and took the more democratic forms of association that the progressivists would sanction. In both cases the formative phase had still to be negotiated, but the profession's structural reaction to it changed markedly.

But although it is true that, historically, professions have tried to solve the problems of autonomy, monopoly, and control central to the formative era, it is not entirely correct to say that associations coping with those problems in 1870 were dealing with exactly the same difficulties as those organizations confronting them in 1920. Insofar as pioneering associations accomplished professional upgrading for themselves, it is probable that they provided examples for other jurisdictions; the diffusion of professional advancement across the country gave newly forming or consolidating associations a head start. Within a profession, therefore, those organizations founded at a later date will have less difficulty solving the formative problems than their pioneering counterparts. An interaction effect therefore occurs between the cohort of an association's founding and historical period. The same historical milieu may turn an elite to an open association, an open to a universal association, or an elite to a universal body. Presumably those organizations with longer and more established traditions will be less vulnerable to environmental forces.

Over the last 150 years, therefore, we may propose that the legal profession in its collegial form has steadily increased its adaptive capacity. There have been three powerful social movements in American society that have had a democratizing effect on lawyers' collegial organization: Jacksonian democracy, progressivism, and the civil rights era of the 1950s and 1960s. In the first assault on professional privileges and associations, climaxing in the 1830s, professional bodies of any consequence collapsed, virtually without exception. During the second burst of democratic reforms from 1900 to 1920, and two decades thereafter, the older associations did not collapse but for the most part adapted, albeit cautiously, trimming their compositional sails to the new ideological winds. Some changed more radically to the all-inclusiveness of the integrated bar; but even these adaptions were far removed from the total abolition of professional associations a century earlier. By the third movement, and its stress on minority rights, almost all associations had the resilience to be able to adjust to the new demands and their consequences for associational structure and government without the massive dislocations and radical changes in formation that characterized the 1920s. As I shall show in the next chapter, associations like the CBA did face internal crises of governance and even threats of secession. But the consequences of those challenges were limited. Part of the explanation may lie in the relative force of the social movements themselves. It is equally, if not more, plausible to conclude that, along with the other resources associations had accumulated, they had also effectively expanded their ability to adapt to severe societal changes.

Resource Accumulation

What magnitude of resources has been accumulated at the end of this century of bar organization? Although it is difficult to obtain quantitative indicators of all resources, data from 1983 do exist on size, administrative staff, budget, and inclusiveness of all state associations and major metropolitan associations. Table 4.4 classifies subnational bar associations into (1) unified state bars, (2) voluntary state bars, and (3) local bar associations.

Variations among unified bars is enormous. The California State Bar Association dwarfs all others with its 89,000 members, $22 million budget, and three hundred-member staff. Five other unified bars average thirty thousand members and an expenditure of $4.5 million; ten others have approximately ten thousand members and a budget between $1 and $2 million. Of voluntary state bar associations, the modal group has an average of eight thousand members and an operating budget approaching $1 million per annum.

Many local associations have resources that supplement their state associations. The four largest metropolitan bar groups average fifteen thousand members and multimillion dollar expenditures; and the fifteen groups with more than 3,500 members had mean budgets of $500,000. Of all metropolitan associations, table 4.5 indicates that, in 1983, the CBA had the largest membership, at 17,638, the largest staff, at 126 persons, and the highest expenditure, of $4.5 million.

The tremendous advances in inclusiveness are also apparent in the last column of the table. Eight of the nineteen associations had in excess of 80 percent of all those practicing in the city as members. Except for two New York associations, every other body included more than 60 percent of practitioners in their local areas. These data have been presented for individual associations. But because two or more associations can exist in the same state, resources for political action are additive across associations. In New York, for instance, 61,322 lawyers were combined into seven state and local associations (many lawyers are doubly or trebly counted) that had combined full-time staffs of 208 and an expenditure of $7,729,392. In contrast to the voluntary bars of New York, California has a compulsory state association and fourteen metropolitan and country groups. Altogether their members numbered 123,576, their staffs added to 428, and their combined budgets for 1983 were $28,148,216. Altogether, the figures for 1983 indicate that, in theory, American state and metropolitan associations can mobilize very substantial resources. In one year, 179 associations represented 869,000 lawyers and spent $129 million. Funds, members, staffs, and inclusiveness can be translated into enormous pools of labor, into extensive individual and organizational networks, and into substantial facilities. Above all, they concentrate almost the total quantam of professional expertise and knowledge contained in a geographic jurisdiction into a single organization. By any standards, these are marks of very considerable success from a century of constructing authority and accumulating resources.

TABLE 4.4. Summary of Membership, Staff and Budget Data on Individual Responding Bars, by Category

	Number in Category	Membership		Staff Employees		Expenditures ($)	
		Total	Average	Total	Average	Total	Average
Unified state bars							
50,000 and more members	1	89,259	89,259	305	305.0	22,127,223	22,127,223
15,000–49,999 members	5	148,584	29,717	356	71.2	22,709,225	4,541,845
5,000–14,999 members	14	133,254	9,518	315	22.5	20,696,734	1,478,338
4,999 and fewer members	13	33,002	2,539	104	8.0	5,758,793	442,984
Subtotal	33	404,099	12,245	1,080	32.7	71,291,975	2,160,363
Voluntary state bars:							
15,000 and more members	4	102,382	25,596	143	35.8	11,135,590	2,783,898
5,000–14,999 members	11	90,445	8,222	139	12.6	9,542,640	867,513
4,999 and fewer members	8	18,091	2,261	34	4.3	2,161,336	270,167
Subtotal	23	210,918	9,170	316	13.7	22,839,566	993,025
Total, state bars	56	615,017	10,982	1,396	24.9	94,131,541	1,680,920
Local bar associations:							
10,000 and more members	4	59,217	14,804	321	80.2	11,990,177	2,997,544
3,500–9,999 members	15	72,218	4,815	169	11.3	8,493,839	566,256
2,000–3,499 members	21	51,980	2,475	115	5.5	5,750,875	273,851
1,000–1,999 members	26	35,405	1,362	85	3.3	3,850,463	148,095
500–999 members	35	26,203	749	64	1.8	2,843,949	81,256
300–499 members	22	9,170	417	33	1.5	1,480,187	67,281
Total, local bars	123	254,193	2,067	787	6.4	34,409,490	279,752
Grand total, all responding bars	179	869,210	4,856	2,183	12.2	128,541,031	718,106

SOURCE.—ABA 1983 Bar Activities Survey, American Bar Association, Chicago.

TABLE 4.5. Membership, Staff, and Budgets of Metropolitan Bars with 3,500 and More Members

Bar Association	City	Members[a]	Staff[a]	Budget ($)[a]	% of Lawyers in SMSA, 1980[b]	% of Lawyers in City[b]
Bar Association of San Francisco	San Francisco	5,925	16	953,843	37.4	63.5
Los Angeles County Bar Association	Los Angeles	17,271	50	3,000,000	66.2	112.8
San Diego Bar Association	San Diego	3,657	9	222,700	63.7	89.0
Denver Bar Association	Denver	4,472	6	276,905	58.0	81.1
Atlanta Bar Association	Atlanta	3,915	6	596,659	49.6	65.9
Chicago Bar Association	Chicago	17,638	126	4,449,738	53.4	71.3
Boston Bar Association	Boston	5,200	9	508,000	39.8	66.9
Detroit Bar Association	Detroit	4,200	9	675,000	37.6	87.2
Hennepin County Bar Association	Minneapolis	4,532	9	458,000	51.6	93.9
Bar Association of Metropolitan St. Louis	St. Louis	4,002	15	897,000	77.7	98.5
Association of the Bar of the City of New York	New York	13,636	107	3,340,439	28.8	31.4
Nassau County Bar Association	Mineola, N.Y.	3,870	10	50,000	58.0	...
New York County Lawyers Association	New York	10,672	38	1,200,000	24.3	31.1
Bar of Greater Cleveland	Cleveland	4,444	12	550,000	55.9	70.2
Allegheny County Bar Association	Pittsburgh	5,218	12	803,741	88.6	111.1
Philadelphia Bar Association	Philadelphia	8,200	29	946,000	64.5	93.2
Dallas Bar Association	Dallas	4,510	6	590,345	48.2	67.9
Houston Bar Association	Houston	6,452	8	405,000	58.8	63.9
Seattle-King County Bar Association	Seattle	3,621	13	560,646	67.9	83.4

[a]Source.—American Bar Association 1983 Bar Activities Survey.
[b]Source.—Barbara A. Curran et al., The Lawyer Statistical Report: A Statistical Profile of the U.S. Legal Profession in the 1980s (Chicago: American Bar Foundation, 1985).

5 The Contradictions of Inclusiveness

Associations that shift from elite to open and universal forms do so in part to gain attributes they do not have. The logic of the shift appears straightforward and unproblematic. So do its consequences. In practice, however, the simplicity of the transition to inclusiveness becomes very complicated indeed. As associations become more inclusive of a profession, their membership tends also to become more representative, thus giving them a compositional mandate to speak authoritatively on behalf of professionals in their catchment area. As I have argued, the authority of representativeness should combine with greater fiscal strength, broader social networks, and a greater depth of manpower resources for organizational projects. Invariably, associations do gain those advantages.

On the other hand, inclusiveness may lead professional bodies into a contradiction. While they gain an authority to speak on behalf of a professional constituency, they simultaneously draw inside the organization the full range of conflicts and polarities that divide and segment a profession. Compositional heterogeneity in the wake of inclusiveness may consign an association to internal stalemate. At the very point at which it appeared to have the greatest potential for influence, an association can be threatened with consensus and collective action on nothing but the most mundane and uncontroversial matters. The cure for the weakness of elite bodies may produce impotence in their organizational successors. In this scenario, open and universal portfolios of resources are recipes for collective failure, a truly ironic climax to a national movement committed to professional power.

The extent to which a profession can resolve this contradiction is a critical condition of its capacity to exert effective collective influence in either primary or secondary spheres. If associations cannot circumvent the pitfalls that inclusiveness lays for them, then a macrosociological capacity to bring expertise to the service of power or professional solutions to the crises of ungovernability is nullified from the outset. Consequently, we are posed a question within a question. I have broached the general macrosociological problem of whether professions can play a role beyond that of monopoly in state or national government. Within this issue, however, is the prior question of whether inclusive associations have the organizational or internal political capacity to act at all.

In this chapter I establish, first, the extent to which the Chicago Bar Association (CBA), among other bar associations, achieved not only an inclusive but also a representative membership in the postwar period, second, some of the internal conflicts and differentiation that inclusiveness brought, and, third, the likely consequences of both developments. In part 3, I contest the proposition that inclusiveness leads necessarily to organizational incapacity and professional powerlessness.

Inclusiveness and Representativeness

By 1950, both unified and voluntary state bar associations incorporated on average more than half the professionals in their states. Figure 5.1 presents a Johnson's cluster analysis of all state bar inclusiveness profiles from organizational birth in the late nineteenth century to 1980. A cluster analysis is useful when there is no theoretical basis for classifying data. By performing a cluster procedure on data collected on bar inclusiveness for each decade and state since 1880, we can identify groups of observations that share similar attributes. It becomes easier to discern similar patterns or profiles of change in state bar inclusiveness over a century. The solution presented in the figure reports the two dominant patterns (although a more refined analysis indicates that these can be further subdivided into five profiles—three for unified bars and two for voluntary associations). One pattern is composed principally of unified bars and the other principally of voluntary bars. Although differences between each profile are small in the nineteenth century, by the mid-twentieth century they are striking. Whereas at mid-century voluntary bars could claim an average of 58 percent of state practitioners in their organizations, the comparable figure for unified bars was 113 percent (with 13 percent of members from out of state). But whereas change in the ensuing thirty years remained minimal for unified bars, it increased drastically for voluntary associations—from 58 percent to 84 percent.

The development of metropolitan associations was rather uneven, as table 5.1 demonstrates. Two associations, those of Boston and Philadelphia, included more than 40 percent of the profession by 1900. Other associations, except for those in New York, followed a pattern quite similar to that of state voluntary associations: between 30 and 40 percent of city lawyers were incorporated by 1920; more than a majority of lawyers were included by 1950; and a continuing drive for inclusiveness was maintained into the 1980s.

Inclusiveness, however, does not necessarily imply an identical degree of representativeness. A professional body could include half the lawyers in a jurisdiction, but they might be confined to solo practitioners or firm lawyers. Of course,

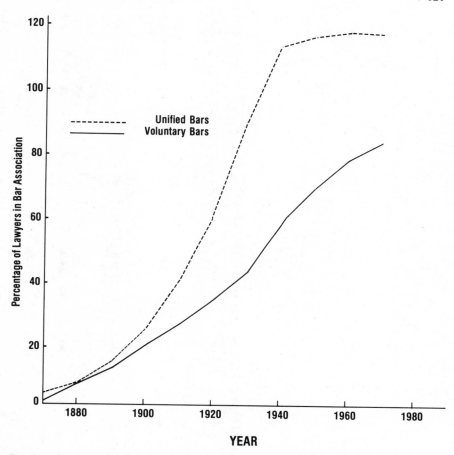

FIG. 5.1. Johnson's cluster of profiles of state bar association inclusiveness, 1880–1980. See Stephen C. Johnson, "Hierarchical Clustering Schemes," *Psychometrika* 32 (1967): 241–54. The unified bars are Alabama, Arizona, California, Florida, Kentucky, Idaho, Louisiana, Michigan, Mississippi, Nebraska, Nevada, New Hampshire, New Mexico, North Carolina, North Dakota, Oklahoma, Oregon, Rhode Island, South Dakota, Texas, Utah, Washington, West Virginia, Wisconsin, and Wyoming plus Iowa and Vermont. The voluntary bars are Arkansas, Connecticut, Colorado, Illinois, Indiana, Kansas, Maine, Maryland, Massachusetts, Minnesota, New Jersey, New York, Ohio, Pennsylvania, and Tennessee plus Georgia, Missouri, Montana, South Carolina, and Virginia. Sources: U.S. census for relevant years; and published bar reports, formerly in the Cromwell Library, American Bar Foundation, and now in the Northwestern University Law Library, Chicago, Illinois.

the closer inclusiveness approaches 100 percent, the more likely will be the accompanying representativeness. Nevertheless, while organizations are in the middle range of inclusiveness, they may still be heavily biased in their representation of lawyers. Data are not available on the composition and representativeness of most American bar associations, and so it is impossible to discover whether representativeness kept pace with growth in size and inclusiveness. The

TABLE 5.1. Growth and Inclusiveness of Selected Metropolitan Bar Associations, 1880–1980

	1880	1900	1920	1951	1960	1970	1980
Boston: Boston Bar Association (1876)							
Lawyers in bar	769	1,472	2,560	4,661	5,063	5,277	7,817
Members	298[a]	667	922	3,193	...	3,513	5,230
Percent	38.8	45.3	36.0	68.5	...	66.6	66.9
New York: Association of the Bar of the City of New York (1870); New York County Lawyers Association (1908)							
Lawyers in bar	4,270	8,024	12,025	25,586	33,631	38,547	39,851
ABCNY members	716[a]	1,641	2,333	5,041	6,921	9,471	12,286
Percent (ABCNY)	16.8	20.5	19.4	19.7	20.6	24.6	30.8
NYCLA members	...	...	3,664	7,405	9,778	9,678	10,549
Percent (NYCLA)	...	...	30.5	28.9	29.1	25.1	26.5
Philadelphia: Philadelphia Bar Association (1802)							
Lawyers in bar	1,641	2,106	1,963	3,740	4,502	5,312	7,727
Members	...	916[b]	...	...	...	4,495	7,200
Percent	...	43.5	...	...	...	84.6	93.2

Los Angeles: Los Angeles County Bar Association (1878)							
Lawyers in bar	...	...	1,901	5,887	6,676	10,014	14,730
Members	...	...	...	2,700[a,c]	4,200–4,500	9,500[a]	16,612
Percent	...	...	...	45.9	65.2	94.9	112.8
Chicago: Chicago Bar Association (1874)							
Lawyers in bar	1,035	4,418	6,266	11,642	13,207	14,375	19,476
Members	...	635	2,576	6,189	7,637	9,881[a]	13,889
Percent	...	14.4	41.1	53.2	57.8	68.7	71.3
San Francisco: Bar Association of San Francisco (1872)							
Lawyers in bar	661	1,488	2,147	3,289	3,832	5,322	8,825
Members	175	200[a]	925[a]	...	2,600[a]	...	5,600
Percent	26.5	13.4	43.1	...	67.8	...	63.5

SOURCE.—Information on the number of lawyers is taken, for 1951–80, from *Lawyer Statistical Reports*; for 1880–1920, from the U.S. census (lawyers resident in central city and suburbs over 25,000 population); and, for 1880–1920 in Chicago, from Edward M. Martin, *The Role of the Bar in Electing the Bench in Chicago*, (Chicago: University of Chicago Press, 1936). Information on the size of bar associations is taken, for 1800, from the American Bar Association's *Directory of Bar Associations*; for 1900–1920 in Chicago, from Martin, *The Role of the Bar*; and, for other years, from the relevant bar association reports.

NOTE.—The date in parentheses following the names of bar associations is the year of founding. Missing information is indicated by ellipsis points.

[a] Approximately.
[b] 1902.
[c] 1952.

data on the postwar composition and inclusiveness of the CBA therefore provide a unique opportunity to examine the extent a once elite or noninclusive association became truly open; thereby we can test directly some hypotheses that have been advanced about the CBA and indirectly those of the organized bar more generally.

How successfully had the CBA attained representativeness by 1950 and in the following quarter century? Jerome Carlin actively contested the representativeness of the CBA in the research he undertook in the late 1950s. On the basis of a study of solo practitioners in Chicago, Carlin observed that only three of his eighty-four lawyers had any active role in the Illinois State Bar Association and the CBA; the others would more often be found in the ethnic associations. Between solo practitioners and ethnic associations, on the one hand, and firm lawyers and the CBA, on the other, existed a "wide and unusually unbridgeable gap." For the solos, the organized bar was dominated by "blue noses" and "snobs"—"blue bloods" who practiced in large firms and whose clients were railroads, insurance companies, and large corporations. Because the CBA elite was controlled by wealthy, corporate, firm-dominated lawyers, it was allegedly unresponsive to the problems of the nonelite. The CBA had fought social security and implemented a dual system of justice—one for rich lawyers and another for the poor; it had attempted to block the progression of the little man to the bench by abolishing judicial elections. In the view of the common man, concluded Carlin, "the bar associations have failed to protect the small practitioners from the encroachment of non-lawyers, have done nothing about improving his economic position, and apply a more stringent standard in judging his conduct than in judging the conduct of lawyers in larger firms." Carlin's conclusions, even though drawn on a small and biased sample of lawyers, reflected accusations leveled in the 1930s—accusations of bias towards white, Anglo-Saxon, Protestant, well-to-do firm and corporate lawyers.[1]

Carlin's thesis has been projected onto the national profession by Auerbach's sweeping indictment of bar leaders over the last century. In his historical critique, Auerbach maintains that the established bar associations traditionally have been weapons in the hands of a professional upperclass who used them initially to exclude, and later to control, an insurgent "underclass" clamoring for, and eventually succeeding in gaining, admission to the profession. Auerbach's evidence is for the most part impressionistic. Nevertheless, he characterizes the membership of the older professional associations, and subsequently their leaders, as dis-

1. Jerome Carlin, *Lawyers on Their Own* (New Brunswick, N.J.: Rutgers University Press, 1962), 175–76, 184.

proportionately drawn from Anglo-Saxon and upper-middle-class origins, elite law schools, large law firms and corporate practice.[2]

The Chicago Bar Project allows the closest examination yet of the relations between inclusiveness and representativeness over the quarter century from 1950 to 1974. I combine information from two data sets to look at levels of representation on a number of criteria. The Chicago Bar survey, conducted by Heinz and Laumann, consisted of a random sample of 777 lawyers drawn from the Chicago legal profession. Administered in 1975, the survey asked lawyers sets of questions on their legal education, careers, practice, opinions on legal issues, involvement with the organized bar, social networks, and various background attributes such as parents' education and ethnicity.

I compiled a second data set from the biographies of all officers and members of the CBA Board of Managers between 1950 and 1974. By combining the data sets, systematic comparisons can be made of Chicago bar members with CBA members, CBA Board members, and CBA presidents. The latter comparisons are pursued in chapter 11.

For present purposes, I reanalyze the 1975 survey not to establish the degree of representation in the mid-1970s, as Heinz et al. have already done,[3] but to approximate the degree of representation in the mid 1950s, when the bar association was less inclusive, and to follow changes in representativeness as inclusiveness changed. This may be done from a single-point survey by breaking the 777 respondents into practice cohorts: all lawyers interviewed in 1974, who were CBA members and in practice in Chicago during 1954, are assigned to a 1954 cohort—and similarly for 1959, 1964, and 1969. While this approach does have the merit that it simulates repeated cross-sectional surveys of the Chicago bar and its change, it also has biases: it cannot include members of the bar and CBA who were members of the earlier practice cohorts but had retired, moved, or were deceased by 1975. Still it does offer a useful method of analysis short of true cross sections for each year.

It has been asserted that the memberships and the elites of professional associations have been skewed. They have underrepresented lawyers who were recent immigrants, who originated from eastern or southern Europe, whose parentage was lower class, who graduated from night schools, who practiced outside larger law firms on behalf of individuals, or who were government attorneys and house counsel.

2. Jerold S. Auerbach, *Unequal Justice: Lawyers and Social Change in Modern America* (New York: Oxford University Press, 1976).

3. John P. Heinz et al., "Diversity, Representation, and Leadership in an Urban Bar," *American Bar Foundation Research Journal* 1976 (Summer): 717–85.

TABLE 5.2. Father's Occupation: Chicago Bar and CBA Members, 1954–74

Practice Cohorts and Father's Occupation	CBA Members		Chicago Bar	
	%	N	%	N
1954:				
Professional, technical	31.2	48	26.5	71
Lawyer*	*17.9*	*28*	*13.7*	*37*
Administrative, sales	40.9	63	38.8	104
Clerical	2.6	4	3.4	9
Craftsmen	9.7	15	13.4	36
Operatives, laborers	6.5	10	9.0	24
Farmers	5.8	9	4.9	13
Farm labor, service	3.2	5	4.1	11
	100.0	154	100.0	268
1959:				
Professional, technical	31.9	68	27.5	95
Lawyer	*17.2*	*37*	*13.5*	*47*
Administrative, sales	43.2	92	40.8	141
Clerical	3.8	8	3.2	11
Craftsmen	8.9	19	12.4	43
Operatives, laborers	5.2	11	8.4	29
Farmers	4.2	9	4.0	14
Farm labor, service	2.8	6	3.8	13
	100.0	213	100.0	346
1964:				
Professional, technical	32.7	91	28.8	130
Lawyer	*18.2*	*51*	*13.6*	*62*
Administrative, sales	39.9	111	40.9	185
Clerical	3.2	9	2.7	12
Craftsmen	10.4	29	11.7	53
Operatives, laborers	6.5	18	8.2	37
Farmers	4.0	11	3.5	16
Farm labor, service	3.2	9	4.2	19
	100.0	278	100.0	452
1969:				
Professional, technical	34.6	133	31.1	186
Lawyer	*19.0*	*74*	*14.8*	*90*
Administrative, sales	39.6	152	41.4	248
Clerical	3.4	13	2.8	17
Craftsmen	8.9	34	10.0	60
Operatives, laborers	8.3	32	8.2	49
Farmers	3.1	12	3.0	18
Farm labor, service	2.1	8	3.5	21
	100.0	384	100.0	599

TABLE 5.2. *Continued*

Practice Cohorts and Father's Occupation	CBA Members		Chicago Bar	
	%	N	%	N
1974:				
Professional, technical	36.3	180	32.1	245
Lawyer	*17.3*	*87*	*14.0*	*108*
Administrative, sales	41.1	204	41.7	318
Clerical	2.4	12	2.4	18
Craftsmen	8.1	40	9.8	75
Operatives, laborers	7.1	35	8.0	61
Farmers	2.6	13	2.9	22
Farm labor, service	2.4	12	3.1	24
	100.0	496	100.0	763

*Values for lawyers not included in totals.

CLASS REPRESENTATION

Has the organized bar in Chicago continued to draw its members from a more exclusive social class in recent years? Table 5.2 indicates that, except for a limited overrepresentation of lawyers in the CBA from the highest category of father's occupation, the CBA more or less matched the class background of the Chicago profession at large. In the CBA, as in the bar, approximately 30 percent of attorneys had professional or technician fathers; another 40 percent had fathers who were administrators, managers, or salesmen; between 10 and 12 percent had fathers who were craftsmen; and approximately 9 percent had fathers who were laborers and operators, farmers, or farm workers.

These class recruitment patterns of lawyers in Chicago have changed very slightly since 1954. There is a minor increase in the percent of lawyers coming from the highest class group and an equally slight decline of those coming from craftsman backgrounds. Change in the distribution for CBA members is comparable to the change observed in the bar.

LAW SCHOOL REPRESENTATION

Is composition of the organized bar weighted against lower prestige, local, and night law schools? The composition of the CBA does not reproduce exactly the educational profile of the bar, as measured by law school attended, but it comes close to doing so. For the bar, recruitment distributions remain relatively stable throughout the period (see table 5.3). Approximately 10 percent of Chicago lawyers attended three eastern schools, Harvard, Columbia, and Yale. Another 12–15 percent came from Northwestern University, with a similar percentage

TABLE 5.3. Law Schools of CBA Members and Chicago Bar, 1954–74

Practice Cohort and Law School	CBA Members		Chicago Bar	
	%	N	%	N
1954:				
University of Chicago	12.5	19	10.1	27
Northwestern University	17.1	26	14.6	39
Other local	40.1	61	45.7	122
Eastern elite	16.4	25	11.6	31
Midwestern	12.5	19	12.7	34
Other schools	1.3	2	5.5	14
	100.0	152	100.0	267
1959:				
University of Chicago	12.3	26	9.6	33
Northwestern University	18.4	39	15.7	54
Other local	40.6	86	46.4	159
Eastern elite	15.1	32	11.1	38
Midwestern	10.8	23	11.7	40
Other schools	2.8	6	5.5	19
	100.0	212	100.0	343
1964:				
University of Chicago	11.2	31	9.8	44
Northwestern University	17.3	48	14.6	66
Other local	42.6	118	46.8	211
Eastern elite	14.4	40	11.1	50
Midwestern	10.1	28	12.4	56
Other schools	4.3	12	5.3	24
	100.0	277	100.0	451
1969:				
University of Chicago	9.8	38	9.0	54
Northwestern University	16.8	65	13.9	84
Other local	41.3	160	46.9	283
Eastern elite	13.2	51	10.1	61
Midwestern	13.2	51	13.3	80
Other schools	5.7	22	6.8	41
	100.0	387	100.0	603
1974:				
University of Chicago	9.5	47	8.7	67
Northwestern University	16.3	81	14.1	108
Other local	40.8	203	46.0	352
Eastern elite	11.5	57	8.6	66
Midwestern	15.3	76	14.9	114
Other schools	6.6	33	7.7	59
	100.0	497	100.0	766

from the major midwestern state universities, such as Wisconsin, Michigan, and Illinois, and a slightly smaller percentage from the University of Chicago. But by far the largest proportion of lawyers, 45–46 percent, came from four local schools—two Catholic private universities, De Paul and Loyola, and two other private schools that offer night classes, John Marshall and the Illinois Institute of Technology at Chicago-Kent. Change in the supply of Chicago lawyers from the respective law schools is negligible, but there is a slight decline of recruitment from the eastern schools and the University of Chicago, accompanied by a corresponding increase from other midwestern schools.

Within the CBA, lawyers trained at Chicago, Northwestern, and especially Harvard, Columbia, and Yale are a little overrepresented; and lawyers who have graduated from other Chicago law schools are consistently underrepresented over time by 5–7 percentage points. The educational recruitment patterns have changed very little over the three postwar decades.

LEGAL PRACTICE REPRESENTATION

Table 5.4 demonstrates that, as far back as 1954, the scales of legal practice within the bar had tipped in favor of the firm lawyers, the single largest category of legal practice. But those lawyers were followed by the 26 percent in the sample who identified themselves as solo practitioners (although that figure probably underestimates the weight of solo practitioners in the bar because of the tendency of the cohort analyses to exclude older and deceased lawyers who would have been practicing in the early 1950s). Of the remaining lawyers, 15 percent were house counsel, and 18 percent worked in some capacity for the government—as state's attorneys, as U.S. attorneys, or as judges and corporation counsel for the city of Chicago.

In the ensuing twenty years this profile took on a different shape: the percentage of firm lawyers increased from 36 percent to 49 percent, while solo practitioners declined by 7 percent. Relative proportions of government and house counsel shifted slightly—proportions in government declining somewhat and house counsel increasing.

When measured against the bar profile, the composition of the CBA is progressively skewed in favor of the firm lawyers. In the early 1950s, 12 percent more firm lawyers could be found in the CBA than in the bar at large, in contrast to 4 percent fewer solo practitioners. The difference of 10 percent between solos and firm lawyers in the profession at large grew to 20 percent between those categories of lawyers within the association. By 1974, the comparable figures are 30 percent and 41 percent, respectively. Both government lawyers and house counsel were underrepresented in the CBA.

TABLE 5.4. Type of Practice: Chicago Bar and CBA Members, 1954–74

Practice Cohort and Type of Practice	CBA Members		Chicago Bar	
	%	N	%	N
1954:				
Solo	26.2	39	25.8	68
Firm	46.3	69	36.0	95
Government	4.7	7	8.7	23
House counsel	12.1	18	15.2	40
Professor	2.0	3	1.9	5
Other	8.7	13	12.5	33
	100.0	149	100.0	264
1959:				
Solo	22.8	47	25.4	87
Firm	51.5	106	40.6	139
Government	4.9	10	7.6	26
House counsel	12.6	26	14.6	50
Professor	1.5	3	1.8	6
Other	6.8	14	9.9	34
	100.0	206	100.0	342
1964:				
Solo	21.5	58	23.9	107
Firm	54.4	147	44.4	199
Government	6.7	18	9.2	41
House counsel	10.7	29	12.5	56
Professor	.7	2	1.6	7
Other	5.9	16	8.5	38
	100.0	270	100.0	448
1969:				
Solo	15.7	60	20.0	120
Firm	53.5	204	43.6	262
Government	10.2	39	12.5	75
House counsel	11.8	45	12.6	76
Professor	1.0	4	1.5	9
Other	7.6	29	9.8	59
	100.0	381	100.0	601
1974:				
Solo	15.7	78	18.8	145
Firm	57.4	286	49.2	379
Government	9.2	46	12.1	93
House counsel	10.8	54	11.5	89
Professor	1.2	6	1.3	10
Other	5.6	28	7.1	55
	100.0	498	100.0	771

SPECIALTIES

No data are available on specialties equivalent to those on practice. Nonetheless, it is possible to make some estimate on the catholicity of the CBA by looking at the size and expansion of its specialty law committees from 1950 to 1974. It is clear from table 5.5 that by 1950 the CBA had organizationally recognized virtually all legal specialties. After that date it formed committees as new fields of specialization developed. Moreover, the committees are not confined to those in corporate or large firm practice. In terms of Laumann and Heinz's treatment of professional differentiation, the CBA in 1950 represented the lower hemisphere of the profession, which delivers legal services to individuals, as fully as the higher hemisphere, which serves corporate clients.[4]

Having said that, however, the changes in committee size over the twenty-five years do have some significant variations. Through the 1950s, the total number of lawyers in substantive law committees increased marginally; but between 1960 and 1965 numbers doubled, and by 1974 the CBA had three times as many lawyers in specialty committees as it had had in 1960. Nevertheless, committee expansion was not uniform. Taking the Heinz and Laumann specialty prestige scale as an index, most growth occurred in high-prestige specialties.[5] Those areas of law ranked first, second, and third on the prestige scale—securities, tax and antitrust—expanded from 13 to 147, from 39 to 205, and from 22 to 155, respectively, over the twenty-five years. Other high-prestige specialties—corporation law, probate, municipal, labor, and real estate law—also swelled dramatically. Of the lower-prestige areas, only criminal and matrimonial law showed comparable changes.

The specialty committees do not precisely match the prestige scale categories: some committees will include lawyers from both "hemispheres." Further, personal injury lawyers and many different types of litigators appear to be grouped together in some committees, even though negligence and personal injury attorneys have a prominent role, as I shall demonstrate, in the leadership of the CBA later in the 1970s. All the same, the committee figures do show that the CBA was generally responsive to all specialties within the profession, that it made efforts to include as many interested and expert practitioners in those committees as it could manage, and that it was largely successful in doing so. Indeed the 22 percent of lawyers belonging to substantive law committees in 1974 demonstrates just how far the association had gone in effecting the structural incorporation of lawyers into the collegial association.

4. Edward O. Laumann and John P. Heinz, "Specialization and Prestige in the Legal Profession: The Structure of Deference," *American Bar Foundation Research Journal* 1977 (Winter): 155–216.
5. Ibid., 166.

TABLE 5.5. Size of Selected CBA Substantive and Specialty Law Committees, 1950–74

	1950	1955	1960	1965	1970	1974
Administrative	15	25	19	29	23	41
Admiralty	. . .	. . .	31	37	27	33
Antitrust	22	22	32	95	105	155
Aviation	18	19	20	28	22	32
Bankruptcy	27	24	28	34	49	44
Civil Practice	37	34	41	94	100	129
Civil Rights	18	26	22	51	44	56
Commercial Code	. . .	. . .	. . .	51	60	64
Constitutional Revision	30	30	29	27	43	28
Consumer Credit	. . .	. . .	. . .	23	31	33
Corporation Law	31	26	36	97	101	115
Corporate Law Depts	. . .	. . .	99	188	216	132
Criminal	27	25	28	47	100	155
Environmental	. . .	. . .	. . .	. . .	. . .	69
Federal Civil Procedure	. . .	18	28	34	52	72
Federal Tax	39	43	44	122	149	205
Insurance	28	25	27	56	58	84
International	26	37	44	53	55	69
Juvenile Delinquents	19	24	27	24	51	38
Labor	21	23	32	71	78	116
Local Government	21	19	28	50	56	84
Matrimonial	21	19	25	60	97	149
Negligence	. . .	. . .	. . .	26	40	. . .
Patents	22	20	21	43	52	52
Probate	41	47	54	124	150	202
Public Utility	21	26	26	25	22	23
Real Property	39	44	49	89	190	199
Securities	13	25	26	44	125	147
State and Municipal Tax	22	22	29	33	52	62
Trusts	25	24	28	43	77	78
Total	583	647	873	1,698	2,225	2,666
Percent CBA membership	9.75	9.37	11.48	20.86	. . .	22.77

SOURCE.—CBA committee books, 1950–74.
NOTE.—These committee numbers are not strictly additive for any given year as it is possible for individuals to have multiple committee memberships.

Precise estimates of change in the representation of different nationalities, religious groups, and political affiliations are limited. Despite this, the Report on the Chicago Bar Project shows that, of the ethnic groups, it is not the Anglo-Saxons who are overrepresented but the Irish. Blacks were underrepresented. Religious groups—Catholic, Jewish, and Protestant—had identical representation within the Association. And, interestingly enough, it is not the Republicans who are overrepresented, but the Regular Democrats—the Chicago Democrats loyal to the political organization presided over by Mayor Daley from the mid-1950s to the mid-1970s. But in neither the case of ethnicity nor that of political preference is overrepresentation or underrepresentation particularly dramatic.[6]

On the criteria for which data are available, therefore, it seems clear that the hypothesis of elite bias in the composition of the CBA membership can be rejected—at least insofar as it applies to the later 1960s. The association could claim that it spoke for the legal profession in Chicago, not only because it included more than 50 percent, and eventually 70 percent, of its members, but also because its membership mirrored, on most key attributes, the composition of the legal profession in the city.

Differentiation and Division

The preceding section established one side of a paradox—that extensive professional influence appeared to demand an inclusive and representative association of lawyers. In so doing, however, an association risks foundering on the other side of the paradox—that inclusiveness draws inside the professional association the divisions extant in the profession at large. A secession in the 1960s by young lawyers from the CBA to form a counterbar association vividly demonstrated that neither an association nor its leadership can afford to be unrepresentative.[7] The elaboration of the divisions within the bar and its collegial association strongly suggest that neither could the CBA afford to be representative.

This section details the other side of the paradox—the potential cost of representativeness. Extensive detailed data are not readily available on the differentiation of the profession in earlier decades; but highly detailed descriptions of professional differentiation are available from Heinz and Laumann's study of the Chicago bar.[8] While there are obvious flaws in the assumption that differentiation of the bar in the 1970s will not have changed from the 1950s, use of the Heinz

6. Heinz et al., "An Urban Bar," 732.

7. Terence C. Halliday and Charles L. Cappell, "Indicators of Democracy in Professional Associations: Elite Recruitment, Turnover, and Decision Making in a Metropolitan Bar Association," *American Bar Foundation Research Journal* 1979 (Fall): 697–767; Michael Powell, "Anatomy of a Counter-bar Association: The Chicago Council of Lawyers," *American Bar Foundation Research Journal* 1979 (1979): 501.

8. J. P. Heinz and Edward O. Laumann, "The Social Differentiation of the Chicago Bar" (paper presented at the annual meeting of the Southern Sociological Society, New Orleans, 1978), "The Legal Profession: Client Interests, Professional Roles, and Social Hierarchies" (revised version of a paper presented at the annual meeting of the Southern Sociological Society, New Orleans, 1978), and *Chicago Lawyers: The Social Structure of the Bar* (New York: Russell Sage; Chicago: American Bar Foundation, 1982); Edward O. Laumann and John P. Heinz, "Fields of Law Practice: Volume of Professional Activity, Intensity of Specialization, and Patterns of Co-practice in a Major Urban Bar" (paper presented at the annual meeting of the American Sociological Association, San Francisco, 1978).

and Laumann data does present, in stark relief, principal divisions still extant in the bar at the end of the period.

The 1974 survey found that, of those lawyers with relatively strong or clear ethnic origins, 26 percent defined themselves as northwest Europeans, including those of English origins, while an almost identical percentage originated from southern and eastern Europe. Internal differences were also pronounced on religious and political values. Thirty-one percent of the bar was Roman Catholic, 24 percent was Jewish, and 32 percent was Protestant. Consequently, on issues such as abortion, legalization of homosexuality and the smoking of marijuana, and, more generally, the use of the criminal law to enforce moral standards, it is not surprising to find significant disagreements. When Chicago lawyers were asked if they thought that "preservation of traditional moral values of the community is a legitimate objective of criminal law," 50 percent believed that it was not and 37 percent believed that it was; the latter position was more likely to be held by Roman Catholics and conservative Protestants.[9]

Political configurations were even more complex. In the 1974 survey, 21 percent of the sample was Republican in national politics, 40 percent was independent, and 36 percent was Democratic. Local political commitments are more difficult to untangle because many of the lawyers practicing in Chicago do not live and vote there. Even so, 16 percent identified themselves as Regular Democrats, 10 percent as Republicans, 40 percent as independent Democrats, and 17 percent as independents.[10] On these figures, the bar appears to be highly democratic and more liberal than conservative. But that conclusion must be juxtaposed with the distributions on political and economic attitudes. On their attitudes to unions, a traditional point of difference between the political left and right, the bar divided. Fifty-four percent believed that the unions had become too big, and 26 percent thought that they had not. Again the bar divided, though somewhat more evenly, on whether labor gains were good for national prosperity: 36 percent agreed that they were not, and 38 percent believed that they were. A similar division appeared in response to the statement that "competition rather than federal government regulation protects consumers"; 44 percent disagreed, and 46 percent agreed.[11]

On other issues, however, there seemed a preponderance of opinion, if not consensus, of a more liberal cast. Seventy-eight percent of the 1974 sample believed that the government should help the poor and disadvantaged, although a clear majority, 61 percent, felt that the problems facing society should be solved locally and not by the federal government. In the post–civil rights era, 63 per-

9. J. P. Heinz and E. O. Laumann, unpublished data, American Bar Foundation.
10. Heinz et al., "An Urban Bar," 724.
11. Heinz and Laumann, unpublished data.

cent did not agree that "an excess of civil rights legislation is threatening the free association of individuals."[12]

It is exceedingly difficult to find any coherent configuration of beliefs at this level of analysis. It is even more dubious to assume that these attitudes were stable in the mid-1960s and the 1950s. There is considerable doubt, for instance, that civil rights legislation would have had such a ringing endorsement in 1964 or that the profession would have had such a liberal hue during the early 1950s and the McCarthy era. Nevertheless, the attitudes do confirm the general argument: on every attribute but one, a substantial segment of the bar—never less than a quarter—stands opposed to the rest of the profession. On major issues of political and economic philosophy, the profession is split almost exactly down the middle.

Similar differences of opinion appear on more proximate issues—the goals of the bar association itself. The 1974 survey found that there were differences by local political party: regular Democrats were much more likely to take positions that favored maintaining the status quo in the courts, for instance. There were differences by age, a criterion that has already been shown to be critical in view of the younger lawyers' "rebellion." The younger lawyers in the survey urged a more liberal and activist role for the organization than did their older brethren, and they placed greater importance on bar leadership to improve the lot of disadvantaged groups and to take stands on controversial issues. There were also differences by "classes" within the bar. Blacks, solo practitioners, and lower-income lawyers tended to place greater stress on the CBA taking activist stands on public policy issues, on preventing unauthorized practice, and enhancing the status of the profession.[13]

Yet for all the disagreement there was some general consensus on the main goals of the organization, goals that coincided with those advanced a century earlier, at the origins of the CBA. Chicago lawyers rated as the four most important objectives, in descending order, to improve the quality of the bar, to improve the quality of the judiciary, to improve the efficiency of the courts, and to enhance the status of the profession. The fifth-ranked objective, thought to be important by 80 percent of the bar, was to initiate legislation. Thus there was some agreement that the organized bar should direct its energies mainly to its primary sphere—the court system. Efforts by segments of the bar to extend the influence of the profession more widely into civil rights matters or other relatively controversial areas of the law would almost certainly embroil the profession in internal conflict not only over whether the CBA should be engaged in wiser matters of public policy but also over what stands it should take on such policy issues.

12. Ibid.
13. Heinz et al., "An Urban Bar," 748–63.

It is clear, therefore, that the representativeness attained by this open association divided it on most criteria—class background, ethnicity, political and religious beliefs, and the proper objectives of the CBA. This finding would seem to be a prescription for decision-making despair, casting into doubt the possibility of any organizational consensus on significant and contentious issues. Mobilizing such a divided profession would, in these circumstances, appear to be out of the question.

The Poverty of Resource Wealth

I have conceded, with association leaders and the bar integration movement, that inclusiveness may be of enormous value to professional bodies. Numbers can solve internal fiscal crises, provide representational legitimacy, diversify organizational and collegial networks, concentrate professional expertise, enhance organizational infrastructures, and resolve the manpower needs of a differentiated association with numerous goals. In a word, for professional associations size is the principal underwriter of influence. Of course, that proposition must be carefully specified: size can be converted into effective action in some circumstances and not in others. Without size, however, and the resources it brings in its train, the American profession of law has believed the scope of its influence will be severely limited. The history of the organized bar in America is therefore a story of the quest by lawyers, through different periods, with some faltering, foot lagging, and even passive resistance, at different rates, and in various regions, for more inclusive bases of collegial association.

Yet the very wealth of inclusiveness is at once its poverty. The weakness of strong associations comes precisely because at the point of its maximal inclusiveness an association has internalized the complete range of diversity within a profession.

Yet my discussion of inclusiveness to this point has proceeded rather ingenuously. Clearly, it is possible to think of instances in which inclusiveness per se would not at all be problematic. Complete inclusiveness of a small group with identical values would very likely present no great difficulties of mobilization, other things being equal. Indeed, the same might be true of a rather large group with similar attributes. I have therefore been using the concept of "inclusiveness" as a shorthand for a more intricate set of relations among four variables— size, inclusiveness of an organization, heterogeneity of a membership pool and representativeness of the membership pool. Inclusiveness becomes a source of weakness only under certain conditions and permutations of those variables.

An initial condition stems from the attributes of membership pools. A population from which an organization recruits members will range from extremely homogeneous to highly heterogeneous in its interests and values. Heterogeneity itself takes many forms, from complete diversity, where every individual has a different position, to a multiplicity of parties, where individuals are grouped into discernible blocs, to a two-party system. Even these unduly simplify many political situations as parties and blocs can shift from issue to issue.

But it does not follow that greater inclusiveness of a diverse recruitment pool necessarily produces contradictions. An association might conceivably—and in the case of the organized bar almost certainly did—go from less to more inclusiveness by drawing very heavily from only one component of the pool, that is, by incorporating in the association individuals whose values are consistent with those of the organization. Inclusiveness then might succeed by being blatantly unrepresentative—as indeed an elite association is by definition. Needless to say, the homogeneity of values demanded of new members must pertain to the goals of the association itself; they might be highly diverse on other matters that are completely irrelevant to the organization, in which case they are of no consequence.

Nonetheless, if a recruitment pool is diverse, then there comes a point at which the putative benefits of inclusiveness must be held to outweigh the potential costs of representativeness, when the bid for even greater inclusiveness forces the association to accept diversity. Here again no immediate deleterious consequences may follow: if the representatives of a new set of values remain a small minority, or if they are prepared to subjugate their interests as the price of admission, or if they are ready to accede dominant power to the elite, the representation of diverse interests will not debilitate collective efforts.

Inclusiveness does create a problem for an association, however, when the recruitment pool is heterogeneous in its interests, when representation of that heterogeneity is more fully expressed within the organization, and when the diverse blocs within the association are not prepared to accede without question to the decision of leaders.

Thus if size and organizational structure are held constant, then the paradox of inclusiveness becomes a major problem for professional associations as a function of a particular permutation of three variables: heterogeneity of a pool, inclusiveness of the association, and representativeness of the association. In the nature of things, however, it is plausible to expect that larger organizations have a greater probability of internalizing diversity than do smaller organizations, other things being equal.

My analysis therefore proceeds on the assumptions that (1) recruitment pools of American lawyers are quite heterogeneous, as the Chicago case exemplifies; (2) greater inclusiveness, after a point, draws heterogeneity inside the organizations, as the representativeness of the CBA indicates; and (3) representation through inclusion of heterogenous populations will internalize conflict and dissent. Inclusiveness therefore pays high dividends in the accumulation of critical resources; but it exacts substantial costs in the mobilization of diverse constituencies.

The situation is complicated further by the enduring collegial function of a professional group—the so-called solidary incentive. We have seen that a comprehensive professional association will usually become an umbrella organization sheltering all the principal specialties. In that sense the organization acts as an integrative force, countervailing the inexorable progression toward differentiation historically occurring in the profession. As the committee lists of the CBA demonstrate, most open and universal associations will eventually recognize emerging specialties with their own organizational niches.

Paradoxically, however, the effort at integration may have exactly the converse effect. Inclusiveness may intensify specialization. A comprehensive association providing an organizational location for specialists thereby facilitates the association of experts who might not otherwise have occasion to meet regularly. The extent to which practicing professionals in the same specialty do meet will vary from profession to profession: those in which work occurs in teams and professionals are forced to collaborate may be more integrated outside the professional association than those in which professionals have an adversary relation or isolated practice. Not only does the comprehensive association, however, draw together those who practice in the same area, but it may also include academics and other professionals who might otherwise be peripheral. A specialty committee of lawyers can therefore incorporate those in private practice as well as academics, those who are employed by government, by corporations, and, of course, judges. Hence an inclusive comprehensive association can help define and organize a specialty. It may offer that organizational element necessary for a specialty to gain a sense of itself. At the point of integration, therefore, the open or universal association becomes a limited agent of specialization.

The inclusion of specialists, with their own organizational location, produces more than an opportunity for interests to coagulate. By integrating specialists, expertise is concentrated and then multiplied. Committees act as clearinghouses of information where ideas and knowledge are exchanged and extended. They allow practitioners to speak and develop their private languages. Incrementally, though the steps may be scarcely perceptible, practitioners who become more at ease in speaking with each other may become less able to communicate with other branches of the profession. A mutual incomprehension of specialists and the generalists who govern an association can be more troublesome than open partisanship and the clash of clearly articulated differences. Nevertheless, as I shall show in chapter 11, incomprehensibility and private languages may be a positive benefit to a committee if not to the association itself.

At the end of the first century of renewed organized bar activity, therefore, legal associations faced the other side of the dilemma that had exercised their predecessors in the 1870s. While an elite association can more easily reach consensus because its members do not reflect the full diversity of the profession, the force of its consensus may not be sufficient either to effect change itself or to mobilize others who can. The intervening one hundred years of professional expansion and progressive division of labor and the transformation in professional bodies that have accompanied them place the inclusive associations on the other horn of the dilemma: there is a wealth in the numbers and representativeness that inclusiveness may ultimately bring to an association. But inclusiveness internalizes all those lines of cleavage—work organization, specialty, ethno-religious, political—that the elite associations had drawn at the edges of their organizations. The crisis of the comprehensive professional association reproduces in microcosm aspects of crises in the wider society. The consequence, like that of the "ungovernable" society, is to nullify professional influence except on those few innocuous goals on which consensus can still be forged. Inasmuch as those goals are likely to be more concerned with general professional well-being, professional associations would be confined to an almost exclusive external preoccupation with monopoly. The transition from the formative to the established association would be impeded—or reversed.

Let us recapitulate the argument to this point. Professions in industrial societies have grown enormously in both size and organization over the past century, developing and then substantially monopolizing expertise in given segments of the division of labor. The coming of age of these organized bearers of special knowledge has coincided with the unprecedented demands on the expectations of the state in Western democracies, such that their capacity to govern is frequently retarded. At this conjunction, professions appear poised to step into that role anticipated by prescient observers over the last eighty years: the belief that the advance in the division of labor uniquely endowed professions to bring knowledge to the service of power and thus break the bottleneck that complexity had imposed on government. The division of labor therefore carried the seeds of its own redemption.

However, the ability of professions to realize this function is not unproblematic. It depends on three factors: first, the foundation of a given epistemology, the construction of an expert authority, and the capacity to translate it into moral authority; second, the ability to exercise influence in a professional primary sphere of influence and then to extend it beyond to secondary spheres; and, third, the success with which a profession can build an organizational vehicle to carry its influence to government in the various spheres.

In part 2 I have shown that the organizational precondition of professional authority can take three forms, elite, open, or universal associations; that each carries with it a distinctive portfolio of resources; and that the historical emergence of professional influence can be seen in terms of a transition from elite to open or universal associations, from exclusivism to inclusiveness, and from one cluster of resources to another. That transition was in part determined by a perceived inadequacy of the bar elite to do much more than achieve the limited goals of professions that mark their formative stage, namely, establishing monopoly and lifting educational standards, controlling admission to the profession, guarding occupational boundaries against unauthorized practitioners, and gaining state powers of internal regulation. These ends, from the point of view of recent theory, are not inconsequential. In Parkin's formulation, closure by an occupation remains one of the most hallowed objectives of an occupational group.[14] Professional monopoly has thus rightly deserved some degree of the attention given to it by class theorists, like Giddens and Parkin, and sociologists of professions such as Larson, Parry and Parry, and Berlant. It is also arguable, however, that equally as important to the formative phase were activities less directed to market control or professional upgrading and more committed to reform and upgrading of the courts.

The established profession, however, is one that has achieved considerable occupational closure, consolidated some measure of monopoly, and is relatively—though not ever entirely—impregnable. In certain circumstances, the established profession can proceed, largely taking closure for granted, to exercise its influence beyond monopoly. Put in my terms, it can convert expert authority into moral authority and commit both to the state, perhaps in both primary and secondary spheres. A key circumstance, however, is that of developing a portfolio of resources appropriate to the more expansive goals of the mature profession. That, we have seen, inevitably means a move away from elitist to mass models of organization. Yet that transition leads associations directly into the contradiction of inclusiveness. An apparently necessary condition of professional influence becomes its primary obstacle.

We are left then with numerous questions. Can a profession transcend the paradox into which inclusiveness plunges it? What are the means by which it does so? Have professions been able to cross the line between expert and moral authority? Has that transition in turn enabled them to extend their expertise to problems in primary and secondary spheres of influence while concomitantly contributing to the solution of those societal issues on which governments have

14. Frank Parkin, *Marxism and Class Theory: A Bourgeois Critique* (London: Tavistock, 1979).

foundered? In sum, what can a profession do with the luxury of resources that inclusiveness brings it?

In part 3, I will present a comprehensive overview of the judicial and legislative activities of the CBA in the postwar period to demonstrate how far an inclusive association may contribute to strains and stresses of governability. Chapters 6 and 7 focus on the legal profession's primary sphere of influence—the administration of justice. In the following two chapters, I indicate that the profession could extend both forms of authority even further into various secondary spheres that, at once, contained particular crises in American society and represent some of the central issues facing any modern Western democracy. Having posed the dilemmas and contradictions of inclusiveness in part 2, and shown that they did not confine entirely the influence of the profession in part 3, I turn in part 4 to explain how an association can resolve the problems endowed on it by inclusiveness and to trace, more speculatively, the general implications of these findings for a macrosociology of the established profession in a society under stress.

Part Three

Spheres of Influence

6 The Autonomy of the Court System

The potential for influence of an inclusive bar association can be tested in the crucible of three crises in postwar America. The *crisis of legitimacy* emerged from within the legal system itself, for it was law that had been impugned by political patronage and manipulation of the judiciary, and it was law that effectively was in default through the incapacity of the courts in many jurisdictions to cope with the demands on them. The *crisis of state and individual rights* had at least two dramatic manifestations in the decades of the 1950s and the 1960s: the first came with the wholesale abrogation of individual rights and disdain for the rule of law in the name of state security; the second appeared with the social movements of the 1960s and their mobilization to redefine the role of the state in securing civil rights for its entire citizenry. The *fiscal crises* did not have the national scope of the former two. But across the country various of the states found themselves unable to respond to new pressures for governmental intervention because their fiscal adaptability was highly constrained. The threat of state bankruptcy therefore prefigured some of the subsequent crises that have been identified with the nation-state.

The confrontation of these strains in contemporary America by the legal profession was played out in microcosm by the Chicago Bar Association (CBA). Through its wide-ranging judicial concerns, it endeavored to confront the decline in the legitimacy of the law. Through its review of state and federal legislation on individual rights and its monitoring of McCarthyism in Springfield, Illinois, and Washington, D.C., it attempted to assert one image—albeit a lawyer's image— of the ways in which the states should reconsider the claims its citizens should have on it and that it should have on its citizens. Through its efforts to revise the constitutional provisions on taxation in Illinois, the professional association hoped both to relieve a budgetary crisis and to respecify the relations between the constitution, the legislature, and the courts.

At the same time, exploration of one professional body's insertion into these tensions allows us to explore the scope of professional action along the dimensions of institutional spheres. In its concern with the court system and the judiciary, the bar association was functioning in its primary institution, a role considered in chapters 6 and 7. With its venture into civil rights—matters of political convictions, housing, and educational and employment opportunities—and the infrastructure of a state economy, the association had clearly moved out into a range of secondary institutional spheres. The nature of those forays and their relative success will be discussed in chapters 8 and 9, respectively. The extent and form of state bar activism throughout the United States, when it took the form of legal rationalization, is reviewed in chapter 10.[1]

The Crisis in the Courts

The courts provide the institutional setting in which the influence of the organized bar should theoretically be at its greatest. As the primary sphere of activity for lawyers, the profession has substantial public legitimacy for an active role in court reform. Lawyers are officers of the courts; they bear partial responsibility for the operation and procedures of the administration of justice; and it is from the legal profession that judges ascend to the bench. By a variety of standards the profession would appear to have a broad mandate to shape court organization and to review judicial behavior.

Potentially, the organized bar can exercise both expert and moral influence on the judiciary. The professional association has a range of technical contributions to make to court organization, court jurisdictions, court rules, court procedures, and other aspects of the administration of the courts that facilitate or impede the prompt and just administration of justice. On the technicalities of court administration, it is unlikely that a bar association would find resistance to its contributions from the judiciary, the profession at large, or the public. Indeed, its active role in improving the functioning of the courts should conceivably be welcomed by all parties.

Such is not necessarily the case for the moral or normative interests of the bar in the courts. The opportunities for moral intervention by the profession are clear. The profession may act entirely on its own volition as a moral arbiter of judicial behavior and the ethics of court personnel. An emboldened organization of lawyers might even aspire to an influence on one of the most critical of public policy issues surrounding the courts—the degree to which local metropolitan

---

1. In pt. 3, I focus on the external action of the CBA and therefore deliberately mute the internal debates, clashes of interests, and divisions of opinions. These are discussed more fully in chap. 11 and yet more extensively in Cappell and Halliday, "Professional Projects"; Terence C. Halliday, "The Idiom of Legalism in Bar Politics: Lawyers, McCarthyism, and the Civil Rights Era," *American Bar Foundation Research Journal* 1982 (Fall): 911–89; and "Parameters of Professional Influence: Policies and Politics of the Chicago Bar Association, 1945–1979," (Ph.D. diss., University of Chicago, 1979).

and state courts should have independence from the influence of political parties, the legislature, and the executive. On these matters, where the activities of the profession exceed straightforward technical matters clearly within its role of expertise, it appears likely that its influence would be strongly contested, its legitimacy undermined, and its effectiveness severely circumscribed.

Nevertheless our knowledge of the extent of technical and moral influence exercised by the bar on court organization and policy remains obscure. There is a great deal known about a limited number of aspects, and very little known about a great many other features, of lawyers' collective intervention in the administration of justice. Several studies have noted the variable effects of organized bar action for changes in the mode of judicial selection and for review of judges selected for or elected to the bench.[2] Much less focus has been given either to more fundamental or to more mundane changes in the administration of justice. In no case has there been a general treatment that subsumes all bar activities in the courts—trivial and transformist—within a holistic interpretation.

That the lapse in research has more than academic significance can be seen by the local manifestations in Illinois of the more general stresses in courts throughout the United States. By the late 1940s, the CBA confronted a court system overburdened with litigation and ill adapted to the lengthening strides of social and legal change. Illinois courts were subject to a rising crescendo of criticism. William Trumbull, an academic and legal reformer writing in the early 1950s, noted that "there has been virtual unanimity in finding (1) defects in the quality of justice caused by the obsolescence of the judicial system created in 1848 and only slightly modified in 1870 and 1905; (2) inordinate delay and expense in litigation; (3) wasteful burdens on the taxpayer by reason of duplication of facilities and services; and (4) inflexibility, requiring the arduous process of constitutional amendment to meet changing needs."[3]

Evidence could be adduced for every charge. The organization of the Illinois courts was highly confused. Outside Cook County, 101 county courts were organized in seventeen circuits and complemented by thirteen probate courts, twenty-six city courts served by fifty-four judges, four hundred magistrates, and more than three thousand justices of the peace. Alongside its county court, Cook County had a circuit court, a superior court, probate, criminal, and juvenile

2. Edward M. Martin, *The Role of the Bar in Electing the Bench in Chicago* (Chicago: University of Chicago Press, 1936); R. Watson and R. Downing, *The Politics of the Bench and the Bar: Judicial Selection under the Missouri Non-partisan Court Plan* (New York: Wiley, 1969); Joel Grossman, *Lawyers and Judges: The ABA and the Politics of Judicial Selection* (New York: Wiley, 1965). See, more generally, the bibliography in Allan Ashman and James Alfini, *The Key to Judicial Merit Selection: The Nominating Process* (Chicago: American Judicature Society, 1974), 329–37.

3. William M. Trumbull, "Why Lawyers Should Support the Judicial Amendment," *Illinois Bar Journal* 46 (February 1958): 434.

courts, and a municipal court in Chicago with parallel city courts in Evanston and other smaller county towns. Jurisdictions frequently overlapped; mistakes with reference to the jurisdiction of a court too often warranted the dismissal of one trial and its commencement all over again.[4]

Apart from some coordination in the Municipal Court of Chicago, trial courts were separate and independent. Lack of coordination among courts and the absence of judicial authority to reassign judges and cases to ensure an even distribution of work across courts left the judicial system impotent to cope with its backlog of cases, a situation further exacerbated by its structural and statutory rigidity. Only in the fact that it was the ultimate court of appeal was the Illinois Supreme Court supreme. Without administrative authority, administrative machinery, or adequate statistics on the flow of cases, the court was helpless in the face of judicial inefficiency and public and professional dissatisfaction. In addition, the judiciary before the 1950s depended largely on the legislature for change and reform, and, characteristically, the legislature's propensity for flexibility and adaptation was limited; procedural and administrative changes demanded by the courts were inevitably converted into political debate over substantive issues.

Statutory provisions further limited Supreme Court control over its discretion in reviewing cases on appeal. Over the preceding eighty years, automatic jurisdiction over approximately forty classes of cases had been imposed on the court by the legislature. A 1947 University of Chicago study demonstrated that the Supreme Court spent between 84 and 90 percent of its time on compulsory appeals.[5] In these circumstances, the court could not exercise its judgment in favor of cases involving important questions of law or matters significant to the community. Neither could the court free itself from its "jurisdictional straitjacket" and the weight of appeals to exercise the administrative and rule-making authority it had sometimes claimed.[6]

The tension between legislative and judicial claims to Supreme Court rule-making authority had never been satisfactorily resolved. The ambiguity of the provisions of the 1870 Illinois Constitution on rule-making powers allowed both

4. Samuel Witwer, "The Illinois Constitution and the Courts," *University of Chicago Law Review* 15 (Autumn 1947): 53; Wayland B. Cedarquist, "The Need for Judicial Reform in Illinois," *DePaul Law Review* 2 (Winter 1952): 39; Barnabas F. Sears, "A New Judicial Article: From the 1848 Horse and Buggy Days to 1955," *American Bar Association Journal* 40 (September 1954): 755; R. N. Sullivan, "Constitutional and Statutory Bases of Illinois Courts," *University of Illinois Law Forum* 1952 (Winter): 463; Palmer D. Edmunds, "Jurisdiction of the Courts," *University of Illinois Law Forum* 1952 (Winter): 480.

5. "A Study of the Illinois Supreme Court," *University of Chicago Law Review* 15 (Autumn 1947): 163.

6. Edmunds, "Jurisdiction of the Courts," 480.

the legislature and the courts to lay claim to such authority, but the Supreme Court was careful not to force any confrontation by directly denying legislative power.

Conditions of judge appointment and tenure matched the political vulnerability of a legislatively dependent supreme court. While the Illinois Constitution of 1818 had provided that judges would be elected by the legislature, political parties gradually came to dominate the electoral process. For the majority of Cook County judges, election to the bench has been a reward for an extended apprenticeship delivering votes in the precincts, prosecuting crime in the U.S. and states attorneys' offices, handling municipal matters in the Corporation Counsel's Office of the City of Chicago, and, in general, proving unswerving loyalty to the Democratic organization. Since the party has carried Cook County offices for several decades, nomination by a ward committeeman—and most wards have their representative judges—virtually guaranteed appointment. Once on the bench, the party still retained some control over the behavior of judges. Before 1964, it could drop a judge from the judicial lists when he came up for reelection, or the chief judge of the municipal court, since he was usually a trusted party loyalist, could assign a recalcitrant judge to less pleasant tasks.[7]

Tenure on the bench was not dependent on good service; it was instead a function of changing political currents and loyalties. Thus a capable but politically independent judge held office tenuously. Once on the bench, there was little collegial or higher court control over behavior. The cumbersome procedures of legislative impeachment were rarely implemented. Within broad and diffusely defined constraints, judges were "laws unto themselves," especially in the lowest reaches of the court system. In these lower echelons, the tribunals of the Illinois judiciary were staffed by justices of the peace and magistrates who were often, if not usually, lay persons acting on a part-time basis as local requirements demanded. Critics of the judiciary did not have a redeeming word to say for the system of justices of the peace. Appeals from their courts, which cited errors in law, clogged the higher courts with multiple trials. Part-time justices of the peace, who frequently had political authority or economic concerns in their local towns and counties, were themselves continually embroiled in conflicts of interest. Decisions, it was alleged, were based on common sense rather than on legal criteria.[8]

Critics were most outraged, however, by the methods of fee compensation.

7. See the lucid and informed discussion of Chicago Democratic machine politics by Milton L. Rakove, *Don't Make No Waves, Don't Back No Losers: An Insider's Analysis of the Daley Machine* (Bloomington: Indiana University Press, 1975). See esp. 221–32.

8. Mildred J. Giese, "Why Illinois Proposes to Abolish Justice of the Peace Courts," *Illinois Bar Journal* 46 (May 1958): 754; 46 (June 1958): 806.

Most justices of the peace and magistrates were remunerated from the fines they levied, either directly through a percentage of the fine or indirectly through salaries based on income from fines. Enterprising justices of the peace could increase their income by increasing convictions and levying larger fines; some local officers of the law had members of the police force on a retainer to ensure a reasonable flow of business. Even when fees were collected without doubtful expedients, the required documentation of court affairs was so haphazard that underreporting of income was widely suspected; cross-checking income levels between jurisdictions was obviated by the great discrepancies in sentences throughout the state for the same misdemeanor. Complete lack of higher court control over the justices of the peace and magistrates only compounded problems already evident in the review of judicial behavior in the higher courts.

The Illinois situation therefore brings into sharp relief the convergence of an empowered bar association with tensions within the judicial branch of government. In short, the dependence of higher courts on the legislature and all courts on political parties, the chaotic internal organization of the entire state court system, and the manifest inadequacies of judicial personnel at all levels add up to a system under such a strain that in many respects it was under default of its principal functions. The crisis in the courts thus provides a test case for the thesis I have been advancing: that governments heavily burdened by new demands and unable to adapt themselves to changed circumstances may find some solution in the growth of professional influence and the application of professional expertise.

I shall argue that in fact the CBA did seek to deploy resources it had accumulated with the intention of solving the crisis in the Illinois courts. In this sphere the profession exercised expert and, subsequently, moral authority. Moreover, its actions had a coherence that spanned the full range of professional efforts from minor day-to-day matters of relative insignificance to massive reform programs stretching over decades. The coherence does not result from the deliberate and rational planning of a central policy-making body within the body; neither is it explicitly articulated in either the aims of the association or their periodic explication in various CBA policy statements. Nevertheless, there is a unity of effect that can be discerned from ostensibly dissimilar forms of bar activity in the courts.

To presage the argument, the profession responded to the crisis by endeavoring to effect an institutional shift of the judiciary away from legislative, executive, and party influence; concomitantly, it sought to draw the court system further within the sphere of professional control. Autonomy and control are the two organizing principles of the legal profession's judicial activities.

The bar sought *judicial autonomy* from political control by the complementary interplay of two subsidiary rationalizing processes—structural differentiation and bureaucratization. It attempted to differentiate the judiciary from politics at each level of linkage between the two, from court rule-making dependence on the state legislature to local party appointments of court personnel. At the same time, the profession encouraged the internal bureaucratization of the court system throughout the state both to deal with the difficulties in the administration of justice and to enable the courts better to exert their autonomy from political control.

Concurrently, the legal association sought to embrace the judiciary within its orbit of influence. The pursuit of *professional control* in the courts also divided into two main components. The politics of negativism presented the critical face of the legal profession to the courts, focusing on judicial probity and the quality of judges admitted to the bench. The politics of affirmation presented the benign visage of collegial activity in the courts.

The evidence of the CBA and the Illinois courts indicates that the resources of the open professional association were massively mobilized to engage the problems of the judicial branch of government. The profession thus not only confronted an imminent crisis but also engaged an enduring constitutional dilemma over the proper balance of power between the judiciary, executive, and legislative branches.

In order to present a holistic interpretation of organized bar concerns with the court system, I collected three levels of data in a "pyramidal" design from the CBA archives for the years 1950 through 1970. First, I undertook a simple content analysis of a 50 percent sample of all judicial topics discussed by the Board over the two decades. Second, I collated all available files for a more detailed review of one hundred judicial issues randomly sampled from board agendas. Third, I closely examined three peak events. The three most significant cases, principally concerned with the theme of autonomy, are discussed in greatly abbreviated sketches in the remainder of this chapter. In the following chapter I seek to place them in the context of the entire array of CBA actions as they are reflected in the two samples.

Paths to Reform

The pursuit of the autonomy of the courts from political influence and legislative controls can be accomplished by several different methods. One alternative is to revise the constitutional article governing the courts in order to change methods of judicial appointment, the internal organization of the courts, and other facets of the judicial article that define the relation of the courts to politics broadly conceived. A less sweeping alternative is to effect changes through statutory reforms, especially those statutes pertaining to civil practice and procedure that provide the internal ordering of court practice. More important, in addition civil procedure legislation may also bear on the rule-making autonomy of the Supreme Court from the general assembly. A third option is to proceed without legal sanction—to try to draw the judiciary away from political pupilage by imposing a moral code on the judiciary that proscribes the more egregious aspects of political party influence on the bench.

The CBA tried, with varying degrees of success, to employ each of these alternatives in the postwar years. Its most far-reaching and publicly controversial campaign was for an amendment of the judicial article of the Illinois Constitution. More discreet were its efforts to revise the Illinois Civil Practice Act and Supreme Court Rules and its proposal to impose canons of judicial ethics on the Illinois judiciary.

THE JUDICIAL ARTICLE OF THE CONSTITUTION

The boldest, most far-reaching, and ambitious bar initiative was an immodest drive by leading Illinois bar associations to effect sweeping changes in the state court system at the highest level—constitutional revision.

After three-quarters of a century of repeated failure to effect any kinds of lasting changes in Illinois courts, the would-be reformers of the bar had become convinced that a radical revision of the entire court system was the only solution. This change could be achieved only by amendment to the judicial article of the Illinois Constitution. In mid-1951 the bar association, under some public pressure, proposed a new judicial article drafted by the CBA's Development of Law Committee and approved by its Committee on Constitutional Revision. The draft article included major sections on the organization and jurisdiction of the Illinois Supreme Court, appellate courts, and trial courts, the selection and tenure of judges, the selection and tenure of state's attorneys, and some general provisions on removal from office, salaries, and clerks.

The four most significant and controversial points in the draft article were selection of judges, tenure of judicial office, rules of the court, and reorganization of the courts. Selection of judges was to follow the "Missouri Plan," itself adopted from a "Chicago Plan" of 1922. The draft proposed that there be a nonpartisan Judicial Nominating Commission of seven members that would submit names to the governor for selection. Each commission—for the Supreme Court, appellate courts, and local courts, respectively—was to have seven members: three lawyers, three laypersons, and the chief judge of the relevant court. Tenure for judges already appointed to the bench would be by election, judges running without party designation on their own record. Section 4 proposed that "the Supreme Court should have authority to make rules governing the practice and procedure in all courts," thus providing for the removal of administration and procedure of the courts from the legislature and, by implementing this provision in the constitution, assuring the independence of the courts from subsequent legislative fiat. The fourth major change proposed reorganization of all Cook County courts into one integrated system, with other counties having the option to integrate courts by referendum.[9]

The intentions of these proposals were clear from exchanges in the Board. The contemplated statewide appointment of the Supreme Court justices, which would replace the previous system of appointment by districts, was designed to remove judges from local political interests and sponsorship. It was also hoped that the court would sit in Springfield, thus further weakening local pressures, both symbolically and actually. Tenure provisions were intended to relieve a "good" judge from the "whim or caprice or circumstances of his party happening to have a landslide for him or a landslide against him." Integration of the courts, it was hoped, would increase orderliness and eliminate disputes over jurisdiction. One judge on the drafting committee stated: "Not only is each court a body by itself, subject only to review of the decisions of a single judge, but the judge of each court is almost a law unto himself. . . . The aim of this draft is to put the judicial system where it was always contemplated it should be, as a separate, distinct division of the state, with authority vested somewhere to guard its proper administration without resort to the legislature. The judicial department of this state has been treated more or less as a stepchild by the legislature."[10] Repeatedly, the bar association emphasized its desire to "freeze" the proposed changes in the constitution in order to prevent piecemeal alteration and amendments by successive legislatures.

This draft, too late to be introduced at the 1951 legislative session, was circulated to the bar and after some minor amendments sent to an Illinois legislative commission. But the commission, balking particularly at the provision for merit selection, dropped the article in its entirety when the organized bar insisted it would withdraw all support for an article that did not include merit selection.[11]

The joint bar committee, although discouraged, brought back a slightly revised draft for the 1955 legislative session that proposed, subject to a 1958 referendum, that judicial candidates be chosen by a commission and their nominees

9. Committee on Development of the Law, "Draft of Proposed New Article VI of the Constitution of Illinois," Report 50–89, 25 May 1951, Chicago Bar Association, Chicago.

10. Transcripts of meetings of the Board of Managers, 24 May 1951 (hereafter cited as Transcripts).

11. "A New Judicial Article." The degree to which merit selection of judges, or the "Missouri Plan" actually does take the politics out of judicial appointments has been extensively evaluated by Watson and Downing, *The Politics of the Bench and the Bar.* They maintain that the Plan, as it operated in Missouri, did not take politics out of the courts. What it did was not eliminate but transform politics. Among the changes that occurred and would have been applauded by most lawyers were:

be approved or disapproved by the electorate.[12] Nominating commissions would be larger and bipartisan. No changes were made on magistrates and justices of the peace. The bar leadership, which expected little opposition from the legislature, was astounded at the vociferous opposition from legislators, who demanded that nonpartisan election of judges be held in the trial courts, that the reorganization provisions give more local control so that the county board rather than the court would determine the number of magistrates, and that the circuit court rather than the Supreme Court would choose the chief judge. Further, they stipulated that the clerk of the court must be elected by the city rather than being appointed by the court or selected according to legislative provisions. Refusing to concede so much on selection and reorganization, the bar again withdrew its article.

Undaunted but wiser, the joint committee revised the article yet again for the 1957 legislative session, but still in a relatively minor fashion.[13] The article would mandatorily submit the question of merit selection to the voters; a commission would select nominees, but they would be elected by the public rather than be appointed by the governor; and the justices of the peace of more than five years experience, even though not lawyers, would be eligible for appointment. The bar, the joint committee, and the CBA were all split on how much should be conceded to the legislature, but it was agreed in the CBA board that, in the face of strong opposition, selection would be dropped and a "last-ditch stand" would be made on court reorganization.

This time, the article got as far as a joint committee of the House and the Senate, but the bar was completely surprised by the savagery of the attack on a previously uncontroversial area—the absolute rule-making authority of the Supreme Court. On June 24, 1957, the legislature adopted its own version of a judicial article that completely excised any mandatory provisions for selection. This article placed selection in the hands of the legislature and demanded a two-thirds

---

(1) narrowing the range of parties who have special interests in judicial appointments and giving particular attention to the opinions of the bar and the judiciary; (2) setting outer limits on the candidates governors could choose (hence screening out the most incompetent); (3) increasing the age and experience of judges appointed to the bench; (4) improving the quality of appointments; and (5) giving judges life-tenure and hence considerable independence. In addition, the Missouri Plan moved appointments away from the vagaries of local partisan politics to the state level—something thought likely to make appointments more enlightened.

12. Louis A. Kohn, "Judicial Article Campaign Renewed," *Illinois Bar Journal* 43 (January 1955): 307.

13. Louis A. Kohn, "The 1957 Campaign for the Adoption of the Judicial Amendment: A Call to Action," *Illinois Bar Journal* 45 (May 1957): 626; "The Proposed Judicial Amendment: Governing Boards of the ISBA and CBA Endorse Senate Joint Resolution 47: A Report to Members," *Illinois Bar Journal* 46 (September 1957): 8; Trumbull, "The Judicial Amendment."

vote in both the House and the Senate before provisions of a new article could be submitted to the people.[14] Bar defeat was anticipated by the more cynical, but they did not expect the determined and systematic efforts of politicians to bind court actions to the legislature. Many lawyers thought the new inserted rule-making provisions actually robbed the courts of powers that they had had under the 1870 constitution. But the provisions for reorganization were still an advance, its supporters believed, over the present system, and, as the "Missouri Plan" looked like it would never get through, they reasoned that the bar should take what it could get. After heated debate, the bar formally agreed to support the legislative article, which was submitted to the voters in a referendum in late 1958. The public voted 346,953 against and 1,000,710 for the article. Approval fell short of the required 66 percent majority by less than 1 percent.

There were many in the bar, including some of those on the joint committee, who greeted the defeat with relief. The extent of their reservations become obvious in the new article drafted for the 1961 legislative session. This article virtually mirrored the bar article submitted to the legislature in 1957 *before* any of the radical legislative amendments. Their changes allowed smaller geographic constituencies to have a more direct voice in the selection of Supreme Court judges; associate judges might be selected by the county rather than the judicial circuit and could sit in centers other than the county seat; and persons employed in municipal corporations or by federal, state, and county governments were eligible for selection. The provisional changes reflected steps taken to relieve the fear local governments had of losing control over certain aspects of the judiciary.

When introduced in the legislature, the bar found its judicial article opposed by a "City Hall" article with major differences in the method of selection, tenure of judges, the rule-making power of the Supreme Court, and who should have the right to choose the chief judge of a circuit. An Illinois state senator and Daley confidant, handling the lobbying for the bar, described the compromise plan to the Board in the following way:

> We finally came up with the proposal that if we give up on the selection, they will accept tenure. If we give up on the rule-making power in the Supreme Court, they will leave it as it is at the present time— no mention of it at all in the Constitution. If we give up on the bare majority and accept the two-thirds majority for subsequent amendments, they will consent to the chief judge being appointed by the Supreme Court. In addition to that, they agreed to put into their resolution, the constitutional terms of office for the judges, ten years for the Supreme Court and six for Circuit Court. They also agreed to let

14. Seventieth General Assembly of Illinois, "Senate Joint Resolution 47 in the House with House Amendments as further amended by Conference Committee Report and Adopted by the Legislature," 25 June 1957.

the Supreme Court have the right to shift Appellate Court Judges from one district to another, and they also agreed that the judges in the circuits could be shifted from one area to another. They also agreed to eliminate magistrates except in non-judicial functions, such as taking pleas of guilty and making bail, and so forth.

. . . My personal opinion is, if we can get this we have a real victory.[15]

The compromise article, conceding much less than the 1957 version, was wholeheartedly supported by the bar, passed both the House and the Senate, and after a vigorous campaign for implementation received a two-thirds majority in the referendum. The article was implemented on January 1, 1964.

The provisions of the judicial article, as it emerged from the last-minute compromises and refinements of the Illinois legislature, represented a radical change in the Illinois court system.[16] The legions of overlapping county, municipal, city, village and town courts, and superior and lower courts were organized into a single, concise court system with three levels: the Supreme Court, an appellate court, and a single, unified trial court of general jurisdiction. The new trial or circuit courts had unlimited jurisdiction of all justiciable matters; jurisdictional problems and trials de novo were completely abolished. Appeals as of statutory right, which had overwhelmed the Supreme Court, were severely restricted in favor of cases involving important or novel questions of law. Those burdensome cases no longer being settled in the Supreme Court went to the appellate court. The three-tiered system was coordinated by a supreme court with complete administrative authority and the machinery of an administrative office. With the consent of circuit court judges, the Supreme Court could move personnel from one trial court to another as the numbers of cases demanded. While the legislature did not explicitly grant general rule-making power to the courts, the Supreme Court was able to build on its own decisions concerning its constitutional authority. Many features of the reorganization did appear to increase its independence from the legislature.

Reorganization of the courts paralleled changes in the conditions of judicial office. The legislature did not adopt the bar proposal for merit selection, but election for incumbent judges was to be noncompetitive, with the judges running without party identification. Neither did the courts obtain rights to appoint clerks or even to appoint judges to vacancies on the bench caused by death, retirement, or resignation; after a resignation the court would have to bear the loss of person-

15. Transcripts, 22 June 1961.

16. An excellent comparative analysis of the 1964 judicial article with its revisions in the 1969 constitutional convention is contained in Rubin G. Cohn, "The Illinois Judicial Department—Changes Effected by the Constitution of 1970," *University of Illinois Law Forum* 1971, no. 3: 355.

nel for up to the two years until another general election. Conditions of retirement and salaries were left in the hands of the legislature. The article did, however, allow the courts to substitute, in effect, the principle of legislative control over judge discipline with the principle of judicial control. The court gained the right to form the Illinois Courts Commission, constituted entirely of judges, which would hear and decide complaints against judges—though not against magistrates—and would administer the appropriate sanctions.

The bar associations were elated by the reforms. The reorganization of the courts was greeted, perhaps overgenerously, with the often-quoted phrase of a New York attorney as "the envy of the nation." But the reform of judicial organization and administration had been bought at considerable cost; most notable was the failure to ensure the detachment from political influence that court rule-making powers and merit selection of judges might have achieved. In 1965, and again in 1967, the bar associations attempted to push merit selection through the legislature, but in both cases the bills did not get out of the committee onto the House floor.[17] It was not until late 1969 that the bar associations made another joint proposal for revision of the judicial article, this time in response to the demands of a constitutional convention that was considering extensive modifications of the Illinois Constitution. There had been several problems in the 1964 judicial article, and the significance of judicial reform was thrust again into the public arena after the extensively publicized resignations of two Supreme Court justices accused of accepting bribes.

The reforms implemented in the 1970 Illinois Constitution took several provisions of the 1964 judicial article to their logical conclusion. The structure of the judicial system remained unchanged. The attempts to restrict appeals as of right, however, implemented in 1964, did not sufficiently lighten the load of the Supreme Court. The 1970 article provided that appeals as of right would apply only to judgments imposing the death sentence. All other appeals from the circuit court to the Supreme Court would be subject to the discretion and rule-making power of the court. The Supreme Court thus gained almost complete control of its jurisdiction for the first time. It also gained greater administrative authority. Whereas in 1964 it had power only to assign judges from one court to another of equal status with the consent of the chief judge, in 1970 it gained the right also to assign judges to higher courts without the approval of the chief judge.

Several changes were made in the role of the magistrates. The three-tiered system of 1964, which had magistrates at the third and lowest rank, was replaced by a two-tiered system with only two categories of judges—circuit judges and associate judges. The legislature, which had claimed some rights of control over the

17. Rubin G. Cohn, *To Judge with Justice: History and Politics of Illinois Judicial Reform* (Urbana: University of Illinois Press, 1973).

magistrates, forfeited those rights to the courts when the new associate judges came under the control of the higher court, which already regulated the activities of circuit judges.

In the wake of judicial scandal, control of judicial behavior was a major issue. The judiciary was given the right to adopt rules of conduct for judges, thereby reinforcing its long-standing claim to the right of self-enforcement, "unhampered by legislative intrusion." The 1970 reforms gave the courts further control over their personnel. Under the 1964 article, clerks at each level had been elected; under the new provisions, clerks of the Supreme Court and at appellate court levels would be appointed by their respective chief judges, although the legislature would still retain the right to decide how circuit court clerks would be appointed—usually by election.

Apart from two relatively minor and, some thought, retrogressive changes, the methods of judicial appointment remained fixed as they had been in the previous constitutions. A change was made, however, in the method of filling mid-term vacancies on the bench. The 1964 practice of waiting for another election before having a vacant position filled had proved very burdensome for the courts. The convention gave the legislature the discretion to choose an appropriate means of proceeding, but in the event of the legislature failing to act within a certain period, the Supreme Court could appoint a judge to the vacancy.

All in all, concluded constitutional expert Rubin Cohn, the 1970 Illinois constitutional article was a praiseworthy advance over its 1964 precursor. While it enacted some measures that were puzzling and others that frustrated reformers, and although it did not make the radical change toward merit selection of judges, it went far along the path to greater separation of powers between the judiciary and politics and made substantial progress toward organizational coherence of the court system. The strenuous efforts of the organized bar over a twenty-year period were rewarded by a marked transformation in the Illinois court system from a quagmire of inefficiency and political patronage to something much closer to a national exemplar of the modernized court system.

THE ILLINOIS CIVIL PRACTICE ACT

If the highest-order activity by the organized bar was directed to constitutional revision, a second, less fundamental, but nevertheless still comprehensive mode of reform is wholesale statutory revision.

Before the Illinois Civil Practice Act of 1933, Illinois essentially used common-law pleading, employing a complex of instruments and procedures developed in different contexts and adapted to fit twentieth-century circumstances. Despite the adaptations, however, "pleading at common law was very technical and difficult. There were innumerable pitfalls that the shrewd lawyer might lay for his opponent and, in which unless he was careful, he might himself be caught. There was an enormous amount of litigation over procedure itself, and it seems . . . that of all the barren subjects to litigate, procedure is the most barren." [18] It was estimated that since 1848 the New York Code of Civil Procedure had cost its citizens $100 million to find out what it meant. The 1933 Illinois revision of the unwieldy and technical limitations of civil procedure was intended to simplify trial practice, to speed up progressions of actions, to reduce work of the trial courts, especially through the extensive use of discovery procedures, and to render legal relations more precise. [19] The courts were also hampered by lack of self-determination in rule making. Traditionally, court rules were statutory and the court demonstrated great reluctance in contradicting or even adapting them. The bar, on the other hand, insisted that the constitution allowed the courts to "tell the legislature to mind its own business." Legislative control of court rules inhibited the necessary flexibility, adaptation, and modernization of pleading that changing social and economic conditions inevitably demanded.

In 1933, a joint committee of the Chicago and Illinois bar associations presented the Illinois General Assembly with a complete revision of civil procedure law in Illinois, which, when subsequently adopted, transformed the procedures in "one of the blackest common-law states" into the most modern, systematic, and innovated pleading procedures in the nation. [20] For our purposes, however, apart from the codifying—and rationalizing—effect, the article of most outstanding significance was the departure from "immemorial tradition" by granting rule-making power to the Supreme Court of Illinois. Article 1, number 2, stated: "The Supreme Court of this state shall have power to make rules of pleading, practice and procedure for the City, County, Superior Appellate and Supreme Court supplementary to but not inconsistent with the provisions of this Act, and to amend the same, for the purpose of making this Act effective for the convenient administration of justice and otherwise simplifying judicial procedure." [21]

---

18. Edson R. Sunderland, "Observations on the Illinois Civil Practice Act," *Illinois Law Review* 28 (March 1934): 864.

19. Albert E. Jenner and Walter V. Schaefer, "The Proposed Illinois Civil Practice Act," *University of Chicago Law Review* 1 (May 1934): 752.

20. I am indebted to Owen Rall, chairman of the Joint Committee on Illinois Civil Procedure, 1955, who was also a consultant for the drafting of the 1933 Illinois Civil Practice Act, and to Albert Jenner for their comments on this legislation.

21. Illinois Civil Practice Act 1933, 2(1). In the 1955 revision, only two words were changed: "shall have" became "has." The significance of this apparently harmless change was indicated in the comments on the draft act of 1955: "The subsection of the present act grants to the Supreme Court by wording prospective in character the power to make rules. The proposed change in the first sentence of subsection (1) is designed to make clear that *the power of the court to make rules governing practice, pleading and procedure is one which is inherent in this court rather than one which rests in legislative grant*" (italics mine).

The new system, according to its proponents, would be a hybrid—partly a legislative and partly a court rule system; but the bar intended that it would be just the first step along the path to even greater judicial autonomy. Edson Sunderland, one of the drafters of the new legislation, wrote:

> Illinois has followed the same course as Connecticut, New Jersey, and New York. It has conferred considerable rule-making power upon the Supreme Court while at the same time the major part of the field of procedure still remains under the control of the legislature. Every reform is a compromise. The tradition for statutory regulation, which had continued unbroken through the entire history of the state, was probably too firmly established to justify any attempt to entirely supplant it. Through the exercise of the limited power granted, the court will be able to build up a technique for dealing with procedure through rules of court, and as the public becomes convinced of the court's ability to make rules which will produce a business-like administration of justice, the legislature will be less reluctant to delegate fuller power.[22]

Subsequent revisions of the law and practice of the courts, it was hoped, would gradually erode legislative control over the courts in the area of civil procedure.

In 1950, a joint committee of the bar associations was formed at the request of the Supreme Court to review the operation of the 1933 act and to change it where necessary. Over a three-year period, the revision went through several stages, the first of which occurred after a conference of appellate court judges called by the committee agreed on a uniform set of rules for the appellate courts for the first time in seventy-six years.[23]

The subsequent 1955 Revised Illinois Civil Practice Act and Supreme Court rules did not perceptibly take the courts further along the road to autonomy. They do indicate, however, the extensiveness of bar effort and the special relation of expertise it had with the judiciary and the legislature. The bar submitted to the Illinois General Assembly 148 pages of draft legislation with comments and 140 pages of draft court rules.[24] Both had been revised with four broad principles in mind: first, successful advances of the Federal Rules of Civil Procedure over the 1933 Illinois Act were to be incorporated, but some rules, such as a few pertain-

22. Edson R. Sunderland, "The Provisions Relating to Trial Practice in the New Illinois Civil Practice Act," *University of Chicago Law Review* 1 (November 1933): 191. See also Edward W. Hinton, "Pleading under the Illinois Civil Practice Act," *University of Chicago Law Review* 1 (March 1934): 580; and George Ragland, "Discovery before Trial under the Illinois Civil Practice Act," *Illinois Law Review* 28 (March 1934): 875.

23. Owen Rall and Theodore J. Tsoumas, "A Symposium on the Revised Illinois Practice Act and Supreme Court Rules: A Forward Step in Civil Procedure: Introduction and Historical Background," *Northwestern University Law Review* 50 (November 1955): 586.

24. *Tentative Final Draft of Proposed Amendments to Illinois Civil Practice Act and Rules of the Supreme Court of Illinois* (Chicago: Burdette Smith, September 1954).

ing to discovery, which had worked less well, were excluded; second, an effort was made to revise the act in the light of judicial constructions subsequent to the 1933 act; third, those measures tried at the appellate court level in some interim revisions made by the committee in 1952 were also included; and fourth, there appeared to be a general attempt made to speed up the dispatch of cases by eliminating undue technicalities.[25] The act passed through the legislature without fundamental change. As one committee member observed in the course of a board debate (and in a high revelatory statement of the authority embodied in expertise): "The Legislature took the whole Act largely based on faith in the Committee and in the recommendations of the two Associations, and I think there were about four minor changes in the whole volume. They took it very largely on faith of the whole procedure."[26]

THE CANONS OF JUDICIAL ETHICS

In its panoply of reform instruments, the organized bar could complement constitutional amendment and comprehensive statutory revision with recourse to nonlegal codes of action, as it did with the bid to institute a code of judicial ethics. After a mass resignation by judges in the 1930s after the association had recommended suspension of four judges for misconduct, CBA leaders had been extremely reluctant to pressure the judiciary into accepting a code of ethics. Several drafts of canons had been prepared over the years, but they had never been presented to the bench. In 1952, the president appointed a carefully chosen committee of "reliable" lawyers and appellate court judges—who were felt to be less potentially troublesome than trial judges—to this sensitive task. After four years of deliberation, the committee presented to the Board of Managers a set of canons adopted from the American Bar Association standards, with the most notable difference that the CBA had been less severe on political activities in order to make their canons "accepted and workable" in Illinois.[27]

The draft submitted to the board on March 27, 1956, contained thirty-three canons. The first section dealt with judicial temperament. It recommended the avoidance of impropriety, the cultivation of patience and impartiality, and the demonstration of industry and promptness. A second area specified relations

---

25. Peter Fitzpatrick and James M. Goff, "Discovery and Depositions," *Northwestern University Law Review* 50 (November 1955): 628; Edward W. Cleary and Arthur R. Seder, "Extending Jurisdictional Bases for Illinois Courts," *Northwestern University Law Review* 50 (November 1955): 599; John M. O'Connor and Edward G. Proctor, "Appellate Procedure," *Northwestern University Law Review* 50 (November 1955): 639; Philip W. Tone, "The New Amendments Top the Civil Practice Act," *Illinois Bar Journal* 43 (August 1955): 900; Albert A. Jenner and Philip W. Tone, "Pleading Parties and Trial Practice," *Northwestern University Law Review* 50 (November 1955): 612.

26. Transcripts, 8 September 1955.

27. "Report of the Committee on Canons of Judicial Ethics," 24 March 1956.

with other parties, exhorting judges to be considerate and courteous to counsel, without avoiding prudent criticism where it was warranted. A further and more sensitive section insisted on the impartiality of the judge and his responsibility to be free from economic or political influence. This section prescribed that a judge not take part in any judicial act in which his personal interests might be involved and that no other personal or partisan demands should intervene. He should be scrupulously careful with ex parte hearings or communications: "A judge should not accept duties or obligations which will interfere, or reasonably appear to interfere with the proper performance of his official duties" (canon 23). Accordingly, he should not be involved in possible conflict of interest in the role of business transactions.

Most controversial, however, were the canons on political activity. Canon 27 on partisan politics was much less restrictive than its American Bar Association counterpart. "Judges should avoid making political speeches, making or soliciting directly or indirectly, payment of assessments or contributions to party funds, the public endorsement of candidates for public office and participating in party conventions. He should neither accept nor retain a place on any party committee nor act as party leader, nor engage generally in partisan activities." The committee goes on to conclude that, if the judge does engage in such activity, his behavior will not subject him to criticism. Canon 28, on candidacy for office, was also adapted to local circumstances. The canon did "not proscribe the candidacy for other office of one holding judicial position, or require that he waive his compensation while he is such a candidate." It did specify, however, that he should make an effort to avoid any suspicion he is using his office to get elected, and if he is running for nonjudicial office, it would be proper to absent himself, as far as possible, from judicial duties during the campaign. The position of an American Bar Association canon that a judge running for nonjudicial office should resign did not, in the committee's opinion, "have the support of precedent in Illinois and is neither workable nor desirable at this time." [28]

Before sending this draft on to the judiciary and the Illinois State Bar Association (ISBA), the board discussed the canons at length, disagreeing most vigorously over the clause on candidacy for office, which indicated that a judge might properly absent himself from the bench during a campaign. Some members felt this would leave critical gaps on the bench; others asserted that it would give the judges carte blanche to campaign at the public's expense and would bring public criticism onto the bench and bar. In both cases the critics thought the judge should resign, a conclusion rejected by attorneys who thought the bar ought to "encourage good men on the bench to be available for higher office." [29]

28. Ibid.
29. Transcripts, 27 March 1956.

It was agreed, finally, that the clause should be struck from the canons. The Joint CBA/ISBA committee appointed to reconcile different bar association drafts foundered on the same issue. One intransigent ISBA representative "vigorously attacked" the idea that a judge could run for nonjudicial office, a stand already taken in twenty-four other states and supported by the Illinois press. The joint committee reversed the original CBA position by maintaining that a judge should resign and sent its recommendation back to the CBA board, which voted, after an entire meeting devoted to the issues, to sustain the joint committee decisions.[30]

In the meantime, the Judicial Conference of Illinois formed a committee to draft its own canons of ethics, partly, it was said by the lawyers, to avoid the indignity of having standards forced on the bench by the bar. It moved perceptibly away from the CBA/ISBA canons, disagreeing with them in four areas: publicity in the courtroom; engaging in business and the practice of law while on the bench; engaging in partisan politics; and candidacy for public office. After submitting its revision to the bar for comments and polling Illinois judges, the judicial conference adopted on June 5, 1959, its own canons, which were significantly different in some respects from the bar position.[31] Bar canon 24 forbade any solicitation for business or private enterprise by judges or court personnel; the judicial canons exempted judges altogether from this provision and restricted court personnel "only within the confines of the court." Bar canon 27, which tried to indicate reasonable limits on partisan political activities of judges, was thought by the judges, on a vote of thirty-five to eighteen, to be unrealistic; it was replaced by a more general and innocuous canon that stated that a "judge avoid as far as possible taking part in general political campaigns." It also allowed political participation other than that directly necessary for candidacy for judicial office. The judges split twenty-nine for and twenty-seven against the original bar canon that demanded that a judge resign during a campaign for non-judicial office, but reference either to resignation or to leave in such campaigns was deleted.

In a mood of resignation, the bar dismissed the relevant committees and urged no further efforts at that time. Castigating the bench might be counterproductive, and there still remained hope that judges working within the judicial conference or some future widely publicized judicial scandal would provide the stimulus for the liberation of the bench from political control. Whatever the shortcomings of the judicial canons, the bar had at least forced the judiciary to act with probably tighter strictures on judicial behavior than it would have of its own initiative.

30. Ibid., 11 June 1958.
31. Canons of Judicial Ethics, Illinois Judicial Conference, 1959 (available at CBA with "Report . . ." in n. 27 above).

Despite the protestations of the judiciary, the CBA now had a set of norms it could publicize and use as its own standards of practice in its quest for some control over judicial demeanor.[32]

The Structure of Administrative Rationalization

Each of the three preceding cases differs significantly from the others. They sought to institutionalize change at different points in the legal system, they ostensibly were independent of each other, and they evidenced quite different degrees of success. Yet from a sociological perspective each represents an element of an underlying pattern of structural change—or attempted change—and in so doing has important consequences for the restoration of legitimacy in the legal system through the establishment of a more autonomous judicial and court system.

The general shape of change fashioned by the three issues can be parsimoniously interpreted in terms of two concepts: structural differentiation and bureaucratization.

Differentiation is a central term in Weber's sociology of law, as I argued in chapter 1. Indeed, for Schluchter, Weber presents a developmental theory of law in which differentiation both within and between the legal and other spheres provides an organizing principle of change.[33] The division of criminal and civil law provides an instance of the former in traditional law; the division of sacred and secular law offers an example of the latter in natural law. If differentiation occurs in the content or substance of law, it also becomes manifest in the roles of officials and forms of organizations in the administration of justice. In Western advanced capitalist societies, therefore, Weber's sociology of law and sociology of domination (through rational-legal organizations) can and should be brought together. The formalization of legal administration proceeds through the differentiation of legal apparatuses initially from patrimonial, then religious, and finally political substantive values and organizational control. Bureaucratization of the legal system structurally complements the formal rationalization of substantive law.

The Chicago case allows the intricate exploration of a general theory in a mundane setting. If Weber's general theory can illuminate and theoretically order the disparate events of a local jurisdiction, then it not only offers a new perspective on a great deal of legal change in the United States but also draws local and state events into a more encompassing system of meaning—one that transcends subnational and national boundaries and ultimately reaches to the rationalization

---

32. Transcripts, 15 July 1959.

33. See the valuable discussion of this concept in Dietrich Rueschemeyer, "Structural Differentiation, Efficiency, and Power," *American Journal of Sociology* 83 (July 1977): 1–25.

of Western civilization itself. At the same time, the case study can specify the processes identified by Weber in a detail the historical sweep of his own writings would not allow.

For present purposes we may proceed with the basic definition of structural differentiation offered by Neil Smelser. It is "a process whereby one social role or organization . . . differentiates into two or more roles or organizations. . . . The new social units are structurally distinct from each other, but taken together are functionally equivalent to the original unit." [34] In some theories, such differentiation will increase the organizational capacities and make more rational and predictable the newly differentiated structures over the fused structures they superseded. Of course differentiation may occur at other levels as well, including institutions and values. Yet it is useful to consider the problem facing both the legal system and the organized bar in the United States, particularly in jurisdictions where local courts have been dominated by party politics, as one of *incomplete differentiation:* that is, the separation of government functions envisaged by the doctrine of separation of powers was structurally incomplete in such jurisdictions as Illinois where politics infused the judiciary at all levels. Hence structural differentiation in this context is that process whereby the partial fusion of the two branches of government is attenuated and the structural autonomy of the legal system reasserted.

Structural differentiation may proceed in tandem with bureaucratization. In Nonet and Selznick's terms, that implies adoption of a form of organization in which purposes are explicit and identified with clear and limited jurisdictions, in which authority is hierarchically subdivided, in which rules are codified, in which decision making is systematized and routinized, and in which the personnel are officials who are full-time professionals, who have no personal constituency, whose appointment is based on merit, and whose careers are ordered by principles of seniority and tenure. [35]

The interplay and complementarity of those two processes—though scarcely perceived by bar leaders in these terms—nonetheless moved the court system perceptibly away from its partial fusion with politics and gave the system itself a new internal rationality and autonomy. The analytic structure and coherence of the bar's reform program can be seen by examining in more detail, and with a conceptual eye, the combined consequences of the three issues.

---

34. See also Wolfgang Schluchter, *The Rise of Western Rationalism: Max Weber's Developmental History* (Berkeley: University of California Press, 1981), chap. 5.

35. Philippe Nonet and Philip Selznick, *Law and Society in Transition: Toward Responsive Law* (New York: Harper & Row, 1978), 22. Compare Max Weber, *Economy and Society,* ed. Guenther Roth and Claus Wittich (New York: Bedminster, 1968), 224.

STRUCTURAL DIFFERENTIATION

Differentiation between the courts and the political system occurred both in organizational structure and role definition. *Organizational differentiation* took place at each level in the court system. The Supreme Court achieved greater autonomy in setting court procedures and making court rules. The 1933 Civil Practice Act marked the first stage of this development, and by 1970 the judicial article had increased the independence of the courts to the extent that the Supreme Court had, with some exceptions, general administrative authority. It also had the means to exercise authority over the entire state court system, although some areas of discretion remained outside its control. Greater autonomy devolved to the higher courts with the 1964 and 1970 judicial article provisions. These provisions enabled the court to decide which cases it would hear. In effect, this jurisdictional authority allowed the Supreme Court considerable flexibility in determining differentiation of judicial functions among the courts.

The court system also received increased powers to regulate its personnel. Control of individual behavior was exercised through tribunals explicitly formed for that purpose. Some freedom was allowed the courts to set conditions of work, and while they had practically no voice in salaries for judges and clerks, they had some control over conditions of retirement. The courts did not break the control of the political system over appointments to the bench, but they were given limited powers to make appointments to vacant seats on the bench, and although all financing came from the state and local political authorities, the Supreme Court had some discretion in its allocation.

Some differentiation further occurred between the local courts and their respective town and county governments, although the attenuation of political ties at this level proceeded more slowly than in the higher courts. In effect, the bureaucratic power invested in the Supreme Court to assign judges, to establish functions of circuit courts, and to control some allocation of funds modestly weakened—at least formally—the strong relation between the courts and political organization at lower levels in the system.

Whereas organizational differentiation was most apparent at the highest levels of the court system, *role differentiation* was most pronounced at its lowest reaches. The Canons of Judicial Ethics and the judicial article both demanded some added segregation of the judicial role from other roles. First, the modest restrictions placed on judges who wished to continue participating in political affairs marginally widened the gap between the public role of judge and the private role of political advocate. Successive canons and regulations emphasized the conception that a bureaucratic role cannot be effectively undertaken when the limits of public and private sentiments in judicial actions and decision making are confused. Second, abolition of the justices of the peace clearly designated members of the judiciary as legal experts whose decisions would derive from specialized training rather than the folk wisdom of the lay judge. Invocation of the criterion of expertise as a condition of the judicial role unequivocally identified legal thought with the practice of adjudication with legal training. Third, the proscription of part-time judging provided further support for the conception of judging as a distinctive career. This proscription prevented fusion of the role of judge with other occupational roles and arrested the blurring of substantive values with legal values. Fourth, restriction on concurrent practice as an attorney and judge segregated legal practitioners into either adjudicatory or counseling practices. Provisions for a longer and fixed tenure for judges, which in turn was based on adjudicatory performance rather than extralegal activities, led to a fifth aspect of differentiation—the possibility that judges might pursue careers within the judiciary without continuing to maintain their legal practices or political affiliations.

The extent of role differentiation correlated inversely with the status within the court system. Roles of higher court judges had already been relatively well defined, but fusion of the role of judge with that of lawyer and nonlawyer was most pronounced at lower levels of the system. Thus the reforms were directed mostly to circuit court judges, magistrates, and justices of the peace. Some steps were taken toward greater independence for court personnel from local political control, but because court appointments were closely integrated with the political patronage system, the abolition of political appointment of clerks did not advance very far. The 1964 constitution explicitly stated that court clerks could continue to be elected; the 1970 constitution modified this only slightly, providing that clerks in the Supreme Court and the appellate courts might be appointed by judges but that the vast majority of clerks in the circuit courts would be elected as they had always been.[36]

BUREAUCRATIZATION

The process of external differentiation is a necessary, rather than a sufficient, condition of bureaucratization; it provides the structural prerequisite for complete bureaucratization of organization structure, procedure, and roles.

The judicial article reordered the main outlines of the court system by instituting a hierarchical pyramid of authority. The fragmentation of the earlier courts

36. A valuable study by Wesley G. Skogan ("The Politics of Judicial Reform: Cook County, Illinois," *Justice System Journal* 1 [September 1975]: 11–23) examined the before and after effects of the judicial articles on the quality of judicial candidates in Cook County. Because the merit selection provisions did not pass, its implications remain untested in Illinois. Despite improvements in court

was replaced by statewide coordination that limited the independence of any court. Constitutional reforms regulated the precise circumstances in which the authority of a higher court power was manifested in its clauses on appeals, discipline, and administration. Whereas hierarchical structuring of the courts resulted in changes in the treatment of appeals and the exercise of administration, lateral structuring took place through the provisions on jurisdiction. Courts of equivalent authority or stature had the limits of their functions defined in order to obviate clashes either in the chain of command or in their areas of proper jurisdiction.

The broad outlines of the new bureaucratic structure of the courts were set inflexibly in the constitution. Bureaucratization proceeded within these limits with the development of organizational procedures through court rules. The process began in 1933 with the Civil Practice Act. Rules were extended to areas of civil pleading for which procedures were not well specified or were absent. Uniformity was imposed on all appellate courts throughout the state; statutory civil procedure was essentially codified to eliminate confusion and to compile, in one document, all operative rules of pleading. The increments of rule-making authority given the Supreme Court in the 1950s and the 1960s ensured a continued flexibility sufficient to adapt, revise, and modernize court rules and, consequently, to resist the intrusion of substantively grounded decision-making in the future.

Finally, bureaucracy was realized in further development of a distinctive judicial role. In Weber's sociology, the officials of a bureaucratic administrative staff—the purest example of legal authority—are appointed and function according to the following criteria:

> (1) they are . . . subject to authority only with respect to their impersonal official obligations, and (2) are organized in a clearly defined hierarchy of offices with (3) clearly defined spheres of competence. (4) Candidates are selected on the basis of technical qualifications . . . ; they are appointed, not elected, (6) They are remunerated by fixed salaries in money. . . . (7) The office is treated as the sole, or at least the primary occupation of the incumbent. . . . (8) It constitutes a career . . . , promotion is dependent on the judgment of superiors. . . . (9) The official works entirely separated from ownership of the means of the administration and without appropriation of his position. (10) He is subject to strict and systematic discipline and control in the conduct of his office.[37]

---

organization and the recruitment of somewhat better quality judges to the courts, the party background of judges changed only in that the better conditions on the bench "raised the level in the party at which these jobs appear to be appropriate sinecures." (p. 20). Moreover, despite the change to nonpartisan retention elections, Skogan concluded that judges still needed to show some party loyalty and responsiveness.

37. Weber, *Economy and Society,* 224.

The points of similarity between the reformed judiciary and this "pure form" of bureaucratic role attests to the significant transformations realized by the judicial article and other reforms. Formal demands of the judicial article departed from this conception of the bureaucratic official only in Weber's fourth point—the competency basis of appointment. The process of role crystallization, begun with the differentiation of judicial from political and attorney roles, was consolidated in an integrated judicial role.

Bureaucratization was complemented within the court system by differentiation and fusion. *Vertical organizational fusion* was represented by the compression of the municipal, county, circuit, and appellate courts and the Supreme Court into only three levels—the circuit courts, the appellate court, and the Supreme Court. Jurisdiction for appeals, previously divided among these courts, was greatly simplified, and the number of possible appeals steps was reduced. Vertical fusion of the levels of judges was partially contingent on these organizational changes. *Vertical role fusion* occurred in two respects: initially, the levels of magistrates, justices of the peace, lower- and superior-court judges, appellate court and Supreme Court judges were consolidated into three levels; by 1970, the three levels, which were intended to correspond to functions and responsibility, were further consolidated even further into two levels—circuit court judges and associate judges.

Before reform, courts had specialized in several different areas of law such as probate, tax, traffic offenses, and others. After reform, *horizontal organizational fusion* integrated all courts into the general category of circuit court, although some would continue to carry out specialized functions under their new nomenclature. *Partial horizontal fusion* complemented horizontal organizational integration. The excessive specialization of judges in an integrated court system could be highly inefficient where some flexibility in assigning judges to courts with especially heavy caseloads was needed. The rotation of judges through courts such as divorce and probate had always been resisted by those judges reluctant to sit in such low-prestige courts. On the other hand, there had been pressure from judges sitting in more prestigious courts that de facto judicial specialization be recognized by the chief judge. In the formal provisions of the judicial article, no such specialization was recognized; but it is certain that the ostensible "de-differentiation" of judicial roles was less pronounced in practice than it appeared in the constitution.

Differentiation occurred primarily between the courts and political institutions, whereas fusion took place primarily within the court system. In a very few instances, however, this association was reversed so that differentiation occurred within the courts, while fusion took place between the court system and organizations outside it. Through the 1950s, appeals as of right to the Supreme Court were set by the legislature. In 1964, the more than forty categories of these appeals were drastically reduced to cover a narrower range of more significant issues. The failure of even this provision to stem the flow of cases led to the 1970 constitutional provision that severely limited appeals as of right and gave the Supreme Court discretion to hear those cases having constitutional or pragmatic import. With this measure, the Supreme Court concentrated on a more circumscribed set of cases and gave appellate courts authority to decide those categories of cases discarded by the Supreme Court.

The autonomy given the highest court to set its own agenda contrasted with the loss of autonomy, through partial fusion, in the area of judicial discipline. The 1964 judicial article had given the Supreme Court complete control over the discipline of judges, thus reducing the influence exercised over the judicial behavior by the profession and political organizations. Widely publicized revelations of malfeasance by two Supreme Court justices led many observers to cast doubt on the ability of judges to regulate themselves. The changes implemented by the 1970 constitution aimed at reducing court autonomy by introducing laypersons into the control process while taking it out of the hands of the Supreme Court. A nine-person inquiry board for the hearing of complaints and conducting of investigations would include only two judges and would be totally independent of the Supreme Court. For the first time—apart from impeachment proceedings—formal control of the judiciary would fall partially outside its jurisdiction. Complaints would go to a tribunal, this time consisting entirely of judges who were formally independent of the Supreme Court.

The complementary contributions of structural differentiation and bureaucratization to judicial autonomy can now be brought into sharper focus. At each level of contiguity between the courts and politics or governments, the process of external differentiation began to break up the comfortable union of judicial activity and political purpose, to relocate the locus of decision making in court affairs, and to substitute new criteria for decision making on the courts. Fused political and judicial roles were either abolished or separated. The abortive campaign for merit selection would have almost completely severed judicial appointments from political patronage; the successful campaign for tenure did ensure that judges, once elected to the bench, would retain their seats by running against their records of judicial performance rather than by engaging in competition over political commitments. Individual courts, previously isolated from sister courts and vulnerable to local community interests, found their political relations and financial dependencies across the boundaries of the court system replaced by authority relations inside the court system. At the institutional level—the statewide complex of organizations and roles—further emancipation from legislative control over rule making allowed the court system sufficient autonomy to chart its own course toward self-defined goals in the administration of justice. In sum, external differentiation partially segregated roles, organizations, and the entire institutional complex of courts from the political system with which it had been extensively fused.

One aspect of the separation of courts from politics was completely independent of bureaucratization—although the occurrence of separation reinforced the movement toward formally rational organization. The tenure and merit selection provisions were intended to minimize explicit political control or adherence to political criteria in decision making over appointment of judges. Both these ends could be accomplished without bureaucratization of the court. Other aspects of external differentiation, however, were either produced by bureaucracy or reinforced by it. Emphasis on rules endogenous to the court system and the imposition of bureaucratic judicial roles implicitly demanded the dislocation of exogenous influence and ties. At the same time, under the authority of a more independent Supreme Court and through the clarification of jurisdictions, the court system gained an internal coherence of its own.

The conjunction of independence and internal coherence enhanced the institutional integrity of the entire system. Coordinated, the courts could more readily withstand intrusions into their domain, especially at lower court levels. Together, structural differentiation and bureaucratization moved the courts to repel illegitimate political incursions and thereby asserted some relative autonomy for the court system. Put in Weberian terms, a system of justice permeated by irrationality and substantive political values shifted its principles of organization and decision making toward the values of formal rationality. Bureaucratization effected the transition—albeit incomplete—from irrationality to rationality; structural differentiation permitted the substitution—again incomplete—of substantive rationality by formal rationality.

Patterns of Change

The analytic clarity of changes from one theoretical type of organization to another was blurred in empirical reality. Underneath the broad sweep of legal change, currents moved swiftly in some areas, drifted more sluggishly in other areas, and advanced not at all in some respects. Even countercurrents could be discerned at certain points. Far from being unilinear and irreversible, structural differentiation, like bureaucracy, proceeded in several directions at varying paces.

The baseline—no discernible change at all—was relatively rare. This is not to say that no area in which change might have occurred remained untouched. Rather recruitment to the bench was one of the very few areas in which the bar pressed for reform with little success. From the 1920s, it had repeatedly argued for merit selection to the bench, and the various drafts of the judicial article exhibited a good deal of ingenuity to realize this goal. But after the 1970 constitutional convention through the mid-1980s, the bar still appeared to have made no progress.[38]

A consistent path to increased rationalization, without substantial reversals, characterized the second pattern of change. The rule-making powers and autonomy of the higher courts best illustrate the pattern. The 1933 Illinois Civil Practice Act gave the courts unprecedented rule-making discretion over pleading despite the fact that such powers continued to be shared with the legislature and the new act extended only to civil procedure. Little further progress took place in the 1950s, especially after the legislature dramatically repudiated the 1957 bar proposals for increased autonomy. The 1964 judicial article explicitly avoided confronting the question of court rules; but by 1970 it had increased discretion in several areas.

The span of change in major court reorganization was much shorter. The breakthrough occurred in 1964 with the judicial article and was further refined in 1970. Changes in the role of judge also witnessed a steady progression toward a distinctive and autonomous role. The joint committee's Canons of Judicial Ethics precipitated a minor self-imposed segregation of political roles from judicial roles by the bench. But the abolition of justices of the peace in 1964 and the consolidation of three tiers of judges in a two-level hierarchy in 1970 (so that the lowest levels in the court system would be responsible to the Supreme Court for review) went far beyond the expectations of the bar. Over thirty years, the general authority of the Supreme Court pressed inexorably to the limits of the court system.

The extent to which the courts could regulate the behavior of their members without interference from either the profession or the legislature exemplifies a third pattern of change. In the 1950s, effective control of judicial behavior very often came from the organized bar on one side and the political parties on the other; the Illinois Courts Commission of the 1960s substituted judicial control for outside review. But this autonomy was thought to be excessive, and the major scandals of judicial misconduct that immediately preceded the 1970 constitutional convention reinforced a critical evaluation. The 1970 constitutional provision for discipline of judges therefore represented a reversal of the pattern toward greater judicial self-regulation. The two-step procedure, modified from the more radical proposal of the bar that no judges be given responsibility for discipline,

38. For more recent developments, see Robert W. Bergstrom, "The Struggle for Judicial Reform," *Illinois Bar Journal* 66 (September 1977): 22–37; John C. Mullen and Thomas A. Clancy, "The McCourt Bill: A Practical Merit Selection Plan," *Illinois Bar Journal* 66 (September 1977): 12.

involved several nonlawyers. Both the Judicial Inquiry Board, which was to investigate complaints and press charges, and the Illinois Courts Commission, which was to hear charges and sit in judgment, were independent of the Supreme Court. The autonomy that bureaucratization demanded was therefore contingent. An autonomy that fostered abuse by the judiciary could precipitate the intervention of outside groups into the court system, thus reversing rationalization.

More complicated patterns of change were also evident. For instance, the court reforms removed many of the direct opportunities for intervention in the courts given the local political parties, only to transfer the contact of the political organizations with the courts to another level. Salaries, which had sometimes been paid or supplemented by funds from local political authorities, were placed in the hands of the state legislature. The dependence of many individual courts on local political goodwill for increased salaries was generally replaced by increased dependency of the collective court system on the one state legislature. Increased autonomy at one level might decrease autonomy at another. At the same time, the negotiating position of a unified judiciary fortified by the bar would very likely be more effective at the state level than in individual courts.

Concern with patterns of change has more than theoretical significance. Relative rates and sequences among different strands in a reform movement can significantly influence the outcome of the general trend toward greater rationalization. The Illinois events demonstrate that the relative timing and coordination of external differentiation and bureaucratization are crucial for the development and persistence of greater formal rationality. Bureaucratization accomplished under the aegis of a political or religious institution may merely reinforce the hegemony of the relevant substantive ideals in the entire bureaucracy. By contrast, structural differentiation without concurrent bureaucratization may leave courts isolated and the court system fragmented, thus leaving little common basis on which to assert values of procedure indigenous to the system of justice alone. If the courts become unified into a statewide bureaucracy when differentiation is incomplete at the highest levels—no matter how much differentiation there has been lower down in the system—then the judiciary continues to be susceptible to political control, which now would need to be exercised only at the apex of the hierarchy. By reinforcing the 1933 movement toward Supreme Court autonomy with the 1964 and 1970 constitutional provisions on separation of powers and, in turn, reorganizing the court system simultaneously along bureaucratic lines, the Illinois court system could begin to develop and to maintain its independence from political control. Bureaucratization without concurrent external differentiation facilitates political control; external differentiation reinforced by bureaucratization facilitates institutional autonomy.

Consequently, although it was not successful in all that it attempted, the fact that the organized bar succeeded as much as it did is remarkable given the extraordinary ambition of its political program. At each of the three levels at which the bar engaged the courts—constitutional, statutory, and voluntary—it accomplished a partial realization of its agenda, whether through an amended adoption of its proposals or through the adoption of a countermeasure that nonetheless incorporated much that the organized bar had initially proposed. In its primary institutional sphere, therefore, on issues some of which were highly controversial, the bar demonstrated the capacity of a profession to bring its expertise to power by the exercise of both expert and moral authority.

Seen from a different theoretical vantage point, this account of professional collective action also vindicates Rueschemeyer's thesis that the process of social differentiation, which has often been conceived as a response to a rather disembodied principle of efficiency, must also be viewed in the perspective of power constellations that have interests in accelerating or impeding differentiation.[39] The partial character of the organized bar's success reflects, on the one hand, the power of its own resources, just as, on the other hand, its partial failure indicates the interests—whether of some judges, party machines, or entire branches of government—ranged against professional collective action. While the principal lines of bar action can be parsimoniously interpreted as a bid for legal rationalization, through the interplay of structural differentiation and bureaucratization, the equivocal outcomes of professional mobilization underline the contingency of social change on the balance of power between the profession and contrary interests, not to mention struggles within the bar.[40] As I shall show in the following chapter, however, effective professional influence extended far beyond the peak events recounted in this chapter. The bid for autonomy was accompanied by a drive for control.

39. See Dietrich Rueschemeyer, *Power and the Division of Labor* (Stanford: Stanford University Press, 1986).

40. Cf. Cappell and Halliday, "Professional Projects"; Halliday, "Idiom of Legalism." For instance, it is not without significance that many Machine and black lawyers energetically resisted merit selection because they believed it would reduce their access to the bench in favor of more advantaged leaders—such as those who dominated the bar association in the 1950s and 1960s. See Watson and Downing's (*The Politics of the Bench and the Bar*) account of clashing interests among segments of the bar over implementation of the "Missouri Plan" in Missouri.

7 The Normative Economy of Judicial Control

A drive toward autonomy of the court system characterizes one principal component of professional politics of expertise in the primary institutional sphere. Reforms of the judicial article of the Illinois Constitution and of the Illinois Civil Practice Act and attempts at the formulation of judicial canons of ethics represent peak efforts of the Chicago Bar Association (CBA) to effect change by widening the gap between the judicial system and the politics, thus drawing the court system, in which lawyers have their principal locus of institutional activity, closer to professional influence.

Alone, however, autonomy represents only a fraction of professional action. The three peak events must be set in a far more holistic context; and autonomy must be placed in tandem with a complementary principle of action—or, at least, explanation. Immediately, many questions arise. How much effort do professions devote to legal institutional change? What is the total volume of action by the organized bar in its primary sphere of influence? Does the spectrum of action in the courts have a unity that embraces autonomy? Is there a dynamic that holds various structural components of apparently random activity in a creative tension? While peak events clearly reveal a corner of collegial action, what place do they have in the totality of professional effort?

A unity can be discerned in the greatly variegated programs of the CBA over the decades. When the major efforts are placed in the general context of all bar association judicial activities, it becomes apparent that bar efforts directed toward autonomy are complemented with a complex extension of bar controls over the court system. Autonomy and control have, therefore, if not an explicit mutuality of purpose, at least a complementarity of effect.

The process of control in turn has an internal logic and dynamic of its own. On the one hand, the profession can perform a negative and regulatory function by imposing sanctions on deviant judicial behavior and by endeavoring to block the appointment or election of any judges to the bench who seem to be unqualified.

On the other hand, a profession can balance this oppositional role with attempts to better the judiciary and to act as an ally for judges in their bid to improve conditions of service, court organization, and court procedures.

The concurrent professional politics of negativism and affirmation are integrated into what may be labeled a *normative economy of judicial control*. The two forms of politics do not run in constant conjunction. Rather the adequacy of the former is a function of the efficacy of the latter. The bar's efforts at ethical or normative control over judges are to a large extent contingent on the credit earned by the profession in its efforts to upgrade the administration of justice. The normative economy can be perceived both objectively, in the balance of negative and positive activities, and subjectively, in the periodic comments of bar leaders who express an inchoate sense that balance is required in the bar's dealings with the bench. Thus the optimal condition of a normative economy occurs when there is an approximate balance between the moral income earned through good works in the courts and the moral loss incurred through the gatekeeping and regulatory functions of the bar. If the profession is to discipline judges and to reject unsuitable aspirants to the bench, then it requires a level of positive activity approximately commensurate with its ethical controls of judges. An economy severely out of balance—especially in debt—can lurch toward organizational bankruptcy, at least in influence over its primary institutional sphere.

The internal dynamics of professional control over the primary institutional sphere can be elaborated and illustrated by an overview of the entire normative economy of the CBA. In the previous chapter I considered only three peak events—albeit issues on which the organized bar expended many resources over a number of years. By themselves, however, they reveal only a limited amount. The two other levels of data, considered in this chapter, complement the major case studies in several ways. As the CBA has been a rather centralized organization, and as the judicial action of the association can be generated from many committees and from within the leadership itself, a sample of board agenda items provides the best index of the total volume and content of judicial issues handled by the organized bar over an extended period. The sample is composed of 50 percent of all board agenda items, randomly assigned from board minutes, for the period from January 1950 to December 1969—some 1,238 items.

Because the items coded in the sample were drawn from the agenda books of the board, there was little information available on the actual content of each issue, on internal CBA negotiations, on board decision making, on the success of an initiative, or on the types of mobilization. A second sample of one hundred issues, drawn randomly from the agenda list and stratified for the periods 1950–54, 1955–59, 1960–64, and 1965–69, gives much more detailed information from the issue files held by the CBA and the transcripts of the board. The issue files in fact constituted issue histories: they consisted of compilations of all reports and correspondence relating to a given problem. When combined with the CBA board transcripts, they provide a rare inside view of elite professional politics.

In sum, the interpretation offered here of the entire array of bar judicial activities builds on a pyramidal design that comprises three levels of data: (1) an attempt to estimate a universe of action by sampling the 1,238 items from the board's agenda; (2) a sampling of the sample to yield one hundred cases for closer attention (also dealt with in this chapter); and (3) the selection of three peak events that were outstanding in their prominence and that also had some theoretical coherence (treated in the previous chapter).

In this chapter I will set the major issues in the general context of professional action on the judiciary. The outlines of the normative economy of judicial control will be traced by a brief discussion of the volume and distribution of agenda items from 1950 to 1970. I will then elaborate the components of the normative economy in more detail by an interpretation of the one hundred issue histories. This pyramidal sampling design therefore provides at once the luxury of sketching the parameters of the entire endeavor while simultaneously being able to underline with greater precision its various elements. We can view both the forest and the trees, allowing each to set the limits for the other. The methodological tension produced by this means points up the balance not only between affirmation and negativism but more generally between the two faces of an established profession, both monopoly and beyond it.

An Overview of Judicial Politics

The most elementary question about a profession's role in its primary sphere is also very often the most elusive to answer. As a result, the literature on contemporary professions offers no response to the question, How much activity does a typical professional association engage in? My attempt to provide a first approximation of a response, found in Table 7.1, indicates that the organization's leadership considered separate judicial items at the rate of about fifty to seventy-five per annum. There were approximately twelve hundred considerations over twenty years, and if we assume that the leadership met perhaps forty-five times each year, it is obvious that one or two judicial issues were discussed at each board meeting. Judicial matters were therefore a constant factor in elite decision making and an index of the importance given to the primary sphere by this profession. The courts never left the agenda books.

It must be quickly observed, however, that this index is an absolutely minimal indicator of general organizational activity. Before coming to the board with rec-

TABLE 7.1. Fifty Percent Sample of Agenda Considerations of Judicial and Court Issues by the CBA Board, 1950–70

	1950–51 to 1954–55		1955–56 to 1959–60		1960–61 to 1964–65		1965–66 to 1969–70		Total	
	%	N	%	N	%	N	%	N	%	N
Autonomy (judicial article)	8.8	18	8.3	10	14.1	21	2.2	3	8.4	52
Judicial elections	33.5	72	34.2	41	30.8	46	37.0	50	33.8	209
Judicial ethics	14.4	31	9.2	11	10.1	15	11.1	15	11.6	72
Judicial conditions of office	10.2	22	3.3	4	8.7	13	9.6	13	8.4	52
Court organization and procedure	19.0	41	22.5	27	22.8	34	18.5	25	20.5	127
Court congestion	9.3	20	10.0	12	2.0	3	2.2	3	8.1	38
Court positive, other	1.4	3	7.5	9	3.4	5	8.1	11	4.5	28
Other	3.7	8	5.0	6	8.1	12	11.1	15	6.6	41
Total	34.7	215	19.4	120	24.1	149	21.9	135	100.0	619

SOURCE.—Minutes, Board of Managers, Chicago Bar Association.
NOTE.—N equals the actual number of items sampled.

ommendations, the 60 percent of items coming from committees (rather than from within the board itself) may already have absorbed dozens or hundreds of lawyer-hours of work to produce a report, not to mention negotiations with judges and court officials before approaching the bar leadership. In addition, for some agenda items, such as judicial elections, there will have been very extensive administrative commitments by association staff. Thus any estimate of total committee, administrative, and leadership output will be very substantial.

The considerations have been coded by topic. In rank order of frequency, judicial elections (33.8 percent of considerations) are by far the most important, followed by court organization and procedures with 20 percent, and judicial ethics, contributions to court conditions, and court congestion with approximately 8–12 percent each. Matters to do with autonomy of the judicial system—at least those aspects arising from the judicial article alone—account for approximately 8 percent of considerations, although the judicial article, which preoccupied the association for twenty years, will have collectively absorbed many thousands of hours of committee effort. It is apparent that the frequency of consideration is not constant across five-year periods, despite the rather stable overall distributions from 1950 to 1970. Yet the changes in relative priorities of issue areas are limited. Only autonomy and court congestion show radical departures from the marginal distributions.

Approximately one-third of all leadership considerations were recurring items, that is, multiple considerations of the same issue. If we control for these, we are left with a net volume of separate matters in the region of forty per year (table 7.2). With some exceptions, however, most notably that of autonomy, the patterns for the volume of distinct issues follows that of leadership considerations, although the marginals are somewhat flattened. In other words, the relative significance of each component of bar association action on the judiciary remains little changed over two decades.

When we begin to aggregate areas of content, several clues appear that sustain the notion of a normative economy. If there is any credence in the argument that the politics of professional control can be represented as a normative economy in which the two hands of professional action must be in approximate balance, then it would follow that the components of "credit" action should be roughly in proportion to "debit" activities. Table 7.1 provides some initial support for this contention: excluding autonomy for the moment, the general class of actions I have designated as negative, namely, those to do with judicial elections and ethics, add to a percentage of total effort rather close to the sum of effort on the remaining items, which have to do almost exclusively with the positive class of actions. In view of this symmetry and the quite stable distributions over time, this rather fallible indicator of professional effort suggests that the professional association

TABLE 7.2. Fifty Percent Sample of Issues on Judicial and Court Topics Considered by the CBA Board, 1950–70

	1950–51 to 1954–55		1955–56 to 1959–60		1960–61 to 1964–65		1965–66 to 1969–70		Total	
	%	N	%	N	%	N	%	N	%	N
Autonomy (judicial article) '	.9	1	.0	0	1.0	1	.0	0	.5	2
Judicial elections	40.2	47	32.1	26	38.5	40	37.5	39	37.4	152
Judicial ethics	12.0	14	9.9	8	12.5	13	11.5	12	11.6	47
Judicial conditions of office	10.3	12	4.9	4	7.7	8	9.6	10	8.4	34
Court organization and procedure	24.8	29	27.2	22	26.9	28	20.2	21	24.6	100
Court congestion	5.1	6	9.9	8	2.9	3	1.9	2	4.7	19
Court positive, other	2.6	3	9.9	8	3.8	4	10.6	11	6.4	26
Other	4.3	5	6.2	5	6.7	7	8.7	9	6.4	26
Total	100.0	117	100.0	81	100.0	104	100.0	104	100.0	406

SOURCE.—Minutes, Board of Managers, Chicago Bar Association.
NOTE.—N equals the actual number of items sampled.

had reached by 1950, and was able to maintain in the subsequent two decades, a steady-state normative economy in long-term equilibrium. Of course, the "steadiness" of the state is partially a function of the aggregation of years into five-year periods. But given the length of many issues, which may stretch from months to years, it would be expected that an economy might well go into debit or credit for a short period provided that the general balance was more or less maintained over the longer term.

In the remainder of the chapter, I will use the sample of one hundred issues, first, to elaborate the content of each class of matters and, second, thereby to bring evidence to elaborate the concept of a normative economy.

The Politics of Negativism
DEMEANOR ON THE BENCH

The sample of cases on bar review of judicial behavior indicates that professional control over the judiciary can extend in successively widening circles of control that encompass increasingly inclusive aspects of a judge's professional and private life. In its narrowest circle of influence the bar can closely monitor the interaction and treatment of lawyers by judges in the courtroom. That interest can be expanded to the treatment meted out by judges to any other persons appearing in court. The profession may broaden its circles of influence even further to include the financial affairs of judges, their political activities, and even, in certain circumstances, their personal behavior and comportment quite outside the formal performance of judicial office.[1]

Bar interests begin in the courtroom. Complaints came from two main sources: individual lawyers who had a grievance against a judge and members of the public who had experienced or witnessed "unjudicial" behavior. In the first case below the bar moved swiftly to react in response to an indignity publicly heaped on a member of the profession in court.

> Attorney Arthur Gestol was called to the bench by Judge Taxin in order to explain why he wanted a new trial. The judge immediately launched into a tirade, denied the motion for retrial, and when the attorney attempted to defend himself he was placed in contempt of court and fined $50. As Gestol did not have the $50 on him, Judge Taxin ordered the bailiff to take Gestol into custody, whereupon the bailiff slapped on a pair of handcuffs in full view of the court, marched the attorney down the corridor past other lawyers and litigants, and, after a clothing and body search, placed Gestol in a cell with a group of criminals.

1. All the proper names of individuals in this section have been changed owing to the sensitive nature of the documentary materials. For the same reason, footnotes will refer only to the respective files and transcripts from which these cases are drawn.

Gestol was outraged. He wrote in vain to the chief judge of the circuit court and then followed it up with a formal complaint to the CBA, which in turn referred the matter to its Judiciary Committee. After a hearing in which the committee had called Gestol, the judge, the bailiff, a court reporter, her employer, and the presiding judge, to give evidence, the committee concluded that without excuse, "Judge Taxin inflicted a gross indignity upon the complainant" and that his action contravened at least two canons of the Judicial Ethics.

The CBA Board privately censured Taxin, placed a copy of the detailed committee report in the judge's personal file held by the CBA, and communicated its findings to the chief judge. In addition, the CBA President drew to the attention of the chief judge the concern of the organized bar about the general manner in which judges treated lawyers.[2]

In this case, a striking feature of the profession's internal system of justice—besides the dim view it took of the public shaming of an attorney by a judge—remains the privacy of the proceedings. While the judicial indiscretions took place in a public setting, neither the public nor the bar could know that a complaint was laid, that a de facto trial had been undertaken, and that a judge had been censured. The only witnesses to this private proceeding between the bar and the bench were the complainant, the witnesses, members of the bar association, and the two judges. Members of the association itself, quite apart from the public, would have no awareness that such an action had been taken or, in the case of the public, that it ever would be likely to be taken.

Not all cases are so invisible, however, and especially not those that involve prominent members of the public or individuals who have access to the media. Neither are all sanctions private.

In late 1950, the *Chicago Tribune* asked a reporter to undertake an investigation of the courts. Williams, the reporter, chose to sit in on a trial being undertaken by Judge Casey. When Casey observed that Williams was making notes on the course of proceedings he called Williams to the bench and subjected him to a battery of questions about his identity and purpose in the court. When the judge found that Williams claimed to be with the *Tribune,* Casey rang the paper but could not find anyone to verify Williams' claim. Consequently, the reporter was sent to the bullpen, then brought back, threatened with contempt of court, and released.

CBA leaders read about Williams' experience the next day in the *Tribune* under the by-line "How Public is Treated in A City Court." The Judiciary Committee instituted an inquiry, calling the judge, bailiffs, clerks of the court, a state's attorney and Williams as wit-

---

2. File 67–12; Transcripts of meetings of the Board, 12 January 1967, 9 February 1967 (hereafter cited as Transcripts).

nesses. Casey's refusal to attend was deemed to be an admission to guilt and the Board voted to censure him publicly through a press release.[3]

The Williams case represents the second step in the extension of professional control beyond the narrow confines of lawyer-judge relations. In the first case the bar association stepped in to defend the rights of a lawyer; it served notice to the bench how the profession would define the limits of judicial incursions on the vulnerability of attorneys. In the second case it is clear that the profession's concerns can extend beyond matters of direct effects on lawyers and that the organized bar can intervene in situations in which judges overstep what the bar considers to be acceptable bounds of judicial practice. The action of the CBA had another significance: it occurred before the implementation of the Code of Judicial Ethics; the judgments made by the lawyers could not be sustained by any code of ethics on which there was a consensus between the bar and the bench or even on which there was a consensus among lawyers. Ultimately, the decision on judicial norms rested on the subjective judgments of bar association leaders.

The expansion of professional monitoring of the judiciary can extend even further—to the behavior of judges as it is affected by their relations outside the courtroom. The profession has been particularly sensitive to infringements of judicial ethics in two areas: conflicts of economic interest and conflicts of political and judicial interests. In a system in which appointment to the bench occurs through election, judges face numerous temptations to profit financially from their position on the bench. Quite apart from the fact that pay is often notoriously low compared with the earnings of a moderately successful practitioner, tenure on the bench in an electoral system can also be precarious. In many jurisdictions judges can expect to spend a significant sum on their campaigns for election; yet once elected they have limited legitimate opportunities to regain the monetary costs. Moreover, because they might lose their position on the bench in the next judicial election, it is not surprising that some members of the bench find it difficult to sever ties with their former law firms and even more painful to relinquish certain investments or financial commitments that might involve conflicts of interest. For judges who do dispense with alternative forms of income, there are opportunities, especially in the daily bustle of the lower courts, to make some money on the side. The vagaries of appointment to the bench, the uncertainty of one's tenure once on the bench, and the paucity of pecuniary rewards from work as a judge—all conspire to place judges in a position structurally conducive to deviance.

In courts in which judges are called on to appoint lawyers to administer an

3. File 50–114, Chicago Bar Association, Chicago; Transcripts, 5 October 1950, 26 October 1950, 2 November 1950, 8 November 1950.

estate or to act as trustees or receivers, the problem is pronounced. Although an errant judge might not handle such a matter himself, he can pass it on to deserving friends and family members who may then in turn channel some of the rewards back to the original benefactor.

> In the early 1950s two Chicago newspapers alleged that Judge Peter O'Brien had passed largess on to his relatives and that he had receiverships pending in his court in which his family had financial interests. The matter was initially taken up by the CBA. But with the news that the Illinois legislature was to undertake impeachment hearings against O'Brien, the CBA offered its services and assistance to the government committee and passed the initiative to it. Nonetheless there was a strong sense within the bar that a political committee acting on the case of a politically appointed judge would produce a "whitewash." For that reason, the CBA asked to be given all the transcripts of the House Judiciary Committee, it had an unidentified observer sit in the House proceedings, and it threatened to take up the case on its own if the House inquiry failed to do so adequately. The CBA presumably must have been satisfied with the ultimate disposition of the case because it did not appear again in its files.[4]

Whereas the bar association held itself in reserve during the House impeachment hearings, in other cases the entire responsibility for investigation and sanctioning devolved on the CBA—or was seized by it.

> Judge Patmos, alleged the *Daily News,* had found a novel way to supplement his income by fining $100 the mostly poor and black people who came before him and then, some days later, remitting the fine, giving most of it back to those he had convicted—except that, in a number of cases, the individuals originally fined had not been informed of the remission. Someone else had appropriated the fines.
>   Judge Patmos asked the CBA to investigate the allegations. The CBA appointed a special committee which undertook a thorough examination of court records and interviewed various court personnel, in the process uncovering even more "difficulties." Faced with censure, Patmos retained one of Chicago's leading trial lawyers to rebut the critical report produced by the committee. After a series of meetings between Patmos, his counsel and the committee, the CBA Board voted to inform the chief judge of the municipal court and the clerk in charge of lower court personnel that Patmos had acted improperly and that he would be censured publicly through the press.[5]

A court with a high turnover in cases provides one set of opportunities for judicial misdemeanors; but courts in which appointments of receivers and trust-

---

4. File 52–62; Transcripts, 24 April 1952, 17 July 1952, 28 August 1952.
5. File 50–101A; Transcripts, 24 August 1950, 7 September 1950, 14 December 1950, 21 December 1950, 28 December 1950, 19 April 1951, 10 May 1951, 15 June 1951.

ees offer other opportunities of unethical practice, such as smaller suburban and county courts, have problems of their own of a somewhat different nature. Before the 1964 judicial article went into effect, lawyers often acted as part-time judges or magistrates. Sometimes they were even seconded onto the bench in a full-time capacity for a limited period. In both cases, these lawyers-cum-judges on occasion were alleged to have a conflict of interest. Again, given the relative anonymity of court proceedings and the limits of higher court control, abuses might easily go undetected and, if detected, unchecked. The controls available to the profession are reflected in the case of an apparently unwitting conflict of interest in a Chicago suburban court.

> An Evanston attorney, George Arthur, wrote to the CBA complaining that he was handling the defense of a case before Judge Gordon Smythe whose firm was representing the complainant. Applying three criteria—legislative prohibitions, court decisions, and the Canons of Judicial Ethics—the CBA ruled that Judge Smythe was doing nothing illegal but that the conflict of interest was in violation of public policy and the bar canons. Because Judge Smythe's conflict was unwitting, and he gave a commitment to the CBA that he would take certain steps to see that it would not recur, the CBA Board agreed that he could stay on the bench until his term ended.[6]

Whereas each of the preceding three cases illustrates an economic conflict of interest or a chance to make some pecuniary gain at the expense of litigants, in systems of judicial appointment through election judges can also confront political conflicts of interest every bit as severe as economic conflicts. The entire system of de facto political appointments to the bench in jurisdictions in which the judiciary is controlled by a political machine inevitably leads to undercurrents of tension between the bench and some segments of the bar. In Chicago some of the more blatant blurrings of the distinction between political influence and the rule of law were addressed in the Canons of Judicial Ethics—indeed those very canons that had provoked the most controversy during the implementation debate concerned the uneasy juxtaposition of politics and judging. Yet despite the fact that the Judicial Conference and the bar association adopted significantly different "political canons," the bar continued to adhere to its own normative code. Where judicial behavior departs from the normative standards set for the bench by the bar, the profession may still proceed to exercise its jurisdiction without the "consent" of the judiciary. Its action is thus completely unilateral—although it still falls within the general conditions of the normative economy I have been elaborating.

In practice the need for judges to raise funds in their campaigns for judicial

6. File 60–31; Transcripts, 22 December 1960, 7 December 1961.

office or reelection leaves open numerous loopholes for abuse. If judges can allow their court personnel to take up contributions from lawyers practicing in their courts, then the potential for corruption multiplies. Even if judges use less aggressive methods, such as the formation of bar committees to solicit contributions from lawyers for their favored candidates, attorneys can find themselves in an awkward position. As a Chicago lawyer wrote to the CBA:

> During the present campaign, scores of "volunteer" committees have appeared on the scene in behalf of practically all of the candidates and, particularly, in behalf of the sitting judges seeking re-election; they have bombarded the members of the bar with requests for contributions, or at least for the purchase of "cocktail party" tickets for parties to "honor" this or that judicial candidate. There have been three or four "parties" each week, almost all of them having the objective of raising funds. It strikes me as the apex of naivete to assume that the organizers of these committees, or the proponents of these candidacies, are motivated entirely by unselfish considerations.
>
> The lawyer who does not join some of these committees, and who does not buy tickets from court clerks and bailiffs, nor make donations to campaign funds, must be conscious of the fact that the successful judicial candidate must necessarily feel an obligation to those who have helped him materially. Almost subconsciously the judge remembers that lawyer Jones, now appearing before him, has contributed or has prevailed upon others to contribute funds for his election.
>
> . . . Is there nothing that the bar association can do to stop this costly and noisome nuisance?

A number of CBA committees took up the problem and the general issue of the limitations of public credibility in a bench dominated by a political machine that forced its judges to curry popular favor. After advice from its committees, which in turn had consulted the Canons of Judicial Ethics, the Canons of Professional Ethics, and the opinions of the American Bar Association Committee on Professional Ethics, the CBA board recommended, first, that an addition be made to the bar Canons of Judicial Ethics proscribing solicitation by clerks or bailiffs; second, that the two main bar associations in the state meet with the Judicial Conference to effect some changes in their canons; and, third, that the president of the CBA should approach political leaders and ask them to refrain from imposing assessments on judges running unopposed for reelection against their own records. The president also was given some discretion in using the press to add pressure on politicians, should it be necessary.[7]

The implementation of the Canons of Judicial Ethics therefore represented a middle path between, on the one hand, the radical change that the proposed CBA

7. File 63–20; Transcripts, 11 October 1962, 4 April 1963, 22 June 1964.

judicial article would have had on the abolition of judicial elections and, on the other hand, complete resignation by the profession to all the abuses that appeared to accompany a politicized judiciary. In themselves the revisions to the canons added little but a more explicit standard by which professional monitoring of the bench might be gauged. Moreover, the new canons did more than alert judges to a new area where professional vigilance might be exercised; they also provided a formal statement judges themselves could use to balance pressures on them to raise money and wage campaigns by political parties.

I have shown that professional control of the judiciary can extend from review of judges' demeanor in the courtroom to economic and political conflicts of interest, whether or not they occur in court. In extreme cases, however, bar surveillance of the judiciary can extend further still. For instance, the CBA Canons of Judicial Ethics, developed without the authority of the bench, mandated a critical role for the profession even in excess of its overview of judicial performance. Canon 4, "Avoidance of Impropriety," read: "A judge's official conduct should be free from impropriety and the appearance of impropriety; he should avoid infractions of law; and his personal behavior, not only upon the Bench and in the performance of judicial duties, but also in his everyday life should be beyond reproach."

Effectively, this canon gave the bar association license to intervene in the private life of a judge in those circumstances in which the bar could demonstrate that a judge's actions might bring disrepute to the bench. A most dramatic example of this level of intervention occurred in Chicago with a former presiding judge of the municipal court.

> In November 1964 the CBA president received a letter from a presiding judge indicating that he was to conduct a hearing on his former superior. Because of the delicacy of the situation, the presiding judge requested that the CBA appoint an unidentified observer to sit in the court. The two CBA representatives subsequently reported to the Board that the judge on trial, and his three friends, had entered a tavern in the early hours of September 22. They got into an argument with other patrons over the relative merits of Goldwater and Johnson, and, as they left the inn one hour and five rounds of Scotch later, became involved in a scuffle with Goldwater adherents. One of the Goldwater supporters pulled a gun. Tomas, the judge, struck him, the man fell, suffered extensive head injuries, and died forty minutes later.
>
> The judge in the preliminary hearing concluded that Judge Tomas should stand trial for manslaughter. The Cook County Grand Jury, however, voted not to indict him and the Chief Judge of Circuit Court referred the entire matter to the Illinois Courts Commission, which in its turn ruled that the evidence warranted no further action.
>
> The CBA accepted the ruling that Tomas was not guilty of a crime

but took up the case on the grounds that Tomas had violated numerous canons of judicial ethics. After its investigation and interviews with Judge Tomas, who retained counsel for the hearings before the CBA Committee, the Judiciary Committee and the Board each divided on whether to issue a private censure or a public disclosure of Tomas' failure to meet the prescribed standards of judicial conduct. Two and one-half years after the original incident, the Board confirmed the majority report of the Judiciary Committee and issued a private censure.[8]

Besides the conspicuous disjunction between the punishment and the "crime," this last case underlines more vividly the general proposition that the bar's contribution to the monitoring of judicial demeanor can and does far exceed the bounds of narrow technical service. Within a geographic jurisdiction roughly coterminous with the drawing area of the bar association membership, the organized bar may intervene not only in the activities of any lawyer but also in the affairs of any state judge. It is also clear that the foundations for the scale of intervention exist not entirely in a statutory or judicial mandate but in convention, not merely by delegated state powers but through the negotiative strategies of the organized bar.

Despite the potential breadth of bar efforts at judicial control, how effective are the profession's self-designated powers of review? The evidence indicates that the bar is taken seriously indeed, not only by the judiciary, but also by several other interested groups. The association often requested and received reports and records of prior investigations undertaken by civic groups, crime commissions, and other watch-dog groups. It could obtain transcripts of government committees or commissions, although on occasion access was denied. Lawyers had access to vital court records; in the case of Judge Patmos, for instance, three attorneys searched all entries—a total of 25,000—on the motion sheets of a court for an entire year.

Furthermore, judges and their court personnel responded with alacrity to requests from the CBA for interviews. While the CBA did not possess subpoena power to enforce attendance at its hearings, rarely did a judge refuse to attend. With him could come court personnel of all ranks and even prosecuting counsel. But perhaps the most significant indicator of the significance some judges attached to the bar inquiries was in the retention of the counsel: in at least one case, a judge hired one of the most distinguished—and expensive—attorneys in the city.

Whether in response to a request from the CBA or in anticipation of its in-

8. File 64–124; Transcripts, 8 December 1966, 2 February 1967, 9 February 1967.

quiry, judges investigated by the association regularly took steps to alter the offending behavior. In addition, some but not all alleged offenders stepped down from the bench during the course of the CBA inquiry. And, finally, the seriousness ascribed to CBA intervention in the courts was reflected in the general display of deference to the association by judges called to task by it. In only one instance did a judge completely defy the CBA; almost automatically the organization took his defiance as an admission of guilt, and it administered a severe public rebuke.

The influence of the bar in establishing a lower threshold of judicial demeanor derives in part from its skillful deployment of a range of informal sanctions. What sanctions does the bar have to administer? First, whether it does so intentionally or not, the professional association can make use of the ambiguities inherent in the authority with which it is endowed to discipline lawyers. The CBA often approached a judge against whom a complaint had been laid, without specifying whether the standards against which the offense had been committed were legal—that is, in violation of the lawyers' code of ethics—or moral. The ambivalence this produces for the judge anxious to avoid any legal proceedings will incline him to comply with bar inquiries as long as he is in doubt about the sanctions that could be attached to his noncompliance. But the ambiguity between legal and moral authority does not explain entirely the compliance of judges. Even after the 1964 judicial article clarified the limits of CBA legal powers over judges qua judges, limiting its powers almost entirely, judges still deferred to bar inquiries.

In part, explanation of this deference must depend on a second sanction. The bar association can privately and publicly humiliate a judge. In most bar activities, the judges who are present receive considerable deference, especially from those lawyers who practice in their courts. At times, CBA committee records reveal that obsequiousness degenerated into scarcely concealed ingratiation. For a judge, and perhaps more so for one who is not a member of an association, the request to appear as a "defendant" in a private hearing of the bar may be as humiliating as the tongue lashings occasionally administered to lawyers by judges in the courtroom. In the informal "trials" held by the bar, the word of a judge is tested against the word of his court subordinates—clerks, bailiffs, court reporters, and others. The humiliation of a trial may be compounded, in turn, by a finding against the judge. Even when the censure is to be private, the CBA usually notified the chief judge of the relevant court of the investigation and of its findings. But of course a professional association also has access to the press, through which it may administer a public rebuke. Quite apart from the indignity this imposes, the adverse publicity, in an electoral system resting heavily on positive publicity as a condition of re-election, may undermine or destroy an entire judicial career. Ultimately, then, much of a professional association's capacity to extend its moral authority in the primary institutional sphere depends on the sanctions that the profession can impose by virtue of its involvement in a form of judicial appointment that many of the very same associations are endeavoring to abolish. This leads us to the third and most potent sanction a bar association has in an electoral judicial system.

ADMISSION TO THE BENCH

Between the two extremes of judicial control—constitutional revision and occasional discipline—stands the middle ground of judicial evaluation. If the bar cannot transform the system, yet remains dissatisfied with a minimal role in judicial control, then its best alternative appears to be to work within the electoral process. The long-standing approach adopted by many American bar associations has been to exert influence over the quality of judges slated by the parties and elected by the voters.

The evolution of judicial evaluation was noted briefly in chapter 3 and has been treated thoroughly by Martin's account of the bar and judicial elections from 1874 until 1930.[9] The general trend in bar polls has been to increase the degree of evaluation in proportion to the growth in the numbers—and relative anonymity—of judges standing for election. From 1906 the bar association's Candidates Committee began to prepare evaluations of each candidate standing for the bench. From the 1930s, in addition to a biography of each candidate, lawyers were asked to respond to a series of questions on judicial nominees that considered their legal abilities, personal characteristics, and general reputation within the bar. Periodically in the interwar years the CBA also tried to match the electoral power of the political parties with its own public campaigns to have elected the candidates it considered most suitable, but it did so with indifferent success.

After 1950, the CBA withdrew completely from public campaigns in judicial elections. Still using the bar poll, it directed its efforts at the party slate-making apparatus. If a private organization could not compete with the political organization in the open market of getting votes, then it seemed much more sensible to direct most effort to the early stages of the nomination process, during which private consultations would be more efficacious than public confrontation. Nevertheless, the intrusion of the bar association into judicial slate making was not

9. The history of the CBA and its involvement in judicial polls until 1932 is contained in Edward M. Martin, *The Role of the Bar in Electing the Bench in Chicago* (Chicago: University of Chicago Press, 1936).

always welcomed; and even when it was acknowledged, it formed no part of the formal process of judicial selection.

Each political party in the county allowed its judicial convention—in fact, the county central committees—to make a decision on the slate of nominees forwarded to it by its nominating subcommittee, a body carefully designed to reflect diverse sections within the party.[10] The orderly facade of the formal process, however, disguised a highly volatile and more complex set of procedures, a process into which the CBA was able to inject its judgments. Each year numerous ethnic, religious, and community groups confronted the committee with convincing reasons why a favorite son should be nominated as "their representative" on the judiciary. Each group could point to its past history of representation—or lack of it. It could argue that a ballot with their candidate on it would be politically appealing to the community or group they represented. It could guarantee strenuous efforts to get out the vote for a ballot to which its members were personally committed. It might even offer the inducement of a sizable campaign contribution to underline their sincerity—a commitment that could run as high as $25,000. Besides pressure groups, the party itself had certain lawyers it wished to reward for able service on its behalf. It also needed to balance its "political" candidates with two categories of "nonpolitical" nominees. Good public relations dictated that each year several prestige or high-status candidates would catch the public eye and so demonstrate the quality of political decision making to the public. And the high degree of ethnic consciousness in the city compelled the Democratic party to present ethnic lawyers with high public visibility, even though those attorneys might have contributed relatively less time in service of the party organization. Moreover, candidates had to be molded for the kinds of constituencies they were to run in. Candidates running in absolutely safe elections would likely differ from those who faced stiff competition or those who were running hopeless races.

Election of New Judges

After 1950, both Republicans and Democrats agreed that potential candidates for the bench would first be screened by the CBA for fitness as judges. Names from the parties went directly to the executive director of the CBA, then to its Candidates Committee. In composition, the CBA committee bore certain resemblances to the parallel nominating committees of the parties. Besides the presence of dis-

10. A detailed account of the process of judicial selection in Cook County is contained in Wesley G. Skogan, "Party and Constituency in Political Recruitment: The Case of the Judiciary in Cook County, Illinois" (Ph.D. diss., Northwestern University, 1971).

tinguished CBA members, including a number of past presidents and members of
the Board of Managers, the committee drew on trial lawyers from a broad spectrum of legal specialties and political convictions—a microcosm of the Chicago
electorate. Final judgments rested with the board. To facilitate continuity between the committee and the CBA leadership, several members of the current
board, most notably the president and the executive secretary, sat with the committee. Together they constituted a range of lawyers—and judges—sufficiently
diverse that several attorneys in the selection process would have had some personal experience with at least one of the vast number of candidates.[11]

Each lawyer standing for judicial office received from the committee an extensive questionnaire on a wide range of topics: details of age, birthplace, education, date of admission to the bar, and history of legal practice; information on
the number of jury and nonjury cases tried by the candidate, together with the
courts and areas of law in which he tried them; and lists of public offices, membership in professional associations, special achievements and recognitions, and
miscellany—such as articles in bar journals—that might add further strength to
a candidate's case. Matters of legal ability and personal attributes could be further explored by contact with referees—among them a mandatory list of five,
and later ten, opposing counsel. Matters of integrity elicited a searching batch of
questions: "Have you ever been a party to, or otherwise personally involved in,
legal proceedings of any kind? Have you ever sued or been sued by a client of
yours? Have you ever been disciplined by any court or administrative agency?
Has your professional or judicial conduct been the subject of complaint at any
time before any Bar Association committee or public officer? Have you ever appeared before any grand jury or been interviewed by any investigating, prosecuting or law enforcement agency?"

Supplemented by informal inquiries, data from prior screenings, and inspection of CBA files on complaints against lawyers, the responses from the
questionnaire provided the agenda for a candidate's interview before the committee. Because a candidate's demeanor might provide a clue as to his or her
performance on the bench, impressions on personalities and maturity formed a
significant component in the committee's final judgment, especially in the realm
of judicial temperament. On one occasion the committee even bluntly cross-
examined a candidate to the point of provocation to confirm for itself reports that
he had a quick temper—an opinion sustained by his increasingly angry rejoin-
ders. Interviewers pointedly probed into areas of weakness in a candidate's legal

---

11. I am indebted to John McBride, executive director of the CBA, for his comments on the
changing processes of judicial evaluation by the CBA over recent years.

experience, as when an attorney had brushed with a CBA disciplinary committee or with some other legal agency. In fact, to consolidate the linkage between judicial demeanor and admission to the bench, the chairman of the Judiciary Committee, which handled breaches of judicial ethics, sat with the Candidates Committee. Votes of either qualified or not qualified required a two-thirds majority of the approximately twenty-five-member committee. After 1962, the qualifications scale, which in the past had sometimes had many more fine gradations, was reduced to three categories: qualified, not qualified, and a nonfinding—a residual category utilized when a two-thirds majority could not be mustered either for or against a candidate. With its vote, and a short biography, names were forwarded to the board for confirmation.

After the first board decision on those candidates to be found qualified for slating, candidates turned down by the CBA had opportunities to appeal the verdict to the Candidates Committee or, in some circumstances, before the board itself. Not every candidate requested a rehearing; not every candidate who did had the request granted. Few managed to reverse the initial CBA judgment.

CBA screenings and evaluations were succeeded by the bar poll. Every member of the association received a booklet describing the candidates, the CBA's recommendations, and a ballot. While the content of the poll has changed in minor respects over several decades, the basic questions remain very similar. "Have you had any personal contact with him/her? Does he/she possess legal ability? Has he/she a judicial temperament? Is his/her reputation at the bar good? Do you have confidence in his/her integrity?" Results, tabulated by the Canvassing Committee, came to the board for its final judgment. Before 1962, results of the poll had only an advisory status; the board might heed or ignore them. After 1962, results were binding; candidates not getting a majority on the question "Is he/she qualified?" were automatically dropped.

The number and proportion of candidates who did not receive the association approval varied from year to year and from one court to another. On the face of it, one might expect that the quality of candidates—and therefore the proportion of CBA endorsements—would vary in direct relation to the standing of a court so that higher courts would attract better lawyers. Yet the CBA applied more stringent criteria to higher court aspirants. Although the association has not maintained accurate records on the proportion of lawyers approved in each election, the contrast of higher- and lower-court evaluations does not reveal any clear pattern. For the Supreme Court election of 1951, only nine out of thirteen candidates were approved; that same year a much lower proportion—seventy-two out of 120 candidates—received CBA support for the circuit court elections. In 1968, the only other year that the committee reported comparative statistics, 145

out of 192 candidates were found qualified for the circuit court. As great a proportion of higher-court as lower-court candidates could receive recognition. On
the average, however, not more than one-third of the candidates had their aspirations denied.

When CBA lists of approved candidates were completed, recommendations
were passed on to the Democratic and Republican parties; the party leadership
was explicitly requested to honor the judgments of the organized bar. Commitments that the parties would not slate candidates judged unqualified by the bar
had been received from politicians since the 1940s. But they were not always
honored. In 1952, party leaders confirmed that they would maintain their prior
agreement not to slate unqualified attorneys, only to breach that commitment
when they entered a contender on the Democratic ticket who had been found not
qualified by the CBA. On the other hand, in 1953 the CBA informed the parties
that five persons running for reelection did not have the confidence of the bar. In
deference to the questionnaire results, which informed the committee's publicized judgments, all five judges were dropped. These two elections epitomized
the shifting sands of the bar and party agreements. In some elections commitments would be recognized and sustained by political leaders; in other elections
political contingencies or personal commitments outweighed even public an-
nouncements of party compliance with bar decisions. Whatever the particular
case, however, the political parties, for a variety of reasons, have usually given
the organized bar an informal, and usually binding, extralegal role in the judicial
selection process—a tenuous agreement unlikely to be readily abused by either
the bar or the parties.[12]

12. An indication of developments after our period, as well as the extensive efforts made by
the organized bar in judicial evaluation, is provided in a thorough and informative overview of
CBA procedures in 1982. Because it encapsulates many of the themes developed here, I quote it
extensively:

   Fashioned by resolution of the Board of Managers of the Chicago Bar Association,
   the present form of the Committee on the Evaluation of Candidates was initiated in
   1976–1977, the result of extensive research and analysis of the attributes and qualities
   required of a judge. Certain procedures and criteria had been developed to identify
   those qualities most desirable for each present and potential member of the judiciary.

   The Committee on the Evaluation of Candidates consists of 150 Chicago Bar Association members divided into two divisions. The Investigation Division is made up of
   eighty attorneys who comprise forty teams of two. These teams are assigned the files
   of the individual attorneys or judges to be screened. A file may include only the
   twenty-page application and questionnaire submitted by a new candidate for judge, or
   it may include several lengthy new and old applications and questionnaires of sitting
   judges, along with reports of prior investigation teams, comments of court watchers,
   clippings from newspapers, and letters from interested parties. This file serves as the
   basis for further research and development by the investigative team.

   Most of the investigative work is done on the telephone to verify the information in
   the file. On occasion, however, the candidate is personally interviewed and observed

Reelection of Sitting Judges

The screening process of judges standing for reelection—for retention—differed only slightly from that for new candidates. Lawyers were asked to rate the sitting judges on a set of more specific criteria: technical qualifications (Does he possess legal ability?); work habits (Does he open court promptly? Is he diligent in the dispatch of business?); temperament (Is he attentive and fairminded?); and character traits (Do you have confidence in his integrity?). The committee went even further, in 1966, when the chairman enlisted the services of the Younger Members Committee to study every decision appealed from judges who came up for reelection. Results were tabulated, added to a file that included references, press clippings, and adverse publicity concerning any complaints recorded with the

---

in the court room. The investigative team follows up leads on particular aspects of an individual's life which may not be fully described in the file.

From this research the investigators prepare a written report. Investigators are asked to comment on certain specific qualities and are encouraged to add other facts and impressions gleaned from their work. The investigators' written and verbal reports are presented to a panel of the Hearing Division for its review.

The Hearing Division includes seventy members of the Committee, none of whom are investigators although most have served as investigators in prior years. The members of the Hearing Division meet as evaluation panels in the early evening several times per week during the judicial evaluation seasons. These seasons precede the slating of candidates, the general elections for contested positions, and the retention balloting. Two Hearing Division panels are assembled in separate meeting rooms where, during the course of an evening, each panel will evaluate several candidates. Since all members of the Hearing Division are urged to attend these meetings and to serve on a panel, there are at least fifteen, and often as many as thirty, members on each panel.

An officer of the Committee on the Evaluation of Candidates is usually designated to chair a Hearing Panel. The selection of the particular meeting room and the particular Hearing Panel is done by lot. Thus never have two panels had identical membership, and each evening session of meeting and evaluating judicial candidates is an original endeavor. In the course of an evening, a Hearing panel may conduct as many as five hearings.

Immediately before each session, the members of the Hearing Panel are given copies of the pertinent portion of the completed questionnaire of each candidate who will appear before them that evening, the report of the investigative teams assigned to each candidate's file, and any other important material. After a review period, the team that investigated the next candidate is invited to share with the Panel any comments which may not appear in the written report. The investigators are questioned on their report before the candidate makes a personal appearance.

The candidate then meets the Hearing panel. At that time he or she is questioned extensively by the Chairman and other members of the Hearing Panel about experience, background and ambitions. These questions flow through all areas which panel members feel are relevant to the evaluation of each candidate's qualifications to serve as judge in a particular court. As a result, the questioning process is different for each candidate.

CBA's Judiciary Committee, and included with the answers to a questionnaire administered to the judge. The CBA retained the right, which it occasionally exercised, to request a confidential medical report on the health of judges who were older or had a health problem. Judges then appeared before the committee to explain any questionable events unearthed in the CBA investigation. The committee exercised special vigilance over health, any notorious actions in which a judge might have been involved, any contempt citations he might have issued to lawyers, and any kind of cantankerous or capricious mannerisms. After the committee voted on a judge's qualifications, its recommendations went to the board for confirmation, together with draft biographies for the second bar poll. Before implementation of the judicial article, the poll took the form of a bar primary. Paired Republican and Democratic judges ran against each other for CBA sup-

---

After a reasonable period of give-and-take between the candidate and the Hearing Panel, the candidate is permitted to make a statement or comment concerning his or her candidacy. The candidate is excused and a full discussion of the candidate's qualifications is held. The investigators, who have been present throughout and who often participate during the questioning of the candidate, join in the discussion. When all Hearing Panel members are satisfied that the candidate has been thoroughly considered, the ballots are cast.

The final evaluation of a candidate is made by all of the Committee members who participated in the hearing process. Each member is asked to vote, by secret ballot, on whether a candidate is "Highly Recommended," "Recommended," or "Not Recommended" for judicial election or retention. All ballots are tabulated by the Hearing Panel Chairman after the conclusion of all hearings for an evening. The combined scores create a composite evaluation in one of the three categories. Regardless of ranking within a category, the tabulations are then given to the President of the Chicago Bar Association, to the General Chairman of the Committee on Evaluation of Candidates and to the candidate as "Highly Recommended," "Recommended," or "Not Recommended."

In the process, literally tens of thousands of hours are spent every year by volunteer attorneys. The investigative process for each candidate takes a minimum of twenty hours. The Hearing Panels of twenty or thirty lawyers spend an average of forty-five to sixty minutes to complete the review of each candidate. This is a big job. If it were not so very important there might not be so many individuals willing to give their time to it.

For instance, from August, 1981, to June, 1982, the Committee on the Evaluation of Candidates screened 258 candidates for judicial office. In numbers this is the same as having one candidate for each of two-thirds of the existing judicial positions now held in Cook County. These screenings included twenty-three candidates for the position of Judge of the United States District Court; seventy-two candidates for the contested elections for the Circuit Court of Cook County and the Illinois Appellate Court; seventy-eight candidates for the positions of Associate Judge of the Circuit Court of Cook County; and most, recently, seventy-seven sitting judges seeking retention as Judges of the Circuit Court of Cook County or Judges of the Illinois Appellate Court in the November, 1982, general elections.

(Paul C. Kimball, Jr., "Footnotes and Dicta," *Chicago Bar Record* 64 [July/August 1982]: 6–9.)

port. With the abolition of contested elections for sitting judges, ballots went out to CBA members with only one question. Should Judge _____ be retained?

After 1962 the results had more than an advisory significance. The CBA announced that it would accept its members' verdict even if the Candidates Committee or the board was reversed—and occasionally they were. Results of the poll went to the parties and the press, which then as now publicized in its headlines the disqualification of sitting judges. The CBA consistently rejected one or two lower-court judges in each election. Thirteen out of fifteen circuit court judges were recommended for reelection in 1951; ten out of twelve received recommendations in the 1957 municipal court election; all but one—who withdrew—were approved for the 1960 municipal court election, although only nine out of twelve had their bids for retention approved in that same court the following year. Seventeen out of nineteen circuit court judges and seven out of twelve associate judges standing for reelection in 1968 gained a sufficient degree of support in the CBA poll. Responsiveness of the parties to these judgments was as uneven for sitting judges as it was for new candidates. The five judges the CBA recommended be removed as candidates in the 1953 superior court election were dropped, as were the three municipal court judges found unqualified in 1961. But six out of eight judges whom the CBA rejected for retention in 1964 were elected.

AGENTS FOR JUDICIAL CONTROL

A system in which judges are elected to office therefore provides the most efficacious sanction available to the profession. Yet in a city dominated by a long-standing political machine, CBA sponsorship, one would think, could be safely snubbed by politically secure judges. But for reasons of their own, political leaders of both parties came to more or less informal agreements with the bar that they would slate only candidates whose qualifications had been approved by the bar association. Of course, in practice, parties could afford to ignore bar recommendations on particular candidates and still have that candidate elected by a healthy majority. But most individual candidates could not be sure that they were sufficiently valuable to the party to warrant a repudiation of the bar's judgment of "unqualified." Indeed, one senior judge of the federal court pointed out that Mayor Daley had occasionally used the bar association as a means of acquitting his political loyalties to a precinct captain or ward committeeman without placing that person on the bench. The mayor would assure an ambitious ward committeeman of complete support. If the bar association found him unqualified, however, then the mayor, so he would say to the candidate, could scarcely retract his public commitment to the legal profession. The mayor made political capital in every way: if he did not want a candidate, he could get rid of him without any personal offense; if he did want a candidate badly enough, he might ignore the findings of the bar association.

Except for a very small number of Mayor Daley's close associates, however, individual judicial candidates could not guarantee their election if the CBA ruled against them. Uncertainty again placed nominees in a position of vulnerability. They generally responded to the aura of doubt by removing every impediment to nomination. Being assured a "qualified" rating by the bar association thus became a matter of considerable importance. Because demeanor on the bench, judicial temperament, and other qualities became the criteria on which lawyers judged judicial candidates, adverse reports of misdemeanors in a candidate's file might weigh against him. Most judges who intended to stand for reelection therefore tried to make sure that their files were unencumbered by censures of any sort. Consequently, when the bar association initiated an inquiry about a judge, most judges became paragons of cooperation, while at the same time mounting as persuasive a defense as they could muster.

With these sanctions it is clear that the organized bar can supplement modes of control internal to the judiciary with a number of cumulatively reinforcing moral codes. In a system of judicial control in which legislative impeachment and judicial peer review are the only modes of judicial discipline, judicial control is effectively in default. With these normative systems alone, there remains a moral no-man's-land in which judges can stray with little risk of apprehension. The legal profession may occupy the vacant sphere by providing its own interlocking matrix of controls. The CBA and the American Bar Association Canons of Professional Ethics, together with the "case law" that has emerged from each system of ethics, provide ethical bases on which to judge the judges insofar as their behavior can be sanctioned under ethical standards applicable to the legal profession. Alongside the ethical code for lawyers, the profession has added its own Canons of Judicial Ethics. These in turn have been specified and elaborated by the few cases of judicial misdemeanor available in the collective experience of bar association decision makers. Within the interstices of judicial self-regulation and legislative impeachment, therefore, the bar associations inserted their own extensive codes and "common law"—a complex of American Bar Association opinions, CBA rulings, Supreme Court decisions, and informal bar precedents.

But while the self-appointed character of "bar law" may have detracted from total bar influence, it has also placed professional associations outside certain procedural strictures of Anglo-American law. If anything, bar freedom from the limits of procedural law actually increases its scope as an agent of judicial control in numerous respects. First, the bar associations can act as *independent* agents of control. They do not require the initiative of other organizations; they can and do act autonomously without any externally derived mandate. Their very independence from law in judicial disciplinary proceedings allows them to set their own rules of procedure—to dispense with the minutiae of due process and the usual conventions of trial. The latter inform bar procedures but do not confine them. Consequently, no evidence is necessarily inadmissible. The straitjacket of formal justice yields to the demands of substantive expediency.

But not all bar association judicial cases followed the inexorable succession of self-initiation, internal investigation, and "sentencing." The bar also acts in a more circumscribed capacity as an *intermediary* agent. The legal associations may commence actions, gather evidence, and make preliminary findings. If the judge appears culpable under law, the organized bar can present a relevant formal body, such as the Supreme Court, the Courts Commission, or the Judicial Inquiry Board, with the facts it has collected. In such cases the association may prod the responsible agency to a degree of activism it would otherwise avoid. Occasionally, the organized bar takes a *complementary* and *advisory* stance. In the cases of Judge O'Brien, for instance, it turned over its information to the legislative committee. The members of that committee, in turn, requested CBA advice on the line of questioning and procedures that would be appropriate.

It is, however, the fourth form of agency that is of most significance in bar efforts at judicial control. The professional associations act not just as complementary but as *successive* agents of control. Their independence from procedural limitations enables the organized bar to try a judge twice for the one offense. Whatever the outcome of a hearing before a court of law or a judicial disciplinary body, the profession retains the right subsequently to conduct its own private trial. The judge, like a lawyer falling awry of the law, may advance from acquittal in the state courts to trial in collegial courts. The professional normative system therefore places the judges in a position of normative double jeopardy. The private courts of the profession effectively parallel the public courts of the state. In so doing, the profession fills some of the vacuums of normative control that might permit an autonomous judiciary a freedom from accountability, threatening both the administration of justice and the legal profession.

Nevertheless, the case for professional normative control should not be overstated. The number of cases appearing before the Judiciary Committee over the twenty-year period was very small indeed. Of the hundreds of judges on the bench between 1950 and 1970, the proportion appearing before the CBA was extremely low. Although no adequate statistics have been kept, in most years it appears that less than half a dozen cases came before the Judiciary Committee. Fewer reached the board. Even for those few cases that did come to the attention of the CBA, the organized bar was extremely cautious about making decisions.

Its investigations were painstaking; its "trials" were protracted; and even when a judge was found guilty, the bar leadership was very reluctant to administer severe public sanctions. Further, its effectiveness in judicial screening has always been in some dispute. The most pointed and informed criticism has come from the Chicago Council of Lawyers, the breakaway organization of younger and more liberal lawyers who believe that the mild evaluations given judicial candidates have fallen far short of even minimum standards for the bench.[13] The vast majority of judicial candidates in every election were approved by the CBA.[14]

Nevertheless, it can be argued that the effectiveness of the bar association can be gauged neither by the number of lawyers disciplined nor by the number rejected as judicial candidates. In both judicial monitoring and screening, a bar association can have a significant threshold effect. Even an occasional public rebuke of a judge, perhaps no more than two or three per year, can have a symbolic effect on the judiciary entirely out of all proportion to the number of judges disciplined.[15] One senior judge on the federal bench, who was also a former CBA board member, commented in an interview that, while it could not be measured, he believed the CBA had a valuable restraining effect on judges tempted to exploit their apparent autonomy on the bench. Again it can be argued that, even if bar standards were too low, the threat of bar association evaluation and the repeated rejection of some candidates at each judicial election were sufficient to encourage some modicum of responsibility and caution in the activities of pro-

13. See Michael Powell, "Anatomy of a Counter-bar Association: The Chicago Council of Lawyers," *American Bar Foundation Research Journal* 1979 (Summer): 501–42. The CCL criticism of the CBA has received support from such quarters as Chicago's caustic columnist, Mike Royko, who recently wrote before a judicial election that all the judges—except one—who were convicted and sentenced in the Greylord scandal (see n.14) had received "qualified" ratings by the CBA at some prior judicial election. "That's a feeble average," he said. "If lawyers who rate judges were horse players, they'd be broke by the third race" (Chicago Tribune, 5 November 1986, 3).

14. The 1985 "Greylord" scandal, which rocked the Chicago circuit courts, also points to the boundaries of organized bar activism and influence. In a 1985 speech before the CBA Judiciary Committee, the U.S. attorney, Anton Valukas, "sharply criticized" the legal profession for its failure to uncover and report a corrupt scheme by which several judges were bribed by lawyers and police officers over many years. For fourteen years, a presiding judge in the traffic court had fixed drunken driving cases and parking tickets in return for thousands of dollars of payoffs. Yet, Valukas charged, not a single lawyer had "voluntarily come forward to simply complain about . . . misconduct or corruption." (*Chicago Tribune,* 23 November 1985, 1, 4). However, the CBA anticipated the institutional criticism with its president's reminder that the CBA had called on the chief judge a year before Greylord broke "to appoint a Blue Ribbon Committee to inquire into the operation of the circuit court, especially the traffic court and other high volume courts" ("President's Page," *Chicago Bar Record* 66 [November/December 1984]: 126–29). In fact, the organized bar has not infrequently found that it could get action on its judiciary reform programs only when public outcry demands change after well-publicized judicial scandals.

15. In an entirely different setting, but not so very dissimilar social process, compare miscreant judges with Puritan deviants (Kai T. Erikson, *Wayward Puritans: A Study in the Sociology of Deviance* [New York: Wiley, 1966]).

spective judges. In the absence of such controls, however far they may fall below optimal standards, a bench already morally impugned, as periodic scandals rock the Chicago judiciary, would have given much greater cause for a drop in the standing of the courts and the legitimacy of the law. Unfortunately, this argument can be made only rhetorically because it is effectively unfalsifiable. That is not, however, to deny its plausibility. Symbolic politics, trading on electoral uncertainty, can have an efficacy of their own—despite their incommensurability.[16]

The Politics of Affirmation

The data in the preceding section demonstrate the scope of professional attempts to exercise some moral and ethical controls over the judiciary. Almost half of all judicial matters considered by the board concerned either the review of judicial behavior or efforts to have some control over the process by which judges are appointed to the bench. Moreover it appears that, while much of the bar's role was more symbolic than real, it nevertheless did achieve some limited success despite the lack of any general warrant of legal authority for the steps it undertook. The substantial moral enterprise in which the bar association engaged therefore was a product of its own facility in constructing an economy that gave it sufficient symbolic income to expend resources on the politics of negativism. A one-handed policy of ethical proscription without either formal authority or some equivalent basis of influence would have been essentially oppositional and effectively counterproductive.

In lieu of formal authority from the legislature or the courts, a body of lawyers must consequently balance its efforts at institutional control with an affirmative program of positive contributions, principally of a technical nature, if it wishes to have any voice at all. Thus the adaptive upgrading of the judiciary proceeds through both normative controls and technical assistance; indeed, the former will be of consequence only when the latter reaches the level at which the bench must accept the scrutiny of the bar in order to also obtain the advantages a professional association may promise. The bench was placed in the debt of the bar because the lawyers maintained a steady level of activity in the courts in three main areas: first, the association dealt with between eight and twenty proposals a year to modify aspects of court rules or organization; second, each year an average of two, and sometimes as many as ten, initiatives were undertaken to improve the conditions of service of judges, such as salaries, tenure, and the like; and, third, the bar made episodic attempts to relieve the growing levels of congestion in Chicago courts. With its endeavors in these three areas of activity the organized bar

16. An influential discussion of symbolic politics of many kinds, though not precisely the kind discussed here, can be found in Murray Edelman, *The Symbolic Uses of Politics* (Urbana: University of Illinois Press, 1967).

demonstrated to the judiciary—albeit tangentially—the contingent relation between moral and expert influence. While the calculus between the two sides of the equation was quite imprecise and indeed seldom if ever considered explicitly in these terms, the effect was to set in motion a complex system of control and adaptation.

CONDITIONS OF JUDICIAL SERVICE

Canons of judicial ethics represent one of the most widely circulated and systematic prescriptions of judicial behavior. They give notice that deviation from norms imposed by the legal profession will invoke its disciplinary displeasure. In the absence of such a formal code or even after its formulation, many aspects of judicial life remain in ethically grey areas—especially in jurisdictions in which political patronage challenges the independence of the judiciary. Accordingly, individual judges who anticipate a course of action that might conceivably elicit professional or public criticism or who experience indecision about the meaning of canons will seek to reduce their uncertainty and risks. One means of doing so, of securing a degree of ethical certainty, is by adopting a professional association as a normative reference group to which judges might appeal for a ruling on a projected course of action. Professional support would thereby provide some *moral insurance* should the probity of acting in one or another way subsequently be called into question. In effect therefore individual judges could co-opt the professional association into a defense of an isolated or vulnerable bench. In a system in which judicial office and political status are blurred, the need for such insurance becomes more acute. This is nowhere better illustrated than in the relations of judges with the media.

> Before the implementation of the Code of Judicial Ethics in Chicago, a television station approached the CBA with a request to allow thirteen mock trials in the juvenile court to be televised. The station had also requested a judge with extensive experience in that court to act as an adjudicator, a judge with strong political connections to the Chicago Democratic Party. The CBA Board decided that as there were numerous benefits to be gained from such publicity in the juvenile courts, and as various precedents from the ABA Committee on Ethics did not exclude this kind of media attention, the programs could proceed and the judge could participate so long as all scripts were approved by the CBA beforehand.
>
> Although normally wary about the possibility that lawyers or judges could get undue publicity from the TV series, the CBA considered its controls adequate—until it learned from a Board member that rumors were beginning to circulate that the judge to appear on the program was likely to be slated by the Democrats for Governor. The CBA ran the risk, considered one Board member, of ap-

pearing that it had "nothing better to do than permit itself to become a tail on the kite of somebody's gubernatorial aspirations." With that, the Board decided that the program could not go ahead until it was ascertained that the judge would not be standing for public office.[17]

Despite the eventual twist in the case, however, the fact remains that a judge whose name was associated with the politics of a particular party—or any judge—felt that he could not act on his own volition to take part in a program without the prior permission of the professional association.

Request for guidance can also pertain to practices within the courts. On matters over which there is public debate or a sharp division of opinion and most pointedly on issues over which judges and lawyers might risk confrontation, it may behoove the cautious judge first to secure his or her grounds of action. The following instance has to do with an area particularly prone to conflict—the judge's authority to set the levels of fees lawyers may charge their clients in certain tort actions.

> After a judge had been criticized in the press and by lawyers for the ways he apportioned expenses in personal injury suits, he wrote to the CBA requesting a ruling on what an attorney should be able to charge in contingent fee cases. The judge asked (1) whether the usual 25 percent contingent fee ceiling was adequate in some sorts of cases; and (2) whether lawyers might claim extraordinary expenses for special purposes like hiring an investigator. The Board ruled that the Probate Court Rules were clear enough on the first point although there was some ambiguity over the situations in which 25 percent or 33 percent fees could be levied. Additional costs in running a law office should not be added to this fee, although an attorney could reasonably expect to be reimbursed for the costs of independent investigators or the need to take depositions outside Cook County.[18]

In this case, the judge sought immunity from any possible disciplinary sanctions from the bar, as he also defended himself from public criticism by using the bar as a shield. The device of using professional associations as *ethical guarantors* can be a strategy adopted far more widely than this episode implies. The bench perceives itself to be vulnerable to attack from the press because the inherent salaciousness of many cases handled in the courts, coupled with public appetite for exposés of corruption—especially in situations in which the principal actors should be models of rectitude—makes the judicial system a choice object for the

---

17. Transcripts, 7 February 1952; "Report of the Subcommittee of the Board of Managers Regarding Participation by Judge _____ in Television Program Relating to Juvenile Delinquency," File 52–27; Transcripts, 22 May 1952.

18. "Report of the CBA Committee on Professional Fees," Report 63–22, 14 February 1962; Transcripts, 28 February 1963, 17 December 1964.

publicists and consumers of scandal. Having an "independent" body available for moral protection, as was the CBA in its occasional scoldings of the press for their "scurrilous" attacks on the bench, aided a beleaguered bench unable directly to fend for itself.

The bar can also become the protector of the bench when judges nominated by political parties find themselves compromised by the demands of their nominators. In these circumstances, judges may welcome the opportunity to lean back on the moralistic argument that while they personally would be glad to accommodate a political request such a response is impossible because canons of judicial ethics, over which they have no control, and threats of professional discipline, equally beyond control, would preclude it—an argument that ironically reverses that used by politicians who in turn use the bar association to justify dropping candidates from the ballot. On both sides the professional association provides an alibi or, more accurately, absolves either party from responsibility for decisions they find difficult to make. Sometimes this justification for resisting political influence will be presented by an individual judge in a particular crisis; on other occasions the entire judiciary may seize on relief from political pressure that could compromise them all.

Political fund-raising offers an important case in point. A sensitivity to the ambiguities in the status of judge was reflected in the proposal by a board member that the canons of judicial ethics should be amended in order to limit the contributions by judges to political campaigns. According to this member, himself fully aware of the political exigencies of the situation,

> I think the judges deserve this, because most judges don't want to contribute to political campaigns and they are looking to the CBA to make a statement so that they can tell their ward committeeman they are not permitted to contribute. Looking at it from the point of view of the judges, they don't want to contribute, and they want something on which to hang their hats and tell this to the ward committeeman. If they do have this canon, they will be able to say, "Well, there is no opposition to me [in a reelection campaign] and I am barred from contributing to this political campaign." [19]

Of course, such a canon will have a direct pecuniary effect, reducing the financial outlay expected of judges who wish to remain on the bench. That should not divert us from the other implications, however, that moral demands of the bar can provide a countervailing force against the otherwise claustrophobic, continuing constraints on judges from their former political sponsors. [20]

19. Transcripts, 1 December 1955.

20. See, for instance, Transcripts, 29 March 1957, 17 May 1956, 12 September 1957, 24 October 1957.

If the bench needs defense from the press and political parties, it may expect even more vigorous action against a lawyer or group of lawyers directing certain kinds of criticism at individual judges or courts. Both forms of criticism can be greatly resented: judges believe they receive enough unearned abuse from nonprofessional quarters without also encountering it from their legal brethren and sisters. The offense may be all the greater when the attacks emerge from official bar publications.

> Two articles appeared in the *Chicago Bar Record* in 1955 strongly critical of the Illinois Supreme Court. One paragraph read: "The indiscriminate denial by the court of nearly one thousand petitions for writ of error unquestionably has relieved the court of a considerable amount of work. However, in the ruthless denial by the court of petitions, for writs of error, no rational criterion or *modus operandi* is discernible and the court's exercise of its discretion in this particular is such that the advisability of conferring more power upon the court may well be questioned." In the following article, the writer commented that a recent supreme court opinion was not in accord with the facts of the case and that it "overlooked or misapprehended" two doctrines.
>
> After some discussion on the extent to which the court should be free of criticism, the Board asked the *Record* editor to submit in future all doubtful articles to it for review and the president wrote an apology to the supreme court assuring its members that the language in the articles "does not represent the sentiment of our seven thousand members." [21]

The examples of bar activity on behalf of the judiciary that I have adduced thus far are essentially defensive in tone. They anticipate deviance by judges, and they shore up their defenses against assaults from within or outside the profession. More active advocacy of the judicial cause can take both intangible and tangible forms. Concomitant with its occasional acts to forestall the erosion of judicial respect through indiscriminate criticism, the profession can take steps to enhance judicial standing in other ways. One method is by the implementation of a system of honors. Accordingly, from before World War II the Illinois State Bar Association (ISBA) hosted annual dinners in honor of the state supreme court, and from time to time the associations held similar events in recognition of new judges elected to the local courts. Individuals with distinguished judicial records were singled out on the occasion of their retirement for a special luncheon or dinner with bar leaders. Other judges who were appointed to higher courts or who had advanced up a level in the court system were issued congratulations

---

21. Benjamin Wham, "Case Comment," *Chicago Bar Record* 37 (November 1955): 89; Transcripts, November 1955.

on behalf of the bar. Judges were also customarily invited to annual meetings. Through this range of courtesies and convivial gestures, the organized bar actively contrasts its role as critic of an errant judge with its deference to the prestige of an honorable judiciary. With an accretion of minor, but many positive, stimuli it thereby reinforces affirmatively the image of a judiciary that its negative evaluations suggest from the opposite vantage point.

Nonetheless, the intangible rewards of honor and deference go only so far to compensate for the tangible costs of a career on the bench. By taking a judicial position, it is almost always the case that the moderately successful lawyer will suffer a drastic cut in income—apart from the insecurity of the position itself—and many lawyers refuse to go to the bench for that reason. During CBA discussions of a 1963 proposal to increase federal judges' salaries from $22,500 to $35,000, for instance, a board member calculated that a federal judge on a salary of $22,000 would drop his income by two-thirds from the $60,000 he might reasonably have expected to be making in private practice. Yet while many judges are politically well connected as a condition of their judgeships, they are curiously impotent to do anything about low salaries: individual influence will very likely be ineffectual, and collective action would be entirely inappropriate or be seen as blatantly self-serving. The organized bar offers the best single vehicle for the expression of judicial grievances. Indeed the American Bar Association has for a long time taken some responsibility, with the support of state and local associations, for improvements in federal judicial salaries, and the American Judicature Society, the organization historically committed to bar integration, has also given its attention to conditions of judicial office at every jurisdictional level. Thus some form of national infrastructure exists for the translation of requests from the judiciary for better conditions of service into reality.[22]

Within this national context the local associations have primary responsibility. In 1967, for example, some judges approached bar association leaders in Chicago to ask for relief from financial hardships. In response, the CBA formed, with the ISBA, a Joint Committee on Judicial Salaries, Pensions, and Retirement Benefits, which undertook a thorough review of current municipal, county, and state practices, gathered statistics on salaries in other states, drew on reports compiled by the American Judicature Society, inquired into relative rewards of federal and state judiciaries, and compared judicial salaries with those of lawyers having comparable experience. In its fifty-page report submitted the following year, the committee recommended that judges' salaries should increase on a scale up to 50 percent of their present salaries. In addition, various supplementary payments should be implemented or increased for particular jurisdictions. The recommendations were forwarded to the governor, to relevant House and

22. Transcripts, 1 July 1965.

Senate committees, and to the body of legislators and others who composed the Judicial Advisory Council.[23]

Nevertheless, assistance given to the judicial cause by the profession can draw lawyers into the thick of debate between various classes of judges—higher and lower court, metropolitan and state—over the equity of differences in salary scales. As a result, bar associations can find themselves in the unenviable position of having to arbitrate between the conflicting claims of various sections of the judiciary. We have seen earlier how a judge compelled to try a former superior may call on the bar association to monitor proceedings. When the association is expected to adjudicate between competing factions of adjudicators, the precariousness of its position becomes manifest. Thus, while trying to maintain some semblance of the general normative economy between the bar and the bench, the bar association must guard against the devaluation of its normative credit should it be drawn into a factional battle within the judiciary that may alienate all sides. Judicial affirmation too easily can degenerate into judicial displeasure.

The intricate relations between the judiciary and politics in those states in which judges are elected appear again on matters of judicial and magisterial tenure. The judicial article proposed by the bar associations in Illinois had made some marginal gains on the question of judicial tenure: once judges were elected they might run for reelection against their own records without party identification. But the new judicial article allowed continued political intervention in the tenure of lower-level judicial officers because it gave circuit judges the right to appoint magistrates "to serve at their pleasure." Consistent with this, the Cook County circuit court had adopted a rule that magistrates would be appointed and reappointed annually so long as they maintained good behavior. The bar association objected to this on grounds that short-term appointments both discouraged good lawyers from leaving their practices and made magistrates highly susceptible to political influence if they wished to retain their positions. But when approached by bar leaders, the chief judge of the Cook County circuit court rejected the allegation that an untenured magistrate system placed judges at the whim of political leaders, and he urged the bar association to leave the matter well alone.[24] This example shows more than another facet of bar efforts to restrain political influence over the judiciary; it also indicates that in order to effect changes at one level of the courts, such as protecting the interests and upgrading the quality of magistrates, a bar association may find itself again in a similar quandry to that of the previous example, namely, that an improvement of one

23. Transcripts, 2 February 1967, 9 March 1967, 11 May 1967.
24. Committee on Operation of the Circuit Court, Report 66–24, 14 April 1966; Transcripts, 14 April 1966, 23 April 1966.

aspect of the judiciary may complicate a bar association's relations with other segments of the bench.

Like conditions of judicial office, there were intermittent rumblings of dissatisfaction with court congestion over the postwar years throughout the United States. The backlog curve rose steadily, and from time to time the worsening situation was punctuated with temporary surges in the caseload occasioned by sudden shortages of judges or widespread civil disorder. By 1960 there were 65,071 cases pending in the Chicago circuit and superior courts, and it was anticipated that a case filed in 1960 would not come to hearing until 1964 or 1965. A congestion crisis can be relieved in at least four ways: by increasing the number of court personnel; by making more efficient use of the time and skills of court personnel; by speeding up the trial process; and by securing more settlements in civil suits outside of court.[25] The following examples demonstrate how the CBA, like sister associations throughout the United States, employed each of these expedients to lighten the crippling load of cases on the courts.

The most obvious remedy is the appointment of more judges. But that is often not so easy as it might appear, as the Chicago experience demonstrates. In 1960 a comparison of the number of judges in Cook County with the number mandated by the Illinois constitution on a population basis revealed that Cook County was short by forty-three judges or 40 percent less than its allowable maximum. Furthermore, the constitution, instituted in 1870, made no allowance for the vast increase in negligence litigation and other new demands on the courts that would eventuate in the following century. Moreover, in any jurisdiction the actual number of judges sitting at any one time will very likely be less than the full complement on the judicial list: some will be ill; others may have died and not been replaced; and yet others may be under indictment and have taken leave of absence.

> Consequently, the CBA drafted two bills to be introduced into the 1961 and 1963 sessions of the legislature which would increase by forty-three the number of judges on the bench in Cook County—the exact number needed to bring the judicial complement up to the constitutional maximum without changing the constitution. After a complex series of negotiations within the CBA, and between it and the judiciary and Chicago political leaders, the CBA and ISBA had a bill, S.B. 261, introduced into the Illinois legislature which would have provided for eighteen new judges in November 1961. It failed to pass the senate.[26]

25. See, generally, Hans Zeisel et al., *Delay in the Court* (Boston: Little, Brown, 1959).

26. Committee on Civil Practice, Report 60–12, March 1960; Transcripts, 17 March 1960, 10 August 1961, 14 September 1961.

A similar fate befell an effort to lift the pressure off the Chicago municipal courts. In fact their particular crisis well illustrates the more general phenomenon confronting courts throughout the country. On top of the constant problems of delays in personal injury cases, the Supreme Court had increased the jurisdictional scope of the court; in addition, the legislature had granted power to the court to review judgments of justices of the peace in Cook County. Besides the usual number of judges who were ill, six hearing officers were under indictment by a grand jury, and three further judges had been transferred from the civil to the criminal division in compliance with statutory provisions that demanded that criminal cases receive priority in the courts.

> The Municipal Court Committee recommended to the Board that amending legislation should be enacted to increase the number of municipal court judges by eighteen, 12 to be elected in 1962 and 6 in 1964. The bill, introduced to the senate as S.B. 317, offered an amendment in section 12 of the Chicago Municipal Court Act, permitting the city council to increase the number of associate judges from thirty-six to fifty-four. But with its sister bill, S.B. 261, it failed to get through the senate.[27]

Although the legislative measure was unsuccessful, the bar association did persuade the chief judge to adopt the mild change of increasing court hours and bringing in judges temporarily from outlying courts.

The same pattern was reflected in an effort of the CBA to deal with delay in the probate court because of the inability or reluctance of the governor to appoint replacements for judges who had resigned or died. The rotation into the probate court of other circuit court judges was not so helpful because the frequent changes of personnel presented difficulties of continuity and administration.

> With the advice of the Legislative Reference Bureau of the Illinois legislature, the Probate Committee drafted an amendment to the Cities, Villages and Towns Court Act which would ease the appointment of a permanent probate judge. A related bill, also introduced into the 1957 legislative session, S.B. 359, which would have permitted circuit court judges to fill vacancies in probate and county courts pending appointment or election of a new judge, was vetoed by the governor after the adjournment of the 1957 General Assembly.[28]

The middle-range legislative proposals to resolve court difficulties were not successful, although it should be observed that several bills did pass either the House or the Senate or both only to be lost in the other chamber or vetoed by the

---

27. Committee on the Municipal Court, Report 60–26, April 1960.
28. Committee on Probate Committee, Report 54–40, April 1954; Transcripts, 22 April 1954.

governor. The profession could do rather better on issues that did not require political mobilization and the uncertain sanction of the legislature. The Matrimonial Committee was able to have two judges transferred into the family court in order to deal with alimony, maintenance, and annulment hearings and motions in the summer of 1959.[29] And the Traffic Court subcommittee supported moves to institute evening court hearings for preliminary hearings.

Nevertheless, the experiences of the CBA exemplify the kinds of expedients—if not the successes—that the organized bar can make to forestall or redress the bottleneck in the courts. The CBA played the full range of variations on the general theme of altering staffing to meet the crisis: it tried to increase the total number of judges, to fill judicial vacancies more rapidly, to make the deployment of judges more flexible so that they might be swiftly transferred to courts most in need, and to devolve tasks on other court personnel formerly undertaken by judges. Additional measures for more efficient use of a judge's time—increasing hours on the bench and ensuring that more courtrooms are available to judges—round out an array of alternatives that could be attempted, albeit often fruitlessly, at every level of action from constitutional revision and statutory amendment through Supreme Court actions and local administrative initiatives.

Yet there are other causes of congestion, quite apart from judges—or the lack of them. The preference of lawyers and their clients for jury trials, the extended number of pretrial motions before the courts for interrogatories, the fondness of many lawyers for repeated continuances, and the hazards of hung juries each added an increment of strain on the courts. Again the CBA demonstrates the options open to the organized bar in order to solve one or another aspect of the crisis. It also points to the impediments within the bar to the adoption of measures likely to speed up trials.

An obvious step to more expeditious dispatch of cases is to change the role of the jury. For instance, the revision of the 1955 Illinois Civil Practice Act had implemented a provision that trials would automatically be considered bench trials unless an attorney petitioned otherwise. But if there were to be trials by jury, the complications of hung juries, lost time, and costly retrials remained. Yet when House Bill 680 was introduced into the 1955 session of the Illinois general assembly to allow for verdicts on a 75 percent rather than a unanimous majority, the CBA joined with the ISBA to oppose its passage on the grounds that this would depart from a hallowed tradition and would be a derogation of the original concept from which jury trials had been derived, not to mention the fact that such legislation was probably unconstitutional—a view rejected by a minority of

29. Committee on Matrimonial Law, Report 58–19, March 1958; Transcripts, 20 March 1958.

civil litigators who welcomed the change. If matters could not be speeded up at the end of the trial, then a change in the methods of using interrogatories could facilitate progress at the outset. But although the CBA joined with several judges to propose a change in court rules that would allow more time to resolve difficulties between the parties out of court, the Supreme Court demurred.

Expert witnesses provide another means of speeding up trials.[30] In civil trials and personal injury or negligence cases, the word of an expert, such as a doctor, can mean enormous differences in the size of damages awarded a party. There are at least two ways that expert testimony can be elicited: on the one hand, each side, both plaintiffs and defendants, can call its own witness or witnesses, and the respective witnesses may then be examined and cross-examined; on the other hand, a less time-consuming method is for the court to adopt one expert witness whose judgment is brief and determinative. In the latter case, the advantage for the medical profession is simply that the differences in opinion within medicine are not aired and brutally exposed, while the disadvantage for lawyers is that they must rely on the judgment of one practitioner, who might be harmful to their case, when the imprecision of medicine and the difference of opinion among doctors are quite manifest. When the medical community pressured the Illinois Supreme Court to adopt Rule 17-2 in 1961, which would allow an "impartial medical witness" and which undoubtedly would have sped up negligence cases, the trial bar vigorously denounced it. However, when in practice it was discovered that the rule was rarely used and that in the two years it had been in force it had been used only nine times, the ire of the trial bar died away and the board decided that the question was moot and not worthy of being pursued further.[31]

A further way of lessening demands on the courts comes from securing settlements before a case comes to trial. The certificate of readiness is an indication to the court that all the discovery proceedings have been completed, that possibilities of settlement have been explored unsuccessfully, and that the case is ready to go to trial. It was suggested that the pretrial discussions would lead to a greater proportion of cases being settled before filing and that the certificate would ensure that attorneys were ready to go to court—thus avoiding last-minute adjournments and upsets in the court calendar.

> In June 1961 the Circuit Court of Cook County voted unanimously to adopt Rule 5.1 which required the plaintiff's lawyer to file a statement of issues and readiness before the case could be placed on the trial calendar. Judges of the superior court strenuously objected to

30. Younger Members Committee, Report 60–122, December 1960; Transcripts, 1 December 1960, 15 June 1961.

31. Committee on Medicolegal Relations, Report 63–98, August 1963; Transcripts, 8 August 1963.

the innovation and the chief judge approached the CBA for assistance. The matter was considered both by the Civil Practice Committee and a Board subcommittee, each of which recognized the danger of becoming embroiled in an inter-court conflict. On the one hand, the Board opposed the rule because it believed that it did little except offer a new opportunity for lawyers to continually defer cases; it also broke the uniformity of rules across courts which the CBA had drafted and the courts had accepted. On the other hand, it had been presented as a *fait accompli*. Consequently the CBA took no action and whether or not it could claim any credit for the eventual withdrawal of the rule three years later is a matter for speculation.[32]

COURT RULES AND PROCEDURES

While the organized bar displayed a periodic interest in congestion, such was not the case, and nor is it likely to be, with the continuing problems concerning court rules and procedures and changes in court organization. A metropolitan or state bar association can have dealings with the courts on these matters along two principal dimensions: first, it will take on responsibilities, but of different kinds, for state courts and federal courts; and, second, its scope of action will vary from contributions to the amendment or implementation of a single limited change through to initiatives on complete revisions of court rules or modifications of court procedures. Indeed a third dimension may crosscut both of these. Bar associations will on some occasions be reactive and on others proactive, although we shall see that reaction and action do not vary independently of the first dimension. Table 7.1 has shown that the CBA devoted a substantial proportion of its judicial activity in this rather general area—approximately one-fifth of all issues coming before the board—and in fact ongoing attention to court organization is second only to judicial elections in the rank order of the CBA's work with the judiciary.

It will usually be the case that a professional association will maintain its primary focus and expend its resources most liberally on that level of institution most salient to its own constituency. Thus a national bar association will be more concerned with federal than state courts, just as a state, county, or metropolitan association will devote most attention to the state, county, or metropolitan levels, respectively. The CBA exemplifies this pattern: the association paid some attention to both limited and general changes in federal court procedures and rules, although proportionately it stressed the latter. In both cases its role was reactive rather than generative. For example, when the CBA was a recipient of proposed new federal rules of civil procedure in 1964 and 1965, the Committee on Civil

32. Committee on Civil Practice, Report 61–95, September 1961; Transcripts, 21 September 1961, 28 September 1961.

Procedure prepared a sixteen-page report that looked in detail at nine of fifteen proposed changes and most particularly at Rule 23, on class action suits. Eventually the committee approved six of the nine changes, and its views were ratified by the board and sent on without discussion.[33] Similarly, the CBA passed its views back to the Judicial Conference of the United States after the conference had circulated a fifty-eight page report calling for new Uniform Rules of Evidence for U.S. district courts.[34] In neither case did the CBA commit any more of its resources than the effort of the committee specifically involved, although that was extensive. On other occasions there may be significant interaction between local and national changes in court rules and procedures. The 1933 Illinois Civil Practice Act, on which leading CBA and ISBA lawyers had worked, significantly influenced the subsequent Federal Civil Procedure Act, some of whose innovations in turn were incorporated into the 1955 revision of the Illinois Civil Practice Act.

When a state or local association does act proactively, it will most often be on a minor matter. For instance, the CBA had no difficulty in sending on to the Federal Judicial Council a 1961 proposal from the Committee on Federal Civil Procedure recommending an addition to federal rule 15 (a) that would eliminate, it was hoped, unnecessary appeals by "affording a claimant one last chance to amend his pleading after he has undergone the educational experience of unsuccessfully defending an attack on the sufficiency of his pleading."[35]

In terms of effort, volume of matters, and expenditure of resources, the bar association will concentrate on a jurisdiction more or less coterminous with its membership constituency. The range of matters can be as extensive as the rules, procedures, and organizational aspects of the courts themselves. The volume of issues considered by the Chicago association averaged approximately ten per year and sometimes reached eighteen or twenty. As we shall see, even this estimate is absolutely minimal. The scope of matters concerned can be exemplified by two more major projects in the 1960s. The first instance concerned the Juvenile Courts. The Juvenile Court Committee of the CBA had been a prime mover in the drafting and implementation of the Juvenile Court Act of 1965, which had "provided a much needed codification of the rights of individuals involved in juvenile proceedings and the powers of the court to act with respect to juveniles," achieved some balance between the rehabilitative and preventive objectives of juvenile law, and offered "a much more workable tool for lawyers" than the

---

33. Committee on Federal Civil Procedure, Report 65–53, May 1965; Transcripts, 6 May 1965.

34. Committee on Federal Civil Procedure, Report 62–116, December 1962; Transcripts, 13 December 1962.

35. Committee on Federal Civil Procedure, Report 61–51, April 1961; Transcripts, 21 April 1961.

state of affairs it superseded—at least according to the lawyers themselves.[36] Nonetheless, certain anomalies and uncertainties remained in court procedures. Accordingly, with the cooperation of the presiding judge of that court, the Juvenile Court Committee drafted a set of rules, covering hours in court, appearances, complaints, motions, inspection of records, privacy of hearings, and other topics.[37]

A curious twist to the affair then occurred. The CBA referred the newly drafted rules to its Committee on Revision of Circuit Court Rules, which opposed them on the grounds that they were poorly drafted and that the topics were not the proper subject of formal court rules. When the CBA board was called to adjudicate between the two committees, it found, quite remarkably, that, although the vice-chairman of the Circuit Rules Committee was chairman of the Judges' Committee on Circuit Court Rules, and although the Circuit Rules Committee had been very active and successful for thirteen years, it had never been formally instituted within the bar association and therefore had never sent either annual reports to the board or asked for the authority of the bar association leaders for its actions over more than a decade! After reviewing this conundrum, the board formally appointed the committee, gave it the autonomy to continue acting pretty much as it always had, and asked the Juvenile Court Committee to redraft some of its rules. The rules were then to be submitted to the chief judge with the suggestion that they be adopted as a general order governing the juvenile division of the circuit court.

This case points up several features of bar action in the courts. At the very least it demonstrates that the index of bar association action I have used, based on board agenda items, must be conservative: a significant committee had been operating for many years without ever having any of its proposals or reforms entered on the board agenda books. It also indicates the fraternal relation that can exist between the courts and the profession: the senior judge with responsibility for court rules in the circuit courts was simultaneously the chairman and vice-chairman of two judicial and bar association committees, thereby at once giving the judiciary committee the advantage of having bar expertise and the bar committee the advantage of having direct access to the circuit courts. So close indeed was the relation between the two communities that it appears the CBA committee had a closer affinity to its judicial counterpart than to the board of its own organization. In virtue of this relation, the traffic of activity between bar and bench could be substantial.

36. Committee on Juvenile Delinquents, Report 65–10, February 1965; Transcripts, 18 February 1965.

37. Committee on Juvenile Delinquents, Report 68–14, March 1968; Transcripts, 28 March 1968.

Bar association interest can extend as far as the geography of the courts. When Chicago lawyers found in 1959 that a new county court building was planned for the downtown area of Chicago but that the criminal courts, located seven miles out of the central city area, would not be included in the new complex, the two committees most concerned with criminal law persuaded the CBA to press for a change in the plans so that all courts could be centralized in the one building. On the grounds that it would be much more efficient to have the courts in the central area, the CBA approached the mayor, the president of the Cook County Board of Commissioners, the chief judges, other bar associations, and the commissioner for the Department of City Planning to press for reconsideration of the decision. With no success the association took its case to the press and lobbied directly through the Public Services Commission and indirectly through the Citizens of Greater Chicago. Press support and active mobilization notwithstanding, the criminal courts remained where they were—thirty minutes from the central area by cab and forty-five minutes by public transport.

The Politics of Affirmation and Negativism

We have seen in this chapter that, in addition to peak events, the professional association maintains a steady and considerable level of activity in virtually every aspect of court organization and judicial performance. Indeed the chapter has not exhausted the scope of such effort: it has mentioned nothing of bar controls over court personnel other than judges, or of association efforts, however rare, to influence court decisions through the submission of amicus briefs, or even of bar endeavors to influence the internal architecture of courthouses. It has not mentioned a plethora of matters, many petty and most relatively inconsequential in themselves, that characterize the ongoing liaison between the professional association and its primary institutional sphere. Yet not only do these actions also, like those noted in more detail, have a place in a more general structure of action, but that action itself has an internal coherence. However insignificant any component of the profession's efforts in the courts, therefore, they all may be ordered within that more comprehensive system of action I have designated the normative economy of judicial control.

The economy had its origins, it can be supposed, in the awareness that, while the profession shared the same fate in standing as the court system, it could do little about it. The economy emerged, perhaps despite itself and with very little concept of design, as the profession recognized that its technical indispensability, and perhaps political value to the bench, gave it the necessary credit to sustain its attempts at moral upgrading of the judiciary. In that sense, the moral and normative authority of the profession grew out of its expertise and, later, its political force. Hence an economy developed that loosely encapsulated each component of the profession's dealings with the courts and judges; every element of affirmation added an increment, however imperceptible, that could later be used to offset the negative functions the bar took on itself.

Efforts on the one side to improve conditions of judicial service, to relieve congestion in the courts, and to improve rules, procedures, and organization (the politics of affirmation) earned the profession the right to monitor on the other side demeanor on the bench and admission to the bench (the politics of negativism). As the elements of bar activity are drawn into this system of action they take on a dynamic relation to each other. If affirmation earns the bar high credits, then it may act all the more forcefully to enforce judicial ethics and standards of admission to the bench. If negativism eats away at the credit that positive activities create, then the bar is compelled to balance the ledger by committing its resources to greater affirmative action. The very stability of efforts, positive and negative, by the CBA over twenty years suggests that, even though such an economy may not be consciously perceived, even by bar leaders, there nevertheless exists a market in which the bar and judiciary exchange intangible benefits and tangible "goods" and in which credits and debits are constantly balanced such that, ultimately, the bar produces from its side of the normative economy some control over the judiciary and the judiciary finds some solution to the stresses.

Yet as I showed in chapter 6, control itself represents only one aspect of a larger process: control over the judiciary is balanced by attaining some autonomy for the judiciary. More exactly, the general logic of the profession's activity in its primary institutional sphere is to dislocate relations between the judiciary and party politics, to take judicial rule-making powers out of the hands of legislatures and vest them in the courts, to differentiate the roles of lawyers and judges, to increase the internal capacity of a court system through bureaucratization, to resist external incursions on its independence, and to complement the thrust toward judicial autonomy with professional control, where conditions in the courts, where efficiency in the administration of justice, and where the character and demeanor of judges themselves fall more fully within the purview of the professional association. In a word, the self-appointed collective professional mandate vis-à-vis the judiciary is to complement judicial autonomy from politics with professional control of the judiciary.

It follows not only that the bar has succeeded in penetrating to every corner of its primary institution but that it has added a moral authority to its technical expertise. That is to say, while the profession has tried to use its special knowledge and the experience of practitioners to increase court efficiency, reduce inconsistency and contradictions in rules, expedite the administration of justice, and order the entire system of rules and aspects of court organization in general codes, its prescriptive and policy functions have far exceeded the narrow limits that a strict-constructionist interpretation of expertise would place on it. The contributions of the profession as a normative reference group for the judiciary, as a monitor of judicial performance, and as a gatekeeper to judicial office manifest the more mundane representations of moral authority.

When, however, a profession launches itself over two or more decades into a series of massive reform programs that would substantially alter the institutional location of the judiciary vis-à-vis the other branches of government and that would determine the various forms that institution will take, then it has taken a giant step over the divide between narrow technical assistance and generally moral authority. The bar reaches to constitutional and policy questions central to the self-understanding of society itself. The relation of the judiciary to the executive and the legislature, not to mention party politics, is a critical problem of political philosophy and an enduring tension in American politics. For a profession to find itself actively advocating a particular configuration of relations between the three branches of government, pressing its own solution to the separation of powers, demonstrates dramatically the capacity of an occupation that claims a monopoly over given expertise to convert a relatively limited warrant into a wide-ranging activism that addresses an enduring problem for the contemporary state.

At the same time, the recognition of this general structure of organized bar actions in the judicial system must be tempered with some realism over the successes of the profession. While attempts by the lawyers were comprehensive in their scope, achievements were less notable. Reasons for this will be considered further in chapter 11: some stemmed from the attributes of the open association itself, whereas others were a reflection of the rather special case of Chicago machine politics. Nevertheless, we may very approximately summarize the distribution of bar association successes in terms of a reversed J-curve. On minor issues to do with court rules and procedures that do not require legislative mandate or that are uncontroversial, the bar association will have most success. Topics of discussion and matters of concern can easily be considered and implemented in a free flow of information, advice, and assistance between the court officials and the profession. Because most such matters do not attract attention, they do not attract opposition. On major issues, such as the Illinois Civil Practice Act, the Supreme Court Rules, and the judicial article, the profession will act less often but with far more investment of resources and with some moderate to considerable success. It was the intermediate efforts that were neither wide sweeping nor trivial, yet required legislative approval, that most often came to nothing.

On the other hand, the professional association's failure must be interpreted with some care. It is clear that the voluntary body could not simultaneously take on the Chicago political machine and numerous other interest groups in the state and expect to win on every successive occasion. But from the point of view of the profession and the structure of autonomy and control, success may be less salient a criterion for judgment than intention and effort. Clearly, for the profession to retain any legitimacy within the judiciary and even among its own members, it must win occasionally—and it did. On the other hand, inasmuch as the profession was driving toward autonomy and control it needed not just political power but the ability to influence through persuasion. And the ability to persuade in turn depends on the goodwill earned by the profession in the courts. That flows in part from its efforts—and not necessarily its successes. For the judiciary, on whom many of the changes depended, bar efforts were an index of good faith and a commitment to the interests of the courts as well as to those of the profession. In short, therefore, while bar successes fell far short of attempts, the successes they did achieve, coupled with the demonstration of goodwill in efforts that failed, together sufficed to maintain that aspect of the normative economy that would allow the profession continued intervention in the court system.

8 Crises of Rights

In the foregoing two chapters I have presented an empirically grounded argument that an open professional association can commit resources to every quarter of its primary institutional domain. In so doing, the profession employs its cognitive and technical mastery of legal knowledge to offer a solution, albeit in part, to many of the smaller problems and some of the larger crises facing the judiciary. If anything, however, professional action in the primary institution, where it has full and marginal legitimacy for expert and moral authority, respectively (table 2.1.), is the lesser task. What of its potential influence in secondary institutional spheres, where legitimacy is contested or nonexistent? If a profession can contribute to the relief of stresses and strains in those aspects of government impinging on it directly, then it accomplishes a significant but not remarkable feat. If, however, a profession can step outside its limited domain of principal activity, and if it can also bring both its skills and a policy perspective to influence change, then that is much more consequential. Influence in secondary spheres is thus a considerably more exacting test of the capacity of the contemporary legal profession to bring knowledge to the service of power.

The crises faced by the profession in the postwar decades provide a context for us both to explore the contributions they may make to a state under stress and, more generally, to show the scope and types of professional legislative activity. As in the discussion of the judiciary, I will present several levels of data in ascending order of detail and magnitude. (1) For an overview of all bar legislative efforts, I display a statistical summary of all legislation brought to the Chicago Bar Association (CBA) leadership for two decades. (2) As an indication of what the bar might achieve in its efforts to influence "middle-range" substantive law, I consider the CBA's role in one specialty area, that of civil rights. (3) As an instance of professional contributions to substantive rationalization of law, namely, codification and the proliferation of uniform laws, I discuss the CBA's drafting of the Illinois Criminal Code. (4) Finally, in chapter 8, I consider the influence of the CBA on constitutional revision, not as it pertains to the judiciary, but as it controls the economic infrastructure of the state of Illinois and the fiscal crisis that confronted that and other states in the 1960s.

The Universe of Legislative Action

As we have seen from the range of CBA substantive law committees, an open professional association has the organizational bases and specialist interests to support a breadth of legislative action across the entire gambit of legal specialties. In practice, however, in what areas of the law does an association seek to take legislative action? With what volume? And to what legislatures? Are bar association attempts at law reform confined to lawyers' law, or do they include more substantive and policy areas? In order to answer these questions in the broadest terms I adopted two methods. First, in a parallel design to that on judicial items, I did a content analysis of all legislative issues coming before the CBA board between 1950 and 1971. Second, I accumulated data on the activities of the Legislative Committee, the CBA's principal organizational vehicle for general law reform. Together these two sources provide a comprehensive—though not complete—empirical basis for a synopsis of organized bar action.

The population of legislative items reaching the CBA leadership include a variety of concerns with legislation and law reform. Some are pieces of legislation initiated from within the CBA for introduction to the state General Assembly; others are reactions by the profession to bills introduced at each legislative session. There are discussions of CBA policy concerning whole areas of the law, such as its attitudes to civil rights legislation; and there are reactions to draft or model legislation submitted for the comments of the CBA by other organizations. Not all these items result in professional action. Sometimes in fact an explicit decision is made not to act. On other occasions matters just lapse, or issues are never satisfactorily resolved. But with the exceptions I will note below, this simple content analysis provides the best single measure of legislative scope and volume.

Table 8.1 indicates the distributions of legislative issues over twenty years by point of origin and legislature of destination. Approximately 1,107 issues came before the board at a rate of between fifty and sixty each year, a volume of activity very close indeed to that on judicial issues. The great majority of matters were concerned with state legislation (81 percent), a focus consistent both with a professional association's tendency to focus on those institutions and jurisdictions that fall within the drawing area of its membership and with the probability that a metropolitan or state association will put its resources to more effective use at the state rather than the federal level. It might be expected from the hypotheses discussed in chapter 5 that an enduring elitism in formerly elite associations would

TABLE 8.1. Legislative Issues on CBA Board Agendas, 1950–71, by Committees and Legislatures

Committees	Federal (%)[d]	N	State (%)[d]	N	Total (%)[e]	N
	Legislatures					
Civil Litigation	14.3	3	85.7	18	1.9	21
Civil Rights	27.5	14	72.5	37	4.6	51
Constitutional Revision	3.5	2	96.5	55	5.1	57
Consumer Credit	. . .	. . .	100.0	19	1.7	19
Corporation Law	. . .	. . .	100.0	16	1.4	16
Criminal	3.6	1	96.4	27	2.5	28
Development of the Law	. . .	. . .	100.0	29	2.6	29
Federal Tax	95.0	19	5.0	1	1.8	20
Industrial Commission	. . .	. . .	100.0	18	1.6	18
Legislative[a]	4.0	6	96.0	145	13.6	151
Matrimonial	. . .	. . .	100.0	41	3.7	41
Municipal Court	. . .	. . .	100.0	25	2.3	25
Patents	86.7	85	13.3	13	8.9	98
Probate	2.7	3	97.3	108	10.0	111
Real Property	. . .	. . .	100.0	80	7.2	80
State and Municipal Tax	. . .	. . .	100.0	39	3.5	39
Trusts	8.0	2	92.0	23	2.3	25
CBA board	23.1	9	76.9	30	3.5	39
Selected joint committees[b]	4.3	1	95.7	22	2.1	23
Other[c]	29.2	63	70.8	13	19.5	216
Total	18.8	208	81.2	899	100.0	1107

SOURCE.—Minutes, Board of Managers, Chicago Bar Association.

[a] On many occasions, especially when proposed bills are intended to be part of the CBA-ISBA joint legislative program, substantive law committees will send legislative items to the board jointly with the Legislative Committee. As the intention of this table is to show the substantive origins of items, all such jointly sponsored items have been recoded into the appropriate substantive law committees. Legislative committee items are those that come from that committee alone.

[b] This table does not include the major legislative initiatives emerging from joint CBA-ISBA committees on the Illinois Criminal Code and Code for Criminal Procedure, or Revision of the Civil Practice Act and Supreme Court Rules, or Judicial Salaries, Pensions, and Retirement Benefits. It includes only five occasions on which the joint committees on the judicial article appeared on the board agendas.

[c] Includes submissions by the following committees: Adoption (11), Antitrust (8), Bankruptcy (6), Circuit Court (6), Commercial Code (5), Federal Civil Procedures (11), Federal Legislation (11), Juvenile Delinquents (143), Labor (13), Local Government (10), Negligence (11), Public Utility (9), Securities (6), Traffic Court (8), Unauthorized Practice (9), and others.

[d] Row percentages.

[e] Column percentages.

leave its residue in the focus of its leadership. In that case the CBA board would be expected to concentrate its attention on higher prestige areas of the law, especially those concerned with the practice of corporate law. But that is not the case. Table 8.1 shows that the diversity of issues over specialty fields in law matches the diversity of an open association's membership. Some of the committees with the highest volume of matters—patents (ninety-eight), probate (111), and constitutional revision (fifty-seven)—are concerned with high prestige areas of practice; and other committees also with high rates of activity—matrimonial (forty-one), criminal (twenty-eight), civil rights (fifty-one), and consumer credit (nineteen)—are at the lower end of the prestige scale. It should also be observed that the vast majority of items are generated from committees and not from the CBA leadership.

How stable are demands for board action from its committee? Does the association itself maintain a steady pattern of legislative involvement? As the association completes its transition from an elite to a mass membership, are specialties whose practitioners were previously excluded increasing their proportional share of CBA legislative reform? Table 8.2 sets out the proportion of items emanating from different committees in four-year periods from 1951 to 1970. Each four-year period includes two legislative sessions of the Illinois General Assembly, which met only in odd-numbered years. It might be expected that, as substantive law committees have quadrupled in size from 1950 to 1970, the legislative activity might increase similarly. However, the column marginals indicate that legislative demands on the board have been rather more commensurate with the increase in size of the CBA: the number of items in the last period is approximately 60 percent higher than the number in the first. Frequency of legislative issues stayed relatively stable in the first three periods until the early 1960s and then took off; they were still rising rapidly in 1971. Yet those committees and areas of law that have taken a relatively larger share of board agendas over the period—civil rights, constitutional revision, consumer credit, and corporation law—do not confirm that less prestigious committees are emerging at the expense of those with higher standing. Similarly, patterns of proportional decline include lower prestige committees, such as criminal law, and higher prestige committees, such as probate. In general, the relative changes have been minimal: there are very few strong deviations from the row marginals, although of course there are many fluctuations from one period to another without any clear trend.

The coded agenda items provide a helpful overview, but they are not an entirely accurate index. They treat all items on the board agenda as equal in scope or significance. They do not allow us to distinguish between legalistic and more substantive considerations. They also underestimate the volume of activity since a substantial degree of activity is not funneled through the leadership. A sum-

TABLE 8.2. Proportions of CBA Board Considerations of Legislative Reports from Selected Committees, 1951–70

Committees	Years												
	1951–54		1955–58		1959–62		1963–66		1967–70		Total	
	%	N	%	N	%	N	%	N	%	N	%	N
Civil Litigation	1.1	2	1.1	2	3.6	5	1.5	3	2.5	8	1.9	20
Civil Rights	3.7	7	3.8	7	4.3	6	9.3	19	3.2	10	4.8	49
Constitutional Revision	3.2	6	3.8	7	2.9	4	7.8	16	7.3	23	5.4	56
Consumer Credit	..		..		..		1.5	3	3.5	11	1.4	14
Corporation	1.1	2	..		..		2.0	4	3.2	10	1.6	16
Criminal	7.0	13	1.1	2	..		2.4	5	1.9	6	2.5	26
Development of the Law	1.6	3	.5	1	1.4	2	3.4	7	2.9	9	2.1	22
Federal Tax	.5	1	2.2	4	3.6	5	1.0	2	1.9	6	1.7	18
Industrial Commission	2.1	4	5.4	10	..		..		1.3	4	1.7	18
Legislative	3.7	7	19.6	36	15.7	22	16.6	34	13.7	43	13.8	142
Municipal Court	6.4	12	1.6	3	8.6	12	5.4	11	.6	2	3.9	40
Patents	3.7	7	10.9	20	14.3	20	7.8	16	10.8	34	9.4	97
Probate	21.4	40	12.5	23	.5	7	9.3	19	6.7	21	10.7	110
Real Property	9.1	17	4.3	8	.7	1	3.9	8	13.0	41	7.3	75
State and Municipal Tax	2.7	5	.5	1	5.7	8	1.0	2	4.1	13	2.8	29
Trusts	3.2	6	2.2	4	1.4	2	3.4	7	1.9	6	2.4	25
CBA board	11.2	21	2.2	4	2.1	3	2.0	4	1.3	4	3.5	36
Selected joint committees[a]	.5	1	1.6	3	5.7	8	2.0	4	1.9	6	2.1	22
Other[b]	13.9	26	22.3	41	20.7	29	18.5	38	18.4	58	18.6	192
Total	18.1	187	17.8	184	13.6	140	19.9	205	30.6	315	100.0	1031

SOURCE.—Minutes, Board of Managers, Chicago Bar Association.

[a] This table does not include the major legislative initiatives emerging from joint CBA-ISBA committees on the Illinois Criminal Code and Code of Civil Procedure, on Revision of the Civil Practice Act and Supreme Court Rules, on Judicial Salaries, Pensions and Retirement Benefits. It includes only five occasions on which the joint committees on the judicial article appeared on board agendas.

[b] Committee legislative items were recoded as in table 8.1, n. c.

mary review of the CBA Legislative Committee and the joint bar associations' legislative program provide one useful corrective to these biases.

The CBA has had a committee concerned with law reform or legislation since 1874. After 1945, the Legislative Committee's functions diversified and became more elaborate, culminating in a joint legislative program with the Illinois State Bar Association to introduce a package of bills drafted by the bar into each biennial session of the General Assembly. The Legislative Committee was one of the most powerful in the bar association; it has been composed of all CBA members who were also state legislators, and it included leading specialists in most areas of the law. The committee did not originate legislation but rather acted as an intermediate body between the substantive law committees that initiated legislation and the CBA board. In its mediational capacity, it made decisions on which bills to recommend be included in the legislative program and which legislators should be approached to sponsor bills that had more or less chance of passage. The Legislative Committee endeavored to coordinate, with the board, the overall approach of the association at any given legislative session. Much of its contribution was strategic. Thus the committee has been careful not to introduce legislation so controversial that it might detract from higher priority bills being pressed by the organized bar in Springfield, the state capital. On occasions it has had virtual veto power over proposed actions by other committees that might place in jeopardy the joint bar program. In addition, the bar associations have employed legislative counsel, a lawyer-cum-lobbyist who "makes a careful choice of legislative sponsors to introduce bills (bi-partisan where possible); he follows the bill at each stage through the two houses, appearing before committees on behalf of the two associations or arranging for some appearance by representatives of the sponsoring bar associations." [1]

The character of the joint bar legislative program between 1951 and 1969 is outlined in table 8.3. The number of bills sent to the legislature have more than doubled, from twenty-three in 1951 to fifty-six in 1969, although the success rate is much more variable, ranging from bad years in 1951 and 1957 to the highly successful years of 1961 and 1963. Yet, as a committee chairman observed after the 1967 legislative session, "Measured on a statistical or quantitative basis, the results of the two years just ended were certainly successful. . . . Qualitatively, the record is perhaps less good, as many of the bills were of a minor or technical nature. . . . Our successful efforts seem to be confined to the special, technical, procedural and bread-and-butter bills which affect lawyers in their particular areas of practice." [2] That judgment accorded well with the comments of the 1951

1. CBA Legislative Committee, annual report (1965).
2. CBA Legislative Committee, annual report (1967).

TABLE 8.3. Joint Chicago Bar Association and Illinois State Bar Association Legislative Programs, 1951–69

Legislative Session	Bills in Joint Program	Bills Passing General Assembly	Bills Not Passed or Vetoed	Bills Enacted	Success Rate (%)[a]
1951	23	10	11	12	52
1953	23	22	5	17	74
1955	32	24	9	23	72
1957	27	22	13	13[b]	48
1959	35	23	9	26	74
1961	30	26	4	26	87
1963	20	19	1	19	95
1965	36	29	7	29	80
1967	29	8	. . .	. . .	. . .
1969	56	37	19	37	66

SOURCE.—Annual reports of the Legislative Committee, Chicago Bar Association, 1951–69.
NOTE.—Missing information is indicated by ellipses points.
[a]The success rate is calculated by the Legislative Committee with some variations in the denominator. Some bills in the joint program, for instance, may not subsequently be introduced. The more conservative measure is used here (bills enacted as a percentage of bills in the joint program).
[b]Information is not available on one bill that was to be voted on in a referendum.

committee chairman who recognized that "the bills most important to the Association are among those not passed."[3] Added to the formal legislative program, the committee undertook perhaps an even more daunting risk in the 1950s. The committee, and subsequently a subcommittee, began to screen every bill introduced to the General Assembly. Any that appeared to have some significance for substantive law committees was channeled to them. The numbers are substantial indeed: of 2,314 bills introduced in 1957, 328 Senate bills and 334 House bills were referred to committees; in 1961, 1,252 bills—almost a third of those introduced—were referred. The board, however, was much more chary about expending resources on reaction to bills in which the CBA did not have a major interest or investment, especially in years in which it had a massive bill like the Criminal Code before the house. In 1957, for instance, while many committees wanted the association to take action, it did so only on fourteen bills: six were supported by the CBA and passed; eight were opposed and lost. The pattern and breadth of referrals to substantive law committees from the legislative committee can be seen from table 8.4 when 575 of the 2,158 bills introduced in 1955—27 percent of the total—were scrutinized by bar specialist committees.[4]

3. CBA Legislative Committee, annual report (1951).
4. CBA Legislative Committee, annual report (1950–71).

TABLE 8.4. References from Legislative Committee to Substantive Law Committees, Sixty-ninth Illinois General Assembly, 1955

Name of Committee	Number of Primary References[a]	Number of Secondary References[b]
Administrative Law	7	3
Adoption Laws	6	1
Anti-Trust Law	2	0
Aviation Law	16	1
Bankruptcies and Reorganizations	2	0
Civil Practice	25	5
Civil Rights	19	7
Constitutional Revision	3	0
Corporation Law	15	7
Criminal Law	82	4
Defense of Prisoners	1	0
Development of the Law	1	0
Industrial Commission	9	5
Insurance Law	34	3
International and Foreign Law	1	0
Judiciary	38	2
Juvenile Delinquents and Adolescent Offenders, Law Relating to	6	4
Labor Law	38	11
Local Government	44	5
Matrimonial Law	11	0
Municipal Court	6	0
Patents, Trade-marks and Trade Practices	2	1
Personal Injury Practice	17	4
Probate Practice	34	3
Professional Fees	2	0
Public Law Offices and Public Service	1	0
Public Utility Law	35	2
Real Property Law	30	24
Securities Law	1	0
State and Municipal Taxation	82	6
Trust Law	3	22
Unauthorized Practice	2	0
Total	575	120

SOURCE.—Legislative Committee, annual report (1956), Chicago Bar Association.

NOTE.—A total of 2,158 bills were introduced in the Sixty-ninth General Assembly. Amendments to bills offered in the originating house and amendments offered in the nonoriginating house are excluded from this figure.

[a] Of the 2,158 bills, 575 were referred by the subcommittee to the chairmen of standing committees that appeared to have a *primary* interest in the subject matter of the bills. Approximately 27 percent of all legislation introduced was thus referred.

[b] Where other committees might have a secondary interest, their attention was called to a given bill by way of a secondary reference. There were 120 instances of such referrals.

While the bills that are part of the bar associations' joint program are not very significant, it is clear nonetheless that the bar association maintains a very substantial interest in legislative proceedings. Indeed it may not be inaccurate to say that the profession monitors state legislation even more closely than it does the courts. These tables provide some index of the volume of separate legislative matters dealt with by the board, but they underestimate the scope of activity in two ways. Most of the bills that were screened by the committee and passed on to substantive committees did not appear on the board agenda books; they were administratively handled by the Legislative Committee and the Legislative Planning Conference established in 1957 to ensure that bills were handled with dispatch and that the board did not become congested with legislation. The other basis of underestimation comes from the significance of major legislative initiatives. The bills of greatest magnitude were handled not by the Legislative Committee but in most cases by special highly expert and somewhat autonomous joint bar committees. These often massive pieces of legislation were in no way comparable to the bulk of technical and limited pieces of legislation emerging from the Legislative Committee. It is to them that I now turn.

The Cold War: Law on the Defensive[5]

Relations between the state and the individual emerged as one of the fundamental dilemmas underlying the convulsions of the postwar period. In the Cold War, the civil rights era, and the codification of criminal law, the same dilemma recurred in different guises. How is it possible to expand state powers, arrest subversion, establish racial equality, and maintain social order without, in so doing, excessively abridging the rights and invading the privacy of the individual citizen? On which side of the dilemma did the organized bar commit its authority? And with what effect? By following through the legislative activities of the Civil Rights Committee and the bar leadership we may observe the different postures a bar association can take when its resources are claimed for commitments that extend to the most controversial public policy issues—issues that include changes in community housing patterns, school integration, and sexual relations between adults.

FEDERAL ANTISUBVERSIVE LEGISLATION

In 1946 legislation was enacted to make the House Un-American Activities Committee (HUAC) a permanent standing investigatory body within Congress. On 2 December 1954, the U.S. Senate condemned Senator Joseph R. McCarthy of Wisconsin for unsenatorial behavior. Between these two historical markers

5. Pages 227–45, 253–60 draw on the more extensive discussion of civil rights legislation in Halliday, "Idiom of Legalism."

was a turbulent decade—from the trials of Foley Square to the Hiss indictment for perjury, from the hearings conducted by the HUAC to the Rosenberg trial, from the Army-McCarthy hearings to successive legislative attempts to stifle Communist impulses and organization in American society: "The temper of the time was suspicious, excited, emotional, pathetic, and hard. There was rage and outrage, accusation and defiance, a Babel of shouting anger in those tense years," an outcome not surprising, perhaps, in view of the clash between fundamental political values that occurred and indeed always remain latent in the political life of the United States.[6]

A remarkable degree of consensus emerged from the CBA in the late 1940s and early 1950s in its response to the antisedition hearings in Washington, although at best the consensus was fragile. Two convictions were voiced on the loyalty programs. On the one hand, many lawyers in the bar and several on the board believed that the goals of the legislative hearings were proper; a purge of radicals was necessary, and they greeted it with sympathy. But the commitments to these substantive ends were offset by rather general distaste for the way the loyalty proceedings were conducted—for the unjudicial, often theatrical, demeanor of the legislators and for the rather cavalier suspension of the rule of law in the process. This objection to legislative procedures by those who were in sympathy with its ends coincided with the substantive objections of civil rights lawyers and civil libertarians. From their perspective, a direct attack on the values motivating the hearings of the HUAC was politically unfeasible. For them a more covert approach to the abuse of legislative hearings through the medium of procedure, thus effecting substantive ends by legalistic means, was not only possible but in all likelihood the only approach that could find support from the more conservative section of the profession. For differing reasons, therefore, and despite its internal polarities, the professional association managed to construct and maintain a united front in opposition to the excesses of the congressional hearings. Throughout the late 1940s and 1950s the bar maintained a general policy stance that judicial rules of procedure, consistent with notions of due process—conspicuously absent from the HUAC—should be imposed on all such legislative investigations.

The specific position of the CBA on particular bills was grounded in a set of recommended safeguards published in the *Chicago Bar Record* in 1948, which specified the conditions legislative hearings would need to satisfy in order to protect individual rights.[7] The CBA manifesto demanded, among other things, that

6. Earl Latham, *The Communist Controversy in Washington: From the New Deal to McCarthy* (Cambridge, Mass.: Harvard University Press, 1966), 3.

7. "Recommendations for the Protection of Civil Rights in Legislative Investigations," *Chicago Bar Record* 30 (November 1948): 71–72.

all witnesses should have right to counsel, hearings must be in public, proceedings should be accurately recorded, individuals whose names were mentioned in testimony should have the right of reply, witnesses should be able to challenge subpoenas, and testimony from a witness should be confined "to testimony of substantial probative force" and to "facts within his knowledge." Apparently in contrast to its later position on Anastoplo, the CBA also asserted that inquiries may not be made as to an individual's "private, unexpressed beliefs, whether they be personal, philosophical, religious or political," except where such inquiries were relevant to an individual's public duties. Neither should the committee make public statements on the reputations of individuals unless certain restrictive conditions were met. At the time of publication in the *Chicago Bar Record,* the Civil Rights Committee had recommended that these guidelines also be transmitted to the press, to legislative committees of state and federal bodies, and to other bar associations. But in a pattern that will become familiar in matters of great controversy, the CBA leadership demurred. Its guidelines, once adopted and circulated to its members, did not reach Congress, the Illinois General Assembly, and sister bar associations, even though it agreed in substantial part with subsequent calls by the Association of the Bar of the City of New York and many law school deans.[8]

Nevertheless, when Congressman Case introduced House Resolution 1017 in 1951, a comprehensive statute to regulate congressional investigations, the CBA adopted a position consistent with its earlier policy stance.[9] Subject to some amendments, the CBA endorsed measures that subjects of investigation should be clearly stated, that witnesses have counsel and be able to cross-examine other adverse witnesses, and that witnesses have right of rebuttal either by calling their own witnesses or by filing sworn statements that would become part of the record. In the event, the Case bill did not pass in 1951 or in the following two years. In 1954, however, several comprehensive bills with similar intent were introduced to Congress: the Kefauver bill (S.R. 10), the Morse-Lehman bills (S.R. 83 and S.R. 64), the Scott bill (H.R. 447), and the Kefauver-Yates bills (S.R. 256 and H.R. 567). But while the Civil Rights Committee discussed all the bills and reported to the board that none of them warranted full bar support—they went either too far or not far enough—there is no record that the CBA took a

---

8. George B. Galloway, "Congressional Investigations: Proposed Reforms," *University of Chicago Law Review* 18 (1951): 499–502.

9. Committee on Civil Rights, Report 51-152, December 19, 1951; "Report of Subcommittee of Board of Managers Respecting Report of Committee on Civil Rights (51-152)," 24 March 1952; Transcripts of Meetings of the Board of Managers, 1 May 1952 (hereafter cited as Transcripts); *Congressional Record* 97 (1951): 110.

position on any of them.[10] In contrast to the CBA in the hearings of the House Committee on Rules on House Resolution 29, a bill introduced by Representative Keating, of nine organizations giving testimony, there were two bar associations, the District of Columbia Bar and the Association of the Bar of the City of New York. In addition, a statement was filed by the Pennsylvania Bar Association.[11]

But if there was some consensus within the bar on procedural guidelines, it foundered on the issue of whether hearings might be televised. Again the dilemma emerged: publicity could have salutory effects on the campaign "to ferret out corruption and evil"; at the same time a medium that reached vast audiences played into the hands of demagogues and allowed crusading legislators to invade the privacy of individuals and pillory and irreparably harm the reputations of witnesses. Not only the CBA but also the national bar split on the issue: the New York State Bar Association and the American Bar Association were opposed to publicity; but by a narrow majority the Association of the Bar of the City of New York approved televised hearings. With a deftness that it was to apply time and again to divisive issues, the CBA leadership equivocated by making a statement of principle and then depriving it of its force by procedural constraints. By a vote of thirteen to three, the board approved the resolution that "the CBA is opposed to the televising, photographing or broadcasting of the testimony of witnesses called before investigating committees of the legislative branches of the federal, state or local government, unless and until there are statutes or ordinances furnishing safeguards which effectively overcome the dangers of these practices, when unregulated, to the rights of individuals." Unlike the guidelines of 1948, the board did allow a news release to carry the substance of its decision on 1 May 1952.[12]

More serious threats to privacy came with legislative initiatives to broaden legislative investigatory powers through immunity provisions and enforcement powers by wiretapping. In these cases the bar rediscovered its earlier consensus and the association acted to oppose both proposals. With the endorsement of President Eisenhower and Attorney General Brownell, Representative Keating of New York introduced House Resolution 6899 to the House of Representatives in 1954, a bill that proposed that individuals who claimed the privilege against self-incrimination should be compelled to testify or produce records or documentary

10. Committee on Civil Rights, Report 54-99, 28 June 1954; Transcripts, 12 August 12 1954, 26 August 1954.

11. Hearings before the Subcommittee on Legislative Procedure of the House Committee on Rules, 83d Cong., 2d Sess. (1954), H.R. Res. 29, Contents, 98, 105, 133, 269.

12. Committee on Criminal Law, File 51-111, n.d.; Transcripts, 24 April 1952; "Report of Subcommittee of Board of Managers," 24 March and 1 May 1952; Transcripts, 24 April 1952; Board of Managers press release, 29 May 1952; Committee on Civil Rights, File 51-152, 9 May 1952.

evidence.[13] The Civil Rights Committee did not deny the value of immunity legislation in criminal proceedings in grand juries and courts, but it had strong reservations about these powers being granted to a legislative body. If such powers were necessary, then officials should have to convince a judge and get a court order.

The Civil Rights Committee's reservations struck a chord of sympathy within the board. Several board members pointed out that the immunity legislation was only one of a packet of bills, all of which concerned basic principles of law and civil rights and which together might effectively erode basic liberties in American society. As one board member said:

> I am opposed to this step-by-step cutting down of the rights of the citizens of the country . . . what happened on the Western Continent of Europe received great aid from laws that were passed which seemed innocent and expedient at the time, which cut out from under the basic rights of the individual citizen, and when the parties now in power stepped in, they found enough to convince the people that what they were doing was more or less legal at the beginning. . . . [F]rom a partisan standpoint, . . . it is becoming quite apparent that the incumbent Attorney General has a number of bills which do at least touch the individual rights of citizens of the country. And he is going to push those bills undoubtedly in the best of good faith, but if he succeeds in all of them, this one, the wire tapping bills, and so on, before he leaves office there are going to be quite a few nicks in what is left of individual rights.

As another argued from quite another perspective, "there is something barbarous in forcing [a man] to destroy his own reputation. . . . [A] man is entitled to be free from destroying his own reputation by having to publicly confess all errors of the past."[14]

Organized bar opposition to the bill was conveyed by the CBA to all members of the Senate Committee on the Judiciary, the House Committee on the Judiciary, and senators and congressmen from Illinois. In the debate over the immunity of witnesses, Representative Celler quoted from the minority report of the House Committee on the Judiciary to the effect that "the testimony of the Chicago Bar Association before this committee gave much needed clarity," particularly on the point of whether "the effect of full immunity would be to nullify state criminal law in the substantive sense." On several occasions, other representatives referred to reports by the Association of the Bar of the City of New York, which, like the CBA, had concluded that "we believe that recent events have not demon-

13. *Congressional Record* 100 (1954): 20, 13322–23; 101 (1955): 2934.
14. Transcripts, 6 May 1954.

strated the need for congressional power to grant immunity." But despite this measure of solidarity and consensus between the two most prominent metropolitan bar associations, the bills as revised were passed in the House on 4 August 1954, by 294 votes to 55, with eighty-five members not voting.[15]

The wiretapping legislation, introduced as House Resolution 8649 in early 1954, would permit the attorney general to use evidence gathered from wiretapping in criminal cases concerned with national security; a parallel bill in the Senate would allow the attorney general to intercept wire communications on the authority of a federal judge. On the advice of the Civil Rights Committee, the board adopted a resolution disapproving the legislation on the grounds that it did not contain safeguards that would minimize the infringement of individual rights and the invasion of privacy, "which is one of the factors making American citizenship so valuable." The bill quickly moved through the House Committee on the Judiciary, was debated before the House on 7 April 1954, and was passed by it the following day. The two major metropolitan bar associations again are acknowledged in the House debates, despite the rapidity of the measure's passage in the House. An Illinois representative noted that the CBA Committee on Federal Legislation, of which he was a member, had been reviewing the bill; a report from the Committee on Federal Legislation of the Association of the Bar of the City of New York was inserted in the Congressional Record; and another speaker noted that resolutions from bar associations around the country were coming in, all of which wanted time to comment on the wiretapping bills.[16]

The principal involvement of the CBA came with the hearings of the Senate Committee on the Judiciary on four bills dealing with wiretapping. The form in which the CBA cast its reaction to the bills is instructive. In the conclusion to its report, submitted as a statement to the Senate Committee on the Judiciary Hearings on Wiretapping for National Security, the CBA stated:

> The burden of proof in showing the Congress that there is a need for legislation authorizing wiretapping should be borne by those advocating it. Since such legislation would necessarily derogate from the individual's freedom and right of privacy, it should be considered only after a congressional determination that the advantage in safeguarding our national security outweighs the disadvantage to individual rights. If such legislation is then determined necessary, careful thought must be given to minimizing the accompanying impairment of individual privacy and freedom.
>
> Those bills now under consideration by Congress are not accept-

15. *Congressional Record* 100 (1954): 13326–27, 13330–32. Committee on Civil Rights, File 54-61, 26 April 1954; Transcripts, 6 May 1954; Board of Managers Press Release, 7 June 1954.
16. *Congressional Record* 100 (1954) 4300, 4422, 4794–4828, 4890–4914.

able. In their present forms, they fail to contain even the following minimum safeguards: (1) Supervision by a court upon written showings by the Government; (2) prohibition of unauthorized wiretapping together with clarification of the Federal-State relationship on the subject; (3) limitation of scope to specified crimes regarding national security; (4) provisions to assure security of material obtained; (5) limitation of authorization to the FBI; (6) limitation of the duration of both the act itself and the periods of each judicial authorization; and (7) prohibition against the use of evidence obtained prior to the effective date of the act.[17]

As in its responses to the immunity legislation, the organized bar achieved a degree of prominence in the committee hearings. Of ten statements submitted to the committee by voluntary associations, three were from bar associations—the CBA, the National Lawyers Guild, and the Association of the Bar of the City of New York. Their contributions to the Senate Committee on the Judiciary hearings may well have had some influence on the tie vote in that committee on the bills. When, on 9 August, the committee rejected by seven votes to seven the motion to table the House bill, it was clear that the committee was impossibly split and that any further action on the bill was abandoned. So ended the principal lines of involvement by the CBA in federal antisubversion and sedition controversies in the decade following the close of World War II.

ANTISUBVERSION MEASURES IN ILLINOIS

Whereas the CBA was virtually lost among the national lobbies in Washington, even if it was one of the few bar associations to attain national prominence, it became much more closely and publicly drawn into Cold War controversies in Illinois, where it was much less anonymous. The issues were similar, but the costs of bar involvement threatened to be expensive, and thus bar strategies were carefully calculated. While reactions to state antisubversive legislation mirrored its policy on federal legislation, a strategic caution couched its substantive conclusion in the most unobjectionable terms—terms that would reconcile the uneasy coexistence of outspokenness in matters of principle with sagaciousness in matters of tactics.

McCarthyism visited Illinois most notably in the person of state Senator Broyles, whose package of bills introduced into each session of the General Assembly from 1949 to 1955 were intended to flush out "communist defenders" and "subversives." To meet "treachery, deceit, infiltration into government and other institutions, espionage, sabotage, terrorism, and other unlawful means,"

17. Committee on Civil Rights, File 54-61, 26 April 1954; Transcripts, 6 May 1954; Board of Managers Press Release, 7 June 1954.

Broyles offered legislation with enforcement provisions to combat sedition and ensure loyalty.[18] The sedition sections made it a felony knowingly to engage in acts that would make one a subversive person, while the loyalty provisions would make subversive persons ineligible for state employment, require government agencies to determine the loyalty of their employees, and ensure that no subversive persons were appointed to them. A special assistant attorney general could be delegated powers to take charge of antisubversion drives in the state.[19]

Carefully prefacing its criticisms with the assurance that "it subscribes wholeheartedly to the objectives sought by these provisions," the Civil Rights Committee submitted recommendations to the board that amounted to a series of systematic, scholarly, and cumulatively devastating attacks on the Broyles bills. The sedition provisions, it said, were hopelessly vague and ambiguous. "By what acts," it asked, "does one 'espouse' or 'subscribe to' a 'doctrine'?" The measures merely duplicated Illinois statutes on overthrow of the government, and, in fact, if more was intended by the bills than present statutes already covered, then they were probably unconstitutional. The loyalty paragraphs were frightening, giving enormous powers to individual agencies such as school boards and to officials from town treasurers to sanitary district inspectors. Even more drastic were the implications for educators in proposed bills introduced in 1951; they would permit public school teachers or university professors to be dismissed for teaching "any doctrine to undermine the form of government in this state . . . by force or violence." In sum, the section was "dangerous, unworkable and violative of traditional notions of due process." Enforcement provisions were also suspect in numerous respects, adding few genuinely new and useful powers but offering much scope for abuse and discretion.[20]

Whatever the inadequacies of the particular provisions outlined in Broyles's fruitless seven-year attempt to enact his programs, the underlying objection of the civil rights lawyers was derived from a fundamental philosophical position that undergirded their predilection for casting opposition in formal or procedural terms.

> These bills . . . seek to protect the state, not from the crimes of communists, but from the "doctrine" of communism. . . . It is extremely difficult to legislate against the expression of precepts or principles without infringing the basic liberties guaranteed by the Constitution. Even if the deficiencies in draftsmanship which now characterize these bills were to be cured by amendment, their curtail-

18. Senator Paul W. Broyles, "Brief Statement of Facts concerning Origin of Senate Bill 102 and Digest of Act," n.d.

19. Committee on Civil Rights, File 53-29, March 1953.

20. Committee on Civil Rights, Report on Senate Bill no. 102, 15 May 1951; Committee on Civil Rights, File 51-23, 21 February 1951, and File 55-32, 28 February 1955.

ment of individual rights would still be unconstitutional unless it could somehow be shown that the security of the nation demanded the suppression of ideas.

The fundamental principle upon which this country has relied for its faith is the uncoerced loyalty of the overwhelming majority of its citizens. This is also the fundamental distinction between free nations and their totalitarian opponents. It is only when a government distrusts its people that it feels impelled to silence dissent, to stifle criticism, to enforce conformity in thought, word, and deed. Isolated instances of betrayal and disloyalty, shocking though they may be, should not blind the legislature to the fact that the people of this state are still loyal to their country and that the security of the nation will not be jeopardized by their continued enjoyment of historic liberties.[21]

CBA board reactions to the Civil Rights Committee reports evidenced almost as much constancy as the reports themselves. In 1949 the association had gone on record opposing the first Broyles bills, a precedent the civil rights attorneys never allowed the leadership to forget. Even after Senate Bill 102 had passed in 1951, the CBA forwarded the strongly critical Civil Rights Committee report—along with a minority report offering amendments—to a House committee and the governor, who used the points raised in opposition by the bar association in his veto message to the state senate. Significantly, the CBA board itself refused to take a position on the reports even though the majority report offered a stinging rebuke of Broyles.[22] The CBA did oppose the comprehensive antisedition bill of 1953, in so doing providing a legal basis for the resolution of the Senate of the University of Illinois opposing the infringement of academic freedom the bills contained. When Senate bills 58 and 59 surfaced in 1955, the CBA sent word of its opposition to all state legislators and to the governor. Once again it became a useful rallying cry for dissent. A Chicago city counselor asked the city council to approve a resolution in opposition to the bills for reasons that included the opposition of the CBA and numerous other civic groups.[23]

Despite its predominantly reactive role in the McCarthy era, the Civil Rights Committee did take the offensive in 1954 and 1955 with the drafting of a Code of Fair Conduct to be adopted by state legislative investigating committees. The code would give statutory force to its long-standing policy of limiting the scope of legislative investigatory powers. But the Legislative Committee opposed including the code in the joint program, and, with similar legislation introduced in the General Assembly, the bill died. Yet the civil rights lawyers did have the con-

21. Committee on Civil Rights, 13 April 1951, 10.
22. Transcripts, 14 May 1951.
23. Resolution introduced to the City Council of Chicago by Alderman Leon Depres, 12 May 1955.

solation of a rare success in Chicago. The Emergency Committee on Crime of the City Council of Chicago requested advice from the CBA on the rules it should adopt in its investigations. The Code of Fair Conduct, lost to the legislature, was submitted to the council, which adopted its basic principles with only minor variations.[24]

As persuasive as the Civil Rights Committee views were in formulating one arm of CBA policy on subversion, those views did not eclipse rival forces within the association that aligned themselves against the procedural fettering of anti-subversive organizations. Despite the apparent identity of the board with the Civil Rights Committee, the public position of the CBA was Janus-faced. From the civil libertarian lawyers, and even from the board, came a relatively subdued but nonetheless stolid resistance to public scapegoating at the expense of the rule of law. From other segments of the association—the *Chicago Bar Record* and the Committee on Character and Fitness—came another perspective, which belied any universal agreement within the profession against the forces of patriotic immoderation.

The editorially autonomous voice of the CBA, the *Record,* remained largely aloof from the thrust and parry of loyalty politics. Yet its editors did not exclude the shrill voice of Benjamin Wham from publishing three articles, spaced over eight years, passionately denouncing subversives. With such emotive titles as "The Pro-Community Conspiracy in our Midst" Wham fulminated against Alger Hiss, Dean Acheson, certain "Harvard New Dealers," Felix Frankfurter, the Tydings Committee "whitewash," and various opponents of the McCarran committee's investigations of Communists and pro-Communists.[25] But the *Record* did allow detailed rebuttals in effect from Northwestern University law professor (and an author of the Criminal Code) William Trumbull and a careful refutation by another lawyer of Wham's interpretation of Supreme Court decisions.[26]

The limited circulation of the *Record* held in check widespread dissemination of the deep rifts within the profession that the board had been able to conceal. The Anastaplo case, however, thrust the stance of the CBA into national prominence, giving the bar association a reputation that completely overwhelmed its cautious—and often invisible—contributions to legislative restraints and the protection of rights. The CBA had excluded George Anastaplo from admission to the bar—a cause célèbre that went from the CBA to the U.S. Supreme

24. Committee on Civil Rights, "Proposed Code of Fair Conduct for State Legislative Investigating Committees," File 54-99, 24 May 1954.

25. Benjamin Wham, "The Strange Case of Alger Hiss," *Chicago Bar Record* 32 (February 1951): 199–209, and "The Pro-Communist Conspiracy in our Midst," *Chicago Bar Record* 34 (November 1952): 55–66.

26. William H. Trumbull, "The Loyalty Crisis," *Chicago Bar Record* 36 (October 1954): 16–34.

Court—after Anastaplo refused to answer a question before the CBA's Committee on Character and Fitness on his membership in the Communist party or his belief in a supreme being.

How can these seeming contradictory tendencies be reconciled? Through its delegated legal functions to act as moral gatekeeper to the profession, the bar association could maintain a substantive position that seemed at odds with the CBA stands on the limits of legislative investigatory power. In fact, the paradox of the Janus-faced organization is not so inexplicable. The bar was deeply divided over the limits to which certain rights should be protected. Even the apparent identity of purpose between the Civil Rights Committee and bar leaders should not mask an incipient, yet basic, disagreement: while the civil rights lawyers used procedural means to effect substantive ends—the cessation or moderation of political inquisition—the more conservative lawyers leading the bar generally approved the apparent goals of the investigatory committees but quarreled with the means by which the committees pursued those ends. When the Committee on Character and Fitness faced the same kinds of questions with Anastaplo that congressional committees had confronted for years, it adhered to a judicial procedure but reached the substantive conclusion with which many, perhaps most, CBA leaders would probably have been most comfortable. In other words, the relative primacy given procedural constraints on congressional investigatory hearings, or the substantive ends to which those hearings were directed, effectively marked the positions of the two wings within the bar.

The Civil Rights Era: Law on the Offensive

With the advent of the civil rights initiatives of the late 1950s and 1960s, the bar faced—and failed to resolve—two enduring problems. On the one hand, there was division and internal ambivalence within the organized bar elite over the proper role of a professional association in matters of public policy. On the other hand, there were fundamental rifts within the association on the substantive goals—or at least the means to achieve them—contained in the respective civil rights bills. On their attitudes toward broadened governmental powers, the positions of conservative and liberal lawyers reversed completely from the McCarthy period. In the 1950s, the civil rights bar was committed to the checking of governmental intrusion into the areas of beliefs, political views, organizational membership, and loyalty; during the 1960s, by contrast, civil rights lawyers advocated an enhancement of governmental capacity to intervene on behalf of the rights of one class of individuals. Moreover, the federal government intruded even further into areas characteristically thought to be the exclusive bailiwick of the states. On checking governmental powers, particularly using procedural lawyers' weapons, most of the bar could agree, albeit for different reasons. But on a more powerful national government that would restrict employers' choice of whom they would employ, that would limit those to whom one could sell one's home, and that might also legislate with whom one's children sat at school, consensus was impossible.

FAIR EMPLOYMENT AND HOUSING

Active involvement of the bar association in civil rights issues began in 1958 with two pieces of Illinois legislation on job discrimination. For the Civil Rights Committee, the reluctance of the Illinois legislature to pass bold laws against job discrimination demanded a statutory expedient that would circumvent state sluggishness. Such a measure, believed the committee, could be found in an amendment to the Revised Cities and Villages Act in order to provide local authorities with the powers to enact the ordinances that their state legislature showed great reluctance to do. In the words of the committee: "The proposed bill is an enabling act authorizing municipalities and other local governmental bodies upon an appropriate finding to enact legislation dealing with acts of discrimination against persons because of their racial, religious, or ethnic backgrounds." Most discrimination occurred in Chicago. An employment discrimination ordinance had been passed by the city council almost fifteen years earlier, but it had doubtful validity in dealing with private cases other than those directly contracting with the city. The committee's response would give local municipalities wide discretion in the enforcement of civil rights issues.[27]

The expansive scope of the committee's draft provisions was a rallying point for opponents within the CBA. The Legislative Committee let it be known that the bill had no chance of passage, that it would give wide powers to local enforcement officials—in effect "local home rule"—when it was not safe to do so, and that it would proliferate heterogeneous local ordinances around the state. Moreover, the Criminal Law committee representative said it was the feeling of his members that "they would like to know what a group of lawyers like the CBA is doing, handling a bill as controversial as these two bills, and having them emanate from the CBA." Furthermore, he told the board, "they feel this is entirely without your scope." The proposal failed to pass the board by a margin of three votes.[28]

During the 1959 legislative session, the committee returned to the board to advocate CBA support for civil rights bills already introduced to the General Assembly by other parties. The Equal Job Opportunity legislation, House Bill

27. Committee on Civil Rights, "Report on a Proposed Act to Amend the Cities and Villages Act with Respect to Denial of Certain Opportunities," File 58-84, n.d.

28. Transcripts, 4 December 1958, 15 January 1959. See also Legislative Committee, File 58-84, no. 19, 12 August 1958.

H.R. 2 and Senate Bill S.36, both supported by the governor and Mayor Daley, aimed at merit employment practices, particularly in the Chicago area. The administration bill would provide that "it shall be unfair employment practice for any employer, employment agency or labor organization to deny equal employment opportunities to individuals because of race, color, religion, national origin or ancestry." [29] An Illinois Equality of Employment Opportunity Commission would enforce provisions of the act. The Civil Rights Committee report pointed out that at least thirteen other states had similar legislation and that it had brought about a drastic improvement in minority employment. On the other hand, the Legislative Committee cautioned restraint and urged the board not to support the legislation. In its compromise solution, the leadership resolved to approve the principle of the Civil Rights Committee report but not to publicize that decision unless asked. In other words, noted a critic of CBA timidity, "We support a position and then refuse to tell anyone about it. What sort of position is that?" [30]

The CBA acquitted itself no better when a Fair Housing Practices Act was introduced into the 1963 session of the Illinois legislature. The bill would prohibit "any person engaged in the business of selling or renting real estate" from engaging in an "unfair housing practice." The bill was directed less at homeowners than at real estate brokers and mortgage lenders. A housing practice would be construed as "unfair" if the seller refused to sell or made some discriminatory special condition of sale on grounds of race, creed, color, national origin, or ancestry. If a financing institution discriminated against an applicant on similar grounds, it would be in violation of the law. The bill would provide for a Fair Housing Practice Commission of five members who would "initiate on its own and receive, investigate and dispose of complaints of unfair housing practices." The commission would have legal powers of enforcement, including subpoena power and ability to issue "cease and desist" orders. [31]

The Civil Rights Committee recommendation that the CBA should publicly support the legislation and "actively" work for its adoption threw the board into disarray, with some of its members arguing passionately for the committee's position and others opposing it just as strongly. This kind of bill, they said, was far from the proper concern of a legal association, it would harm its public image and its relations with real estate organizations and the financial community, and the form of the actual bill itself was "terrible." Caught between the two political wings of its membership, the association contrived to place itself on the morally "right" side of the issue without committing itself to the specific bill pending in

29. Committee on Civil Rights, File 59-60, 22 April 1959.

30. Board Subcommittee on Equal Job Legislation, File no. 59-60, n.d.; Transcripts, 11 June 1959.

31. Committee on Civil Rights, File 65-33, n.d.; Transcripts, 25 April 1963, 2 May 1963.

the general assembly. The board issued a carefully worded and much debated announcement that housing discrimination was "a grievous wrong and contrary to American ideals." Law could be a constructive force in eradicating this wrong, but such law must meet several other criteria and warranted careful study. Consequently, the CBA's diffuse endorsement provided little moral impetus, no technical support, and of course no commitment of any of its other resources. The bill and similar measures failed in 1963, 1965, and 1967; by 1975 a Fair Housing Practices Act had still not been passed in Illinois.[32]

After the protracted debate around this issue, and with impending federal civil rights legislation, the association was forced to debate explicitly its degree of involvement in social change. A motion from two of the most conservative members of the board precipitated a general review of the association's role. The motion read: "[I]t is the sense of this Board that the CBA not participate in matters pertaining to racial discrimination except insofar as it may directly pertain to the functions of the Bar Association itself."

In the opening remarks before a special board meeting called to debate the motion, the main sponsor argued that he had only one thing in mind—it was not within the objectives of the CBA to participate in this kind of action. He did not condone discrimination, he said, but concluded that "I cannot see how, by any stretch of the imagination, the Bar Association should become involved in a question of racial discrimination within the limits of this language." Getting into such a controversial subject, with its social, political, and economic ramifications, would be like getting "a wildcat by the tail."

Of course, pointed out an opponent of the motion, the precedents of the CBA itself could not sustain a constricted vision of its purpose. The Corporation Act of 1933, the Uniform Commercial Code of 1961, the Code of Criminal Procedure of 1961, the revenue article drafts, the trust laws, the divorce laws—all areas where the CBA had been a key advocate and proponent of change—burst out of the narrow confines of a strict constructionist reading of the objects and purposes. In a capsule of sociological jurisprudence, the symbiosis between the CBA and the community was summed up by another opponent of the motion: "The people look to the Bar Association; we are supposed to be an influence in the community, and we grow with the community and the community grows with the law." By virtue of their education, their specialized knowledge, and their heritage, lawyers can remain on the sidelines of public debate—but they do so irresponsibly. "I think from the time the Constitution of the United States was enacted, all social legislation, progress, was all done by the lawyers. The lawyers

32. On H.B. 257, see also Committee on Civil Rights, File 65-18, 24 February 1965; Transcripts, 29 April 1965, 6 May 1965; Committee on Civil Rights, File 67-29, 31 January 1967; Transcripts, 9 February 1967, 16 February 1967.

comprise most of the Congress and the Senate. And the people look to us for guidance; they are always asking, 'what is the Bar Association going to do about it?'"[33]

The motion, however, was less than deftly drawn. It demanded not generality, not specificity, but total noninvolvement. And, for the great majority of the board, that was completely unacceptable—at least in theory. Rejecting by a vote of nine to two the motion that it should withdraw from civil rights issues that treated racial inequality, the CBA board signaled its intention to venture beyond the uncontroversial palisades of lawyers' law. But the vindication of good intention would come not with the nobility of stated purposes but rather with the courage of political action. The actions of the association in subsequent years would seriously call into question the salience of the board's vote for an enlarged conception of its role in social change.

The first test of the CBA's convictions came with a report from the Civil Rights Committee—which had taken the board vote very seriously indeed. On 8 October 1963, two months after the decision on CBA policy, the committee presented the board with an agenda for social action. That agenda would demand a statement of CBA policy on racial equality to be issued to all CBA members, a statement that would acknowledge public protest as a basic right of all Americans. Chicago lawyers, it said, should engage in public interest litigation and the association should file its own suits against discrimination. Further, the CBA should review, with an eye for revision, all Illinois civil rights statutes. And the Civil Rights Committee would meet with all major law firms to discuss their employment practices. The committee forwarded its manifesto to the board for immediate consideration, but there is no trace that the policy proposal ever reached the board's agenda book. Somewhere between the committee and the leadership, the idealism of the civil rights bar met with the realism of bar association politics. The convictions of the board's lofty and abstract ideals faltered at the bar of political advocacy.[34]

THE FEDERAL CIVIL RIGHTS ACTS

More direct tests of the CBA's commitment to civil rights reform came with the massive civil rights bills introduced into Congress in the following three years. The 1964 Civil Rights Bill, initially introduced to Congress as House Bill 7152, was one of the legislative landmarks of the civil rights era. Even the CBA Civil Rights Committee excelled its usually demanding standard for thorough reports with a submission to the board that ran to seventy-four pages of description, evaluation, and recommendations. With a unanimous vote, the committee pressed

33. Transcripts, 7 August 1963.
34. Committee on Civil Rights, File 63-120, 8 October 1963.

the board for early action on its report so that it might have the maximum contribution to make to the legislative process in Washington.[35]

The main provisions of the administration bill, contained in its eleven titles, ranged over all facets of discrimination problems, subject to constitutional constraints on federal intervention in state affairs. The bill would secure voting rights for Negroes (Title 1), rights to public accommodations and business and service facilities (Title II), and a variety of other rights in any operations concerned with interstate commerce. Title IV mandated school desegregation. The bill continued the Civil Rights Commission and provided for a commission on equal employment with investigative and limited enforcement powers (Title VII), and it gave the federal government powers to withdraw federal funding of programs in certain instances.[36]

National debates over House Bill 7152 centered on three issues. For the lawyers, the constitutionality of provisions that squeezed the utmost flexibility out of the Constitution for enhancement of federal powers provoked fierce disputation. For the states, the greatly increased powers of the federal government to intervene in states' affairs raised a cause for alarm not unlike that generated by the reform legislation of the New Deal. For the public at large, the discussion over the extent of government action to be used to redress grievous wrongs without abrogating individual rights generated a tremendous furor.

Each of these topics occupied the board. Within the leadership, objections divided between those whose disagreements with the total bill were implacable (and who used particular objections to subvert its general effect) and those who were largely in accord with the purposes and provisions of the legislation but had reservations about specific clauses or titles. The extent of division and heat of argument were commensurate with the extensive powers the bill would give the federal government. The board met in two rare, full, special meetings and devoted considerable time to it on three other occasions.

In a long speech prefaced by the comment that he thought the committee report was "sincere" but "unscholarly," a leader of the opposition conceded the value of Title I on voting rights but found Titles II and VII highly controversial if not radical. The intention to desegregate public accommodations was laudable, he said, but the means of achieving it were not. Besides the immense expense required to implement this legislation, it was virtually unworkable. "It is seriously likely to cause disrespect for law, defiance of law, and loss of prestige in our courts." It would be a momentous error to concede so readily to the civil rights movement and to allow it to "sweep" into law. Title VII had a reach

35. Committee on Civil Rights, Report 64-33, 10 April 1964.
36. *Congress and the Nation: 1945–1964* (Washington: Congressional Quarterly Service, 1965), 1630–41.

nothing short of alarming. "I am sick of commissions . . . and bureaus; I am tired of having people snoop around. And if their purpose is to make sure that my firm doesn't discriminate in employing secretaries or lawyers, well, now, I have a certain right to choose whom I want to employ and with whom I am going to be associated for ten, fifteen, twenty, or thirty years."

The CBA president, unable to maintain normal presidential aloofness from the early stages of debate, strenuously disagreed. Personal freedom, he did not doubt, was a wonderful thing. But black people did not have it. "The realities are that great oppression is practiced and has been practiced for years and years and years, and every time some attempt is made to correct it, we are confronted with the question, 'Why shouldn't I be permitted to live with or . . . to employ whom I like without coercion?'"

But that sort of argument evaded a simple fact: the wage and hours laws "and many other important pieces of social legislation were enacted over the years because voluntarily our people wouldn't make the changes that were required." Another CBA leader and former president stated:

> [D]efeat of Title II or Title VII of this particular legislation, in my judgment, would be a victory for those people who are determined that, one hundred years having passed, for at least another century to pass before we have equality before the law in this country. . . . [We] should confront, not the technicalities, but the broad issues of this legislation. . . . [I]f the lawyers are not going to take the lead in a situation of this kind, then the profession doesn't deserve the front that is put up by us and the image we desire to create, that we are leaders in the community, in the interests of the law and justice and what is right between man and man.

After hours of debate the board passed two resolutions by a vote of eleven to four.

> BE IT RESOLVED, That the CBA believes it to be imperative that the Congress of the U.S. adopt now a bill which makes the necessary improvements in the recognition and enforcement of the civil rights of all its citizens.
>
> BE IT FURTHER RESOLVED, That H.R. 7152 is such a bill, and while not perfect, it should be promptly enacted.

Copies of the resolutions were forwarded to the press and the two senators from Illinois. In addition, the board agreed that a summary of the Civil Rights Committee report be circulated, which might include mimeographing copies of it or including extracts in the *Chicago Bar Association Communicator* or the *Chicago Law Bulletin*. Nevertheless, these actions, while positive, were cautious indeed. The public lobby of the CBA amounted to two paragraphs, two letters to senators, and a two-paragraph news release.[37] In this sphere the CBA lagged far behind both the American Bar Association and the Association of the Bar of the City of New York. The massive report of the Association of the Bar of the City of New York on every aspect of the legislation, including defenses of its constitutionality, received wide distribution in political and legal circles, the CBA committee itself acknowledging its debt to the earlier report. The American Bar Association had urged that all its members and its sister and constituent associations do all they could to push the bill.

An opportunity to redeem its earlier reticence came when the CBA faced an extension of the 1964 act with the 1966 Civil Rights Bill, House Bill 14765. But the CBA chose not to use this opportunity to acquit its self-defined commitment to end racial inequality. Before the board lay an extended statement by Attorney General Katzenbach, presented to the House Judiciary Committee in support of the proposed Civil Rights Act. Katzenbach documented the extensive changes wrought by the legislation of 1964 and 1965, but he also noted the work that still remained. Title V provided punitive measures against the "shameful catalogue of racial killings," sometimes Klan sponsored, that had too often gone unpunished. Titles I and II set out means to eliminate unconstitutional discrimination against Negroes in federal and state jury service. Title III would strengthen the hand of the government in enforcing school desegregation. The attorney general under this new law would be able to institute proceedings against individuals denied equal protection without waiting for individual complaints. Title IV presented a frontal assault on discrimination in housing practices—discrimination in the sale, the leasing, and the financing of residential buildings.[38]

The Civil Rights Committee petitioned the board to endorse enactment of House Bill 14765 publicly and to vouch for its constitutionality—a matter under some dispute. A board subcommittee appointed to draft a CBA position supported the intent and provisions to Titles I, II, III, and V, but it split on the issue of constitutionality and Title IV. With a cloture motion already voted down in the Senate and another motion expected, an argument for postponement gathered some strength with the bar leadership. Instead, a rival motion was introduced to table the subcommittee majority report: the board split evenly, six members in favor and six against. Assuring all members that his motives were only concerned with timing, the chairman cast his vote to break the tie in favor of tabling—an action that left a black lawyer present at the debate charging that this

37. Transcripts, 20 April 1964, 30 April 1964, 29 April 1964, 11 June 1964.
38. "Statement by Attorney General Nicholas deB. Katzenbach before Subcommittee no. 5, House Judiciary Committee, in support of the Proposed Civil Rights Act of 1966," H.R. 14765, 4 May 1966, File 66-65.

use of postponement as a weapon brought to mind the failure—through the triumph of passivity—of forces to stem the development of Nazism in Germany.[39]

Open occupancy legislation, in substantially the same form as a bill introduced into the 1965 Illinois legislature, faced the board again in 1967. The same board, with the same political convictions about the role of the organized bar in substantive change, resurrected the same parameters of debate already thoroughly addressed in the 1963, 1964, 1965, and 1966 civil rights legislation at both federal and state legislatures. Already having committed itself to a general expression of principles in favor of the *idea* of open occupancy legislation, the CBA sidestepped direct comment on explicit legislative proposals, namely, Senator Partee's Senate Bill S.155, and retreated to the secure and tried ground of its enunciation of principles to govern housing legislation. There, for all practical purposes, ended the efforts of the civil rights lawyers to convince the organized bar to commit its authority to substantive social change through civil rights legislation in the decade from 1957 to 1967.[40]

But if these were the fates of intermediate-level legislation, what possible expectations could the organized bar have to influence policy with even more macroscopic legislative programs? Surprisingly, perhaps, the contributions of the profession at the highest levels of action—codification, uniform laws, and constitutional revision—seemed considerably to exceed those less far-reaching proposals I have already considered. It is to these, in the remainder of this and the following chapter, that I now turn.

Codification of Criminal Law and Procedure

> Whatever views one holds about the penal law, no one will question its importance in society. This is the law on which men place their ultimate reliance for protection against all the deepest injuries that human conduct can inflict on individuals and institutions. By the same token, penal law governs the strongest force that we permit official agencies to bring to bear on individuals. Its promise as an instrument of safety is matched only by its power to destroy. If penal law is weak or ineffective, basic human interests are in jeopardy. If it is harsh or arbitrary in its impact, it works a gross injustice on those caught within its coils. The law that carries such responsibilities

39. Committee on Civil Rights, Report 66-65, 25 July 1966; Transcripts, 8 September 1965; "Board Subcommittee Majority and Minority Reports on a Proposed Resolution to be adopted by the Board of Managers of the CBA and on the Civil Rights Act of 1966," File 66-65, 12 September 1966; Transcripts, 15 September 1966.

40. Transcripts, 9 February 1967, 16 February 1967. See also "Resolution Adopted by CBA Board of Managers," Report 67-29, 16 February 1967.

should surely be as rational and just as law can be. Nowhere in the
entire legal field is there more at stake for the community or for the
individual.[41]

Herbert Wechsler, Columbia University's noted criminal law authority, introduced his 1952 call for a model penal code with the fundamental dilemma of
state power in democracies: the powers of social control, necessary for public
order and social integration, are balanced against the rights and freedoms of the
individual, the right to privacy, and the freedom of self-expression and self-
determination. The dilemma in the criminal law therefore reproduces, in another
context, the inherent tensions between state powers and individual vulnerability
made manifest in the civil rights causes of the 1950s and the 1960s.

But Wechsler and others took the argument beyond state and individual rights.
They believed that in the criminal law the relations among the branches of government had become deformed in at least two ways. First, by default and by design legislatures had too readily cast the burden of criminal law responsibility on
the judiciary. Many state legislatures were perfectly content to set ranges of
penalties, to formulate concepts, and to leave the courts to "pour content into the
main concepts used." The very large number of court decisions provided a formal indication of legislative neglect and inattention.[42] Second, legislatures and
courts had, by default, conceded ascendancy in social control to administrative
agencies. "One of the major consequences of the state of penal law today is that
administration has so largely come to dominate the field without effective guidance from the law. This is to say that to a large extent we have, in this important
sense, abandoned law." The combination of legislative inertia and judicial vari-
ability allowed enforcement agencies to determine the delicate balance between
state power and individual rights.[43]

Thus reform of the law, and particularly its codification, implies much more
than statutory tidiness. As Allen puts it:

> In a time when there is a strong disposition of many to withhold their
> allegiance from the legal order, the familiar failures of the crimi-
> nal law in its administration, toward which we have displayed a for-
> midable tolerance for decades, take on a new and ominous signifi-
> cance. We simply cannot afford the deficient criminal statutes that
> burden most American jurisdictions. This is true because such legis-
> lation results in inefficiency and injustice; and inefficiency and in-

41. Herbert Wechsler, "The Challenge of a Model Penal Code," *Harvard Law Review* 65 (May
1952): 1102.
42. Ibid., 1097.
43. Frank J. Remington and Victor G. Rosenblum, "The Criminal Law and the Legislative Process," *Northwestern University Law Review* 1960 (Winter): 481–99.

justice in the criminal law produce intolerable losses in the legitimacy of all law.[44]

In general, codification of law had received little attention since the second half of the nineteenth century. But by the 1940s there were signs of renewed interest in criminal law revision throughout the country, first manifest in the 1942 Louisiana code, followed in 1955 by the Wisconsin code. In the interim, the American Law Institute, a prestigious organization devoted to the modernization of law, was undertaking the massive drafting of the Model Penal Code. That code would serve as the single most important source of inspiration in the postwar efforts of states at codification. Not only did it reexamine all the philosophical and contentious issues that surrounded criminal law—such as theories of punishment and policy issues of what should be placed in the sphere of public control and what should be left in the sphere of private morals—but it also provided specific, modernized, and comprehensive provisions across the entire field of criminal law. Louisiana and Wisconsin provided precedent, demonstrated that codification did not necessarily demand radical change, and afforded a wealth of practical experience. The Model Penal Code provided an expansive digest of legal principles and an authoritative compilation of systematic and coherent statutory provisions.[45]

Illinois, like the overwhelming majority of its sister states, had, as late as 1960, no criminal code in the sense of a "codified, systematic body of law having utility as an instrument of social control in a modern community."[46] The growth and status of criminal law in Illinois exemplified the irrational elements of the law mourned by would-be reformers. Many aspects of the criminal law in 1960 had remained part of Illinois law since Judge Lockwood had presented a draft of laws to the General Assembly in 1827, which was based on the criminal law of New York in 1802, and a volume on Georgia criminal law that he had found in the office of the secretary of state. A substantial revision took place in 1874, and repeated and unsuccessful attempts were made to implement a new code in the 1930s. Other than that, some provisions of criminal law had remained unchanged for 130 years, while a general systematic revision had not occurred in seventy-five years.[47]

Consequently, the inconsistencies and contradictions rife in the criminal laws

44. Francis A. Allen, introduction to "Symposium: Recodification of the Criminal Laws," *University of Michigan Journal of Law Reform* 4 (Spring 1971): 426.

45. Herbert Wechsler, "Codification of the Criminal Law in the United States: The Model Penal Code," *Columbia Law Review* 68 (December 1968): 1425–56.

46. Charles H. Bowman, "The Illinois Criminal Code of 1961 and Code of Criminal Procedure of 1963," *University of Michigan Journal of Law Reform* 4 (Spring 1971): 461.

47. Ibid., 461–62.

of other states were paralleled in Illinois statutes. Revisions of the criminal law were spread through 148 chapters of the Illinois statutes. Various forms of theft were dealt with in seventy-four different sections; fourteen terms could be found to define the mental states required to establish criminality. For stealing a horse, the minimum penalty was three years; for stealing a car, the penalty was only one year. While one section provided that children between the ages of seven and eighteen found smoking in public places should be found guilty of misdemeanors, another section indicated that no person under ten years of age could be convicted of a crime in Illinois.[48] So confusing were the statutes that the status of the law at any one point in time rested heavily in the rulings of the Illinois higher courts: but their interpretations and constructions were constantly changing. So too were the public morals on which the 1827 and 1874 provisions were based: standards of sexual morality, for instance, had changed so radically over many decades that the statutes, even if one could decipher them, seemed archaic.

In 1954, the Illinois State Bar Association and the CBA privately asked the governor and the Illinois Supreme Court publicly to ask bar associations to begin revising Illinois criminal law.[49] The Illinois and Chicago bar associations appointed a joint committee, chaired by Judge Austin, chief justice of the Criminal Court of Cook County, and consisting primarily of judges, academics, and leading members of the bar. A drafting subcommittee of seven was formed and, with assistance from several universities and the financial support of the Illinois Judicial Advisory Council, undertook the task. The committee worked for six years on the substantive law alone. In late 1960, it circulated several thousand copies of its 318-page Final Tentative Draft of legislation and commentary to lawyers, legislators, law enforcement officials, and others for comment and criticism.[50]

The draft code reduced the prolific confusion of extant criminal law to a simplified, coherent, and even elegant design. Title 1 set out the general provisions of the code; title 2 enunciated the principles of criminal liability; and title 3 outlined specific offenses. Within each title, the same degree of systematic orderliness was maintained. Under specific offenses, for instance, the code dealt first with inchoate offenses and then proceeded systematically through offenses directed against a person, offenses directed against property, offenses affecting

48. "Proposed Illinois Revised Criminal Code of 1961, Tentative Final Draft 1960," 4 (hereafter cited as Draft Criminal Code, 1961).

49. Richard B. Austin to Board of Managers, 23 October 1952, file no. 52-98. See also Transcripts, 30 October 1952, 10 December 1953.

50. General treatments of the codification of Illinois criminal law can be found in the following sources: Draft Criminal Code, 1961; Bowman, "Illinois Criminal Code"; Francis A. Allen, "Criminal Law Revision in Illinois: A Progress Report," *Chicago Bar Record* 34 (October 1957): 19–21; and John P. Heinz, Robert W. Gettleman, and Morris A. Seeskin, "Legislative Politics and Criminal," *Northwestern University Law Review* 64 (July–August 1969): 277.

public health, safety, and decency, and offenses affecting governmental functions. These offenses were in turn subdivided, so that offenses directed against a person included homicide, kidnapping, sex crimes, bodily harm, violation of civil rights, and eavesdropping—all of which were defined and further specified, with the nature of the offense, the allowable affirmative defenses, and the sanctions concisely expressed. Underlying each section was a set of policy considerations and a philosophy of punishment.

Codification, assert its sponsors, is primarily an adaptation of form: clarification of language, the elimination of inconsistencies and obscurities, and the rationalization of principles and offenses in criminal law. But form and substance, analytically distinct in theory, became inextricably intertwined in practice. The codifiers of criminal law in Illinois stated, "It was not intended to make any violent departure from the existing common law of crimes in Illinois." [51] In fact, numerous significant changes in philosophy and specific offenses were inserted in the new document.

Two specific changes threatened to subject the code to intense public scrutiny: changes in the definition of sex offences and liberalization of the provisions on abortion. The committee, with the drafters of the Model Penal Code, grounded the new law of sexual offenses on four policy considerations.

1. The protection of the individual from forcible sexual attacks.

2. The protection of the young and the immature from sexual advances of older and more mature individuals.

3. The protection of the institution of marriage and normal family relationships from sexual conduct that tends to destroy them.

4. The protection of the public from open and notorious conduct that disturbs the peace, tends to promote breaches of the peace, or openly flouts accepted standards of morality in the community. [52]

Criminality would be defined by offenses against these principles. But their acceptance signaled a major policy shift in the criminal law: there would be no criminal sanctions against consenting adults engaging in sexual relations in private. Adultery and fornication would remain crimes—but only where their commission was "open and notorious." Similarly, homosexual relations between consenting adults would not be considered criminal if they did not *openly* offend public morality. Sexual activity between humans and animals was also legalized by implication. The code abolished statutory rape and provided three affirmative defenses for taking indecent liberties with a child. In general, therefore, the revi-

51. Transcripts, 27 October 1960.
52. Morris J. Wexler, "Sex Offenses under the New Criminal Code," *Illinois Bar Journal* 51 (October 1962): 152.

sions marked a new toleration for the loosening of sexual standards and a new limit on the intrusion of the state into the private moral activities of its citizens.

The law of abortion was also mildly liberalized. Illinois law had allowed the justification for abortion when necessary to save the mother's life. After a careful review of the law on abortion in other states and of the results of various factual and scientific studies, the joint committee offered three affirmative defenses for abortion: first, an abortion would be legal if it was medically advisable on grounds that it would endanger the life "or gravely impair the health" of the pregnant woman; second, in view of birth defects resulting from diseases such as German measles, the committee would allow the defense for an abortion when the "fetus would be born with a grave and irremediable physical or mental defect"; and, third, abortion would be permitted when pregnancy resulted from forcible rape or aggravated incest. In every case, the abortion would have to be performed by a licensed physician in a licensed hospital.[53]

Other provisions, less demanding of public attention, nonetheless significantly reformed the channels along which prospective criminal law would proceed. The notion of mental states, a pivotal issue in any criminal case, received major clarification. The Illinois code reduced the dozens of confusing alternatives to four mental states, which would be used uniformly throughout the code: intent, knowledge, recklessness, and negligence.[54]

Despite the welter of innovations, some insignificant and some notable, several broader shifts in the character of the criminal law undergirded the extensive array of specific provisions. First, the code implemented a uniform system of punishment: in so doing, it expressed reservations about the dominance of retribution as a theory of criminal justice and acceded to the criminologists' new emphasis on prevention and rehabilitation. Second, and relatedly, the code definitively set the locus, type, and degree of discretion surrounding sentencing. Virtually all sentencing powers would be removed from juries and vested in the court. In turn, the courts would have uniform minimum and maximum limits of punitiveness set by the legislature—but would be given extensive discretion, taking into account the information gathered in presentencing hearings, to fix a specific sentence.[55] Third, and perhaps most important from the point of view of the separation of powers, the code represented the completion of the long path toward the complete transference of common law definitions of crime to statu-

53. Draft Criminal Code, 1961, sec. 23-1; "Committee Comments," Draft Criminal Code, 1961, 298.

54. Draft Criminal Code, 1961, sec. 4-3; "Committee Comments," Draft Criminal Code, 1961, 145–56; Bowman, "Illinois Criminal Code," 465–66.

55. Bowman, "Illinois Criminal Code," 465; Draft Criminal Code, 1961, sec. 1-24; "Committee Comments," Draft Criminal Code, 1961, 111–15.

tory provisions on crime.[56] In order to guide the case law that would emerge from the new code, the joint committee provided an extensive two-hundred-page commentary on the seventy-five-page code, which summarized Illinois case law up to 1960, compared that case law and court decisions in other states with the new code, and explicitly established the intent of the codifiers, and subsequently the legislature, in each of the provisions.

Despite the comprehensive scope of the code, and its potential for a public furor, when the joint committee submitted its draft to the board, abortion and sexual offenses were scarcely mentioned. Approval came quickly. In fact, other than a minor revision on gambling, the board appeared to be predisposed to accept the code before it had even seen it. It occasioned only one substantial appearance on the board's agenda book, and it was passed unanimously.[57]

The joint committee continued its careful planning in the legislature. It secured nonpartisan or joint sponsorship of the code, which was quickly referred to House and Senate subcommittees and then to a joint legislative committee for public hearings. Here three main issues dominated the others. First, the Defense Lawyers' Association resisted the provisions in the code that vested almost complete sentencing power in the judge, not in the jury. Amendments were offered to restore the jury's sentencing power but were defeated by a close vote in the committee and by a more substantial vote on the House floor. Thus the joint committee was able to sustain "a substantial break with the tradition of the criminal courts of the state." The second source of opposition emanated from the National Rifle Association, which saw the code as a way to weaken the weapons control provisions. But after "fanatical" lobbying efforts, their attempted amendments came to nothing.[58]

The third, and potentially most alarming, attack on the code came from representatives of the Roman Catholic Church, who liked neither the liberalization of sexual offenses nor the liberalized provisions for abortion. Without suitable amendment, the church threatened to speak from the pulpit against the entire code. After intense negotiations between legal representatives of the church and the joint committee leadership of the bar association, the two worked out a compromise: if the joint committee would drop the liberalized abortion provisions, the church would not object to the liberalized section on sexual offenses, including "private, consensual homosexual acts." With this accord, the code passed the legislature with little debate and very little amendment. It was, as Heinz et al. have observed, *"as if the Legislature had said to the Joint Committee: 'You settle*

56. "Committee Comments," Draft Criminal Code, 1961, 101–4.

57. Transcripts, 27 October 1960, 15 December 1960, 22 December 1960; Heinz et al., "Legislative Politics," 320; Bowman, "Illinois Criminal Code," 468.

58. Heinz et al., "Legislative Politics," 324–25.

it, and whatever you work out (within reasonably broad limits) we will approve' "
(my italics).[59]

The Code of Criminal Procedure, its 155-page draft and comments presented
to the CBA for approval two years later, was not to receive such easy passage. It
had two main objectives: to modernize the method of reviewing a case and to
expedite and reduce the cost of review. Like the substantive criminal law, the procedural provisions of Illinois law were based on the 1874 act, on which had been
superimposed various independent acts, so that inconsistencies, duplication, and
disorganization were inevitable. The joint committee endeavored to merge statutes and case law on criminal procedure into a consistent and coherently developed set of statutes. The code was a model of clarity. It was organized chronolog-
ically: investigation of a crime, arrest, trial, and posttrial proceedings were
addressed in that order.[60]

Like its sister code, the Code of Criminal Procedure did not purport to implement any radical, even extensive, changes in established procedure—at least
publicly. But one of the draftsmen admitted to the board that "we have made
some drastic changes in the law" on the arrest section.[61] Section 43 provided, for
instance, that a police officer might hold a detainee for up to four hours so long as
the officer believed the detainee "has committed, is committing, or is about to
commit any offense, even though the nature of the offense may be unknown." [62]
On this and other sections, the CBA Civil Rights Committee raised strong objections. It proposed several amendments to the code: that strict controls be placed
on police so detained persons would not be restricted from communicating with
their families or attorneys; that persons arrested should be brought before a judge
"forthwith," without any delay; that police officers should inform persons of
their rights to remain silent and to communicate with an attorney; and that inter-
rogations by police be recorded. All amendments were lost. The Civil Rights
Committee raised questions about changes in the law on search warrants. The
commentary in the Code of Civil Procedure stated that there have been "relatively minor changes in the existing law," but a joint committee spokesman told
the board that the code would greatly expand search powers so that a police officer could "get a warrant for anything that is the product or evidence of a
crime." [63]

With no significant amendments from within the CBA, the code proceeded to
the legislature, where it ran into a gauntlet of opposition on the detention provisions and on the revision of bail bond provisions—which would abolish bonds-

59. Ibid.

60. "Proposed Illinois Code of Criminal Procedure, Tentative Final Draft, 1963" (hereafter cited
as Draft Code of Criminal Procedure, 1963). Transcripts, 6 December 1962.

61. Transcripts, 6 December 1962.

62. Draft Code of Criminal Procedure, 1963, secs. 43-2, 43-3.

63. Transcripts, 14 February 1963.

men—and from state's attorneys who attacked the proposal that defendants be furnished with any confession before a trial. The defense lawyers in their turn resented a new clause that would permit an appeals court to increase as well as decrease sentences on appeal. For all the controversy, the joint committee had done its drafting with technical skill and political astuteness. Together with the well-orchestrated bar campaign for passage, the virtuosity of joint bar committee politics ensured that the code was passed with minimal changes from that approved by the CBA. It was implemented as law on 1 January 1964.[64]

The Idiom of Legalism in Legislative Politics

A thread of continuity runs through these issues. It finds its reference point more in reaction to state powers than in action to extend individual rights. Both political wings of the bar could agree on law used defensively: even if they could not agree over which government powers should be enhanced, they did concur that any expansion of powers be carefully circumscribed. Of course, they reached a firmer consensus on the McCarthy and criminal code debates than the rather shaky front they presented to the civil rights movement. But the bar reached no consensus when law went on the offensive: agreement within the bar on the withdrawal of the state from the bedrooms of its citizens contrasted sharply with divergent opinions on state incursions into places of employment, places of residence, and places of schooling.

A case-by-case review of CBA civil rights initiatives demonstrates, therefore, that the orientation of the CBA was more complicated and more interesting than earlier observers perceived. It is too simple to conclude that the organized bar was for lawyers and not for rights, that it merely used the contrivances of legality to avoid the demands of justice. Although from a public vantage point it may have appeared that the association was either extraordinarily reactionary or hopelessly divided, a case-by-case review of civil rights endeavors shows that the actual orientation of the bar was rather different. The main thrust of CBA activity on federal legislation was not to the Internal Security Act of 1950 or the Communist Control Act of 1954, the linchpins of government actions against seditious organizations; and yet the association did respond to proposed statutes seeking broader investigatory powers whether through wiretapping or compulsory testimony of congressional witnesses. The principal drive, however, was directed toward congressional conduct in the process, or in lieu, of lawmaking. The CBA repeatedly communicated the disfavor with which it viewed alleged abuses or undue invasions of individuals' privacy. In Illinois, where the association stressed rules of fair conduct for legislative investigations, it can also claim

---

64. Charles H. Bowman, "The Illinois Code of Criminal Procedure of 1963," *Illinois Bar Journal* 52 (October 1963): 106–17, and "Illinois Criminal Code," 471–72.

a pivotal role in the perennial—and biennial—defeats of what it saw to be potentially repressive state laws against subversion.

Nevertheless, the vigor with which it defended rights in the earlier decade seemed to be contradicted by its languor toward extending rights in the later decade. Faced with the federal civil rights legislation on voting in the 1957, 1960, and 1965 civil rights acts, the CBA responded not at all. Neither did it contribute to the legislative enactment of federal housing legislation in 1968 or to the more comprehensive civil rights bill of 1966. The only federal statute on which it took relatively energetic action was the 1964 Civil Rights Act. Within Illinois, CBA activism was equally mixed; whereas on the one hand it gave some support for fair employment legislation, on the other hand it provided only slight assistance to the passage of bills on fair housing. Viewed in substantive terms, it ignored voting legislation, it mildly supported housing legislation, and it encouraged (albeit with restraint) employment legislation.

The profession's actions are as significant for their form as for their content. Indeed, the shape of the latter turns on technicalities of the former. In its reaction incursions on rights during the 1950s, the organized bar adopted what might be styled a *standard formula of resistance*. The characteristic bar response had two components. First, the bar faced the main issue of substance in legislation or procedure by treating it obliquely; the general point or goal of a proposed statute, such as rooting out Communist infiltration of government, was conceded at once. The profession refused to be placed in the position in which authors or supporters of a bill could label legal associations as fellow travelers or active dissenters.

But having conceded the worth of congressional investigations or statutes directing against sedition, the second and more important component of the bar formula of resistance came into play: the bar maintained that if the substantive goal warranted severe government intervention then the latter could only be countenanced through strict procedures. The interplay of the two components receives eloquent expression in a letter of the CBA president to an aggrieved commander of the American Legion during debates over antisedition legislation:

> Perhaps no organizations in our land are more vigorous in their opposition to communism or more relentless in their efforts to clean out the subversives than our organized bar associations. On the other hand the bar has traditionally regarded itself as bound to protect the constitutional rights of individual citizens and to oppose legislation that is regarded as violating the constitutional rights of our citizens. Every lawyer is bound by oath to uphold the constitution. The members of the bar cannot approve unconstitutional legislation and respect that oath.[65]

65. Andrew Dallstream, president, CBA, to Irving Breakstone, commander, Cook County Council of the American Legion, 7 April 1953, File 53-29.

The organized bar met every substantive proposal with rules, procedures, codes, and strictures. The bar hedged its support for substantive ends with highly qualified support for the means by which the intent of the legislation was to be realized. Legislative proposals and investigatory committees were wrapped about with a mesh of constricting processes through which the bar demanded they act. Accordingly, the bar supported the idea of and need for congressional investigations, but it repeatedly issued lists of conditions those investigations must meet if they were to continue properly. The bar conceded that indeed potentially draconian measures for intercepting telephone calls might be necessary but then insisted that wiretapping should be permitted only with numerous restrictions on executive autonomy and discretion. The closest the CBA came to direct confrontation of a bill's substance was found in the compulsory testimony legislation, but, for reasons that are considered below, this case is much less an exception as it seems.

In the public expression of its point of view, therefore, the profession was consistently vacuous in its reaction to the ends of justice, the substantive goals of most civil rights statutes it considered. At the same time, however, it developed an extensive idiom of professional expression through the adherence, in public, to procedural and formal conceptions of law. In its formula of resistance the profession places the meat of its reaction in the language of legalism.

First, statutes or procedures can be placed in a constitutional context, with review of the relevant sections of the Constitution that bear on the issue. Second, an association may then provide a summary or elaborate account of Supreme Court judgments and interpretations of the constitutional provisions as they apply to the statutes or procedures in question. Third, a proposed statute can be set in the history of legislation in its area with some comment on the force of preceding legislation and the need for a broadening of the legislative mandate. This context allows the profession sometimes to argue that a proposed bill unnecessarily duplicates existing legislation or that it contradicts other statutes currently in force.

Fourth, at the state level, technical arguments can also be mounted, on comparative bases, that measures adopted in other states are inappropriate in this state or that the experience of other states bears out the inadequacies of this form of legislation. Fifth, attacks can be based on conflicts of law—that the immunity legislation enacted by Congress, for instance, would not provide immunity in the states. Sixth, the form in which the bill has been placed may be subject to criticism on other legalistic grounds such as ambiguity in the major terms of a bill or its failure to meet criteria such as constitutional validity. Seventh, the profession can claim even more expertise in its understanding of the implementation of legislation, its effects on relations between the executive and the judiciary, and the capacity of the administration of justice to cope with the new expectations of its role. It can claim on legal or practical grounds that a bill gives too much discretion to authorities, that it would be impractical to implement, that its intent could be perverted, that the delays in time to have certain procedures carried out would undermine the point of the procedures in the first place. Eighth, all these points, however elementary, can be stated in a language that by its very form connotes expertise and validates its legitimacy. In some contexts and for some purposes legal language is self-validating.

Did the same formula of resistance characterize the bar's response to antidiscrimination legislation? In some cases, general enunciation of principles was followed by a checklist of procedures to be followed. There the direct analogy begins to break down. In the first place, it seems clear that in no case was the bar completely hostile to a civil rights bill: at worst it did not support, but neither did it openly oppose, antidiscrimination laws. When the CBA did take a position, it did so in one of two ways: either it specifically named and indicated its support for a bill (such as the 1964 Civil Rights Act); or it expressed its support for the general principles that a specific bill would implement without endorsing the bill itself (as in the case of employment and housing bills in Illinois). Even when the association took the former stand, however, it never gave unqualified support for proposed legislation; instead, its endorsement might include a rider such as "H.R. 7152 . . . , *while not perfect*, . . . should be promptly enacted." Of these three forms of response—qualified support of a specific bill, support of the principles behind a bill, and failure to take any action for or against—it seems clear that the two last options were more readily employed than support of specific bills. Thus while it cannot be said that the CBA opposed laws against discrimination, neither can it be said that it was generally energetic in support of the extension of rights withheld from minority groups. Indeed, it might even be concluded that the lists of principles and procedures were actually forms of legalistic evasiveness, comparable to similar, although weaker, resistance to some antisubversion measures.

If one of the profession's responses to the tension between state powers and individual rights is to use law defensively, by adopting an idiom of legalism to impose rules *within* branches of government, its other principal defensive mode is to press for adjustment in the balance of powers *between* branches of government. Bar attempts at moderating the distribution of power were of two, somewhat countervailing, kinds. The most dominant direction of bar policy attempted to transfer powers from the judiciary to the legislature. In part, this occurred by putting in statutory form lines of development in the law already initiated by the courts. The most striking example, of course, is the civil rights legislation of the 1960s, which followed the direction of social change set by the Supreme Court in *Brown v. Board of Education* a decade earlier. An even stronger movement from the courts to the legislature came with codification. By codifying the criminal law, the bar systematized the common law. But it went much further: the very notion of codification connoted a shift in emphasis from law finding, the law of the courts, to lawmaking, the law of the legislature. At least in theory, therefore, codification brings some democratization of the law—the creation of law by representatives of the people rather than by legal experts on the bench. In fact, as it has been demonstrated, codification may merely take the initiative out of the hands of particular judges and lodge it with a panel of lawyer experts. But, of course, it is easy to overemphasize the degree of change in the role of courts and legislatures that follows from codification: even the most detailed codes demand that courts retain considerable influence specifying statutes and filling out the interstices of statutory law.

At the same time, the bar attempted to redress some imbalances by extending judicial checks on legislative actions. In response to a legislative proposal to coerce testimony, the organized bar not only attempted to impose rules on the proceedings but insisted that legislative committees first convince a judge of the necessity for compulsion of testimony, thus providing a judicial check on potential legislative excesses. Similarly, the CBA made strenuous efforts to extend judicial controls over the sweeping loyalty legislation proposed by Broyles. In the criminal code provisions on sentencing, the courts were endowed with much greater discretion by the legislature.

The bar also sought, on other occasions, to extend legislative and judicial controls over executive agencies. The judiciary would have to be convinced of the necessity for wiretapping; and under the Illinois Criminal Code it was given more responsibility by the legislature to authorize search warrants. According to Francis Allen, the principal draftsman of the Illinois Criminal Code, the prime motivation of the Code of Criminal Procedure was to arrest the slide of discretion in criminal law toward the police—to reverse, as Herbert Wechsler put it, the trend toward "abandoned law."

Did the CBA exert any influence on the resolution of the tension between the state and the individual? Its influence declined from the criminal code, through the Cold War, to the civil rights era. As to the significance of its efforts on the criminal code, the effect of the organized bar cannot be questioned. With support from external groups, the organized bar initiated and drafted the new law. Except for negotiations with interest groups and the legislature, the profession, almost entirely by itself, totally revised and had implemented an extensive body of the law in Illinois. But its effects on the Cold War era were more limited: on Congress, its effect was minimal, expressed mainly through general resolutions forwarded to Illinois legislators. On the Illinois General Assembly, its contribution appears to have been much more significant. The CBA provided an expert authority around which public opinion opposed to the Broyles legislation could coalesce. The bar strenuously, and in great detail, attacked the Broyles provisions year after year. It did so publicly and, apparently, with considerable effect. Its declaration of principles in 1948 served not only as a manifesto providing unity for its policy but as the framework on which the Chicago City Council based its own investigatory crime committees. But in the field of civil rights, the bar association was mixed at best. Its high moral ideals, expressed with force within the association board room, emerged for the most part as bland murmurs. Although not manifestly opposed to civil rights reforms, it was not highly mobilized either.

We are brought, then, to the heart of the criticism that surrounds the use of legalistic modes of representation by bar associations. Is an emphasis on formal aspects of law—on craft, on legal neutrality, on reason—inherently conservative? A simple response cannot be given in either direction. The emphasis on legalism can be neutral or substantively biased. In one sense it has been seen that an adherence to a formal conception of law is a neutral stand; process and procedure and formal aspects of law more generally are doubled-edged swords. They are weapons that can be taken up by ideological adversaries. Yet a preoccupation with due process or procedure on the formal aspects of law are surely not without their political implications; but it is wrong to assume that those implications are necessarily conservative. The CBA's response to the antisubversion and anti-discrimination issues points up the contrast in the way the profession used the idiom of legalism to substantive ends. In the earlier decade, the organized bar used rules and procedures to a substantive end that must be considered liberal rather than conservative; in the later decade, sections of the profession showed some inclination to use a similar idiom to the opposite political effect, namely, in a more conservative than liberal reaction. In both cases the choice not to engage directly the substantive issues in question did not signal avoidance of the real issues so much as a choice to encounter those issues by a medium in which the profession has a singular expertise and substantial authority.

At the same time, it appears that at another level there was a conservative unity to the bar's reaction to both types of issues; in each case the profession used legalism *against* state initiatives, even though the results, in terms of conventional political philosophy, were entirely different in the two cases. Legalism, it appears, is therefore much better for opposing legislation than supporting it. Thus it is a more appropriate weapon to be used against a government infringing on rights than it is to be used for a government extending rights. If, therefore, an association is bound to exercise collective influence through the idiom of formalism, it appears that this constraint will produce an organizational bias against support of some types of controversial issues and actions in favor of others. This appears to hold at least for the civil rights area.

Once again, however, a qualification must quickly be made. There are many examples in the recent history of the CBA and other associations of legal formalism being used to liberal ends. The criminal codes represent striking cases in point: formal and technical approaches to change become vehicles for substantive amendment in ways that were undeniably—some thought radically—liberal. Those associations whose policies are committed to the advance of formalism, such as codification of laws, implementation of uniform laws, modernization of constitutional articles, the reorganization of courts, the institutionalization of judicial autonomy, and the like, have often pursued substantive ends by a range of these ostensibly formal means. Once again formalism becomes the idiom through which reform is expressed; the actual consequences may be conservative, or they may not.

We can say, then, that the extent of CBA influence was directly proportional to the interaction of two factors: the extent to which the organized bar could represent moral authority in the guise of the legal idioms of expert authority; and the immediate salience of the issues to the public and the profession. The bar achieved such great success with the criminal code because it could engage in the pretense that this was entirely—at least, almost entirely—an expert matter, with few substantive or moral implications, and the latter could be raised with appropriate interest groups or by the legislature. Consequently, the vast technicality of the code enabled the organized bar to make substantive changes without much challenge. The criminal law was perceived as a lawyer's concern. Moreover, the criminal law, in the eyes of the public, principally affects the unruly sector in society; as long as there is some semblance of public order, most people are not particularly engaged by the intricacies of criminal procedure.

With the Cold War, there was much more general public interest; yet again legislative hearings directly affected only a small group of marginal persons. Again, therefore, an expert and technical posture was possible. Under the guise of procedure, of due process, and of the rule of law, the lawyers could make a substantive effect on the scope of loyalty proceedings while protecting themselves from public excoriation by concealing any sympathy for the goals of the legislative investigations.

On civil rights matters, however, law on the offensive would have a vast and immediate effect not only on numerous institutions besides the law but also on members of the profession: neighborhoods, once sanctuaries for whites, could be threatened by the deterioration in property values and by open housing legislation. Businesses, law firms, and government might have to open their doors more widely to minorities; and, most alarming to many, the education of white children might be impaired by the forced integration of schools. The immediacy and personal threats of these putative changes were deeply divisive politically and provoked passionate emotional responses. In these circumstances, even if they had achieved a consensus, the ability of the lawyers to exercise their moral authority under the pretext of technical expertise was quite limited. Those lawyers who wished to use the auspices of the organized bar to sustain the legislative initiatives had either to address narrow clarifications in the legislation or constitutional issues or to make very tenuous logical leaps between the object of the civil rights legislation and areas in which lawyers had an acknowleged authority. Some argued that the rule of law was a more proper means to resolve injustices than recourse to the streets and that, therefore, the organized bar should be active in removing the causes that would drive minorities to the streets. Others presented the logic that, if the slums bred crime, and if lawyers were concerned with combating crime, then it follows that lawyers should be combating slums. Moreover, any attempt at asserting moral authority by means of technical contributions—an area where the legitimacy of the bar was unquestioned—depended on the internal consensus of the bar: one sector of the profession could effectively stalemate another sector by insisting that a given position was less technical than political.

In these circumstances, the CBA role was both reactive and restricted. It was responsive to proposed solutions, not responsible for them. While internal reports on 1960s civil rights issue were extensive, heavily documented, and highly informative, the CBA took efforts to contain their potential influence, either by filing reports, or by approving resolutions summarizing general recommendations of the report, or by giving them minimal publicity. Accordingly, on the 1960s civil rights matters the CBA engaged in symbolic politics, playing almost no expert or educational role for politicians, for the public, or for the profession.

In sum, therefore, issues such as the civil rights movement, which arouse widespread public sentiment and mobilize a diverse range of interest groups, exemplify the limits of the professional association's contribution to public policy. Internally fragmented and unable to effect a transformation of moral into technical authority, the profession as a collective actor was rendered largely impotent. This is not to say that on issues in secondary institutional spheres with less emotive content the organized bar could not gain the measure of legitimacy necessary to make a policy contribution. It is to say that on issues of which the effects are immediate and drastic, over which there is a political rift and both the public and lawyers are implacably committed to emotionally charged, and differing, positions, then the open association will have met the limits of its authority, certainly of a moral nature and, frequently, of an expert character as well.

9 Fiscal Crisis

It has become clear that a professional association can engage in considerable activity outside its primary institutional sphere. Indeed, the Chicago Bar Association's (CBA) relatively high volume of legislative actions took it into some of the most controversial issues of the postwar period. Yet the scope of professional action can extend still further—to the economic foundations of the state itself. The efforts of the CBA and the Illinois State Bar Association to amend the constitutional article on revenue represent another type of maximal case: a profession that can influence the structure of something so fundamental as the revenue base of a state economy is an influential profession indeed. But these actions have other implications for the arguments I have been advancing. Revenue politics provide a new, prominent, and hitherto unrecognized context in which to extend our understanding of the degree to which a profession can exploit the uncertain distinction between expertise and policy. In so doing it may bring its knowledge and skill to involvement in another crisis periodically faced by the modern liberal state.

Joseph Schumpeter called at the close of World War I for a "fiscal sociology" because, he maintained, "fiscal pressure of the state" has made of people what they have become.

> Fiscal measures have created and destroyed industries, industrial forms and industrial regions even where this was not their intent, and have in this manner contributed directly to the construction (and distortion) of the edifice of the modern economy and through it of the modern spirit. But even greater than the causal, is the symptomatic, significance of fiscal history. The spirit of a people, its cultural level, its social structure, the deeds its policy may prepare—all this and more is written in its fiscal history, stripped of all phrases. He who knows how to listen to its message here discerns the thunder of world history more clearly than anywhere else.[1]

1. Joseph A. Schumpeter, "The Crisis of the Tax State," in *International Economic Papers*, ed. Alan T. Peacock et al. (London: Macmillan, 1954), 7.

And if fiscal analysis pries open the mysteries of economies and politics, its leverage is especially critical at certain historical junctures. "The public finances are one of the best starting points for an investigation of society, especially though not exclusively of its political life. *The full fruitfulness of this approach is seen particularly at those turning points,* or better epochs, during which existing forms begin to die off and to change into something new, and *which always involve a crisis of the old fiscal methods*" (my emphasis).[2] Fiscal crises, then, are scarcely new; and a tax crisis for a subnational state in one decade (Illinois) can turn into an urban fiscal crisis in the next (New York) and a national deficit crisis some ten years later (the United States). My concern, therefore, is to take a modest instance of crisis and treat it in Schumpeter's terms, namely, by observing it closely to discover key features of adaptive capabilities by the modern state.

A state may find itself in revenue difficulties for a combination of reasons.[3] One has to do with the types of taxation on which it principally depends; another concerns the mix of taxes or the composition of its tax base. Historically, states have depended heavily on *property taxes*.[4] These are of two kinds: real property tax constitutes a levy on the value of real estate, farms, houses, factories, and the like; personal property tax is raised by a levy on savings, holdings of stocks and bonds, jewelry, furniture, machinery, equipment, and other valuables. Revenue may also be raised from *sales taxes* of which a certain proportion of retail sales are paid to the government. *Income tax* can be of two types: business or corporate taxes and personal income tax. In addition, governments may impose levies on a wide variety of other items, including *occupation and franchise taxes,* where license and other miscellaneous fees are charged for the privilege of carrying on vending or trade.[5]

Governments raise revenue by various combinations of these methods. The choices they make have significant consequences. While property taxes levied on

2. Ibid.

3. For reasons that are not clear, much more research attention and commentary have been given to local or city fiscal crisis, on the one hand, and national crises, on the other, than subnational state fiscal problems. Compare Charles H. Levine, ed., *Managing Fiscal Stress: The Crisis in the Public Sector* (Chatham, N.J.: Chatham House, 1980). Even the 1978 "tax revolt," epitomized by California's Proposition 13, barely redressed the imbalance.

4. On the advantages and disadvantages of various types of state and local taxes, see Robert D. Ebel, "Research and Policy Developments: Major Types of State and Local Taxes," in *State and Local Government Finance and Financial Management: A Compendium of Current Research,* ed. John E. Petersen et al. (Washington, D.C.: Government Finance Research Center, 1978), 1–21; Steven D. Gold, *Property Tax Relief* (Lexington, Mass.: Lexington Books, 1979); Glenn W. Fisher, "The Changing Role of Property Taxation," in *Financing State and Local Governments in the 1980s,* ed. Normal Walzer and David L. Chicoine (Cambridge, Mass.: Oelgeschlager, Gunn & Hain, 1981).

5. A valuable comparative analysis of state and local sources of revenue is found in James A. Maxwell and J. Richard Aronson, *Financing State and Local Governments* (Washington, D.C.: Brookings, 1977), 92–188.

real estate have traditionally been one of the most significant and staple methods of state taxation, property tax tends to be quite inflexible because real estate values can rise and fall relatively rapidly whereas assessments and rates tend to change more slowly. Moreover, the value of real property and its proportion of the average individual's wealth may change greatly over a century or more; while it may have been the prime component of wealth in 1850, it has become much less central by the mid-twentieth century.[6]

Furthermore, like a portfolio of investments, a failure of a state to diversify the sources of its revenues may make it highly vulnerable to any sudden or drastic changes in the base from which most of its revenue is drawn. Taxes also vary in the ease with which they are collected and, correlatively, in the ease with which they may be avoided. Thus personal property tax depends considerably on the declaration of belongings and the valuations individuals place on them; if individuals greatly underestimate those values, there is very little that state authorities can do about it. On the other hand, it is much easier to tax savings, stocks and bonds, and other readily identifiable holdings. Effectively, therefore, it is entirely possible that more taxes will be collected in cases in which value is easily determined than in those cases in which it can be disguised. And that may work an injustice.[7]

But the assumption implicit in this discussion—that governments have complete freedom to impose new and varied taxes and to change, as occasion demands, their revenue "portfolios"—cannot be taken for granted. The authority to impose taxes can be vested in several places. It may be governed by the state constitution; but even there the constitutional revenue article can be written either as a statute, to give legislatures little freedom to adapt, or as a much more open warrant for legislative action. In the former case, a state needing to modify its revenue provisions may be forced to take recourse in court in order to find loopholes in the constitution. In the latter case, however, a legislature easily manipulated by powerful coalitions of interest groups may perpetuate injustice and inequities. Consequently, the balance of constitutional authority and legislative prerogatives is critical, especially as that in turn conditions relations between the state legislature and the state supreme court, thus raising in another guise some of the philosophical and policy issues surrounding the doctrine of separation of powers.

Not only are there ethical or moral questions about the proper relations among

6. Note the general aspects of the discussion in Glenn W. Fisher, "An Economist's Appraisal of the Illinois Tax System," *University of Illinois Law Forum* 1961 (Winter): 543–85.

7. See the useful comparative and historical overview of taxing and spending by state governments in Ira Sharkansky, *The Politics of Taxing and Spending* (Indianapolis: Bobbs-Merrill, 1969), 83–175.

the constitution, legislature, and courts, but each decision on types or mixes of taxation raises further problems of equity. Hence the moral aspect of taxation becomes relevant because some taxes, like sales taxes, are regressive, taking proportionately more from the poor than the wealthy, while others, such as income tax, can be progressive, taking proportionately more tax from those who earn more. Furthermore, taxes may be classified: different tax rates may apply to different types of property, where for instance income earning property would be more heavily taxed than residential property. And taxes may or may not be assessed uniformly, that is, the same taxes to be paid according to the same standards on all types of property within a given class.

It is clear then that both technical and moral matters are closely interwoven in revenue politics.[8] A technical decision that a certain combination of taxes would be easiest to collect will inevitably have effects on the distribution of the tax burden and thus on wider official and policy issues about what sectors of the community should bear more or less taxation. At the same time, decisions about the revenue clauses of the constitution and their amendment will bring up the traditional range of questions in political philosophy about the optimal, most balanced, set of relations among the branches of government and their flexibility under the constitution.

The crisis which faced Illinois and many other states in the postwar period directly confronted questions such as these. They arose not from theoretical but from immediate revenue problems, as the Illinois case indicates. State expenditure in Illinois rose from $225 million in 1942 to $1.9 billion in 1965. The increase was attributed to numerous factors: the high degree of prosperity and its effect on heightened demands for highways, schools, and recreational facilities; inflation; the backlog of public works left undone during the depression and World War II; and growing public reliance on government to solve problems that had been resolved traditionally by other means. Consequently, Illinois government was forced to rest its expanded demand for revenue on its constricted taxation base, inflexibly set eighty years earlier. More and more reliance was placed on the traditional sources allowed by the constitution: the "sales" tax, intergovernmental revenue, motor fuel taxes, motor vehicle and operator licenses, and cigarette and alcohol taxes.[9]

8. On principles—social and economic—of tax reform discussed in the context of the U.S. tax system, see Henry J. Aaron and Harvey Galper, *Assessing Tax Reform* (Washington, D.C.: Brookings, 1985), chap. 2.

9. Glenn W. Fisher, *Taxes and Politics: A Study of Illinois Public Finance* (Urbana: University of Illinois Press, 1969), 23–67, 198–215. For a summary of the continuing crisis by the General Assembly on Illinois state and local finance, see "Report of the Assembly," in "Illinois State and Local Finance," ed. Glenn W. Fisher, *University of Illinois Bulletin* 66 (21 March 1969): 3–6.

The prospect of revenue crisis came to sudden immediacy in the early 1960s. For fifteen years, since the close of World War II, Illinois had been balancing its budget by supplementing inadequate revenue with surplus built up in a general revenue fund during the war. The surplus in the general revenue fund, $147 million in 1949, was down to $15 million when Otto Kerner took office as governor in 1961. Four months later, Kerner announced that the balance in the general revenue fund had reached an alarming level: during February 1961, the daily balance in the fund had dropped to $8 million, and Kerner predicted a $12 million deficit by the end of the fiscal year. Without a significant cut in expenditure, a politically unacceptable alternative, or an increase in taxes, always a politically sensitive issue, Illinois would totter on the brink of insolvency.[10]

In fact, the crisis of the 1960s had been building for decades and had its origins in the uncertain history of the Illinois Constitution's revenue article.[11] The revenue provisions of the 1870 Illinois Constitution, which still governed the state in the mid-twentieth century, had in turn been drawn from sections of the 1848 constitution. Like the constitutions of most other states in the mid-nineteenth century, taxation rested primarily on a property tax, which, in an economy based on agriculture, represented a reasonable measure of the economic worth of the owner. The tax was governed by two principles: there was no classification, and all property had to be taxed uniformly, with some minimal exceptions. All property was to be taxed at the same rate. Alongside this tax, the constitution allowed—indeed restricted—other taxation to a levy on franchises, occupations, and privileges. As this exceedingly narrow tax base became untenable, particularly with shifts in holdings to intangible property, the state found itself unable to adapt. From 1900 to 1970, six attempts were made to amend the revenue article—all unsuccessful. In 1932, the Illinois General Assembly tried to enact a graduated income tax—Illinois' first venture into any sort of taxation based on income—but in a celebrated decision, *Bachrach v. Nelson* (349 Ill. 579, 182 N.E. 909 [1932]), the Supreme Court struck down the legislation and cast doubt on the ability of the legislature to impose any tax other than those few specifically noted in the constitution. In so doing the court reiterated the limitations on legislative autonomy and reinforced the power of the constitution, as interpreted by the courts, to inhibit adaptive revenue policies in the face of social and economic change.[12]

10. A description of the immediate crisis in 1961, and its aftermath, is given by Thomas J. Anton, *The Politics of State Expenditure in Illinois* (Urbana: University of Illinois Press, 1966), 118–46.

11. Janet Cornelius, *Constitution Making in Illinois, 1818–1970* (Urbana: University of Illinois Press, 1972), 56–88.

12. George D. Braden and Rubin G. Cohn, *The Illinois Constitution: An Annotated and Comparative Analysis* (Urbana, Ill.: Institute of Government and Public Affairs, 1969), 420–23.

The legislature looked elsewhere to solve its revenue problems in the 1930s—by instituting sales and use taxes—taxes that were, in fact, not true sales taxes at all but rather taxes "on the privilege of engaging in the occupation of selling tangible personal property at retail." By the 1950s the general sales tax was second only to property tax as a source of state revenue. Yet even this adaptive expedient far from solved Illinois's taxation difficulties. Writing in 1961, economist Glenn Fisher concluded that Illinois was too heavily dependent on general sales and property taxes. Before 1961 the sales tax base was among the narrowest in the country, and Illinois levied no corporate or individual income taxes. Together these factors made the Illinois taxation system among the most regressive in the nation. In addition, taxes contained numerous horizontal and vertical inequities. Sales taxes, for instance, placed a greater burden on lower-income persons than on middle- and upper-income persons. Ironically, many horizontal inequities had also developed from attempts to impose uniformity on property tax. Further, Illinois's narrowed revenue base also rested on taxes such as those on real property whose yields respond sluggishly to economic expansion and rises in prices.[13]

Lawyers were as dissatisfied with the inadequacies in the constitution as economists and legislators. Illinois compared badly to the legal bases of taxation in other states.[14] Only Arkansas was as rigid as Illinois in requiring that personal property be taxed uniformly without classification. General classification was allowed in twenty-nine states and a more limited classification in nineteen others. Uniform classification of real property was required in twenty-four states, while the remainder permitted some form of classification. In striking contrast to Illinois, thirty-four states levied personal income taxes in 1965, and thirty of these states imposed graduated income taxes. Other constitutions appeared more flexible on income tax than Illinois. Illinois remained one of the very few states—probably less than five—that had either debatable or explicitly prohibited income tax provisions.[15]

Underlying all the preceding objections, therefore, was a fundamental impediment. The constitution was unduly rigid: its rigidity greatly inhibited the ability of the state to respond adequately, quickly, and comprehensively to economic and social change. In effect, it was argued, state finances were largely dependent on

13. Glenn W. Fisher, "An Economist's Appraisal." For other general accounts of Illinois taxation and its fiscal crisis of the 1960s, see Rubin G. Cohn, "Constitutional Limitations on Income Taxation in Illinois," *University of Illinois Law Forum* 1961 (Winter): 645–60; Elroy C. Sandquist, Jr., "Taxation of Corporations in Illinois," *University of Illinois Law Forum* 1961 (Winter): 661–78; Glenn W. Fisher, "Public Finance," in *Con-Con: Issues for the Illinois Constitutional Convention,* ed. Victoria Ranney (Urbana: University of Illinois Press, 1970).

14. Cf. Glenn W. Fisher, *Financing Illinois Government* (Urbana: University of Illinois Press, 1960), 101–36.

15. Ibid.

the court's willingness to expand definitions of the constitution rather than on the legislature's best judgment of tax policy. Tax policy, for all intents and purposes, was determined by the courts and not by elected representatives. Illinois was constitutionally, and thus economically, shackled.[16]

In this context, the organized bar would seem to offer a distinctive contribution to change. A comprehensive bar association in a major metropolitan center concentrates extensive expertise in taxation and constitutional law. As a case in point, the two specialized committees of the CBA on constitutional revision and on state and municipal taxation brought together a pantheon of distinguished academics, including two law school deans and several other professors, some leading politicians, including the prospective governors of Illinois, Adlai Stevenson and Otto Kerner, state legislators, the leader of the Chicago Democrats in the Illinois house, and judges, including subsequent Supreme Court justices. The committees could also count among their members a large number of leading tax lawyers, who could bring wide experience to deliberations on tax reform, experience in court interpretations of constitutional provisions and in the actual workings of the tax system on a day-to-day basis. The organized bar arguably had a greater wealth of expertise in taxation matters than any other single body in the state. Furthermore, together the two committees had close ties with major political and economic groups throughout the state.

In the convergence of a governmental crisis with a profession uniquely endowed to assist in its resolution, what sorts of contributions could a professional association aspire to make? Could it go beyond the limits of technical advice in this, a secondary institutional sphere? A professional association's approach to government in these circumstances might take any of the following forms. First, a bar association could draw up its own draft constitutional article and submit it as a basis for the legislature's own article. Second, an association of lawyers might join an alliance of other interested groups to press more vigorously, and with added political pressure, for the legislature to adopt a particular article. Third, a profession could reject a limited advisory role and take an even more independent path by drawing up its own revision and submitting it directly to the legislature through a legislative sponsor without dependence either on other interested groups or on a joint legislative revision drawn from the profession's draft. Rather than going formally or directly to the state house, or, in some cases, concurrent with these steps, there is a fourth possibility—to allow deliberations and ideas emerging from the professional association to be introduced informally

16. See the account of constitutional impediments to revenue reform and fiscal flexibility in J. Nelson Young, "Constitutional Constraints and Fiscal Policy," *University of Illinois Bulletin* 66 (21 March 1969): 45–54.

into the proceedings on a new constitutional article, such as those that surround constitutional conventions.

Between 1951 and 1970 the CBA successively employed each of these strategies with varying consequences. In the following account of each attempt, I will show not only how close the lawyers came to having a radical effect on the shape of the Illinois economy but also some of the substantive and policy implications that flowed from what ostensibly was nothing more than technical assistance.

Professional Strategies of Constitutional Reform

Approaches to substantive constitutional revision are not unproblematical; it cannot be assumed that resolve and political will can readily amend and adapt an outmoded constitution to the needs of the modern state. Yet the principal point of entry into the constitutional politics by the organized bar in Illinois came not with the substantive changes of the judicial or revenue articles but with the formal conditions of changing the constitution itself. Indeed until the latter was resolved it appeared that there was no possibility of any constitutional adaptation under the political sponsorship of any group in the state.

The Illinois constitution had frozen the parameters of all institutions it governed. In the forty-two years from 1907 to 1950, nine constitutional amendments were proposed and all failed, principally because of a requirement for constitutional revision that a majority *of all those voting in the election* must approve a change. That is, revision demanded that there be not a majority of people who entered an opinion on revision but a majority of all people who voted for any candidates in the election at which a constitutional amendment had been put. Because very many fewer people register a vote for constitutional amendments than actually vote for public officials, it requires an overwhelming and massive majority for constitutional change. The failures of referenda in twentieth-century Illinois underlined the difficulty only too well.[17]

The CBA, like other reform-minded organizations, recognized that constitutional change of a judicial or revenue article must therefore be preceded by a change in the way change itself was permitted, namely, an amendment of the constitutional amending process. Shortly after World War II, therefore, the bar association committed itself to leadership in a strong alliance with other organizations to have a Gateway Amendment passed that would ease the difficulties of constitutional revision.[18] It was with that key objective attained in 1951 (another example of far-reaching association influence) that the bar association imme-

17. Charles V. Laughlin and Kenneth C. Sears, "A Study in Constitutional Rigidity," *University of Chicago Law Review* 10 (1943): 142–76; 11 (1944): 374–442.
18. Wayland B. Cedarquist, "The Gateway Amendment: A Resume," *Chicago Bar Record* 32 (October 1950): 18.

diately began to look to the next stage—revision of the judicial and revenue articles of the Illinois constitution. Revision of judicial articles I have already canvassed. The following sections provide an analytic narrative of the means by which it made its contribution to the fiscal crisis in a postwar state.

THE SOLO AND INDIRECT INITIATIVE

The initial strategy used by the bar had three features: under some public pressure, the bar drafted a model revenue article; it did so by itself; and it submitted the draft article to the legislature, with the intent that it be taken over by the joint House and Senate legislative committee that would attempt to draft a bipartisan measure.

In March 1951, long before the fiscal crisis was widely acknowledged as such, the CBA board approved an article that had been drafted by its prestigious Committee on Constitutional Revision. The committee's draft, subsequently to become that of the CBA, proposed to change the current revenue article in several ways. (1) Whereas the present constitution did not permit classification, the new article would permit the General Assembly to institute classified personal property tax. This would allow legislators to divide property into classes so that each class, if necessary, might be taxed differently. (2) The requirement of uniformity on personal property tax would be abolished so that different tax rates could be imposed even within classes. (3) Real estate, with the exception of mineral lands and land used for reforestation, would consist of one class, with the effect that residential real estate, which was non–income earning, and commercial real estate, which did earn income, would be taxed at the same rate. (4) The legislature would retain the right to classify any class of property at zero and thus effectively abolish tax on it. (5) The principle that tax had to be uniform within a class would be abolished. (6) Graduated income tax would be explicitly prohibited.[19]

The overall effect of the draft would be to give the legislature great discretion over the abolition of taxes and the implementation of new taxes and the facility to classify and tax without uniformity, powers so wide in fact that critic within the CBA stated that the draft provisions would allow the legislature, "without any curb of the Constitution, to enact almost any kind of tax except a graduated income tax." Moreover, according to critics, the freedom to classify personal property would allow some classes of property to be disproportionately and heavily taxed while others were protected; the provision on classifying real estate as one class would shift a greater tax burden onto homeowners and away from owners of commercial and income-producing property; and the power of the legislature to classify would shift a function away from local to state government. Hence the

19. Constitutional Revision Committee, File 51-26, 26 February 1951; Transcripts, 1 March 1951.

power of state government would be immeasurably increased with little constitutional check on its discretion. Whatever the substantive effects—and many lawyers asserted that this was a "rich man's" draft—there was consensus that implementation of the article would effect a major shift of power to the state legislature. Indeed, the formal freedoms this lawyers' draft offered the legislature seemed to entail a shift in the tax burden from those who could better afford it toward those who could not—a formal change, in other words, with major policy implications.[20]

Despite objections from within the association, the CBA board adopted the draft article.[21] Under the guidance of leading Chicago lawyer and CBA member Robert Cushman, the article was presented to the Civic Federation, the Association of Commerce, and the Illinois Agricultural Association, among others, as an amendment that would solve many if not all of Illinois's fiscal woes.[22] In a matter of two months a house joint committee had drafted a revenue article that closely followed the original CBA draft, and, with two relatively insignificant amendments, the joint resolution passed the house on 12 June 1951 by a vote of 127 to two and the Senate on 30 June by a vote of forty-five to zero. In the statewide referendum that followed, the voters polled 1,650,000 votes for the amendment and 990,000 against—but 1,900,000 voters did not cast a ballot in the referendum, and it therefore fell short of the necessary plurality.

Not defeated, the bar association came back to the legislature in 1955.[23] Again a draft virtually identical to that of the 1951 CBA draft moved quickly through the Sixty-Ninth General Assembly; again it was presented to the voters; and again it lost—this time much more heavily than in the preceding referendum. The defeat notwithstanding, the bar could draw some consolation not only from the fact that not only had the proposal adopted by the legislature been very close indeed to that drafted by the CBA but also from the fact that the draft had received widespread and effective support by interest groups. Furthermore, in 1951 it had sustained a large, if not adequate, majority of voting support.

---

20. Transcripts, 8 March 1951.

21. Typical objections lodged by the State and Municipal Taxation Committee can be found in Transcripts, 5 April 1951; and State and Municipal Taxation Committee, File 51-26, 12 August 1952, later reprinted as Henry J. Brandt, "Observations on the Proposal to Revise the Revenue Article of the Constitution of the State of Illinois," *Chicago Bar Record* 36 (May 1955): 365.

22. Internal memorandum, 12 April 1951, file 51-26. A comparison of the CBA's draft revenue article with those of the Civic Federation, the Joint Legislative Committee (embodied in House Joint Resolution no. 40), and Article IX of the 1870 constitution is provided by Robert S. Cushman, "The Proposed Revision of Article IX (the Revenue Article) of the Illinois Constitution," *University of Illinois Law Forum* 1952 (Summer): 226–47.

23. Constitutional Revision Committee, file 55-113, 12 October 1955. The board debates over the CBA position on the 1955 revenue article are contained in Transcripts, 27 October 1955, 17 May 1956, 26 July 1956. See also State and Municipal Taxation Committee, File 55-113, 16 February 1956; Committee on Constitutional Revision, File 55-113, 14 March 1956.

THE JOINT INDIRECT INITIATIVE

The result of the 1956 referendum indicated that the public mood was turning against aspects of the proposed article and that organizations in favor of constitutional change would have to adopt a new approach. The CBA did not take the initiative on its own terms in 1959 but rather joined forces with a broad-based alliance of organizations, the Joint Committee on the Revenue Article, which included the Chicago Association of Commerce and Industry, the Chicago Civic Federation, the Illinois Manufacturers Association, the Illinois Retail Merchants' Association, the Illinois State Chamber of Commerce, the Taxpayers Federation of Illinois, the Chicago Real Estate Board, the Illinois Association of Real Estate Boards, and the Illinois Bankers Association. The joint committee draft of January 1959 built on the already-proposed amendments to mollify some of the most vociferous complaints that had been directed toward earlier proposals.[24]

In view of its composition, it is not surprising that the joint committee draft was an artfully contrived document in favor of business and corporate interests. By explicitly prohibiting the classification of real estate, the new constitution would therefore reverse the de facto system of real estate classification in Cook County under which commercial real estate was being taxed at least twice the rate of residential real estate. Consequently, taxation on commercial property and revenue-bearing property would likely shift, in lieu of some other tax, to homeowners. By submitting a proposal for an income tax to referendum, the legislature would probably lose any authority that the 1870 constitution might potentially give it to levy an income tax on corporations or individuals. There would be no exemptions for low-income groups; the burden of income tax would therefore rest disproportionately on their shoulders.

The financial sector, afraid of an unhampered legislative responsiveness to "populist" pressures, defined legislative taxation authority with precision. Critical issues, such as the provisions on classification of real estate, which could maintain a heavier tax levy on income-producing property, were frozen in the constitution where they would be safe from tampering by politicians. The legislature would not have freedom to levy new kinds of taxes; it could merely add two specific taxes to the three specific taxes already authorized by the constitution. The valuation process, another point at which a relatively higher rate of taxation could be shifted to commercial and other property, would be removed from local assessors to the state legislature—an indication, perhaps, that statutory assessment would be more responsive to financial and corporate groups at state rather than at local levels. While the joint committee therefore advo-

24. Joint Committee on the Revenue Article, "Proposed Amendment of Article IX, the Revenue Article of the Illinois Constitution," 15 January 1959, File 57-10.

cated some minimal loosening of the constitution, its draft maintained, and in some respects perhaps even increased, constitutional restrictions on legislative discretion.

Faced with criticism of this draft by the CBA's own State and Municipal Taxation Committee, the CBA board asked a subcommittee to formulate a CBA position on principles of taxation revision. On the basis of its report, the CBA board effectively repudiated elements of the joint committee's proposals to which the CBA itself was a nominal signatory. The CBA board recommended that property should be classified for purpose of taxation. Taxation of real estate and tangible personal property should be by valuation. A legislature should have the right to subclassify real estate and tangible personal property and thus perpetuate the de facto system of classification in Cook County. Authority should also be given the General Assembly to provide a uniform exemption for the levy of a nongraduated income tax, an issue that should *not* be subject to referendum. Finally, for the purpose of clarity, a graduated income tax should be expressly prohibited. Perhaps most significantly, in constitutional terms, the board came out in favor of greater legislative flexibility in its taxing powers, although it did not go so far as the freedoms given the legislature in earlier CBA drafts.[25]

By taking this position, the CBA used its authority to undermine Senate Joint Resolution 19 and House Joint Resolution 48, both of which were substantially drawn from the joint committee draft. In opposition to the draft article, the CBA found itself with the majority. Once again the attempt at reform failed, although the CBA found itself this time on the side of those opposing passage.

THE DIRECT, INDEPENDENT INITIATIVE

At least twice the CBA had endeavored to precipitate change in the constitution by indirect means; it sought to produce a model article for the legislative committees endeavoring to produce a bipartisan, and thus more politically acceptable, set of provisions. Each time it approached the legislature throughout the 1950s, however, it seemed to have less effect than it did in 1951.

From 1961 to 1965, bar leaders changed their approach. They introduced drafts directly to the House through a legislative sponsor without having them screened or amended by an intervening legislative committee. In the first instance, in fact, its contribution was rather involuntary. Noble W. Lee, the dean of John Marshall Law School and a state legislator, wrote to the president of the CBA to inform him that Lee had of his own volition introduced into the General Assembly the CBA proposal to amend the constitution. Lee maintained that "this

25. Committee on Constitutional Revision, File 59-10, 23 March 1959; State and Municipal Taxation Committee, File 59-10, 23 February 1959; Board of Managers Subcommittee, File 59-10, 1 June 1959; Transcripts, 4 June 1959.

product of the CBA comes the closest to being an acceptable compromise of anything that has been discussed in the last ten years," and he urged the CBA itself to combine its support with other organizations to press the CBA bill. In any event, Lee's measure came too late in the legislative session to be considered, and the CBA itself was distracted by its major commitment to ensure passage of the judicial article and the Criminal Code. In 1963 the CBA did take more initiative and forwarded a bill to Noble Lee and other legislators, but, together with the other revenue article proposals of that year, the CBA proposal died before it received legislative approval.

In the meantime, as the 1961 and 1963 general assemblies reluctantly and fruitlessly grappled with their unwelcome fiscal agenda, the crisis continued to build. In a stopgap measure, funds were juggled around to provide a temporary infusion of revenue into the general revenue fund from three special revenue funds. Governor Kerner obtained an increase in the retailer's occupational and use tax, a slight broadening of the tax base, and higher taxes on receipts from hotels, motels, and cigarettes. All these notwithstanding, the basic tax structure that originally had led Illinois into fiscal difficulties remained unchanged.[26]

Between 1964 and 1965 numerous "new" drafts found their way into the public arena.[27] A widely based coalition of organizations from agriculture, education, labor, and business produced a draft, as did the Joint Committee on the Revenue Article. Once again the CBA would not accept the joint committee's suggestions, and it decided instead to submit its own ideas for revenue reform directly to the General Assembly in the form of House Joint Resolution 30, introduced by Representative Harold Katz. But yet again the legislature produced its own joint committee proposal, a measure that promptly received approval by the General Assembly and ratification by the governor. It was set to be voted on in the November 1966 general election.

House Joint Resolution 1 paralleled in numerous respects the 1961 CBA draft. Graduated income tax was excluded, flat rate income tax was permitted, limited classification was possible for tangible personal property, and classification or even abolition was allowed for intangible personal property. But the joint subcommittee of the CBA constitutional revision and taxation committees, which reviewed House Joint Resolution 71, unanimously concluded that "the present proposal falls so far short of being a satisfactory amendment as to not justify support." The House joint resolution, it said, was unduly inflexible, giving the legislature little opportunity to adjust to social and economic changes. It in-

26. Ann H. Elder and Glenn W. Fisher, *An Attempt to Amend the Illinois Constitution: A Study in Politics and Taxation* (Urbana: University of Illinois, Institute of Government and Public Affairs, 1969).

27. Fisher, *Taxes and Politics*, 198–215.

cluded particular special interest provisions—especially for corporations and banks—that seemed completely inappropriate. It took away powers, such as a corporation income tax, that the 1870 constitution already allowed the legislature. Ambiguity and imprecision compounded these inadequacies. Powers of certain government officers appeared unchecked; modes of administering provisions like the state income tax rebate to local municipalities were completely unspecified. Its draftsmanship was faulty and fell far short of the goals of clarity and precision.[28] However, differences within the CBA itself on House Joint Resolution 71 made the position of the board particularly difficult, especially as one of the drafters of the assembly joint resolution was a prominent member of a CBA taxation committee. Ultimately, the board decided the bar could neither give its support to the draft nor oppose it too strenuously. It opted instead for a purely educational role: the association would inform the public about the advantages and disadvantages of the article. Again it was to no avail.

DIFFUSE AND MEDIATED INFLUENCE

The handsome defeat of the 1966 draft revenue article in the referendum relieved those lawyers and interest groups that had found it wanting. But the fiscal crisis remained, and Illinois appeared to have exhausted its options for effecting change. There seemed little doubt that a radical alternative to the conventional mode of constitutional revision was the only way out of the deadlock. That instrument of change was the 1969–70 constitutional convention.[29] The contributions of the organized bar to this new mode of action were of two kinds: one was through the formal collective activity of the bar association; the other was through the informal channels of influence set up by the appointment of many leading CBA constitutional law and taxation lawyers to the constitutional convention. The chronology of events indicates the interplay of both forms of action.

In February 1967, the CBA added its weight to an appeal by a study commission of the General Assembly that there be a sixth constitutional convention in Illinois. The CBA urged the legislature to approve "the calling of an unlimited constitutional convention to be submitted to the people in a referendum at the next general election." Such a convention would allow a singular opportunity to break out of amendatory strictures, and it would provide a unique setting in which to confront directly and creatively the massive problems awaiting solution but blocked by an archaic constitution.[30]

28. Transcripts, 19 May 1966, 26 May 1966.
29. See, in general, Cornelius, *Constitution Making in Illinois,* 138–63.
30. On the revenue politics of the constitutional convention more generally, see Joyce D. Fishbone and Glenn W. Fisher, *Politics of the Purse: Revenue and Finance in the Sixth Illinois Constitutional Convention* (Urbana: University of Illinois Press, 1974).

With the legislative decision to put the possibility of a convention to a referendum vote in November 1968, the CBA began to mobilize. Already the Illinois Committee for Constitutional Convention included as prominent members the chairman and vice chairman of the CBA Constitutional Revision Committee, along with several other leading CBA lawyers—Louis Ancel, Elroy Sandquist, and Samuel Witwer, the last mentioned a key figure in previous CBA attempts to change the constitution. The Constitutional Revision Committee threw itself into the campaign for voter approval. Committee members made over 150 speeches to business, labor, civic, and community groups as well as radio and television appearances. More than five thousand reprints of a 1967 committee report on the need for the convention were distributed to civic leaders around the state. The *Chicago Bar Record* published a series of articles to inform the association's membership on the major issues. The Illinois Committee for Constitutional Convention and the CBA together sponsored a Blue Ballot Bipartisan Support Dinner for Con-Con to which they invited ward committeemen in Cook County, an occasion that also included the governor of Illinois, Republican and Democratic party chairmen from Cook County, and Mayor Daley. The Subcommittee on Convention Structure, Organization, and Procedure prepared memoranda on eligibility for delegate election to the convention, while James Otis of the committee argued a friendly suit before the Illinois Supreme Court to clarify whether public officials could also serve as convention delegates. The subcommittee prepared, and the board approved, enabling legislation to implement nonpartisan delegates' election; and the subcommittee submitted to the convention a set of rules for its organization and procedure. So confident was the committee that the constitutional convention referendum would pass that it appointed nine subcommittees to make recommendations for change in each of the major areas of the constitution requiring revision.[31]

The movement toward massive constitutional reform moved into a new phase: the selection of delegates. A second Constitution Study Commission was created to propose enabling legislation that would govern the composition and procedures of the convention. Again, strong links were established with the CBA: among the study commission's twenty-six members were Thomas Lyons, chairman of the commission and a member of the State and Municipal Taxation Committee, Ancel, James Otis, Sam Witwar, and Dawn Netsch—all influential members of CBA committees. Considerable controversy surrounded the alternatives

31. Constitutional Revision Committee, annual report (1968–69, 1969–70, 1970–71); Howard R. Sacks and Peter A. Tomei, "Report of the Constitutional Revision Committee of the Chicago Bar Association on a Constitutional Convention for Illinois," *Chicago Bar Record* 48 (February–March, 1967): 56–75; Elroy C. Sandquist, "Constitutional Convention—Is It a Revenue Article Problem?" *Chicago Bar Record* 49 (April 1968): 280–85.

of whether election of delegates should be on a partisan or a nonpartisan basis. The CBA constitutional reformers viewed a partisan convention with grave misgivings. Because they saw the triumph of partisanship as the death of creative reform, they worked strenuously, and successfully, to insist on nonpartisan elections. In the final analysis, that policy may have exerted significant influence on the final content of the new constitution. For while as a result of the nonpartisan elections there were still strong factions of Cook County Democrats and downstate Republicans in the convention, a small number of nine independent Democrats from Chicago were able to exercise and influence deliberation out of all proportion to their numbers.[32] Three of these members were committee leaders in the CBA: Peter Tomei was serving as chairman of the Constitutional Revision Committee; Dawn Netsch was currently vice chairman of the Civil Rights Committee; and Bernard Weisberg was immediate past chairman of the Civil Rights Committee. Connections were maintained at other levels: Samuel Witwer, the CBA's elder statesman of constitutional reform, was elected president of the convention; Thomas Lyons was chosen as a vice president.

The CBA, mainly through the activity of the Constitutional Revision Committee, threw itself into the discussions underway in the convention on the major articles of the constitution. With board approval, the Constitutional Revision Committee sent drafts on all present articles, except for the judicial article, which was jointly submitted by a CBA and ISBA committee. Committee members joined the representatives of many other organizations in testimony before the convention, and they also undertook a limited number of additional research tasks to clarify issues before the convention.

If legislative confrontations in earlier years were any indication, the negotiations over a new revenue article should have been long, bitter, and ultimately too conservative. Two events intervened to ensure that that did not happen. In its 1969 session, the Illinois General Assembly enacted an Illinois Income Tax Act in face of the 1932 *Bachrach v. Nelson* decision that such a tax was unconstitutional. In a landmark decision, the Supreme Court in *Thorp v. Mahin* (43 Ill.2d 36 [1969]) overruled the earlier decision and gave the General Assembly virtually unlimited taxing power, except for restrictions in the area of property tax. Two of the most controversial issues that would have emerged within the convention were therefore resolved before it convened: Illinois now had an income tax; and, in effect, it had a more flexible constitution.[33] Discussion of the new revenue article thus took on a different hue—that constitutional flexibility should be specifically vested in the constitution and not be dependent on the changing rulings

32. Cornelius, *Constitution Making in Illinois*, 152.
33. Dawn Clark Netsch, "Article IX—Revenue," *Chicago Bar Record* 52 (November 1970): 103–14.

of the court and that the almost unrestricted taxation authority given the legislature by the courts required some checks, with constitutional limits placed on its discretion.

The 1970 constitutional article that emerged contrasted dramatically with its 1870 predecessor most notably in its conception of constitutional powers.[34] The 1870 constitution had been construed as a grant of powers: it provided not a general authority for taxation but a specific authority for a limited number of taxes. By contrast, the 1970 constitution vested powers of taxation in the legislature and merely provided certain limitations on those powers. In that respect the constitution came to look more like a constitution than a statute, in fact taking on a degree of flexibility for which the organized bar had been struggling for two decades. Thus on the *form* of the constitution itself the new article closely approximated that which the CBA had long been advocating.[35]

Furthermore, the specific provisions of the article that emerged from the constitutional convention—and that were subsequently approved in another referendum—closely paralleled the draft article submitted to it by the joint committee of the CBA. On the taxation of *real property*, both articles agreed that there be uniform taxation by valuation; both allowed some classification, although they varied on what body would have valuation powers and how classification would be applied across different counties. On taxation of *personal property*, both agreed that there should be classification, and both held that after a set period ad valorem taxes on personal property should be mandatorily abolished.[36] The convention article, however, was more flexible on the number of classes, providing open classification and no restrictions on uniformity within classes, thus vesting more power in the legislature. On *nonproperty* taxes, the articles were almost identical: both gave general authority to the legislature to classify; both insisted taxes be uniform as to class; and both provided for reasonable exemptions. On *income* taxes there were differences: the CBA draft had no prohibitions on any such taxes, whereas the convention specifically prohibited graduated income tax but allowed other income taxes subject to certain restrictions.

It is apparent therefore that on most provisions the revenue article that became

34. J. Nelson Young, "The Revenue Article of the Illinois Constitution of 1970—an Analysis and Appraisal," *University of Illinois Law Forum* 1972 (November): 312–40.

35. On expanded judicial powers under the 1970 constitution, as they relate to taxation, see Wayne W. Whalen and Paula Wolff, "Constitutional Law: The Prudence of Judicial Restraint under the New Illinois Constitution," *DePaul Law Review* 22 (Fall 1972): 65–66, 68–71. Compare Sheldon Gardner, "Judicial Developments in the Taxation of Real Property since the Adoption of the Illinois Constitution of 1970," *John Marshal Journal of Practice and Procedure* 9 (Winter 1975–76): 333–50.

36. See Malcolm S. Kamin, "Constitutional Abolition of Ad Valorem Personal Property Taxes: A Looking Glass Book," *Illinois Bar Journal* 60 (February 1972): 432–48.

part of the 1970 constitution paralleled closely the draft article proposed to it by the CBA. More important, the convention article very much reflected the spirit of bar association considerations on the formal properties of the constitution—that it be more flexible and yet that it limit untrammeled legislative authority, thus maintaining some semblance of balance in the relative powers of the courts and the legislature. On some measures, such as the imposition of income tax, the CBA draft would delegate more discretion to the General Assembly; on other issues, such as classification of property other than real estate, the constitutional convention vested more authority in the legislature than the CBA would have done. On balance, however, their conceptions of the relation between a constitution and a legislature and between the General Assembly and the courts were remarkably close. In that goodness of fit, the fiscal crisis confronting the state was defused.[37]

Professional Expertise and Economic Policy

What may we conclude from this case? Two major difficulties in the economic organization of Illinois captured the attention of the organized bar in the 1950s and 1960s. On the one hand, the strictures of a constitution that was unchanged for a century did not give the legislature the ability to cope with the drastically changed structure of the state's economy. On the other hand, because the constitution was so restrictive, Illinois had a system of taxation that was inequitable, costly to administer, and subject to massive evasion. Not only did the state have among the narrowest of tax bases in the nation, but also by 1965 it faced the possibility of bankruptcy. By 1970 both impediments to an appropriate taxation system had been substantially removed. How much could the CBA claim in reform of the Illinois constitution? And by extrapolation, what does the Illinois case tell us about the potential of bar associations to serve the state by the application of their distinctive skills in times of crisis?

It is quite clear that the professional association itself did not change the constitutional article. The debate over its amendments extended to the complete range of interest groups affected by both the collection and the consumption of taxes. In this sense, the CBA was just one among many. But treatment of its contribution cannot be dismissed so easily. We have seen that the bar association was integrally involved in each step of the twenty-year reform campaign. If it was not a primary actor in the front ranks of amendatory organizations, it nonethe-

---

37. Evaluations of changes contained in the 1970 revenue article are found in Whalen and Wolff, "Constitutional Law"; Gardner, "Judicial Developments"; Richard A. Michael and Jerry E. Derton, "House Rule in Illinois: A Functional Analysis," *University of Illinois Law Forum* 1978, no. 3, 587–600; Richard Wattling, "Taxation of Real Property in Cook County under the Constitution of 1970," *John Marshall Journal of Practice and Procedure* 6 (Fall 1972): 87–118.

less made substantial indirect contributions.[38] The import of these has ramifications far beyond the CBA.

The amendment of constitutions is a matter as complex as its implications are far reaching. Few persons have the technical facility to interpret constitutional provisions or the case law that surrounds them. Only a few small groups of experts in any state will have the specialist and drafting skills necessary to translate policy decisions into precise constitutional language. Committees, such as the Constitutional Revision Committee and the State and Municipal Taxation Committee of the CBA, provide organizational niches for constitutional experts—lawyers who are also academics, politicians, and experienced practitioners in constitutional and legislative revision. These expert niches will include attorneys with both the motivation and the knowledge to provide technical assistance in constitutional amendatory processes; the niches offer an organizational base to provide the continuity necessary for reform programs that stretch over long years. At the very least, therefore, a constant stream of reports from bar association committees to their leaderships and from them to other reform organizations provides a cumulative clearinghouse of information on all legal aspects of constitutional change, from past interpretations and operations of the constitution to its comparability with other state constitutions and its future prospects. Professional association experts can, as CBA lawyers did, subject draft articles to searching criticism, explore ambiguities, and point out unanticipated consequences—a function potentially as valuable to legislatures as to reform organizations seeking to persuade them. The CBA constitutional lawyers had the facility to represent policy ideals in precise constitutional terms, while tax lawyers had the experience, in private practice and in the assessor's office, to flag those ideas that were workable and those that were not.

In these respects, therefore, professional associations can act in certain circumstances as professional advisory bodies to government, in effect performing a "think-tank" function, bringing experts together to confront apparently intractable problems and, in response to crises, to prepare research reports, position papers, and detailed analyses that might inform and enlighten the political process. Moreover, a bar association does not require a formal invitation for this sort of role. The profession itself believes it has a mandate—or can construct one—to act in secondary institutional spheres whatever the position of the legislature. The form of the mandate and its potential breadth can be gauged from two bar statements in the course of the revenue article campaign. In the first, a board

38. In their analysis of urban fiscal strain, Terry Nichols Clark and Lorna Crowley Ferguson (*City Money: Political Processes, Fiscal Strain, and Retrenchment* [New York: Columbia University Press, 1983], 191) find that professional associations receive almost no recognition as significant actors in urban fiscal politics.

subcommittee justified the full involvement of the profession in revenue matters on the following grounds:

> The need for revision of Article IX of the Illinois Constitution has for decades been a matter of great concern to the public generally and to the legal profession in particular. The special concern of the legal profession derives primarily from the basically unsatisfactory and unworkable nature of the unclassified property tax, *widespread nullification of the law by the public and by officers of the government, breakdown in judicial enforcement, and the difficulty lawyers face in giving tax advice that is ethical and yet will not work a penalty on conscientious clients.* For these reasons it is proper and desirable that the association tender to the General Assembly its suggestion regarding the constitutional revision in this field [my emphasis].[39]

Thus the lawyers grounded their involvement in what ostensibly appeared to be policy issues in a secondary sphere by maintaining that this was an expert matter in a primary sphere: poor taxation laws affected the legitimacy of the law, the effectiveness of the administration of justice, and the practice of lawyers' work itself. Such a mandate, of course, was used similarly—though with less success—by civil rights activists. Both cases illustrate, however, that a mandate for professionals interpreted this widely gives them access to every institution affected by law—which is to say some aspects of every institution.

But of course given the mandate for involvement as experts, bar participation was not restricted to narrow technical matters. The bar strived to maintain its legitimacy by constantly reasserting that its interests were only narrowly legal. In a news release to justify the CBA direct introduction of House Joint Resolution 30 to the General Assembly in 1965, the CBA stated: "The aim of the association in preparing its recommendations has been to develop *a technically competent draft* of a new Revenue Article which might combine political acceptability with a required degree of flexibility" and the president took pains to underline that "in submitting this draft for legislative consideration, the association does not necessary endorse any of the forms of tax legislation which might be enacted within its framework" (my emphasis).[40] But even though the recognition of the difference between technical and policy matters was frequently alluded to by participants in bar association debates, the ease with which the association could contribute to policy positions through its technical functions was exploited by interest groups within and outside the bar and indeed by the bar itself. On more than one occasion the bar was thrust into a policy stand by individuals or other voluntary associations. When Robert Cushman came to the board in 1951 with the first of many drafts—indeed initiating the twenty-year reform program—he

---

39. Board of Managers, Subcommittee Report 59-10, 1 June 1959; Transcripts, 4 June 1959.
40. Press release, 8 February 1965, file 61-55.

maintained that he wanted only the bar's comments on a proposed article as a *"technical job."* [41] Yet a few days later the CBA was being publicly identified with the actual substantive provisions of that draft proposal. The fine line between "technical" endorsement and substantive advocacy is easily dissolved in the heat of lobbying. On another occasion the bar was drawn reluctantly into an apparent policy position when one of its committee members who was also a legislator introduced a CBA-drafted article to the General Assembly. By allowing itself to be placed on the Joint Committee on the Revenue Article, the CBA could not avoid being identified with the policy preferences of the mainly corporate organizations belonging to that body. Whatever its protestations or even its intentions, therefore, the bar association was drawn into policy matters in virtue of its technical facility.

Even on matters concerning which the association had most legitimacy, namely, advice on the optimal form of constitutional provisions, the position of the bar had political consequences. For example, when the bar argued that the constitution should be more flexible, it implicitly endorsed the greater devolution of power to the state legislature. As one of the drafters of House Joint Resolution 71 in 1965 told the board, "The business community, for instance, is hyper-chary of allowing the General Assembly unfettered, absolutely untrammeled authority in the areas of revenue. . . . The business community, the agricultural community, the political organizations, everybody else, is pretty used to what we have. Nobody wants to be the one who is going to authorize the General Assembly to make sweeping radical changes without any limit set to its authority." [42] Having taxation powers vested in the state legislature rather than local municipal authorities placed the Chicago political machine at a distinct disadvantage. Business groups feared that excessive legislative authority would open it to "populist" demands; consumer groups feared that the legislature would be controlled by powerful interests. Moreover, because in effect a more flexible constitutional article shifted powers from the judiciary, as interpreter of the constitution, to the legislature, it appeared likely that taxation policy would become a good deal less conservative. Advice on what would and would not be administratively feasible could also provide a means of taking a policy stand on technical grounds. By expedients such as these, the bar leadership shifted its stance from a preference for a limited expert role in the 1950s to a quite explicitly normative role in the later 1960s. Yet it justified both functions on the same grounds—special expertise.

A further contribution beyond the professional association's advisory functions emerged from its distinctive character as an open association. The inclusiveness of the mass organization enables it to reproduce internally the full range of diver-

41. Transcripts, 1 May 1951.
42. Transcripts, 19 May 1966.

sity, not only in the profession, but also, through the clientele and affiliations of its members, almost the complete range of interest groups in the state. The weakness of inclusiveness can thereby be turned to advantage. With a diverse membership, which also included many leaders of state political, civic, and business organizations, a bar association may be able to act as a private legislature, aggregating and reconciling demands.[43] The association can provide an informal context for the trial formulation of new ideas at no cost to their proponents. It can enable sponsors of amendments to test the strengths and weaknesses of the opposition. Indeed, by raising proposals within the association, various parties to reform can use its organizational centrality to convey, through informal channels and without risk of public commitment, possible courses of action to other interest groups. Hence negotiations between committees within the association herald the beginnings of possible compromise between wider conflicting interests. Because, for instance, the Constitutional Revision Committee had closer ties to business and the State and Municipal Taxation Committee was closely connected to Mayor Daley's regular Democrats, a compromise between them anticipated a broader ground of consensus between the Cook County party and corporate interests. Hence the common ground on which the committees met in the early 1960s signaled to external groups the likely flexibility in their respective negotiating positions. In this sense, the internal polity of the organized bar prefigured state legislative politics, and it is therefore not surprising that successive bar drafts came to look very similar to several of the bipartisan legislative proposals and indeed the final revised revenue article. The latter, it appears, drew substantially on the former.

Furthermore, alongside the direct, formal action by the professional association lay a channel of influence through the informal and indirect contributions of constitutional and taxation committee members. Such influence is highly resistant to precise calculation. But the bar committees provided a pool, far out of all proportion to the size of the CBA, from which leaders of the constitutional review process were drawn. Robert Cushman, an ardent advocate for the 1951 and 1955 drafts, later became chairman of the 1963 and 1964 Illinois Commission on Revenue. Samuel Witwer, the founding member of the Constitutional Revision Committee and a prime mover for the indispensable Gateway Amendment, provided bar leadership for twenty years and was rewarded in 1969 by being appointed chairman of the constitutional convention. Three members of the Board of Directors to Defeat the Revenue Article in 1966, Louis Ancel, Ar-

43. The invisibility of CBA action and the indirect character of its contributions can be seen by its almost complete absence from conventional interest-groups approaches to politics such as that by Fisher (*Taxes and Politics*), who mentions the CBA just twice—once in connection with House Joint Resolution 30 (1965) and once to say it was deadlocked and therefore "neutralized" in 1966.

nold Flamm, and Howard Sacks, were all active members of the committee. The genesis of the group calling for a constitutional convention in 1967, the Illinois Committee for Constitutional Convention, again included the familiar names of Ancel, Tomei, Witwer, and Otis. Ancel and Witwer were members of the twenty-six-person constitutional study commission created by the Seventy-fifth General Assembly. Peter Tomei, chairman of the Constitutional Revision Committee in 1968 and 1969, concurrently served as a delegate to the constitutional convention, together with other CBA members. It becomes increasingly clear, then, that exclusive focus on the CBA board and the public, formal action of the CBA vastly underestimates the more subtle contributions of the professional association to change through personal and organizational networks. A bar association, the revenue example suggests, may add a diffusionary function to its mediational capacities. Both add up to extensive expert and normative influence.

It is now possible to place the case of the revenue article in the context of the overall pattern of organized bar activities in the courts and legislatures. Part 3 has shown that, in legislative and court matters, the profession can engage in action at numerous levels, from minor and inconsequential changes such as a court procedure or a brief comment on a technical bill, to intermediate-level actions of some substance, through major reform programs that aim at fundamental changes in the structure of social institutions. At the minor and technical levels, activity is constant and ongoing, with a heavy flow of consultation and negotiation back and forth between the collegial body and other organizations. In some areas, such as the CBA's legislative program, it appears that the volume of activity has increased in proportion to the growth in size of the bar association.

Yet it has also been apparent that, above the everyday normative economy of judicial control and the regular business of the legislature, the profession has either initiated or sponsored some far-reaching constitutional and statutory reforms. In a period of twenty-five years, it contributed to revisions of all major articles of the Illinois constitution and indeed of the conditions under which the constitution itself can be amended. It offered several codes or comprehensive acts that were actually drafted by the bar association itself; and in turn it assisted in the implementation of such massive and extensive bodies of legislation as the Uniform Commercial Code, which governs banking and commerce within and among the states. In the terms of the theoretical categories with which I began, there can be no doubt that the profession has inserted its technical and policy perspectives into all areas of its primary sphere. But more than that, it has been seen that a lawyers' association can find itself able to contribute at least a technical, and sometimes a moral, authority in secondary institutions as widely variegated as the economy, the education system, and the social organization of urban areas.

10 The Advance of Legal Rationalization in the United States

The Chicago case offers considerable support to the contention that the organized bar can commit its resources to the extension of professional authority into a plethora of institutions. A significant proportion of that influence was exercised through a process of rationalization—of substantive and procedural law and of legal institutions. The richness of the Chicago Bar Association (CBA) archives has enabled us to specify the elements of rationalization, and their interplay, with a degree of precision. At once we can integrate aspects of general theory in the sociology of law and social organization with the hum and buzz of everyday professional politics. By proceeding in this manner, theory obtains instantiation in actual events; day-to-day activities attain meaning that transcends their particularity. But despite the indispensable contribution of the case study, it has manifest limits. While a careful inspection of professional activism in one setting allows a complex set of relations to be explored qualitatively with some intricacy, it can only hint at the breadth and scale of that activism elsewhere. And while some components of rationalization seem to emerge together in a particular historical instance, there is no surety that they do so in other times and places.

Whereas the case study sought to discover the theoretical coherence of local events, this chapter presents configurations of rationalizing activities by the organized bar throughout the United States. I proceed, first, by operationalizing theoretical concepts for cross-sectional research, and, second, by obtaining estimates of rationalization activity for all state and major metropolitan bar associations.

Measuring Rationalization

My argument advances on the methodological assumption that general theory, potentially powerful in its theoretical scope, has little use unless its central terms and their relations can be specified clearly and operationalized empirically. Otherwise, abstract concepts can degenerate into little more than slogans, unable to be convincingly sustained, rebutted, or qualified; and theoretical debate becomes endlessly scholastic, where finer exegesis and elaborate parsing become preoccupations detached from their explanatory objects. Explanations of social phenomena, therefore, must always be disciplined by the phenomena they seek to explain.

But to discipline concepts with data exacts a cost. There are two recurrent quarrels with empirical operationalization. On the one hand, they inevitably simplify. Empirical indicators cannot capture the fullness or essence of their theoretical referents, although it is not infrequently the case—indeed should be a purpose—that empirical research will lead to refinement and qualification of a theory, forcing it to a higher level of elaboration and specification. On the other hand, empirical operationalizations are held to distort theory—that they imperfectly, indeed inaccurately, account for the correspondence between an idea and its indicator. In substantial part, the latter criticism follows from the imprecision, even inconsistency, of many central concepts, rationalization being a primary case in point.[1] The higher the order of abstraction, the wider the gap between theory and data; hence the greater will be the discretion of the researcher and the more open the researcher's judgment to characterizations not only of simplicity but also of distortion. Yet it must also be recognized that both attacks sometimes are veneers for a more deep-seated unease—they are the idiom through which scholars resistant to any signs of empiricism or positivism express their fundamentally different epistemological assumptions. Indeed, to some theorists, operationalization invariably gives offense.

The issue of operationalization becomes more acute the more a sociologist aspires to empirical scope. A case study allows intensive and intricate exploration of concepts; an interview survey trades a quantum of intensity for extensity; and a mail survey, usually under constraints of cost and time, sacrifices the complexity still available in a sophisticated interview schedule for simplicity and comprehensiveness of coverage. What is gained in breadth, through the adduction of national data to an argument, is lost in depth, through the abandonment of conceptual refinement.

Having assumed the position that theories of general scope must be held accountable by data of comparable breadth, a process of empirical evaluation must seek to compensate for the limitations of any given method. I have attempted to amplify various aspects of rationalization through the case studies of judicial and legislative politics. The mapping of those processes at the national level can be

---

1. Anthony T. Kronman, *Max Weber* (Stanford, Calif.: Stanford University Press, 1983), 72. See also Donald N. Levine, *The Flight from Ambiguity: Essays in Social and Cultural Theory* (Chicago: University of Chicago Press, 1985).

treated only by a survey. For fiscal reasons, it was not possible in my case to interview in person the leaders of all eighty-four state and major metropolitan bar associations. Consequently, I employed a mail survey to bar executive directors. To compensate for the simplifications required in mail-survey questions, I sought (*a*) to use multiple indicators wherever possible and (*b*) to complement the survey data with systematic information garnered from organizations that monitor areas I have subsumed under the rubric of rationalization. The mail survey was undertaken in February 1982 of (*a*) all comprehensive state bar associations and (*b*) all metropolitan associations represented in the American Bar Association House of Delegates with more than two thousand members. The questionnaires, which were mailed to the executive directors—the chief administrators of bar associations—asked questions on legislative programs, self-regulation activities, and efforts at judicial change by their bar association during the decade 1970–80.[2] Of the eighty-four state and metropolitan associations in the population, responses were received from seventy-one, a response rate of 84 percent.

Added to these survey data were extensive amounts of information collated by various organizations of the American legal profession—the 1980–81 American Bar Association *Directory of Bar Associations;* the 1980 *Directory of Bar Activities;* the 1979 *Handbook of the National Conference of Commissioners on Uniform State Laws*—and the 1980–81 *Book of the States.*[3] By complementing the survey results and cross-checking them with information collected on the administration of justice by the American Judicature Society, these additional sources effectively provide systematic data on the population of state and major city associations, with some missing information on certain variables. Altogether in excess of four hundred variables provided cross-sectional data on bar organization, bar programs, and various economic, political, and historical attributes of states.

The concept of rationalization, in the sphere of law, was broken down in chapter 1 into various forms of substantive and administrative rationalization. In contrast to bureaucratic components of institutional rationalization, which have been measured extensively, that rarely if ever has been the case for law and legal institutions. This latter explanatory effort is fraught with difficulties, not only

2. As chief administrators of bar associations and as ex officio members of most influential committees, the executive directors are in the most strategic position to be aware of bar policies at large.

3. American Bar Association, *Directory of Bar Activities* (Chicago: American Bar Association, 1981); *Handbook of the National Conference of Commissioners on Uniform State Laws* (Chicago: National Conference of Commissioners on Uniform State Laws, 1979); American Bar Association, *Directory of Bar Associations* (Chicago: American Bar Association, 1981); Council of State Governments, *The Book of the States, 1980–81 Edition* (Lexington, Ky.: Council of State Governments, 1980).

because the content of Weber's categories is still disputed, but also because their translation from German to American legal contexts inevitably requires a degree of extrapolation and speculation. Codification in the sense of the German Civil Code, for instance, bears a fairly tenuous relation to American "codes," which are by and large far less "formal" and more inductive in their formulation. Neither is it the case that the implementation of uniform legislation across states is a particularly strong form of legal rationalization, although the transcendence of local traditions by rationally contrived statutes to facilitate regularity and comparability across individual jurisdictions certainly contains many elements of substantive or formal rationality. Consequently, none of the following attempts to provide indicators of rationalization in law are definitive or incontestable. They are offered, however, as a point of departure for a systematic national exploration of collegial professional action directed toward ends that are central themes of Weber's interpretation of Western culture.

The Chicago case indicated clearly that organizations of lawyers in Illinois were committed to the rational reorganization of laws, whether through codification, uniform legislation, or constitutional revision. These efforts at *substantive* rationalization,[4] or the reorganization and reordering of the content of law itself, can be imperfectly estimated for bar associations throughout the United States by eliciting responses to the following questions.

Bar executives were asked two questions concerning uniform laws: (1) whether their association had become involved in any way with the implementation of eight important uniform acts promulgated by the National Conference of Commissioners on Uniform State Laws (NCCUSL) in the 1970s and (2) whether their association had generally supported, generally opposed, or had given more technical assistance for these acts. Uniform laws are efforts to reduce confusion and increase predictability and continuity among states in given areas of the law. Organizations such as the NCCUSL draft model legislation in consumer credit or marriage and divorce and seek to have the identical legislation replace extant laws in all states.

Codification was measured (1) by asking bar associations if they had been involved in the codification of state laws quite independent of model acts proposed by national bodies or by means other than adopting acts drafted by the NCCUSL and (2) by eliciting from those active associations the names and numbers of acts

---

4. I use "substantive rationalization" here to denote the rationalization of the substance and procedure of law, not in the sense of substantive or value rationality, although rationalization of the content of law can take substantive or formally rational forms. On these distinctions, see Levine, *Flight from Ambiguity.*

in which they had had an involvement and whether the respective codes were enacted substantially intact.[5]

Constitutional amendments are perhaps the most contestable of rationalization indicators. As we have seen from the judicial article of the Illinois Constitution, bar politics were devoted to changes that were essentially components of a formal rationalization process, and it is likely that other bar associations engaged in reform of the judicial article were most often dedicated to the same end. Other constitutional revisions, however, cannot be assumed to have the same qualities. To the extent that bar associations are engaged in the rational adaptation of outmoded constitutions there are currents of purposively rational intervention. But in formal terms, and without more precise information than a mail survey can provide, constitutional initiatives other than on the judiciary are the weakest and most equivocal of legal rationalization.

Constitutional contributions were elicited in several ways: associations were asked (1) if they had become involved in efforts to amend the state constitution between 1970 and 1981; (2) if they had taken the *major* action of proposing or drafting constitutional amendments in any of nine areas; and (3) if they had taken *minor* action by preparing reports or comments for appropriate authorities, including legislatures and constitutional commissions, on the nine areas of state constitutions and provisions to amend them.

Efforts at *administrative rationalization* of the justice system by bar associations were charted also by a battery of questions in the survey, both drawn from the case study and adapted from the systematic evaluations of judicial and court changes regularly undertaken by the American Judicature Society.[6]

Differentiation was measured by nineteen items, some of which were built into simple scales used initially in the analysis, and others of which were combined into more complex scales used subsequently. The questions tapping organizational differentiation included the following. (1) "Has your association taken any action toward having *rulemaking authority* within the court system vested in the state supreme court without rules being subject to veto by the legislature?"

5. In subsequent analysis, codes of law (e.g., the Illinois Criminal Code) and codes of procedure (e.g., the Illinois Code of Criminal Procedure) are treated together. Yet from a strictly Weberian exegetical vantage point, codes of procedure approximate more nearly Weber's formal rationality, whereas codes of substantive law have a more value rational character.

6. Larry Berkson et al., *Judicial Selection in the United States: A Compendium of Provisions* (Chicago: American Judicature Society, 1980); Susan B. Carbon and Larry C. Berkson, *Judicial Retention Elections in the United States* (Chicago: American Judicature Society, 1980); Robert G. Nieland and Rachel N. Doan, *State Court Administrative Offices* (Chicago: American Judicature Society, 1979); Chris A. Korbakes et al., *Judicial Rulemaking in the State Courts* (Chicago: American Judicature Society, 1978); Charles W. Gran, *Judicial Rulemaking: Administration, Access and Accountability* (Chicago: American Judicature Society, 1978).

(2) "Has your association contributed to any efforts to have *state financing* implemented for the entire court system?" (in contrast to local financing and the political controls that often are entailed by it). (3) "Has the bar association . . . advocated that the power of the legislature on *judiciary budgeting* be limited to appropriations?" (4) "Has the bar association . . . proposed that the *power of the executive be restricted* from participation in the court budget preparation process or from revising a judicially prepared budget?"

Role differentiation was approached at various levels. One had to do with the separation of the judicial role from part-time performance by lawyers or non-lawyers. Thus executives were asked if their association had campaigned for the abolition of nonlawyers filling judicial offices, part-time judicial officers, and a justice-of-the-peace system. Another level had to do with full-time judges and their links with politics in the process of appointment. Accordingly, for the Supreme Court, intermediate appellate courts (where applicable), and courts of general jurisdiction, executives were asked to report if their association had campaigned for the merit selection of judges by any of (i) a nominating commission, (ii) gubernatorial appointment, or (iii) nonpartisan election.[7] An association was given a value of 1 if it answered yes for any effort at differentiation from politics by the courts at any of these three levels. A similar question was also asked of retention of judges, but, because retention bears a more equivocal relation to differentiation and in subsequent analyses did not prove to work very well, the retention measure was not retained.

Bureaucratization, to the extent it is empirically separable from differentiation, was treated in three questions. (1) "As part of a court reorganization program, has your bar association been involved over the last decade in plans to implement a *state court administrative office* with centralized management of the court system?" (2) "Has your bar association taken part in plans for a *unified court system* through the statewide simplification and consolidation of trial courts over the last decade?" (3) "Has the bar association . . . advocated *centralized budgeting* for the entire court system?"

I argued in part 1 that the extent of bar collective action is a function both of state crises and bar empowerment. Empowerment in the contemporary period can be expressed in differing portfolios of resources: elite associations are virtually extinct; but open (voluntary) and universal (unified) associations remain ubiquitous. Data gathered from the survey and secondary sources permit quantitative analysis of bar resources and their relations to level and type of collective action.

---

7. See Berkson et al., *Judicial Selection*, for details on the various forms of nonelective judicial appointment.

Of the bar attributes that might be systematically linked to rationalization propensities, this chapter examines eight that are commensurable and theoretically salient, although they operate at different levels. Three tangible resources are associated with size (see table 4.1): membership; size of budget; and numbers of general administrative staff. All of these are potentially able to be mobilized in support of legislative initiatives. In fact, preliminary analysis indicated that the three size variables were correlated very highly indeed (in excess of .88) and could not be used together. Consequently, I use membership size, logarithmically transformed to counteract skewed distributions at the upper level, as a proxy for budget and staffing.

Three other sets of resources, some tangible and some intangible, are likely correlates of activism. A political infrastructure that enables an association to engage in sustained lobbying at the legislature and that serves also as an index of commitment to legislative revision is measured by a simple indicator of whether the bar association retains a full-time *lobbyist* while the legislature is in session. Inasmuch as both success and readiness to mobilize are partially contingent on the ability to garner public support and build coalitions, it seemed plausible that bar associations with extensive public relations programs might be positively associated with law reform. Two variables were constructed by a factor analysis of responses to twenty-four questions asked of bar associations about their public relations programs by the American Bar Association Division of Bar Services. Two principal factors emerged. One, called *Public Relations Staff,* is concerned with full-time staffing of a publications department and a full-time public relations director.[8] The other, called *Public Relations Programs,* concerns a wide range of activities undertaken outside the organized bar to inform the public of matters concerning the law or lawyers' associations.[9] These programs would serve to raise the public's knowledge of the law and to raise the visibility of the bar association generally. Each scale is the total number of yes responses to these items.

Further, it is consistent with Weber's writings on legal honoratiores to expect that associations whose representativeness integrates the profession as a whole,

8. The principal items loading on this factor were responses by bar associations to the following questions. "Does your bar have a full-time staff person for public relations?" (.825); "formal media/law conferences?" (.450); "Does your bar have a full-time staff person for publications?" (.857).

9. The principal items loading on this factor were responses by bar associations to public relations programs that included the following: "Law Day celebrations?" (.358); "public information pamphlets?" (.385); "speakers' bureau?" (.540); "law for the layperson (adults)?" (.402); "naturalization ceremonies?" (.419); "regular newspaper features?" (.476); "desk book?" (.301); "brochure detailing benefits of membership?" (.468); "Is your bar involved in an ongoing program of teaching or discussing law in your area's schools?" (.485); "Do you publish pamphlets on the subject for students or the public?" (.282).

by incorporating *law professors* and *judges* to be centrally involved in decision making and reform activity, will be in a better position to draft and comment on legislative and constitutional changes than associations in which the academic legal profession and members of the judiciary are less intimately involved in organized bar affairs. Moreover, it also can be expected that a bar that can mobilize its foremost legal experts on statutory matters and its sitting judges on the administration of justice will evince a greater readiness to undertake reforms and have more ability to do so successfully.

Finally, *form of bar association* net of the foregoing variables is included for historical, practical, and political reasons: historically because it was strongly argued by proponents of the unified bar that unification would enable more efficacious efforts at court reform, many of which are consistent with the theoretical categories of differentiation and rationalization; practically because voluntary and unified associations have differing relations with the state; and politically because I have maintained that varying types of bar associations have differing portfolios of resources that have not been fully gauged by the variables above. In addition, voluntary associations are divided into state and metropolitan bodies: they vary in geographic or population densities of their membership and hence in their ability to mobilize; they differ in the services they offer, with metropolitan associations frequently maintaining large libraries and restaurants; and they represent differing levels of collective organization, with metropolitan bars in some states deferring to the reform leadership of statewide associations.

Incidence of Substantive and Procedural Rationalization

How widespread are attempts at substantive and procedural rationalization of state law by bar associations? Table 10.1 lists eight acts considered to be among the most important promulgated by the NCCUSL in the 1970s. They were also among the most debated by the American Bar Association and its various state and metropolitan affiliates. They span a fairly substantial spectrum of state law. The general activism of bar associations on these several uniform acts is of three kinds: positive support; technical assistance; and opposition. In Table 10.1, I assume technical assistance is equal to the difference between the sum of support and opposition and 100 percent. Because both support and technical assistance can be thought to facilitate uniformity, the column indicating opposition to uniform legislation provides the simplest way to summarize the bar stance.

In terms of volume, approximately 20–30 percent of associations were active during the 1970s on all but the Uniform Probate Code, on which fully two-thirds of associations reported activity. Moreover, the orientation of the profession is overwhelmingly positive: in all but one case—the controversial no-fault auto compensation schemes—opposition ranges from 10 to 20 percent of involved associations, support ranges between 40 and 70 percent, and the remainder are technical contributions of various sorts. In order to refine the measure of orientation, a scale was calculated to examine the distribution of involvement by bar associations such that an association could have a value of 8, if all its contributions were positive, through a value of -8, if its contributions were all oppositional. Thirty-eight bar groups fell on the positive side of the scale, ranging from 1 through 8 indications of support, whereas only seven groups fell between -1 and -4 on the scale.

It might have been expected that the level of bar contributions to codification would be lower than uniform legislation. In the latter, acts already drafted by other organizations are presented to bar organizations and thus require a relatively limited degree of mobilization, at least of internal resources. In the former, however, the drafting of a new code, such as the Illinois Criminal Code, can be a massive operation for a private association: it consumes the energy of the relevant committee for several years and requires sustained financial support and volunteer commitment.

Yet responses by bar chief executives show that 35 percent of associations have participated in a codifying effort in the previous decade, a marginally higher figure than the average rate for uniform legislation. As table 10.2 indicates, the thirty participating associations generated some fifty-one codes or contributions to codes. By far, the most prominent substantive area was criminal law, followed by a group comprising tort, product liability, probate, and corporation law, with commercial, tax, and family law accounting for two to three instances each. The great majority of associations (80 percent) report that the codes were enacted largely intact.

Constitutional amendment is not necessarily to be considered a case of rationalization. As often as not such amendments represent an adaptation or modernization of a constitutional article that may or may not be more "rational" or "formal." Yet, as will become evident below, a revision of the judicial article for the most part has included rationalizing provisions, and, as table 10.3 clearly demonstrates, the judicial article is by far the most significant area of endeavor in constitutional reform by bar associations.

Major constitutional action, reported in the table, is quite limited. Very seldom have bar associations drafted any article other than the judicial article. Minor constitutional action, on the other hand, is a more frequent and usual form of participation, but even then, except for judicial article reform, less than 10 percent of associations report activity. Here again, however, the point of chapter 9 must be reiterated: the *indirect* contributions of the organized bar to constitutional reform, which may be highly consequential, will *not* be registered by responses to this question. The results of table 10.3 point to public and direct, not

TABLE 10.1. Activism, Support, and Opposition of Bar Associations to Uniform State Legislation, 1970–81

	General Activism		Active Associations in:		Active
	%	N[a]	Support (%)	Opposition (%)	Associations (N)
Uniform Probate Code	66	68	68	18	44
Uniform Marriage and Divorce Act	29	62	41	18	17
Uniform Land Transactions Act	27	60	47	20	15
Uniform Condonimium Act	26	62	60	7	15
Uniform Consumer Credit Code	28	61	71	12	17
Uniform Rules of Criminal Procedure	21	62	68	11	19
Uniform Motor Vehicle Reparations Act	24	62	14	71	14
Uniform Residential Landlord Tenant Act	22	64	46	23	13

[a]Row, not cell, number. Thus 66 percent of the sixty-eight bar associations responding to the survey were active on the Uniform Probate Code. Similarly, 18 percent of the forty-four associations active on the Uniform Probate Code were opposed to it.

TABLE 10.2. Codification Efforts of State and Metropolitan Bar Associations, 1970–81

	Criminal		Torts, Product Liability		Probate		Commercial, Insurance		Corporation		Tax		Family		Other		Total	
	%	N	%	N	%	N	%	N	%	N	%	N	%	N	%	N	%	N
Enacted	31	13	14	6	10	4	5	2	14	6	5	2	5	2	17	7	100	42
Not Enacted	44	4	0	0	11	1	0	0	22	2	11	1	11	1	0	0	100	9
Total	32	17	11	6	9	5	9	2	15	8	6	3	6	3	13	7	100	51

TABLE IO.3. Bar Association Involvement in the Amendment of State Constitutions, 1970–81

Constitutional Articles	Major Constitutional Actions N[a]	Minor Constitutional Actions N[b]	Total Actions[c] %[d]	N
Bill of Rights	1	3	6.0	4
Suffrage and elections	1	7	10.4	7
Legislative branch	0	4	6.0	4
Executive branch	1	5	7.5	5
Judicial branch	25	31	49.3	33
Local government	0	2	3.0	2
Taxation and finance	1	8	11.9	8
State functions	0	2	3.0	2
Amendment and revision	3	6	10.4	7

[a] An action was considered "major" if an association proposed or drafted a constitutional amendment.
[b] An action was considered "minor" if an association prepared reports and/or commented to the appropriate authorities on articles drafted by the legislature, a constitutional commission, or any other group in the state.
[c] Associations are given a score of one if they took only major action, and one for only minor action, but only one if they took both. These were added to give a total action score.
[d] Percent of all associations answering either or both of the questions on major and minor constitutional actions.

private and indirect, initiatives by bar associations. When the major and minor efforts are added into a composite measure, it can be seen that constitutional revision falls into two classes: first, around 10 percent or less of associations have contributed to changes in articles to do with the bill of rights, the legislature, the executive, local government, state functions, suffrage, finance, and amendment and revision; and, second, the judicial article has commanded the active attention of half of all major state and metropolitan associations throughout the United States.

Incidence of Administrative Rationalization

The contributions of the organized bar to separation of the judiciary from politics at the role level can be seen in tables 10.4A and 10.4B. For relevant associations, that is, associations in which merit selection has not already been established, approximately two-thirds report that they have contributed to the appointment of judges, at all levels of the state court system, by merit rather than by political election. Attempts at professionalization of judicial offices, however, have not been so widespread, although here the results must be interpreted with especial caution because reliable information on states that already abolished

TABLE 10.4A. Bar Association Contributions to Merit Selection in Three Levels of State Courts, 1970–81

Merit Selection	Bar Contribution		N
	No (%)	Yes (%)	
Supreme Court justices	33.3	66.7	57
Intermediate court justices	39.2	60.8	51
Courts of general jurisdiction	35.8	64.2	51

TABLE 10.4B. Bar Efforts to Professionalize Judicial Roles

Abolition of:	Bar Contribution			N
	Yes (%)	No (%)	Do Not Know (%)	
Nonlawyers in judicial offices	31.3	56.7	11.9	67
Part-time judicial offices	25.4	61.2	13.4	67
Justice of the Peace system	39.4	50.0	10.6	66

these quasi-judicial roles before 1970 was not collected and hence the findings underestimate the incidence of rationalization.

The results on organizational differentiation are a little more complex. Between 20 and 45 percent of associations report (see table 10.5) that some forms of differentiation have already taken place in their states. For those associations in states where these measures have yet to be implemented, the results are equivocal. A majority have tried to secure state, rather than local, financing of the courts together with a limiting of legislative rule-making authority. On the other hand, other financial limitations on the legislature and executive have not been a primary object of action.

Two aspects of bureaucratization for applicable associations have garnered substantial support, whereas a third aspect has not (see parts A and B of table 10.6). Between half and two-thirds of associations state that they have supported unification and centralized management of the entire state court system. Only 30 percent have attempted to secure centralized budgeting.

Creation of Rationalization Scales

In the preceding discussion, rationalization is measured by a large number of individual indicators. Because many of these measures are conceptually and empirically related, more complex analysis is simplified and aided by the creation of scales from the indicators consistent with the several dimensions of rationali-

TABLE 10.5. Bar Associations Efforts toward Organizational Differentiation of
State Courts, 1970–81

| | Bar Efforts | | | |
Forms of Action	Yes (%)	No (%)	Not Appli-cable (%)[a]	N
State financing of entire court system	43.5	34.8	21.7	69
Limiting legislature to appropriations	23.4	48.4	28.1	64
Limiting executive budgetary discretion	14.3	52.4	33.3	63
Limiting legislative rule-making authority	32.8	22.4	44.8	67

[a]In these states, the forms of action may already have been implemented, in which case further bar
action would be redundant.

TABLE 10.6. Bar Association Involvement in Bureaucratization of State Courts,
1970–81

| | A. Direction of Action | | | |
Type of Action	Opposition (%)	No Action (%)	Support (%)	N
Unification	7.4	37.0	55.6	54
Centralized management	3.9	27.5	68.6	51

| | B. Bar Efforts | | | |
	Yes (%)	No (%)	Not Appli-cable (%)	N
Centralized budgeting	29.9	46.3	23.9	67

zation drawn from Weber's theory and identified in the Illinois experience. Eight
scales were created as follows.

1. *Uniform Support.*—Bar associations were given a score of 1 for each instance of support for uniform legislation to produce a scale of possible scores
ranging from 0 through 8. Thirty-five percent gave no support, 37 percent provided support in one or two cases, and the remainder contributed in the passage
of three to eight pieces of uniform legislation.

2. *Major Constitutional Action.*—For each report of an action on any of the
nine areas of constitutional revision, bar associations were given a score of 1
such that an organization's score on this scale could range from 0 for participation
on none of the articles through 9 for participation on all possible constitutional
articles. In practice, there were only three values: 63 percent of associations dor-

mant, 27 percent recording one major effort, and the remaining 10 percent contributing to revision of two articles.

3. *Minor Constitutional Action.*—The same coding scheme as in major constitutional actions was adopted for their minor equivalents. In this case, the range was greater, from the 48 percent who did nothing, to another 31 percent who reported one action, to the final group of associations who replied that they took between two and nine measures to ensure constitutional reform.

4. *Codification.*—Bar groups received a value of 0 for no codification attempts and a value of 1 for each subsequent instance of codification to yield a scale ranging from 0 (54 percent of cases), 1 (24 percent), 2 (10 percent), 3 (5 percent), to 4 (6 percent).

5. *Merit Selection.*—Responding associations received a 0 if they were totally uninvolved and a 1 if they reported any sort of involvement in merit selection at any of the Supreme Court, appellate court, or general jurisdiction court levels.

6. *Bureaucratization.*—A ratio scale was calculated from responses to three questions concerning contributions to a state court administrative office, a unified court system, or centralized court budgeting. Associations received a score of 0 if they took no action (36 percent), a score of 1 if they took only one action out of the three that were applicable in their situation (6 percent), a score of 2 if they took one action out of two that were applicable (5 percent), a score of 3 if they took two actions out of three which were applicable, and a score of 4 if they took all the foregoing forms of action applicable in their situation (i.e., one of one, two of two, or three of three possibilities), as did 36 percent of bar groups.

7. *Judicial Roles (Abolition).*—The scale ranged from 0 through 3. For each reported act in support of the abolition of nonlawyers filling judicial offices, part-time judicial offices, and a justice-of-the-peace system, an organization received a score of 1 to a maximum of 3. Fifty-five percent were scored as taking no action, 17 percent made one effort, 7 percent took part in two such activities, and 20 percent reported an involvement in all three.

8. *Organizational Differentiation.*—This ratio scale was created from responses to four questions concerning contributions to vesting more rule-making authority in the Supreme Court, to implementing state financing for the entire court system, to advocating limits on legislative powers over judiciary budgeting, and to proposing restrictions on the power of the executive from revising court-prepared budgets. Associations received a score of 0 if they took no action (33 percent), 1 if they took one of four actions applicable in their state (8 percent), 2 if they took one of three applicable actions (8 percent), 3 if they took two of four applicable actions (16 percent), 4 if they took two of three such actions (2 percent), 5 if they took three of four actions (2 percent), and 6 if they took action

in every instance that was applicable in their state (31 percent)—that is, one of one, two of two, three of three, or four of four possible actions.

Incidence by State

The unit of analysis in the preceding discussion has been the individual bar association. However, frequently, if not usually, there is a division of labor in reform activism within states. For instance, it is not unusual for county and some metropolitan associations, as in California, to defer to their state bodies on law reform issues. Moreover, it might be expected that unified bar associations would be constrained in legislative revision whereas voluntary bars would not, just as voluntary bars might consider themselves less equipped to engage in judicial change than voluntary associations.

Consequently, a somewhat different perspective on legal change may arise if the unit of analysis is changed from individual associations to individual states. Accordingly, I recalculated the incidence of activity on *any* given criterion within a state by giving the state a value of 1 if any association in the state claimed it had participated in substantive or administrative programs. The state-by-state breakdowns are summarized in table 10.7. It can be seen immediately that the incidence of rationalization activity is considerably higher by state than by association. Of the states for which data are available, a substantial majority have experienced some reform activity of uniform laws and of a minor constitutional sort. Approximately 50 percent of states were the locus of some codification or major constitutional action by associations.

Activism is more strongly and consistently apparent for judicial change. In states for which we have information, a substantial majority report activism. If those states on which we do not have information are assumed to have distributions similar to the others, then the majorities very strongly favor reform activity.

Bar Resources and Legal Rationalization

To what extent do levels of activism vary by resources and types of association? For substantive and procedural rationalization the answer from the analysis of variance in table 10.8 is that variation is not significantly different among associations. Nevertheless, there are some patterns that are worthy of comment. Unified bars are mostly above the grand mean: they engage in more constitutional action and codification efforts, but they do less on uniform laws. Metropolitan bars are mostly below the mean except for uniform laws, for which they are about average. State voluntary associations are mixed: they are above the mean for uniform legislation, at the mean for major constitutional actions and codification, and below average for minor constitutional activities.

TABLE 10.7. Substantive and Administrative Legal Rationalization for All States, 1970–81

| State Activity | Uniform | | Code | | Constitutional | | | | Merit Selection | | Bureaucra-tization | | Judicial Roles | | Judicial Differentiation | |
| | | | | | Major | | Minor | | | | | | | | | |
	%	N	%	N	%	N	%	N	%	N	%	N	%	N	%	N
Yes	70	35	44	22	40	20	58	29	66	33	68	34	50	25	72	36
No	18	9	44	22	46	23	28	14	10	5	16	8	34	17	10	5
Missing	12	6	12	6	14	7	14	7	24	12	16	8	16	8	18	9

NOTE.—A state was scored as "yes" if any bar association in that state recorded some positive activity on the relevant rationalization indicator.

TABLE 10.8. One-Way Analysis of Variance of Rationalization by Type of Bar Association

	State Voluntary (M)	State Unified (M)	Metropolitan (M)	Total (M)	F	df	Significance
Substantive rationalization:							
Uniform support	2.4	1.4	1.7	1.8	1.319	65	.275
Major constitutional	.44	.64	.30	.48	1.621	64	.206
Minor constitutional	.81	1.32	.78	1.01	.903	64	.411
Codification	.82	.96	.68	.83	.343	63	.711
Administrative rationalization:							
Judicial separation	.47	.59	.32	.46	2.661	58	.078
Judicial roles	.40	.53	.17	.37	4.422	62	.016
Merit selection[a]	.85	.84	.52	.73	6.934	2[b]	.031
Bureaucratization	.63	.67	.27	.52	7.051	63	.001

[a]Because merit selection is a nominal variable, differences between associations were calculated using the chi-square test.
[b]N = 59.

The statistical relations are significant for administrative or judicial changes. The pattern is clear. In every case unified state associations are significantly above the mean and metropolitan associations are significantly below it. Voluntary associations rank higher than average on merit selection and bureaucratization.

It is entirely possible, however, that the most important factor is not the type of association per se but various other features of associations that are correlated with type of association. Tables 10.9 and 10.10 therefore begin two tasks: first, they provide a preliminary evaluation of whether type-of-association effects are better explained by other variables; and, second, they offer an initial step to the causal modeling of factors statistically associated with differences in rationalization. Predictors (bar association attributes) were entered into regression equations by a stepwise procedure with a .10 significance level for inclusion.

It is immediately apparent from table 10.9 that the models are only modestly successful. Except for major constitutional initiatives ($R^2 = .229$), the R^2 of the remaining equations ranges from .0 to .117. Neither is it the case that type of association has a significant effect when it is entered into the equation simultaneously with other variables. Interestingly, if there is any more general conclusion to be drawn, and that is a doubtful exercise, it is that political and public relations administrative infrastructures are the critical factors. Even here considerable caution is necessary. There are strong correlations between size of membership (logged) and lobbyist ($r = .47$), public relations staff ($r = .77$), and public relations programs ($r = .43$). In turn, size has a modest positive relation with unified bars ($r = .20$), which tend to be larger than the average, and a modest negative relation to metropolitan bars ($r = -.29$), which tend to be smaller. Thus these results might hint that it is not sheer size of resources that matters (and these are more often found in unified bars) but the way in which those resources are channeled—in this case into relations with the public and the legislature.

A more particular explanation helps account for the effects in the model predicting major constitutional action. It has been shown that the judicial article is by far the most important of the constitutional articles on which the organized bar has focused, and table 10.7 indicates that unified bar associations have engaged in far more administrative rationalization, often by means of constitutional revision, than other types of associations. That effect is not lost in the regression model (table 10.9), and, quite plausibly, the close involvement of judges in the association has a significant effect independent of association type.

The models are more successful in predicting rationalization of the court system (table 10.9). The interpretation of the regression equations is also more straightforward. State associations rather than metropolitan or urban county

TABLE 10.9. Regression Models of Constitutional and Legislative Activism on Bar Attributes

	Uniform Support		Major Constitutional		Minor Constitutional		Codification	
	Beta	Significance	Beta	Significance	Beta	Significance	Beta	Significance
Unified bar	a		.27	.042	a		a	
Metropolitan bar	a		a		a		a	
Membership (log)	a		a		a		a	
Lobbyist	a		a		a		.34	.016
Public relations staff	.27	.058	.20	.145	a		a	
Public relations programs	a		a		a		a	
Law professors	a		a		a		a	
Judges	a		.26	.063	a		a	
Constant	1.14		−.32		...		.625	
R^2	.073		.229		...		.117	
Significance F	.057		.007		...		.016	
N	50		50		...		49	

NOTE.—All significance tests in this table are two tailed.
[a]Variables that did not meet the criterion of a .10 significance level to be stepped into the equation.

TABLE 10.10. Regression Models of Judicial Activism on Bar Attributes

	Merit Selection		Abolition		Depoliticization		Bureaucratization	
	Beta	Significance	Beta	Significance	Beta	Significance	Beta	Significance
Unified bar	a		.344	.016	a		a	
Metropolitan bar	−.360	.011	a		−.258	.082	−.392	.005
Membership (log)	a		a		.263	.076	a	
Lobbyist	a		a		a		a	
Public relations staff	a		a		a		a	
Public relations programs	a		.370	.010	a		a	
Law professors	a		a		a		a	
Judges	.280	.046	a		a		a	
Constant	.396		−.22		−.539		.644	
R^2	.226		.237		.178		.154	
Significance F	.004		.007		.014		.005	
N	45		48		46		49	

NOTE.—All significance tests in this table are two tailed.
[a]Not significant at .10 level and not entered into the equation.

bodies occupy themselves with greater vigor in judicial change. It is noteworthy, however, that it is not unified associations but state associations generally (the inverse of "metropolitan bar") that have the most consistent effects. Again, as in the case of major constitutional action on the judicial article, the close integration of judges in a bar's affairs will have a statistically significant effect on the likelihood of the association to press for merit selection or separation of politics from the judiciary in the process of judicial appointment.

The National Portrait of Professional Activism

It scarcely needs reiterating that there are quite difficult problems to be surmounted in the translation of Weber's highly abstract concepts into particular sociohistorical situations and behavioral terms. Added complications arise when one moves from qualitative and historical analysis to the operationalization of behavioral measures for cross-sectional analysis. Furthermore, the development of models to explain differences in rationalization activity is far from easy when so many factors may be relevant, particularly as the comparative analysis reported here is within rather than between sovereign nations. Nevertheless, these findings do represent an effort to span the too-frequent gulf between powerful theories of legal organization and change and the phenomena of everyday activity.

I have identified eight dimensions of movement toward a formally rational legal system: four are in substantive and procedural law, and four are in the judiciary and court system. They appear to be conceptually and empirically independent. The incidence of actions on any of the dimensions can be viewed in several ways—from a null hypothesis through some particular hypothesis about volume. No criterion for evaluation of volume has been offered here. Whether a great deal or very little is occurring in the light of these findings depends on whichever relatively arbitrary perspective one wishes to adopt.

With respect to substantive and procedural rationalization, it can be said that, where bar associations are the unit of analysis, more than half have given some support for the passage of uniform legislation, about one-third have contributed to codification in a major way, and apart from revision of the judicial article the amount of constitutional reform is very limited. If, however, the unit of analysis is changed to the state, then between half and three-quarters of American states have experienced some efforts to rationalize substantive law through the positive involvement of the organized bar.

With respect to administrative rationalization, the degree of activity is perceptibly higher. Three-quarters of associations have sought merit selection of judges, two-thirds have pressed for more bureaucratic forms of organization in the court system, 60 percent have endeavored to remove the legislature and executive from critical aspects of judicial self-government, and almost half have tried to professionalize the judicial office by abolishing part-time and ad hoc staffing arrangements. If we use the state as the unit of analysis, approximately two-thirds of states have been the locus for administrative rationalization by the organized bar between 1970 and 1980.

Nonetheless, it bears repetition that even if there is a net movement in law and legal systems toward formal rationalization—and that is an empirical question, not merely a normative assumption—the survey masks what the case study discloses: within the general drift toward formalism and institutional differentiation, there are countermovements of many kinds. Political pressures toward patronage judicial politics of a substantively rational or irrational kind, informal judicial and dispute-processing initiatives, legislative efforts to limit judicial discretion, a common law developing within the provisions of new constitutional articles and codes—all these sharply modify a unilinear and irreversible conception of legal rationalization. The movements toward greater rationalization are in constant tension with reactions to it—indeed, both Weber's and Habermas's treatments of rationalization and juridification recognize some of the contradictions inherent in it. Nevertheless, my empirical analysis has sought to provide indicators by which disputes over the advance of rationalization can be empirically adjudicated. Those results for the concepts I have operationalized here suggest at the very least that the organized bar has committed its resources quite emphatically to the value of a limited rationalization—limited because a fully rationalized judiciary, for example, would be purely administrative; it would be devoid of juries and adversarial processes, something totally inconceivable to the organized bar in the United States.

The attempts to identify correlates of rationalization from within the bar were quite modest in their yield. It can be said that substantive rationalization seems less to be linked to type of bar association and more to be a function of the infrastructure bar associations can create for mobilization, something that has substantially to do with resources of size and its derivatives. Rationalization of the judiciary does seem very much to be a concern for state rather than metropolitan organizations, and here again there is a hint of a size factor. More important, perhaps, may be the distinctive connection of the unified association to the state.

In degree and breadth of activity, it may be that the CBA and the Illinois State Bar Association have been rather more active than most. But the fact remains that, throughout the United States, collegial organizations of lawyers with extensive resources have been quite energetic in the pursuit of various kinds of rationalization. Sometimes that rationalization has been an end in itself; and at other times it has been a means to some other substantive end. Nevertheless, quite apart from the volume of reform activity, it should not escape attention that bar collective action canvasses a very wide sphere of social activity, which in turn touches in one way or another on almost every citizen: probate, land transactions, condominium ownership, laws governing consumer credit, motor vehicle accident schemes, landlord-tenant relations, tax codes, corporation law codes, and suffrage and election provisions in state constitutions, together with taxation and finance articles also in constitutions. In the administration of justice, which might not directly affect individuals so extensively, there has also been widespread bar mobilization.

In this sense, then, the CBA represents in microcosm a national phenomenon. At the level of subnational government, resource-rich professional associations of lawyers, like the CBA, have been exercising authority in a spectrum of primary and secondary institutional spheres, and they have very frequently done so either by means or to the end of greater legal rationalization. In the process, they evince a pattern of activity quite contrary to that which Weber thought he observed in England. In the United States, by contrast, the collegial and collective expression of professionalization has become causally linked with a modulated advance of rationalization, as it is measured here, in both legal culture and legal institutions.

Part Four

Parameters of Professional Politics

11 Transcending Inclusiveness between Stalemate and Oligarchy

The legal profession in the United States has demonstrated an overwhelming commitment to the presupposition that collective professional influence will be effective only when elite bases of organization are rejected in favor of open or universal associations. In other words, the organizational vehicle best able to exercise expert and moral authority in primary and secondary institutions is an association more, rather than less, inclusive of all professionals. But therein lies a contradiction. While a mass membership provides an association with a luxury of resources, both tangible and intangible, it internalizes within the collegial body the full range of diversity extant in the profession at large. The consequence, as Heinz et al. concluded from their analysis of the Chicago profession, is that

> this growing heterogeneity means that a bar association that is broadly representative of the major elements within the profession is less and less likely to be able to satisfy all of its constituencies. There are too many groups within the profession that have too many conflicts with too many other groups—conflicts that are deep-seated and not subject to compromise. Any action of the association that would be likely to be regarded as "decisive" or "progressive" is also likely to offend one or more of these major factions. . . . Herein lies the dilemma of every professional association. The more its membership reflects the diversity of the larger society, the more limited and noncontroversial will tend to be the set of goals, however important they may be, that it can effectively pursue.[1]

Hence we are led back to the microscopic organizational question nestled within the macroscopic professions' issues. At the outset, I posed the problem of whether empowered professional associations might be able to bring their technical monopolies to the service of an overburdened state. But that issue encap-

1. John P. Heinz et al., "Diversity, Representation, and Leadership in an Urban Bar," *American Bar Foundation Research Journal* 1976 (Summer): 771–72.

sulates another. Does the inclusiveness of an open association preclude it from acting on any issue of any consequence whatsoever? An answer to the latter question establishes a condition of the former. It is also to confront in another setting the classical problem of political organization in voluntary associations, the balance between participation and coordination, democracy and oligarchy.

We have seen from the activities of one professional association in primary and secondary institutions that there are limits to professional influence. Even if the Chicago Bar Association (CBA) did succeed in having a judicial article passed, it did not achieve its ultimate aim—merit selection. Even if it did stimulate the judiciary to enact its own code of ethics, it did not persuade the bench to incorporate a "political" canon. And while it drafted and had enacted two codes of criminal law and criminal procedure, it had minimal success with affirmative civil rights legislation. Although it managed to have twenty or more bar bills passed at each session of the General Assembly, it had much less to boast about when it came to intermediate-level statutes to relieve court congestion.

On the other hand, the CBA can scarcely be counted a failure. It made very substantial contributions to constitutional reform—the Gateway Amendment, the judicial article, the revenue article, and the other articles of the constitution revised at the constitutional convention. It sponsored several major pieces of legislation, from the Civil Practice Act to the two criminal codes. And it drafted scores and commented on hundreds of pieces of legislation while it maintained a steady ongoing traffic of reform in the courts. Its collective influence seems far to exceed that of the naysayers.

How then can the achievements of the professional association—its ability to go beyond "more limited and noncontroversial goals"—be reconciled with inclusiveness? In what circumstances are constituency demands satisfied or rejected? More generally, can we divine some of the conditions under which comprehensive professional associations in the United States can transcend their characteristic organizational inclusiveness? If we can do so, then we will have gone some distance toward being able to specify the organizational conditions under which professional expertise can be brought to the aid of the state.

Immediately, another sociological tension comes into play. If one obstacle to mobilization stems from inclusiveness, one solution leads to oligarchy. Any voluntary association can centralize power so completely in its leadership that it becomes estranged from its members and unresponsive to their interests. Indeed, if we accede to the so-called iron law of oligarchy, democratic processes ineluctably surrender to oligarchic control.[2] Hence it becomes a matter of critical moment to observe whether the professional association can negotiate the fine

2. For a recent review of Michels and criticisms of him, see David Beetham, "Michels and his Critics," *Archives européennes de sociologie* 22 (1981): 81–99 and the references in n. 2.

line between the stalemate of inclusiveness and coordination through oligarchy. Is it possible for an association to act collectively without negating political participation?

With few exceptions, the empirical literature that has followed Michels confirms the ubiquity of oligarchic tendencies in political organizations.[3] Garceau's most influential study on the internal politics of interest groups demonstrates convincingly that, in the American Medical Association, "who says organization says oligarchy."[4] Even scattered members of the CBA charged forty years ago that democracy was slowly losing ground.

Whereas this penumbra of "metaphysical pathos" about democracy might lead us instinctively to predict oligarchy in the CBA, in fact there are grounds for expecting the opposite. The structural component of Michel's theory contends that oligarchy will be facilitated when (1) centralized administration is necessary; (2) outside threats engender organizational militancy; (3) the membership is large and dispersed; (4) the ordinary members are poorly educated, (5) politically unskilled, and (6) politically indifferent; (7) there are few if any local bases of counter organization; (8) elite positions are preferable to usual jobs; (9) elites persist in office; (10) elites control means of administration, finances, and communications; and (11) elites are better educated and (12) more politically adept.[5]

Many of these conditions do not obtain in a professional body like the CBA. If centralized administration is necessary, it is not for militant action. Membership is relatively small and concentrated in the central city of a large metropolitan area. Ordinary members are apt to be as educated and politically skilled as their leaders, although they might not choose to use those skills in the bar association. Most lawyers have nonelective jobs to fall back on if ejected from office; leadership itself is nonremunerative; and each provides less incentive to limit turnover. Elective and administrative functions are divided. And while, unlike the International Typographers Union studied by Lipset, Trow and Coleman, a two-party system was absent from the CBA, committees provided a structural basis for countering elite power, even to the point of nullifying it.[6]

We have seen that the CBA could act, if not always with full force or complete effect. How could it transcend organizational inclusiveness? How successful was

---

3. Robert Michels, *Political Parties* (Glencoe: Free Press, 1949).

4. Oliver Garceau, *The Political Life of American Medical Associations* (Cambridge, Mass.: Harvard University Press, 1941). Compare also Harry H. Eckstein, "The Politics of the British Medical Association," *Political Quarterly* 26 (1955): 345–59.

5. The most systematic formalization of the conditions under which oligarchy will be mitigated (or, obversely, facilitated) remains S. M. Lipset, M. Trow, and J. S. Coleman, *Union Democracy* (Glencoe: Free Press, 1956), 465–69.

6. Empirical research on oligarchy in voluntary associations continues to be quite limited, as Lipset has noted ("The Sociology of Politics," in *Political Man,* ed. S. M. Lipset [Baltimore: Johns Hopkins University Press, 1981], 20–22).

it in doing so, short of oligarchy? In short, are bar associations one of the few exceptional classes of organizations that may *not* succumb to oligarchy?

Inclusiveness has both internal and external implications. Internally, an organizational leadership confronts conflicting and contradictory demands from committees that appear to have mutually exclusive expectations and differing interests. Externally, the heterogeneity of membership draws the association into a complex network of relations, which in turn constrain the scope of professional action. To be able to act collectively and effectively, therefore, the inclusive association must thus be able to mitigate both sets of consequences that follow from compositional diversity. In the following sections I discuss the ways one association coped with each set of limits by, first, considering attributes of elites that may enhance their decision-making capacities and, second, observing methods of organizational management used by elites to pursue broader and more consequential goals. I then turn to consider the effects of organizational networks—a putative resource—on the successes of those bar proposals that do emerge from the leadership.

Elite Attributes[7]

Organizational elites seek to counter some of the deleterious consequences that it appears will result from representativeness in numerous ways. First, when the elite maintains a degree of compositional homogeneity, despite the heterogeneity of the organization, then a governing consensus may be forged more easily. Second, an elite that has a low rate of turnover may be able to develop a distinctive style and even a culture of its own despite compositional diversity. Third, if the elite attains a degree of autonomy from its constituent organizational units and exercises some control over their deliberations and demands, then it may be possible for it to counteract the internal stalemate to which the mass organization seems particularly vulnerable. To what extent were these conditions attained in the CBA?

ELITE HOMOGENEITY

If the elite is homogeneous and does not incorporate the diversity of its membership, then it is possible that decision making may be easier even if it compounds problems in the articulation of the elite with the nonelite and facilitates oligarchy.

By combining two data sets, from the CBA Board of Managers and the Chicago bar survey, respectively, we can systematically compare distributions of leaders and members on several salient attributes. Table 11.1 indicates that, although both CBA members and leaders were disproportionately drawn from

---

7. Part of this section is drawn from Halliday and Cappell, "Indicators of Democracy."

TABLE II.I. CBA Presidents, CBA Boards of Managers, and CBA Members by Father's Occupation, 1954–74

Father's Occupation	CBA[f] President %	N	CBA Board[f] of Managers %	N	CBA Members %	N
1950–54:[a]						
Professional, technical	. . .	2	30.2	13	31.2	48
Administrative, managerial, sales	. . .	1	25.6	11	40.9	63
Clerical	. . .	. . .	2.3	1	2.6	4
Craftsman	. . .	. . .	2.3	1	9.7	15
Operator, laborer	. . .	. . .	. . .	. . .	6.5	10
Farmer, farm worker	. . .	1	. . .	. . .	9.0	14
No information	. . .	1	39.6	17	. . .	. . .
Total	. . .	5	100.0	43	100.0	154
Lawyer	20.0	1	16.3	7	17.9	28
1955–59:[b]						
Professional, technical	. . .	1	34.1	15	31.9	68
Administrative, managerial, sales	. . .	1	15.9	7	43.2	92
Clerical	. . .	. . .	4.5	2	3.8	8
Craftsman	. . .	. . .	. . .	. . .	8.9	19
Operator, laborer	. . .	. . .	2.3	1	5.2	11
Farmer, farm worker	. . .	1	6.8	3	7.0	15
No information	. . .	2	36.4	16	. . .	. . .
Total	. . .	5	100.0	44	100.0	213
Lawyer	.0	0	15.9	7	17.2	37
1960–64:[c]						
Professional, technical	. . .	. . .	25.5	12	32.7	91
Administrative, managerial, sales	. . .	2	32.0	15	39.9	111
Clerical	. . .	. . .	6.4	3	3.2	9
Craftsman	. . .	1	2.1	1	10.4	29
Operator, laborer	. . .	. . .	2.1	1	6.5	18
Farmer, farm worker	. . .	1	6.4	3	7.2	20
No information	. . .	1	25.5	12	. . .	. . .
Total	. . .	5	100.0	47	100.0	278
Lawyer	.0	0	19.1	9	18.2	51
1965–69:[d]						
Professional, technical	. . .	. . .	31.9	15	34.6	133
Administrative, managerial, sales	. . .	1	31.9	15	39.6	152
Clerical	. . .	. . .	6.4	3	3.4	13
Craftsman	. . .	. . .	4.3	2	8.9	34
Operator, laborer	. . .	1	. . .	. . .	8.3	32
Farmer, farm worker	. . .	. . .	4.3	2	5.2	20
No information	. . .	3	21.2	10	. . .	. . .
Total	. . .	5	100.0	47	100.0	384
Lawyer	.0	0	14.9	7	19.0	74

TABLE 11.1. *Continued*

Father's Occupation	CBA[f] President		CBA Board[f] of Managers		CBA Members	
	%	N	%	N	%	N
1970–74:[e]						
Professional, technical	. . .	. . .	29.4	15	36.3	180
Administrative, managerial, sales	. . .	2	45.1	23	41.1	204
Clerical	. . .	. . .	3.9	2	2.4	12
Craftsman	. . .	. . .	. . .	. . .	8.1	40
Operator, laborer	. . .	. . .	2.0	1	7.1	35
Farmer, farm worker	. . .	1	3.9	2	5.0	25
No information	. . .	2	15.7	8	. . .	. . .
Total	. . .	5	100.0	51	100.0	496
Lawyer	.0	0	15.7	8	17.3	87

[a] 1954 only for CBA members.
[b] 1959 only for CBA members.
[c] 1964 only for CBA members.
[d] 1969 only for CBA members.
[e] 1974 only for CBA members.
[f] From Halliday and Cappell, "Indicators of Democracy," p. 721.

higher *occupational groups,* the differences between the leaders and the led are not radical. Unfortunately, interpretation is confounded by the relatively high percentage of missing cases, coded here as "other"; but it does appear that some substantial proportion of these have fathers who were administrative, managerial, and sales workers. Across the period, the relative proportions of leaders and members drawn from legal, professional, and technical backgrounds remains fairly stable. At once the leadership is approximately as heterogeneous as members on this attribute, and there is no clear evidence for their superiority in occupational background. Data that allow a comparison of the elite with the membership on other ascriptive characteristics—national origins, sex, race, politics, and religion—are not available. But the one seat on the board assigned to blacks in 1956 and a further seat assigned to women in 1959 further broadened the composition of the leadership. The data do not allow similar comparisons to be drawn of the criteria of religion, politics, or national origin, although it is known that no religious, political, or ethnic groups were systematically excluded from leadership after 1945.

Differences between bar association leaders and members are also relatively muted on the criterion of *legal education.* Although a very few law schools— Harvard, Yale, Columbia, and Chicago—account for some 30–35 percent of board members until the 1970s (table 11.2), the CBA membership evinces a

TABLE 11.2. CBA Presidents, CBA Boards of Managers, and CBA Members by Legal Education, 1954–74

Legal Education	CBA[f] President		CBA Board[f] of Managers		CBA Members	
	%	N	%	N	%	N
1950–54:[a]						
University of Chicago	. . .	1	14.0	6	12.5	19
Northwestern University	. . .	1	20.9	9	17.1	26
Other local schools	. . .	. . .	27.9	12	40.1	61
Eastern elite schools	. . .	3	18.6	8	16.4	25
Midwestern schools	. . .	. . .	18.6	8	12.5	19
Other schools	. . .	. . .	. . .	. . .	1.3	2
Total	. . .	5	100.0	43	100.0	152
1955–59:[b]						
University of Chicago	. . .	1	9.1	4	12.3	26
Northwestern University	. . .	1	9.1	4	18.4	39
Other local schools	. . .	2	31.8	14	40.6	86
Eastern elite schools	. . .	. . .	20.4	9	15.1	32
Midwestern schools	. . .	1	25.0	11	10.8	23
Other schools	. . .	. . .	4.6	2	2.8	6
Total	. . .	5	100.0	44	100.0	212
1960–64:[c]						
University of Chicago	. . .	2	14.9	7	11.2	31
Northwestern University	. . .	. . .	23.4	11	17.3	48
Other local schools	. . .	1	21.3	10	42.6	118
Eastern elite schools	. . .	1	19.1	9	14.4	40
Midwestern schools	. . .	1	17.0	8	10.1	28
Other schools	. . .	. . .	4.3	2	4.3	12
Total	. . .	5	100.0	47	100.0	277
1965–69:[d]						
University of Chicago	. . .	1	14.9	7	9.8	38
Northwestern University	. . .	. . .	8.5	4	16.8	65
Other local schools	. . .	1	42.5	20	41.3	160
Eastern elite schools	. . .	1	17.0	8	13.2	51
Midwestern schools	. . .	1	12.8	6	13.2	51
Other schools	. . .	1	4.3	2	5.7	22
Total	. . .	5	100.0	47	100.0	387

TABLE 11.2. *Continued*

Legal Education	CBA[f] President		CBA Board[f] of Managers		CBA Members	
	%	N	%	N	%	N
1970–74:[e]						
University of Chicago	. . .	. . .	15.7	8	9.5	47
Northwestern University	. . .	1	21.6	11	16.3	81
Other local schools	. . .	3	33.3	17	40.8	203
Eastern elite schools	. . .	1	9.8	5	11.5	57
Midwestern schools	. . .	. . .	11.8	6	15.3	76
Other schools	. . .	. . .	7.8	4	6.6	33
Total	. . .	5	100.0	51	100.0	497

[a] 1954 only for CBA members.   [b] 1959 only for CBA members.   [c] 1964 only for CBA members.
[d] 1969 only for CBA members.   [e] 1974 only for CBA members.   [f] From Halliday and Cappell,
"Indicators of Democracy," p. 723.

similar pattern, ranging between 4 and 9 percentage points less, until the 1970s. Correlatively, for most of the period except 1965–69, lawyers who graduated from the local proprietary and Catholic law schools are underrepresented in the leadership, although the gap narrows in the last decade. During the first three periods, mid-western schools are overrepresented on the Board, but again the gap closes almost completely by the 1970s. Consequently, there is some evidence of elite overrepresentation, but it is not dramatic, and it is reduced over time.

More compositional bias is apparent on the criterion of *legal practice* (table 11.3). For the 1950s, firm lawyers, who consistently represent between half and three-quarters of the leadership, are substantially overrepresented, but the differences become marginal in the following periods. Government lawyers are consistently overrepresented, three to five times more than their membership in the CBA would lead one to predict—a finding probably a result of the CBA's tendency to include judges wherever possible on the board. In 1950, 35 percent of the bar (cf. table 5.4), 24 percent of the CBA, but only a minute 5 percent of the board were solo practitioners. But although virtually no changes in the relative differences between the board and the CBA occur until 1965, the following decade closes the gap, so that by the 1970s, 18 percent of the bar, 16 percent of the CBA, and 12 percent of the board are solo practitioners. The period closes with the elimination of the most blatant biases in leadership recruitment from different types of legal practice; but it also bequeaths the association with a much more heterogeneous decision-making body.

The data are far more equivocal on the stereotype that the bar leadership is dominated by corporate lawyers. In many respects, it is difficult to confirm or deny such a stereotype because the concept of *legal specialty* remains definitionally imprecise. Instead of using the usual subjective reports of lawyers them-

TABLE 11.3. CBA Presidents, CBA Boards of Managers, and CBA Members, and Chicago Lawyers by Type of Legal Practice, 1954–74

Type of Legal Practice	CBA[f] President		CBA Board[f] of Managers		CBA Members	
	%	N	%	N	%	N
1950–54:[a]						
Solo	. . .	1	4.6	2	26.2	39
Firm	. . .	3	53.6	23	46.3	69
Government	. . .	1	25.6	11	4.7	7
House Counsel	. . .	. . .	9.3	4	12.1	18
Professor	. . .	. . .	2.3	1	2.0	3
Other	. . .	. . .	. . .	. . .	8.7	13
No information	. . .	. . .	4.6	2	. . .	. . .
Total	. . .	5	100.0	43	100.0	149
1955–59:[b]						
Solo	. . .	. . .	4.5	2	22.8	47
Firm	. . .	2	65.9	29	51.5	106
Government	. . .	1	15.9	7	4.9	10
House Counsel	. . .	. . .	9.1	4	12.6	26
Professor	. . .	1	2.3	1	1.5	3
Other	. . .	. . .	. . .	. . .	6.8	14
No information	. . .	1	2.3	1	. . .	. . .
Total	. . .	5	100.0	44	100.0	206
1960–64:[c]						
Solo	. . .	. . .	6.4	3	21.5	58
Firm	. . .	4	46.8	22	54.4	147
Government	. . .	. . .	19.2	9	6.7	18
House Counsel	. . .	1	8.5	4	10.7	29
Professor	. . .	. . .	10.6	5	.7	2
Other	. . .	. . .	. . .	. . .	5.9	16
No information	. . .	. . .	8.5	4	. . .	. . .
Total	. . .	5	100.0	47	100.0	270
1965–69:[d]						
Solo	. . .	. . .	4.3	2	15.7	60
Firm	. . .	3	57.3	27	53.5	204
Government	. . .	2	19.2	9	10.2	39
House Counsel	. . .	. . .	8.5	4	11.8	45
Professor	. . .	. . .	6.4	3	1.0	4
Other	. . .	. . .	. . .	. . .	7.6	29
No information	. . .	. . .	4.3	2	. . .	. . .
Total	. . .	5	100.0	47	100.0	381

TABLE 11.3. *Continued*

Type of Legal Practice	CBA[f] President		CBA Board[f] of Managers		CBA Members	
	%	N	%	N	%	N
1970–74:[e]						
Solo	. . .	. . .	11.8	6	15.7	78
Firm	. . .	4	54.9	28	57.4	286
Government	. . .	. . .	17.6	9	9.2	46
House Counsel	. . .	1	7.8	4	10.8	54
Professor	. . .	. . .	5.9	3	1.2	6
Other	. . .	. . .	. . .	. . .	5.6	28
No information	. . .	. . .	2.0	1	. . .	. . .
Total	. . .	5	100.0	51	100.0	498

[a]1954 only for CBA members.   [b]1959 only for CBA members.   [c]1964 only for CBA members.
[d]1969 only for CBA members.   [e]1974 only for CBA members.   [f]From Halliday and Cappell, "Indicators of Democracy," p. 725.

selves, we created a behavioral index, the Specialty Interest Index, that codes information from documentary sources on actual elite membership in specialty bar associations and bar committees as well as positions of leadership in those groups. Individuals are given a score of 1 for each membership they register in a specialty organization or for their membership on specialty committees or any major bar association. They are given a score of 2 when they have been officers of either specialty committees or specialty bar associations. By giving individuals scores of 1 or 2 on a series of specialties, a profile of specialty interest can be constructed for each individual. By adding together the profiles of all individuals on the board in a given year, a board specialty interest index can be constructed for that year.

It is apparent, from table 11.4, that lawyers with financial and corporate interests have a strong voice within the bar leadership. There were numerous representatives of banking, general corporate, securities, and especially tax law on the board. Of these areas, the tax lawyers maintain the most prominent and consistent presence. But this is no homogeneous elite of corporate lawyers. In fact, the weight of interests in trial law alone—civil litigation, and personal injury lawyers—matches the number of lawyers with explicitly corporate interests, although it should be noted that an undetermined number of litigators will be acting for corporations. In addition, those traditionally disvalued branches of law that cope with personal and family crises—matrimonial and criminal law—are also significantly represented.

Further, if anything, changes over time have reduced the position of corporate specialists on the board in favor of a dramatic increase in the dominance of trial lawyers. Whereas twelve civil litigators emerged in the first five-year period, by the 1970s that number had more than doubled, a pattern duplicated by personal injury lawyers. The single most striking change came in the last five-year period—a time less than appreciatively designated by one observant Chicago lawyer as the "trial lawyers coup."

It is clear, therefore, that, while the organized bar elite may have manifested in the early 1950s some of the characteristics of a more homogeneous, corporate, large-firm elite, by the 1960s the composition of the governing body had changed sufficiently for its heterogeneity to draw into the elite most of the diversity of the profession at large. In that sense the board leadership did not try to solve the problem of organizational diversity by recruiting a strictly homogeneous body. Nevertheless, even in the diversity reported in tables 11.1–4, there was considerable structure. Cappell and Halliday performed a latent class analysis of CBA boards from 1950 to 1979, taking into account four variables—national origins, birthplace, father's occupation, and law school—and considering a fifth, type of practice. The latent class analysis, somewhat analogous to a nonparametric factor analysis, found that three status classes best account for the associations among the four discrete background variables.[8]

Lawyers in Status Class 2, it was found, represent the "aristocratic" or elite bar that are believed to have once dominated elite associations almost completely. These lawyers were almost exclusively drawn from professional or managerial classes, they were at least third-generation Americans, and they were concentrated in the larger firms. Status Class 1 lawyers represented the "ethnic" bar: their parents were more likely to be foreign born, they were more likely to have been born in Chicago and to have nonprofessional parents, and they attended less prestigious law schools. Almost half these attorneys were employed by the government. Status Class 3 lawyers tended to be long-term Americans who were born outside Chicago and who went to eastern elite and large midwestern law schools. But unlike Status Class 2 attorneys, their parents were more often drawn from nonprofessional than professional backgrounds. Moreover, Status Class 3 attorneys were drawn from law firms of all sizes, although those solo practitioners and house counsel lawyers who infrequently reach the elite are overwhelmingly drawn from Status Class 3. Consequently, we can conclude that, while the bar elite was almost as heterogeneous as the membership, it was an ordered heterogeneity that would be more conducive to compromise, coalition, and even consensus.

8. Cappell and Halliday, "Professional Projects."

TABLE 11.4. Specialty Interest Index Profiles for CBA Boards of Managers, 1950–74

	Antitrust		Banking		Civil Liti-gation		Civil Rights		Criminal		Matri-monial, Divorce		Corpo-ration		Labor	
	(1)[a]	(2)[b]	(1)	(2)	(1)	(2)	(1)	(2)	(1)	(2)	(1)	(2)	(1)	(2)	(1)	(2)
1949			1		4								1		1	
1950			1		7								1		1	
1951					6				2				1			
1952			1		5				3	1			1	1		
1953			1		3				1	1	1		2	1	1	
1954			1		1			1	1		2		1		1	
1955			1		3	1		1	1		1				1	
1956			1		6	1	1		1		2		1		3	
1957				1	7		1		1		2		1		3	
1958			1	1	7		1		3		1		2		1	
1959			4		4	1	1		3		2		4			
1960			5		3	2	1	1	2		1		2			
1961	1		2		3	1	1	1			1				1	1
1962	1		2	1	6		1			1	2	1			2	1
1963		1	3	1	8				2	1	1	1			1	
1964	1	1	2	1	8		1		4	1	1					1
1965	1				8		2		2	1	2	1				1
1966		1			7	1	1	1	2		1	1	1		2	
1967		1	2		6	2	1	1	3	1	1		1		2	
1968	1		4	1	4	2	2		3		2		1		1	
1969		1	3	1	4	2	1		2		3		1		1	1
1970		2	2		7	2		1	1		3			1	1	2
1971	1		2		11	1	1	1	1		4			1	2	1
1972	1		2		12	1	2			2	2			1	2	
1973	1		2		10	1	2			2	2				2	
1974		2		8	1	1			1		5				2	
Totals[c]	4	3	17	2	62	8	9	4	12	8	19	2	5	2	15	4

SOURCE: Halliday and Cappell, "Indicators of Democracy," p. 739.

[a] Column 1 under each specialty indicates memberships in a committee or organization related to that specialty or identification as a practicing specialist.

[b] Column 2 under each specialty indicates offices held on a committee or in an organization related to that specialty.

Municipal		Patent		Personal Injury		Trusts		Securities		Tax		Real Estate		Insurance		N
(1)	(2)	(1)	(2)	(1)	(2)	(1)	(2)	(1)	(2)	(1)	(2)	(1)	(2)	(1)	(2)	
					1					2				1		13
		1		1	1					2	1			1		21
		1		1			1			2	1	3			2	21
1		1	1	2			1			3		3		1	2	21
1		1	1	3			1	1		4		1		1		21
	1			1			1	1		2		3				21
	1			2		1			1	2						21
				3		2		1	1		1			1		21
		1		2		1	1	1		3	2	1		1	1	21
1		1		2		3	1	1		4	1	1	1	2		21
1		1		1	1	3	1	1	1	2	1		1	1		21
		1			1	3			1	2	1	1	1	2		21
1						2	1			2	2	3	2	2		21
1		1					2			3	1	2	1	1		21
		1			1	2	1			4		2		4	2	21
				1		2	1	1		3		2	1	4	2	21
			1	1	1	2	1	1		2		3	1	4	1	21
1		1				2	1	1		3		3		3	2	21
2		1		1	2	3		1	1	3		2		3	2	21
2		1		1	2	4		1	1	2		2		3	2	12
1		1		3	1	3			1	2			1	2	2	21
2			1	3		1			1	2	1	1	1	2	1	22
3			2	5		1		1	1	1	1	1	1	2		22
2			1	5		3		1	1	1	1	1	1	2		22
2		2		3		2		1		3	1	2		1		21
3		2		2		1		1		3		2	1	2		21
9	1	9	3	18	5	15	5	5	3	21	7	14	5	19	6	

Totals are not column totals but rather the frequency of specialty interest aggregated for the 219 board members (many board members have been coded with multiple interests, e.g., forty-one board members have been active in three or more specialties).

ELITE TURNOVER AND TENURE

Oliver Garceau demonstrated, in his study some forty years ago, that the average tenure of leaders in medical societies extended for in excess of ten years, thereby enabling a relatively differentiated elite to develop a stability and indigenous culture of its own.[9] If the organized bar, like other professional associations, reduced the rate of leadership turnover, then it might have created the continuity necessary for elite solidarity and be able to transcend the latent divisions the three status classes reflect. But that explanation is not particularly compelling for the CBA. Formally, the association conducts annual elections for leaders; the term of office is one year for officers and two years for ordinary board members. In fact, an informal convention cycles presidents of the association through a four-year succession of offices—the second vice presidency, the first vice presidency, the presidency, and the past presidency. In addition officers may already have been ordinary members. That exception notwithstanding, it can be seen from the transition matrix in table 11.5 that long-term tenure is not especially characteristic of this organization and that turnover is relatively high. If we take a year such as 1958, we can see from the diagonal that there were twenty-one members on the board. By going back along the row it will be seen that twelve members were also on the board in 1957, three in 1956, two each from 1955 and 1954, and one each from 1951 and 1950. Of those lawyers on the board in 1958, thirteen remained on the board in 1959, five in 1960, two in 1961 and 1962, three in 1963, and so on. Turnover is neither so rapid nor so complete over the shorter term that it will entirely forestall some continuity in policy or style. But it appears much too rapid to consolidate control. And high circulation of members would make much more difficult a cohesiveness at the expense of membership interests.

ELITE AUTONOMY AND ACCOUNTABILITY

There is a third means by which elites characteristically counter the conflicting demands of their constituencies. They seek a degree of autonomy from organizational units, they endeavor to increase their decision-making discretion, and they try to nominate their own successors.

Examination of the Chicago leadership indicates that historically, as the association has become more open in membership policies, the elite has strived for more autonomy from the membership and greater centralization of authority. In the late nineteenth century bar leaders were nominated and elected at the annual general meeting. But as the CBA moved away from the elite model in the early

9. Garceau, *The American Medical Association.*

TABLE 11.5. Transition Matrix of CBA Boards of Managers, 1950–74

On Board During:

	1950	1951	1952	1953	1954	1955	1956	1957	1958	1959	1960	1961	1962	1963	1964	1965	1966	1967	1968	1969	1970	1971	1972	1973	1974
1950	21																								
1951	13	21																							
1952	2	10	21																						
1953	2	3	13	21																					
1954	2	2	3	13	21																				
1955	2	1	2	3	13	21																			
1956	3	2	3	3	4	11	21																		
1957	1	1	3	3	3	4	12	21																	
1958	1	1	2	4	3	3	4	12	21																
1959	1	0	2	3	2	2	3	4	13	21															
1960	1	0	1	2	2	3	3	2	5	13	21														
1961	1	0	1	2	1	2	4	1	2	4	13	21													
1962	0	1	0	2	1	1	2	1	2	3	3	12	21												
1963	0	2	0	1	1	1	2	1	3	2	2	1	10	21											
1964	0	2	2	1	1	1	1	1	2	2	2	0	2	13	21										
1965	0	2	2	0	0	1	1	0	2	1	1	0	1	5	13	21									
1966	0	1	2	0	0	1	1	0	1	1	0	0	0	4	5	12	21								
1967	0	0	2	0	0	1	0	0	1	1	0	0	0	2	4	3	11	21							
1968	0	0	1	0	0	0	0	0	0	1	1	0	0	2	3	2	3	13	21						
1969	0	0	0	0	0	1	0	0	0	0	1	1	1	1	2	1	1	3	11	21					
1970	0	0	0	0	0	1	1	0	0	0	0	1	1	1	2	0	1	2	3	11	22				
1971	0	0	0	0	0	1	1	0	0	0	0	1	1	0	0	1	2	2	2	3	13	22			
1972	0	0	0	0	0	1	1	0	0	0	0	1	1	0	0	1	3	1	0	1	3	12	22		
1973	0	0	0	0	0	0	0	0	0	0	0	1	1	0	0	1	2	1	0	1	2	4	14	21	
1974	0	0	0	0	0	0	1	0	0	0	0	1	1	0	0	0	1	1	0	0	1	4	6	12	22

SOURCE.—Halliday and Cappell, "Indicators of Democracy," table 11.4, p. 748.

twentieth century, the board began to appoint nominating committees to select a slate of prospective leaders that would be voted on at the general meeting; by 1917 the official slate drawn up by the Nominating Committee was considered to be elected automatically unless the slate was contested. In effect, therefore, the leadership would be appointed by the nominating committee, itself appointed by the current leadership—indirectly, therefore, a process of elite co-optation.

With few modifications, that form of elite recruitment persisted throughout the 1950s and 1960s, and, despite occasional challenges from rival candidates or even entire rival slates, very rarely did the bar leadership ever find that its nominating committee choices were rejected by the membership. To this extent the board could perpetuate—albeit at arm's length—whatever characteristics of prospective bar leaders it sought. Of course it is clear from the heterogeneity of the board that the Nominating Committee does endeavor to effect a careful balancing of constituency representatives. That notwithstanding, the nominating committee is in the position to choose among representatives of a given segment of the profession in order to produce a leadership more consonant with the style and views of the one that preceded it.

With increased inclusiveness the bar leadership also moved to exert greater control over its committees. By 1943, the bylaws of the CBA gave the board extensive powers to form committees, to appoint their members and leaders, and, if need be, to abolish them. Moreover the leaders insisted that no reports from committees were to be circulated without the prior consent of the board, thus ensuring that channels of communication became highly centralized. In practice the board has allowed very few committees to proceed independently, and effectively it gives a degree of autonomy to joint bar association committees working on major legislative reforms. For the most part, however, committees remain very much controlled by the leadership, especially if committees wish to take action of any sort that might commit the association to a point of view or expend some of its resources.

To even further consolidate the possibility of elite control, the board adopted the practice of appointing liaison members to committees. With two or more committees specially assigned, the liaison member was expected to attend meetings whenever possible, introduce reports from the committee to the board, and make comments on the degree of internal consensus or the tenor of discussion in committee debates. The system of liaison members therefore gives a leadership independent information on committee activities as well as providing the possibility of some control by the leadership over the actual deliberations of committees before matters are sent formally to the board. In practice, some leaders took their liaison responsibilities much less seriously than others; they seldom attended meetings, and they were in no position to affect committee decision making. Nevertheless, on critical matters, the bar leadership had intact an organizational infrastructure with the capacity to tighten controls as issues demanded.

Leadership discretion has expanded in tandem with committee controls. After the first quarter century, the bar leadership acted more as a representative body, coming to the members in only three areas: changes in dues or location of the association; decisions on bar support of particular judges standing for election; and the position of the CBA on major policy matters. Except for judicial elections, bar leaders have progressively exercised more autonomy in their decision making. Whereas the board was required to go to the membership for any changes in dues during the elite period, a series of subsequent bylaw changes gave it much greater freedom to alter dues, subject to certain constraints—such as a fixed percentage increase in any given year.

Much more important, however, were patterns of consultation with members on significant policy issues. Between World War I and World War II, the leadership conducted numerous referenda on the position to be taken by the CBA on such matters as constitutional conventions, prohibition, and whether to support congressional moves to limit the power of the Supreme Court. Nonetheless, the pattern of referenda on the most important policy issues confronting the bar association did not continue into the post–World War II years. On neither of the twenty-year debates over revisions of the judicial and revenue articles of the Illinois constitution did the leadership submit to the membership its decisions, although in both cases drafts were given wide publicity. Indeed the organized bar elite was quite aware that there were strong sections of the bar association opposed to merit selection and some of the early drafts of the revenue article. When the survey of the Chicago bar showed just how much opposition there was within the profession to merit selection, a former president commented that the finding acquitted his decision at the time not to risk a referendum. Similarly, the Illinois codes of criminal law and criminal procedure drafted by the organized bar were widely circulated within the profession—yet CBA members did not get an opportunity to disapprove the document adopted by the board. On the civil rights position taken by the CBA in the middle 1960s, the board actually voted down a motion that association support of the 1964 U.S. Civil Rights Act be submitted to the membership. The arguments summoned against recourse to referenda were straightforward: they cost too much; they were unwieldy and inflexible and impossibly slowed down decision making; they did not lend themselves to intelligent decisions by the membership on highly complicated measures; they could create problems for organizational solidarity, even betraying to outsiders the lack of organizational consensus; and they restricted the autonomy of a leadership given representative authority to act on behalf of its members. Very rarely, if ever, were board decisions ever bound by membership votes.

In sum, then, there is some evidence that the CBA responded to the transition from an elite to a mass membership by increasing its compositional diversity but modestly limiting the rate of board turnover, increasing the effective tenure of officers, assuring a degree of co-optation and self-perpetuation in the recruitment of new leaders, and obtaining more autonomy from constituents as it effected more control over members.

Organizational Management

Even if an organizational elite does adapt in this way, the implications of inclusiveness are not entirely resolved. To ensure a degree of autonomy, elites can (1) attempt to reduce the number of demands made on it by members or (2) endeavor to control the nature of those demands. The Chicago bar leadership attempted both.

REDUCING DEMANDS

An organizational elite can decrease the amount of direct pressure on the leadership by the diversion of selective incentives.[10] The challenge for the leadership is to expand the membership without proportionately expanding demands on the leadership, to be able to appropriate resources from members without them exacting commensurate demands from the leadership. The simplest way to effect this ostensibly impossible feat is by attracting members through the offer of incentives that they cannot get so readily elsewhere. Members use the organization for these limited purposes, but they do not become actively engaged in general policy issues. Thus, at the same time, their membership increases the representiveness and inclusiveness of the professional association, thereby expanding the authority of the leaders. But the added members make few direct political or policy demands on the leadership.

Professional associations have developed a large array of incentives for membership. For instance, the CBA has two restaurants in the center of the Chicago legal district. According to the 1974 survey of the Chicago bar, 34 percent of members—approximately three to four thousand lawyers—used the restaurants at least twice a month. The association also maintains one of the largest law libraries in the city, and at least a quarter of the membership in 1974 used it twice a month or more. The library is especially useful for those lawyers in solo practice, in small firms, or with a lower income who cannot afford satisfactory libraries of their own. The CBA has developed a Lawyer Reference Plan whereby per-

10. For recent discussions of the extensive literature that has arisen since Mancur Olson's seminal work, see Terry Moe, *The Organization of Interests: Incentives and the Internal Dynamics of Political Interest Groups* (Chicago: University of Chicago Press, 1980); Philip R. Jones, *Doctors v. the BMA: A Case Study of Collective Action* (Westmead: Gower, 1981).

sons needing legal services contact CBA staff administering the plan and are referred to lawyers who have been screened by the bar association and listed with the service. Not only does the plan enable individuals to be referred to lawyers who may have experience in the area of their particular problem, but it is also an important means of securing clients for a section of the profession. Ten percent of CBA members, or approximately one thousand attorneys, were listed with the plan in 1974. Moreover, it is important to observe that the lawyers more likely to belong to the Lawyer Reference Plan and to use the library regularly are less likely to participate in CBA committees. Hence these incentives for membership draw into the association lawyers who would not be attracted by committee memberships alone.

Nevertheless, it is from committees, particularly those on the courts and in areas of substantive law, that most demands are generated. Yet while it is apparent that legislative issues, for example, emerge from a broad spectrum of specialty committees, it is also the case that a few committees account for most of the demands. Alongside these particularly active committees are others that may make one demand every five years or none at all. These organizational units may be designated *enclave committees*. For their members, the connection of committees to an organization or leadership is largely irrelevant. Their loyalty is less to the center of the association than to their particular segment of the periphery. The organization merely provides a convenient organizational niche in which members with common interests can meet. It is rarely the case for such lawyers to be preoccupied with general bar association policy except insofar as it directly affects their special interests. The committee structure is in itself therefore a selective solidary incentive and a sufficient condition of membership for many professionals.

That committees are significant for members can be seen from the finding of the 1974 survey that 68 percent of the members had belonged, or did belong, to a committee. Some few of these committees will be highly active: on judicial matters, the Candidates Committee, the Civil Practice Committee, and the Circuit Court Rules Committee; and on legislative matters, the Legislative Committee and committees on patents, real property, and probate law. But the vast majority of other committees are much less visible to the leadership, and many of them exist almost purely for social, collegial, or educational purposes. In these respects, they divert the attentions of members away from the bar elite, once again providing numbers in exchange for limited, but selective, incentives.

Finally, there are those material incentives that any large organization can provide through its buying power—cheaper travel and lower premium insurance schemes, to name but two. In addition to all the members who have little concern with the leadership or the policies it enunciates, there are those who have a membership in name only because their firm automatically pays their dues. They participate minimally or not at all in organized bar affairs.

In sum, therefore, there is some credence within professional associations for Olson's by-product theory of collective action—that some members join an organization in part for reasons other than the purposes or roles that principally engage the attention of the leadership. Precisely because those members are diverted or distracted from those judicial or legislative roles, the association leadership can act with much less constraint than if all members were highly mobilized or politicized—but in contrary directions.

CONTROLLING DEMANDS

Observation of the CBA elite over several decades and many hundreds of different issues indicates that, in addition to reducing demands, the leadership developed complex and sophisticated methods of control.

As a basic condition of most of its other methods of control, the leadership exploited the *structural segmentation* within the profession as it is reproduced within the professional association. Patterns of membership involvement in a bar association lend themselves to segmentation and control. If indeed lawyers do belong to an organization primarily for one or two material selective incentives, such as the restaurants, the library, or the collegial or solidary activities of committees, then their primary focus will be on a very limited segment of organizational activity. Members can belong to several committees, but constraints of time and space do not allow any one lawyer to spread his or her involvements too widely. Apart from sharing common members, however, committees for the most part have little knowledge of each other's deliberations. Apart from annual reports, the occasional special projects, or the information exchanges in units like the Legislative Committee, most committees operate in effective isolation from one another. The failure of the CBA leadership to discover the standing of the Circuit Court Rules Committee for over thirteen years illustrates the point dramatically.

The deliberations of the leadership itself did not counterbalance the information blocks caused by segmentation. Like most committee actions, the deliberations of the CBA board were conducted in private, and neither board agendas nor the outcomes of board deliberations were usually conveyed to the membership. In fact, interviews reveal that even policy positions of the CBA leadership on important matters could not be articulated by a substantial proportion of members. No bar publication sought to bridge the information gap in any comprehensive or systematic way. Consequently, most committees were not readily aware of what sister committees were doing, and, in turn, committees had little idea of board deliberations unless they were directly involved or the matter was so important that the CBA as a whole had to be mobilized—or at least informed. Because the leadership can take action without awareness of the membership at large, therefore, it gains some flexibility in what actions it will take, how it will do so, and when and how its actions will be made known.

Furthermore, committees were given *differential access to the leadership*. In theory, access was identical for all committees; in practice, there were marked differences, although many members, separated in their respective segments, did not know this. Hence, while some committees, such as the Constitutional Revision Committee, could bring their legislation directly to the board, other committees were expected—or they believed it necessary—to proceed through an intermediate screening committee like the Legislative Committee. Members of the Constitutional Revision Committee were on a first-name basis with board members when they appeared to present a case; by contrast, the chairman of Civil Rights and State and Municipal Taxation Committees had to be introduced to the board as strangers. Quite apart from overlap of committee and board membership—which favored some areas of the law more than others—committees were differentially advantaged in their access to the leadership by the attributes of their liaison person. A liaison member might materially assist the case of a committee by indicating that he was fully aware of their deliberations, that they had been undertaken with his advice, and that the committee report was worthy of board approval. But a less prestigious committee such as that on civil rights can scarcely have been assisted by a "sponsor" who indicated that the committee was, in his judgment, unbalanced and that its proposal unsatisfactory. If need be, then, a board liaison person might influence committee deliberations by suggesting anticipated objections from the leadership and by providing more or less support in the presentation of a report before the bar elite.

But even with these differential conditions of access to the board, any controversial issue still opens up the possibility of conflict and stalemate on the most significant matters. The CBA leadership developed several different tactics to mitigate the occurrence or effect of such conflict.

First, conflict can be avoided in highly contentious circumstances if the leadership can entirely *sidestep an issue*. The board may simply state that an issue is outside the technical capacity of the bar—its role narrowly defined. That of course is an inversion of the more usual logic the profession employs when it wishes to expand its influence, namely, that a policy matter is really a technical matter and that therefore the bar has a mandate to act. To forestall internal conflict, however, the elite turns the argument on its head by maintaining that a matter is moral or policy oriented and therefore outside its mandate. However, the facility with which this device can be employed is limited simply because many of the lawyers will be quite aware of the weight of precedent to the contrary—that no matter is so much a policy matter that it cannot be converted into a technical mandate for action.

Second, conflict can be externalized. *Partial externalization* occurs when the bar leadership forms a special organizational unit, such as joint bar committee, that includes all the major interest groups concerned with reform and that is given some limited autonomy to produce a major reform by taking conflicting interests and reconciling them. Only when the compromises have been achieved and the draft legislation is acceptable to all parties will the committee be expected to return to the respective bar elites for final approval. When the compromise draft document is presented to the leadership, as in the cases of the Civil Practice Act, the criminal codes, the uniform commercial codes, and others, approval will be virtually pro forma on the grounds that any objections that the bar leadership could raise will already have been aired. The draft legislation will thus represent a balance of intraprofessional interests. This form of action has the added advantage that it enables very substantial reform efforts to be mounted by the bar; but if the measure becomes too controversial, the leadership of the organized bar is partially absolved of responsibility. More *radical externalization* occurs when, as with the early revenue article, the bar association takes one side of an issue—knowing that there is strong internal opposition to its position—and lets the dissenting segment of the profession carry its fight to the legislature. But this tactic can be dangerous because the bar may risk completely alienating one of its committees. It also signals disarray within the profession to the wider public and thus belies the image of collegial consensus that the organized bar is eager to project. The strategy can be used only rarely and then only when opposition is weak.

Third, conflict can be managed by internal *neutralization of dissent* before it reaches the leadership. One method was to form "balanced" committees that include two opposing wings of the profession in a given area of the law. For example, a leadership might place plaintiffs' and defendants' personal injury lawyers in one committee or management and union lawyers together in a labor law committee. Compromise between opposing factions is therefore a condition of committee activism. The leadership can expect that if a measure does emerge from a balanced committee it will not embroil the elite in intraprofessional conflict because common ground will already have been established within the committee. Less often an elite can adopt the policy it did on revenue reform. In the early 1950s, the CBA board had supported the Constitutional Revision Committee almost unconditionally and in the face of mounting resistance from lawyers in the State and Municipal Tax Committee. By the later 1950s the disagreements were so strong and escalating so dangerously that the leadership demanded that both committees convene a special subcommittee that might hammer out a compromise position to which the CBA could give its unconditional support.

A further option can be to use another committee as a *gatekeeper* to the board. This role in the CBA devolved principally on the Legislative Committee, whose task went far beyond the preparation of the twenty or thirty bills prepared for each session of the state legislature. The committee came to have veto power over many proposed legislative actions that were not part of the joint bar program. Two instances from the Civil Rights Committee illustrate the arguments that can be used to foreclose action of certain types. When civil rights lawyers suggested that the CBA support equal job opportunity legislation, the Legislative Committee counseled restraint on three grounds: first, the CBA could not afford to become a "superlegislator"—to advise on too much legislation too often—because that would dissipate its resources; second, the association should speak only on issues concerning which it had authority, and job opportunity legislation was more social than legal—the CBA would be persuasive in its support but not authoritative; and, third, the bar lobbyist in Springfield could not manage the added burden of the civil rights legislation, and it would cast in jeopardy the CBA's legislative program because of the controversy that would be generated. On another occasion, when civil rights attorneys proposed a code of fair practices, the Legislative Committee indicated that the bill would have no chance of passage and that its nonspecific provisions would make implementation difficult. It has been shown that the Circuit Court Rules Committee had a somewhat similar but more limited role on judicial issues. Because the committee had a highly prestigious membership and included a number of senior judges, a proposal by the Juvenile Delinquents Committee to reform the law of juveniles was effectively vetoed by a sister committee.

Consequently, expertise may be used within the association for exactly the obverse reason that it is employed outside it. Whereas in the latter case professionals use their technical skills to gain a mandate for wider action on policy matters, in the former case the bar leadership can quash policy matters on technical grounds. The justifications for narrowing the scope of action were enunciated not infrequently: proposals exceeded the proper role of the CBA; they were impossible to implement; or they were poorly drafted. Ironically, therefore, the ability of the association to move from technical to moral authority *outside* the organization not infrequently is contingent in some degree on its capacity to move in the opposite direction—from moral to technical matters—*within* the organization.

But there is an added twist to the irony. Some specialist and highly technical committees treat the bar leadership in an analogous fashion to the approaches the bar itself makes to the legislature. Committees like the Patent Law Committee, which came to the board with great frequency, present very arcane reports to the board with the expectation that there will be no one in the leadership who has the expertise to contradict the recommendations of the patent lawyers. Frequently, board members were led to observe that they had no independent basis of judgment on patent matters and that they had to take the Patent Committee reports at face value. Similarly, some sponsors of specialized legislation of a major kind implied strongly to the board that it did not have the resources to quarrel with the committee report—in other words, presenting the argument to the board that it did not have the expertise and information on which to make a proper judgment, similar grounds indeed to the leadership's rationale for not taking the most far-reaching matters to a referendum of members. Within the bar polity itself, therefore, the professionalization of politics that the organized bar sought in state and national legislatures was anticipated in microcosm.

But if a leadership cannot deal with inclusiveness, internal heterogeneity, and clashes of intraprofessional interests by one or another mode of externalizing or neutralizing conflict, then it can bring into play a set of mechanisms, principally through graduated levels and *types of approval.*

1. Proposals may be approved immediately without amendments.

2. Some proposals will be approved subject to certain amendments.

3. Proposals that may be more problematic or touch on the interests of other segments of the association can be sent to those committees for discussion and comments. If the leadership wishes to quash a certain bill it may do so by a careful choice of referrals. Thus the Legislative Committee could be expected to express reservations about any proposals coming from civil rights lawyers, the Municipal Court Committee might well have overturned the CBA's position on the judicial article at certain points had it been given the option, and the State and Municipal Taxation Committee was thought to be at odds with the constitutional lawyers.

4. Another option is delay: a board reluctant to act may refer a proposal to other committees—a quite "democratic" and justifiable step—in order to buy time; it can then stall for a period until the proposal is no longer relevant because action has already been taken by the courts or the legislature, a tactic used in federal civil rights legislation.

5. Delay is sometimes combined with a "wait-and-see" attitude. Thus if a court committee wishes to react to a new court rule or an unpopular change in procedure or organization, a reluctant board may decide that the committee's point is worthy of consideration but that it would be premature to act until such time as the new rule or procedure has been in operation and it can be observed how well it works in practice. As often as not, the matter will die there.

6. On some of the most contentious matters, the leadership adopted the device of rejecting a specific proposal, such as a detailed commentary on legislation or a draft bill, in favor of a general, carefully worded set of principles that would offend no one. We have seen the use of that device during the civil rights and

revenue debates. Nevertheless, this approach can be used only with care. As a board member pointed out, it would look a little foolish if the CBA wheeled out a regular resolution in favor of integration each time civil rights legislation came to the legislature—as foolish as thundering a belief in God and country!

7. If the board declined to allow a committee to proceed to the legislature, it sometimes diverted demands into educational channels so that a committee was encouraged to write up an article or series of articles on an issue, occasionally accompanied by articles of rebuttal.

8. Then there is the expedient of approving a proposal but refusing to publicize it. Or, less dramatically, the leadership will publicize it only under certain specified circumstances, such as a direct request.

9. Finally, of course, the board may reject a report completely.

Although it cannot be demonstrated conclusively, it appears that the attempts of the leadership to control demands are structured according to the size, and especially the prestige, of the committees concerned. It seems almost as if the board implicitly follows something analogous to a graduated reinforcement schedule. Powerful and prestigious committees will be positively reinforced more frequently than those committees that are more peripheral and have lower standing. Rarely did the board attempt to substantially change reports from joint bar association committees, in part because the personnel on those committees were usually distinguished members of the bar. Similarly, it was the immediate reaction of the leadership to accept the proposals of the prestigious Constitutional Revision Committee rather than those from the less prestigious State and Municipal Tax Committee. For committees in areas of the law that are of relatively low standing in the profession, intermittent or even random recognition through occasional success may be sufficient to keep them from being alienated from the bar association.

In this sense the leadership follows a distributive policy. A leadership in an inclusive association will be able to act despite its internal diversity if it satisfies the interests of all and of none. Put another way, every party will be partly satisfied and partially dissatisfied by an implicit schedule of approval and support weighted in favor of the relative standing and prestige of the groups making demands. This is not to say that on every particular issue every party has to be partially satisfied. On some issues no parties will have their interests furthered because the organization is deadlocked. At other times, it seems a leadership will opt for one segment of the profession in preference to another. Yet it appears that a highly heterogeneous organization could maintain the continued commitment of its committees because the distributive system of rewards dispensed by bar leaders positively reinforced, with enough frequency, the differential expectations of committees.

It is apparent, therefore, that the organized bar leadership is not helpless in the face of a heterogeneous and representative membership. The size and breadth of open and universal associations bring substantial accompanying portfolios of resources; they do not, however, completely stultify collective action. While the CBA elite is compositionally and structurally more democratic than has been the case with other professional leaderships, it nonetheless has adapted to the movement from exclusivism to inclusivism in such a way that decision making and action are still possible—and sometimes on highly consequential policy issues on which the association itself may be divided. By maintaining some control over recruitment to the leadership, by ensuring that authority is centralized, and by developing a degree of autonomy from constituent units, the leadership gained the flexibility and discretion to contain disintegrative consequences and deadlocking tendencies that might have followed inclusiveness. When these leadership attributes are combined with a series of tactics and strategies that divert demands and exploit the structural segmentation of the association, then the leadership becomes more the master than the servant of its organizational constituencies.

Nevertheless, inclusiveness also has external consequences. They too may facilitate or impede effective collective action.

The Weakness of Strong Ties [11]

We have seen that, the greater the inclusiveness of a professional association, the greater the internal heterogeneity of its membership. Similarly, the greater the inclusiveness of an open association, the broader will be the scope and density of networks between the association and other institutions and organizations. From the diversification of its ties the organization gains the resources of interdependency and interpenetration. *Interdependency* concerns those interactions between the association qua association and other organizations. Relations will be both formal and informal, but they will be between corporate rather than individual actors. *Interpenetration* on the other hand refers to those ties achieved by the

---

11. This section attempts to suggest another side to the portrayal of strong ties presented in Mark Granovetter's pregnant "The Strength of Weak Ties," *American Journal of Sociology* 78 (May 1973): 1360–80. It also offers a highly negotiative formulation of the relations between a professional organization and its environment. For an approach that deals with issues of reciprocity in more formal terms of exchange theory, see Karen S. Cook, "Exchange and Power in Networks of Interorganizational Networks," *Sociological Quarterly* 18 (Winter 1977): 62–82. A general review of approaches to organizations and their environments can be found in Howard Aldrich, *Organizations and Environments* (Englewood Cliffs, N.J.: Prentice-Hall, 1979). It will be seen that my approach is rather more amenable to resource dependency and mobilization theory, suitably modified, than to a more deterministic population ecology perspective (cf. Michael T. Hannan and John Freeman, "The Population Ecology of Organizations," *American Journal of Sociology* 82 [1977]: 929–64).

common memberships of individuals in organizations of all kinds, in addition to an affiliation with their professional body.[12]

The degree of organizational interdependency and membership interpenetration, I argued in chapter 2, will vary from profession to profession—partly as a function of the particular knowledge that a profession claims and the skills it can exercise. But it is likely that of all professions the legal profession is distinctive in its degree of structural centrality. Inasmuch as law regulates relations, at some level, within and among other institutions, it is probable that the bar association will find itself linked to most other institutions; if this is not so at the organizational level, it will certainly pertain to the individual level. There is no institution, then, to which the bar association will not be directly linked, either by formal or informal organizational ties, by common individual memberships or by the clients of bar association members.

This position of centrality offers the bar association an enormously critical resource, for it implies that the profession can be expected to have a direct and probably strong tie to all major institutions and, further, that those ties will be at the top rather than intermediate or lower levels of the respective institutions. This breadth of network connections provides several advantages for the bar association: wide networks give it access to information, offer numerous possibilities for joint action, alliances, and coalitions, and place the association in such a structural position that its very centrality, as in the drafting of the revenue article, may allow it to play a brokerage role out of all proportion to its voting base. By the same token, legislative and other reform programs undertaken by the bar demand levels and types of resources it does not have. The professional association is consequently at the nexus of a network of reciprocity. Where the bar association can offer specialized technical knowledge of the law, a range of other organizations can provide funding, lobbying, the dissemination of information, the mobilization of the electorate—indeed the full repertoire of political skills and capacities.

12. The concept of *interdependency* draws on network theory, in which entire organizations are treated as actors, nodes, or points. Represented graphically, relations among the bar association and other organizations would appear as:

$$CBA$$

Judiciary ⟷ Regular Democrats

The concept of *interpenetration* draws on the Boolean algebra concept of intersecting sets, where members simultaneously participate in two or more overlapping organizations. Represented graphically, interorganization relations would be seen as:

CBA

Judiciary ◯ Regular Democrats

But herein lies a cousin of the internal paradox faced by open associations. Both interdependency and interpenetration represent the paradox of inclusiveness in its *external* manifestation. Strong ties to a heterogeneous membership provide external organizational expression of the divergences in interests and values that members bring into the organization. To the extent that there is internal conflict, therefore, that conflict can be mirrored through the mobilization of respective organizations by opposing parties in intraprofessional disputes. Thus at once the profession can find itself greatly advantaged by its structural position in general organizational networks and greatly disadvantaged by the contradictory demands or expectations allied organizations can make on it. Just as the professional association is constrained by internal cleavages, therefore, it is also limited by institutional reciprocity and organizational cross-pressures. Consequently, transcending inclusiveness implies not only dealing with internal divisions but also coping with the weakness of strong ties—the bonds of reciprocity. The latter provide both a basis of action and limits to it.

The nature of this reciprocity can be illustrated by a brief consideration of flows of resources between the bar association and the economic sector, political organizations, educational institutions, and the judiciary. I then explore the strategies whereby the professional association can rise above these external manifestations of inclusiveness.

Economic institutions have two kinds of formal relations with the professional association: relations can be direct, between a specific economic organization and the bar association, or they may be indirect, through collective organizations such as the Chamber of Commerce, the Association of Commerce and Industry, the Manufacturers Association, the Bankers Association, and the Real Estate Board. Usually, specific organizations like banks provide the bar tangible assets such as funds; the collective associations provide public support and organization. The professional associations lean most heavily on corporations and financial houses for funds. For example, while the CBA had a very large budget (in excess of $1.5 million) in the mid-1970s, most of its income was and is tied down in fixed budget lines; the fluid or capital reserves available for publicity campaigns are quite limited. Accordingly, the bar must solicit contributions, usually from organizations that have an interest in given legislation. For example, the collective organizations in the economic sector provided crucial support for the CBA in its larger campaigns, such as its efforts to pass the judicial article. In fact, the relation of economic institutions to the professional association is well exemplified in the mutuality engendered when the economic sector had a revenue article it wanted adopted and the legal profession had a judicial article it wished to be implemented. The CBA provided legitimation for the economic organizations; the latter contributed economic and public support for the CBA. Curiously enough, when the judicial article was finally passed in 1961, the CBA suddenly found itself unable to continue its support of the economic institutions. The unions were also potential allies; the support of the CIO brought with it the votes of its members and their door-to-door lobbying for the judicial article.

Political organizations and institutions have a more integral relation with the organized bar. A responsive general assembly or city council can further both professional economic interests and the conditions of legal work. They provide access for special interest groups within the bar to get legislation enacted or to have legislation blocked. Ultimately, as we have seen, the success and influence of the organized bar as an agent of institutionalization depends on the credence given to it by politicians. But it is more than a matter of goodwill by political sponsors. The relation was reciprocated. The bar in its turn provided political organizations with technical assistance on major law revisions. Codification and the implementation of uniform laws enhanced the prestige of legislators within the state. They identified Illinois as a "progressive" state within the Union. The bar frequently needed sponsors for its legislation, thus providing a legislator with technically competent bills with which he or she could confirm his or her activism to constituents. The bar provided a degree of neutrality to politicians; lawyers argued that they more often understood legislators' needs, and, unlike most interest groups, the bar brought a wider and more balanced perspective in its major legislation. In the revenue article and Criminal Code, the bar associations had already acted as a legislature in microcosm; some of the disputes among interest groups was mitigated before the legislation was brought to the House floor. And, of course, it was the bar association that had pressed for the constitutional amendment that had increased the political adaptive capacity of the state government.

The role of academics in the revision of the Criminal Code, and all other comprehensive pieces of bar-initiated reforms, points to the mutually beneficial relations between universities and the profession. The university bolsters the profession's claims to expert authority by underwriting professional claims with the prestige of the university and the charisma of cognitive mastery attained by its faculty members. Some universities maintained a reform infrastructure by donating the time of scholars, providing facilities for conferences, and giving drafting and secretarial support—as did the Northwestern University School of Law during revision of the Criminal Code. Bar associations can reciprocate by offering a political base for professors hoping to translate ideas into statutes. Moreover, law reform work counts in many universities as a factor in the upward professional mobility of the academic. Further, the law schools rely on the general goodwill of those sectors of the profession that control the bar associations for job placement of graduates and the augmentation of law school endowments.

Reciprocal ties between the judiciary and the bar association are the most significant and complex of all. Both individual and collective relations between the bench and the bar are mutually beneficial for each party. Many individual judges are members of bar associations and sit on procedural committees or on committees in their fields of substantive interest. In an electoral system, they benefit from the visibility participation in the bar association gives them, and because the associations frequently screen the qualifications of judges running for office of retention, it may be very useful for them to have colleagues in the organized bar in case there are any problems—a connection equally useful if a judge is attacked in the press or is investigated by an association on a misconduct charge. Bar membership provides a judge with some vocational security.

This individual involvement of judges in the organization facilitates the collective relations of the bench and the bar. The organized bar can exercise some influence over conditions of judicial office and the organization and procedure of the courts. The bar association will often be a more persuasive, public proponent of judicial change than will the judiciary, particularly when, in cases like salaries, action by judges would be interpreted as self-serving. The organized bar then can usually be counted on to champion the cause of the bench in public. As one CBA leader appropriately noted, "If the public come to lose confidence in the bench, they will also lose confidence in us." Paradoxically, however, the closeness of this bench-bar tie also can protect the bench from the bar association; it is particularly difficult for the latter to direct a sustained attack on an institution whose members form a valuable component of the collegial body.

So, too, are close individual and collective relations valuable for the organized bar. Lawyers may gain some slight advantage, particularly in the lower courts, if they are on personal terms with the presiding judge. But the professional association is very much more significant for aspirants to judicial office; the organized bar is a path of mobility to the bench. While it may not be decisive in itself, bar membership can help those who are not well-known in local political circles at nomination and election time and may be even more important for those lawyers who are so political that some time in a professional association may help them in the eyes of the perennial critics of "political" appointments to the bench. This ladder to the bench can be gauged by the observation that, from 1945 to 1970, two board members went to the U.S. Supreme Court, at least five were appointed to U.S. district courts and courts of appeals, and two became chief judges of the former Chicago municipal court system. Many others have gone to other courts and both federal and state administrative agencies. One—Richard Daley—became mayor of Chicago. Bar association involvement anticipates criticism that judges were appointed not because they were good lawyers or conscientious professional citizens but because they were "political hacks," as one commentator less than charitably referred to some nominees for the bench.

Although many different kinds of organizations, representing different institutional sectors, have some form of exchange relation with the professional organization, their salience to the profession varies greatly. Some organizations offer resources the bar cannot do without; others have relatively less with which to trade. Organizations have different media to exchange. The character of the media themselves will partially account for the flexibility with which a professional association can deal with given organizations. Financial support, for example, can be precisely calculated (and hence the extent of bar obligation accurately gauged) and readily converted. Electoral support and public endorsement, on the other hand, are difficult to measure, and the level of reciprocation necessary to balance an exchange remains unclear. Furthermore, some sectors, such as large financial and business organizations, have constant dealings with the leaders of the bar; other organizations can reach no higher into the professional association that peripheral and less powerful segments of the profession. Consequently, the bar leadership faces a somewhat similar set of decisions externally as it does internally: it must gauge which organizations can offer it more, which must be supported more often, and which have little to provide and should thereby get little in return. It is consistent with this proposition that the professional association supported for several years a revenue article that quite clearly favored the business and corporate sector at the very time that business support was critical for passage of the judicial article. It is also consistent with this proposition that the organized bar had little difficulty in being unresponsive to fair housing legislation; presumably its decision not to act adversely affected only a minority of the profession and a section of the population—the poor and ethnic groups—who were disorganized and had little to offer in return.

Nevertheless, some caution should be exercised in pushing this reciprocity conception too far. Under some circumstances the CBA was forced to withdraw support from the very influential economic organizations that had drafted an unsatisfactory revenue article in the early 1960s. The Roman Catholic church, which does not usually engage in formal relations with the organized bar, nevertheless could still act as a veto group for an entire code of draft legislation, so much so that its objections to the Criminal Code had to be met for legislative passage to be assured. In the decision-making discussions themselves, except for relations with political institutions and the judiciary, relatively little explicit concern or calculation was evident.

In practice, therefore, the bar association can adapt to its reciprocal ties with other organizations using some of the tactics that it applies inside its own organization. Its general approaches to its organizational environment must be subdivided into two broad types, each of which has numerous variations. One adaptation to strong ties was to use an *insider* approach, especially in situations in which there were close relations between an organization and the professional association and in which it appeared that the organization that the association wished to influence might be amenable to persuasion. In this case the professional leadership, perhaps without reference to most of its own constituency, discreetly approaches another organization and attempts to effect change through negotiation. A relatively high level of reciprocity between organizations seems to be a precondition for insider approaches because the organization in which change is sought must be persuaded that it is to its advantage to respond positively to the bar initiative or at least that it may be to its disadvantage to opt for inertia; thus the profession must have real or implied sanctions it can apply to a noncompliant organization if persuasion fails. If the change cannot be effected by virtue of the advantages to be attained by maintaining high levels of organizational reciprocity, then it may be effected by the strength of personal ties between leaders of the respective organizations.

However, if ties between the bar association and an organizational object of influence are weak, or if the bonds of reciprocity are strong but the bar association presses for changes that exceed what the object organization is prepared to concede, or if the target organization is or may be under strong cross-pressures not to change, then it will be necessary for the organized bar to adopt the *outsider* approach. Here it acts in much more of the conventional interest-group pattern. It can no longer proceed in secrecy; it must inform and mobilize its own members; and it must build coalitions and alliances with other sympathetic organizations. By taking such a form of action it is subject to the same processes of mobilization as any other pressure group.

The contrast between the two forms of adaptation to external ties can be exemplified by their use in the campaign for autonomy of the Illinois courts. In 1953 and 1955, the first two occasions on which the bar presented a draft judicial article, it used an outsider approach because the bar leadership had relatively weak political ties to the Republicans who dominated downstate Illinois and to the Democratic party machine that controlled Chicago and Cook County. Consequently, the bar had little option but to wage an expensive campaign. Between 1950 and 1964, it raised more than $100,000 by soliciting its members, law firms, clients, banks and corporations. The funds were employed to form front organizations, such as the Citizens' Committee, that would handle lobbying and enable the bar to "drop in the background and allow citizens' groups, the limelight"; to hire public relations firms through the Citizens' Committee; and to build alliances directly or indirectly with civic groups such as the Union League Club and the Commercial Club, with labor groups, and with the Agricultural Bureau, among others. The bar assiduously wooed the media, took out advertising, and arranged speakers programs to disseminate its points of view. It invited various officials, ward and town committee men of both parties, to a dinner at

Barrister Hall. But as chapter 6 recounted, those extensive efforts were not successful in either 1953 or 1955.

Learning from bitter experience, the board changed its strategy completely. The change was possible because the CBA now had a president with powerful Republican connections and a board member who had very close personal ties with Mayor Daley and regular Democrats in the Illinois house. The board believed that if it could negotiate directly with political leaders it might be able to work out a compromise plan before going to the legislature and thus be assured of bipartisan support once it got there. Mobilization of the bar and a costly campaign to mobilize the electorate would only become necessary once the article went to the voters for confirmation. But the costs of direct negotiations would likely include the delegation of considerable discretion to bar negotiators, and the bar would probably pay a heavy price in any compromise proposal. With this strong leadership, the board seized the initiative away from its Joint Committee and took a much more pragmatic substantive position that stressed court reorganization rather than merit selection. The two political insiders on the board asked for its trust and proceeded to negotiate secretly with the mayor and governor. Mobilization of the bar was actively discouraged. The president insisted that any pressure from the CBA membership would tie his hands in negotiations, would alienate the political parties, and would not do any good at all. "You don't start attacking the fellows you are trying to get along with. . . . If we sell them [the political leaders] on the program that you are working out, it won't cost you anything, and if you cannot, you can go down and spend all the money you want to and you won't pass the bill." There is little doubt that the article produced by this method got further than it had before—through the legislature and almost past the voters. But it was so compromised, in the view of leading bar reformers, including the chairman of the joint committee, that it was not considered worthy of their strong support.

The case of the judicial article contrasts strongly with that of the Illinois Civil Practice Act, concerning which there were constant negotiations between lawyers and the judges. Once the legal experts had agreed to a common position, the legislature passed the draft legislation virtually intact. In fact cases such as the Civil Practice Act suggest that the nature of issues will very often determine whether an insider or outsider approach will be employed. If an association has strong ties with another organization, and if the issue is limited in scope and is more a technical than a policy matter, then it is more likely that an insider approach, without mobilization of internal constituencies or external alliances, will suffice. Moreover, because the outsider approach is so costly in terms of the resources it expends, the bar association will prefer to negotiate most often from the inside. Where ties with other organizations are weak or a bar association wishes to exceed the bounds that reciprocity places on it when organizational ties are strong, or when the issue itself is clearly a social or public matter and must eventually be out before the legislature or voters, then the outsider approach will be inevitable. But even in these cases, it may be possible for a professional association to take negotiations to an advanced stage by the inside method (as in the cases of the criminal codes) before finally having to proceed as an interest group in the political marketplace.

Simply because the outsider approach is so costly, therefore, the bar association must budget its resource expenditure closely. An association will not be able to deal with too many major issues at the same time or in quick succession. It may still, however, be able to compress a great deal in a short period. At the 1961 session of the General Assembly, the bar associations had before the legislature a draft revenue article, a draft judicial article, a draft criminal code, the Uniform Commercial Code, and its usual joint bar legislature program. All of these, but for the revenue article, passed. Yet 1961 was exceptional. For the most part, the association must stay within the bounds of reciprocity and must tailor its demands to fall within the lower and particularly upper thresholds of change that other interested organizations will be prepared to concede. It is for this strategic reason, then, among others, that the bar association prefers to work cooperatively with the judiciary and is careful to moderate the nature of its controls over judges.

There is an alternative method—to approach the judiciary in the oppositional way that has been used by the Chicago Council of Lawyers (CCL), a breakaway group of younger and more liberal lawyers from the CBA.[13] But in fact the two contrasting sets of relations with the judiciary may be not mutually exclusive but complementary. Through its reciprocal ties, the CBA can exercise considerable ongoing influence in all aspects of the judiciary and court system; but the maintenance of those same ties does not enable it to take the strong and forthright action that may be required in certain circumstances. That role can be played by the smaller, more homogeneous, and critical CCL, which in its turn, however, does not have the credit and goodwill to be able to exercise the more diffuse and extensive influence of the larger association. In this respect, therefore, a division of labor has emerged within the collegial organizations of the profession that allows it both to profit from the strength of its strong ties to networks of organizations and to give the profession the capacity in some circumstances to compensate for the potential weaknesses of those ties.

    13. Michael Powell, "Anatomy of a Counter-bar Association: The Chicago Council of Lawyers," *American Bar Foundation Research Journal* 1979 (Summer): 501–41.

Stalemate, Oligarchy, and Activism

Does the contradiction of inclusiveness in an open association stifle collective professional action? We have seen that inclusiveness has two aspects, internal and external, and that both have the potential to stalemate elite decision making or organizational action. Nevertheless, it seems clear that, as a bar association shifts from an elite to an open form of organization, it can modify its government to mitigate the consequences of diversity adverse to decision making and action. These changes, achieved through amendments of bylaws, changes in conventions, and the application of control strategies, enable bar elites to maintain some autonomy and control over their constituents. With this added discretion, a bar association leadership can exploit structural segmentation within a comprehensive association by both reducing and controlling the demands on it. By these means, the pessimistic expectations of inaction that result from compositional diversity are not realized. A bar association can take advantage of the resource wealth brought by a democratization of the professional association and at the same time minimize the potentially negative consequences of that shift in composition.

If these adaptations to inclusiveness by the elite ensure it a degree of decision-making autonomy, the shape of that government nonetheless falls short of the strict conception of oligarchy articulated by Michels. The leadership had attributes scarcely more advantageous than the members, whether in recruitment or political skills. In fact, it appears that, as the period advanced, it was under considerable pressure to reproduce in the leadership the distribution of key attributes in the membership at large. Furthermore, the structure of succession maintained a fairly high rate of turnover, even if it was not quite as high as the constitution allowed. In addition, pressure from powerful committees clearly constrained the leadership to respond to expressions of interests that emanated from them. Even when the board could use segmentation and other forms of structural control to limit committees, it did not succeed in stifling organized action by its constituent units, whether it intended to do so or not. Moreover, the existence of a significant committee for an extended period without board authorization clearly calls into question the completeness of its political awareness and penetration of control. This argument cannot be pressed too strongly: the board undoubtedly had structural advantages—in information, financial control, and administration—that it used to adopt and implement policies not infrequently in the face of considerable organizational dissent. Nevertheless, the composition of the leadership, its structural relation to constituent committees, and the relations between associational positions of power and positions in the work force suggest that at worst this is a rather benign and malleable oligarchy and that at best bar associations represent a fairly notable—and further—exception to the "iron law of oligarchy."

Ultimately, however, it is the external ramifications of inclusiveness that are the more severe. Bar associations are caught in a network of organizational reciprocity that may give them access to all other institutions, allow them the possibility of inside negotiative strategies for change, and provide opportunities for organizational alliances where the external alternative must be taken. At the same time the bar association has much less control over external organizations and many fewer resources to commit to conventional interest-group activities. Consequently, in situations in which the bar association must adopt an outsider strategy on issues concerning which there will be general mobilization, its influence will be much more questionable. That will apply particularly in those cases in which the public issue is more a moral than a technical matter and located rather more in secondary than primary spheres.

The prospects of professional associations bringing their influence to bear on major issues and crises of public policy therefore will depend on the extent that they can take inside approaches to problems in primary institutional spheres under the cloak of technical assistance. With this type of action they will be able to implement frequent and sometimes major changes. When, however, bar associations endeavor to exercise moral authority in secondary institutional spheres, and they do so by the outsider approach, then the likely successes of their activities will be much more contingent. The historical task of the associations has been to convert a steadily wider domain of issues from the second to the first mode of action—to accomplish moral and policy ends through the guise of technical means.

12 Established and Civic Professionalism

The state in Western industrial societies has been subject to crises of capacity. All branches of government have come under increasing pressure from the revolution in rising expectations of state intervention. As demands on government have increased in volume and variety, so also have they become more often contradictory and mutually exclusive. With the splintering of traditional forms of interest representation has come a decline in the capacities and centrality of conventional aggregatory structures such as political parties. Each branch of government has both increased in size and become more differentiated—each development in turn posing more acutely the problems of organizational coordination. Accompanying the diversification and replication of functions within and across branches there has been a compounding of difficulties in relations among them, such that one branch, in a struggle for ascendancy with another, can too often achieve no more than a stalemate. It is the latter—a growing incapacity of government to fulfill the functions expected of it—that results in the ultimate condition in which the overburdened state may find itself—a crisis of effectiveness and legitimacy. The chief task, then, of the state under strain will be to find expedients by which to adapt its functions and structures to the new circumstances impinging on it. The principal task of the liberal democratic state is to balance efficacy with participation and technical competence with public accountability.

The crises or strains of governability are ramified through all levels of the state—in the subnational governments of states in the federal union as well as in federal government itself. But the former, the fifty constituent governments of the United States, have remained in the shadow of contemporary debates despite the fact that they have compelling claims to attention in their own right. The pressures on apparently overburdened states have been concretely exemplified by the post–World War II crises in Illinois. The conundrums facing state and federal courts throughout the United States in the last three decades are represented in microcosm by the Illinois court system and judiciary—a system in which law has been wed to politics, in which a growing case backlog has fallen on court organizations ill equipped to respond to it, and in which a rational, bureaucratic, and more efficient form of administering justice has been conspicuously absent. In these circumstances, the inadequate administration of justice too readily becomes translated into a general crisis of legitimacy for the legal system and eventually for law itself. Similarly, the fiscal crises into which national governments have fallen have their analogues with state governments. The latter, in the 1960s and even the 1970s, found not only a shortfall of revenue to meet a surfeit of expenditure but also a structural rigidity within government itself, particularly in its revenue-raising capacities, which inhibited them from adaptations that might meet the new economic and social conditions. Most dramatically of all, the enduring tension between governmental powers and the individual rights affected the states with full force in the two and a half decades after 1945. Essentially, that crisis called for nothing less than a historical redefinition of the respective rights and responsibilities of the state and the individual. The crises of law, economy, and rights do not exhaust the issues of the last three decades. Neither were they local or exceptional. Each has been a particular manifestation in one state of a more ubiquitous phenomenon—if uneven in its intensity—across all states.

The historical point of state fragility coincided with the coming of age of bar associations. In the last half century, major metropolitan and state bar associations have made a transition from elite and unrepresentative organizations to open, inclusive, and representative bodies. In so doing they have accumulated enriched portfolios of resources. These private associations are both inclusive of all major areas of specialty expertise in a profession and replete with the organizational capacities, including substantial financial incomes and assets, to bring expertise to government. From both theoretical and practical points of view, therefore, the problem of an overloaded state becomes an issue for the macrosociology of the professions.

The critical question for that intersection of professions and the state can be broached in terms of two alternatives: juxtaposition or convergence? Are the changes in government and the professions merely correlative but independent, changes significant in themselves but inconsequential in their conjunction? Or has there been a meeting of the two at a time when the one is most resourceful and the other less efficacious? It has been the argument of this book that juxtaposition is being converted into convergence—that at least one profession has signaled its willingness to provide services for the state while the state has indicated some readiness to take advantage of the unique capabilities of professional groups.

My principal thesis can be stated succinctly. The dramatic transformations of the collegial organizations of the legal profession over the last century have endowed professional associations with a wealth of resources. The strengths garnered through resource accumulation have allowed professional bodies to move beyond a preoccupation with monopoly, occupational closure, and the defense of work domains to courses of action more concerned with the functioning of the state itself. This transition from a formative to an established stage of professional development has occurred concurrently with the decline of the authority of the state and the efficacy of government. The established profession, no longer absorbed with monopoly and its maintenance, has the potential progressively to commit its singular expert authority to the tensions of the late, twentieth-century, democratic state. In that convergence of enlarged professional capacities with diminished state capabilities, some professions may have the potential to take on themselves—or have thrust on them—a more prominent responsibility for liberal democratic government. The degree and shape of that commitment, however, generates anew the enduring tension between representative authority derived from the citizen and technical authority monopolized by the expert.

From Formative to Established Professionalism

An essential problem for the neophyte profession is the establishment of control over a sphere of work. It is this, and the cluster of concepts surrounding monopoly, that has become the conceptual pivot around which have revolved many recent treatments of professions and professionalism. The discourse has been cast in two molds, the one neo-Weberian and the other neo-Marxist. The neo-Weberian treatments have focused on the process of economic monopolization; the neo-Marxist discussions have gone on from monopolies of competence to their consequences for the reproduction of bourgeois ideology. Both, however, have been prone to a form of theoretical imperialism that has lost sight of most images but monopoly.

In Weberian terms, guild-type groups are formed as professional instruments of collective action in favor of a set of interests such as economic domination or privilege. Compared to an interest group based on exclusion of outsiders by some external characteristic such as race or class, the guild regulates its membership by inclusion of members on the basis of acquired attributes such as those obtained through "upbringing, apprenticeship, and training."[1] Monopoly by such a group is achieved by a combination of several strategies. An occupation must create its distinctive commodities. In the case of professions, these are services rather than tangible goods. But intangible products such as a legal or medical service cannot be guaranteed because the outcome will not always be favor-

1. Max Weber, *Economy and Society: An Outline of Interpretative Sociology*, ed. Guenther Roth and Claus Wittich (New York: Bedminster, 1968), 344. See Weber's discussion of guilds and monopoly generally at 302–48 and in his *General Economic History*, trans. Frank H. Knight (Glencoe, Ill.: Free Press, 1927).

able. Lawyers lose cases and doctors lose patients despite the best efforts of each. Consequently, an occupation must convince potential clients that the performance of services and recompense for them must be kept distinct. Having created service commodities, an occupation has to maintain strict control over the channels by which they can be satisfied. Supply of service can be monopolized through control of educational and apprenticeship institutions, and scarcity of services can be created by either the regulation of supply or the regulation of demands or both. At the same time, a monopolistically inclined occupation needs to eliminate external competition and minimize internal competition. Competition from outside the occupation would deprive it of the ability to control the supply of services; open competition among workers would drive down prices and fracture internal solidarity.

The instruments of monopoly that have emerged from a century of professionalization are well known. An occupation develops an organizational vehicle with which to press its claims; it seeks to control professional education so far as possible; it strives to obtain licensing powers from the state and hence the right to bring legal sanctions against unauthorized practitioners; and it constructs an internal normative system to regulate relations among professionals. Monopolization therefore demands that an occupation dominate the market for its services, and that may best be attained by the delegation of state powers. The most secure and complete monopoly will be that which is legitimized by the legal authority of the state and enforced by its coercive machinery.

The concept of monopoly has come to have more than economic ramifications. Both neo-Weberian and neo-Marxist analyses of professionalization have a class dimension as well. Occupational closure, which restricts entry to the profession, together with control of education and admission, facilitates collective upward mobility.[2] With the prestige of advanced education and extended training came licensing powers that enabled professionalizing occupations to exclude the lower classes, certain denigrated ascriptive groups, which have historically included women, and certain ethnic and racial groups, thereby making admission to the profession all the more desirable and raising its standing further.[3] Alongside the economic advantages of market control for individual professionals to accumulate capital, the profession as a whole can ascend prestige and economic ladders.[4] Furthermore, one recent argument would have it that with the bureau-

2. The most lucid recent discussion of occupational closure in neo-Weberian terms can be found in Frank Parkin, *Marxism and Class Theory: A Bourgeois Critique* (London: Tavistock, 1979).

3. On the exclusion of women from medicine, see Noel Parry and Jose Parry, *The Rise of the Medical Profession.*

4. See also the treatment of collective upward mobility in ibid., an argument that is derived theoretically from another neo-Weberian approach to class analysis, namely, Anthony Giddens, *The Class Structure of Advanced Societies* (New York: Harper & Row, 1975).

cratization of professional work the concept of monopoly in a "free" professional market no longer has relevance, that the conquest of status through organizational advancement remains the primary goal of professionalizing occupations under monopoly capitalism.

That thesis has been taken a step further. Clearly, professions with control of the market of professional services and with standing at the apex of the occupational prestige scale have a distinctive capacity to shape the ideology of the capitalist order that has served them so well. In this formulation, therefore, professions continue to perpetuate an outmoded notion of service in order to disguise the true form and scale of their control over professional markets and institutions. Their role, this argument goes, is even more insidious: the conception of a professional denotes a worker whose standing in the class system is a result of education and ability alone. Professions stand as the most visible symbols of meritocracy, a class segment not founded on ascriptive attributes but on individual ability and individual achievement. Thus the concept of professionalism reinforces the ideology of the liberal society that individual talent and ability will triumph whatever one's point of origin in the class system. In this sense contemporary professions serve to legitimize the class structure through their idealization of bourgeois ideology. But to underwrite a capitalist ideology represents a more critical function, for, in this thesis, the monopoly capitalist system is maintained in part through the pervasiveness of an ideology that obscures both the ubiquity of monopoly and the myth of meritocracy. Market control by professionals therefore leads to a monopoly of competence, which in turn reinforces an ideology eventually to provide a foundation of legitimacy for the monopoly capitalist order itself. The professions thereby become an ideological pillar of late capitalism.[5]

The monopolistic assumption has become a new orthodoxy in recent sociological interpretations of professions; it is a basis on which is elaborated the more trenchant critiques of professions in advanced capitalist societies. I will return below to the thesis that the prime macrosociological role of contemporary professions is to obscure the chains of capitalism. The more conventional treatments of economic monopoly, however, are not to be denied completely. A theory of professions in advanced capitalist societies does not need to repudiate entirely all economic foundations of professionalism in order to go beyond monopoly. Such a theory rather requires that monopoly be set in its context, that its possible distortions be set alongside its manifest contributions.

Monopolistic interpretations of the rise of professions too readily become wrong headed and unbalanced. In part the fallacy of universal monopoly results

---

5. This has been most forthrightly stated in Magali Sarfatti Larson, *The Rise of Professionalism,* pt. 2 and pp. 208–44.

from a methodological lapse. Ex post facto reinterpretation of a sequence of historical developments allows an observer to assume that monopoly is the overriding motive of most professional actions when it may well be an unintended consequence of some other motivation. In this mode of analysis, where professional actions can be attributed to more benign or malevolent motivations, the latter seem always to be preferred. Higher educational standards may have had a salutary effect on quality of care and on research and the advancement of professional knowledge; professional ethics may have produced higher levels of professional responsibility; and licensure may have protected the gullible from exploitation and personal tragedy. That some of those aspects of professionalism have also had monopolistic effects seems to have largely eclipsed any beneficial consequences. Even if actions are not explicitly monopolistic, that can be reinterpreted as strategic retreat or cunning strategy. Demonopolization becomes indirect monopolization.[6] Moreover, advocates of the monopoly thesis are inclined, at critical points in their arguments, to fall back on an assumption of internal professional cohesion that, in other sections of their discussions, they have been at pains to deny. Consequently, little attention is given to those monopolistic actions by one section of a profession that partially dismantle the monopoly of another section. For example, more prestigious and more powerful specialties within professions may be more readily inclined to adopt measures, such as no-fault laws, that effectively demonopolize areas of less prestigious professional specialties. In sum, then, the defect of an unchecked theory of professional monopolies is that all motivations and most consequences other than those that are explicitly or intentionally monopolistic become debased by that label.

Consequently, the chief lapse of market interpretations of professional activity is not that they draw attention to professional self-interest or to economic motivations or to the consequences of professionalism. To a point, they can be validated empirically. The impediment of vulgar monopolistic theories is that *one* consequence or even intent of professionalism becomes the raison d'être of the entire professionalization enterprise. The part is taken for the whole. Latent consequences become explicit intents; accompanying motives become sole bases of action. Results of professionalization are assumed to be the outcome of a professional "project." In a word, the entire interpretative model is overdetermined.

But this argument is to do more than place the monopolistic component of professionalism in proportion. I contend that the centrality of monopoly to the professional enterprise has a developmental dimension. Control of the market for American lawyers was a prominent task only in the *formative stage* of the profession's development. In the first decades following the renewal of collegial organi-

6. For example, compare Jeffrey L. Berlant, *Profession and Monopoly*, 153–76.

zations for lawyers in the 1870s, substantial proportions of time, effort, funds, and other organizational resources were committed to programs that either were intended to accomplish or resulted in domination of the market for legal services. For legal associations—and it is conceivable that other professions show a similar pattern—early records indicate that a majority of organizational units and committee efforts were committed to the upgrading of educational requirements for admission to the bar, to the attempts of the profession to get statutory or court authority for requisite levels of training, to endeavors that would delegate powers of admission from the state to the bar through such bodies as committees on character and fitness that screened applicants on behalf of the Supreme Court, to efforts to have court rules or statutes enacted that forbade unauthorized practice by unlicensed practitioners and provided channels for their prosecution, and to gain delegated authority from the state to enforce professional ethics. In other words, the profession was committed to the task of constructing an elaborate system of professional and market control. This was not the only component of professional activity, but it was prominent. It was also transitory.

In the legal profession, whose "modern" bid for professionalization emerged principally from the last quarter of the nineteenth century, there has been a perceptible shift away from the primacy or centrality of market and professional control. A preoccupation with market dominance marked only one, and a developmental, stage in the emergence of the profession and the expansion of its associations. Once that stage was reached, and its "developmental tasks" accomplished, the importance of monopoly in collective professional action and to professional identity began to fade.

The shifts away from the formative stage in the legal profession have been reflected in numerous indicators. Evidence from bar associations demonstrates that there has been a steady relative decline in the size and number of committees on professional fees, professional education, and professional discipline.[7] Indeed professions themselves have been engaging in what Powell has called "professional divestiture" of some traditional functions thought to be core elements of monopoly. Some of the divestiture has been involuntary—court decisions have struck down minimum fee schedules, and some associations have had their disci-

7. Compare the changing proportions of committees directed specifically to monopolistic concerns within the Chicago Bar Association (CBA) between 1874 and 1974 (table 3.1) The proportion of committees on discipline, ethics, admission, and the like in later years is even lower than table 3.1 suggests because, while those committees are included in the table, a large number of other substantive, special, and joint committees are excluded. Almost none of these have any direct or explicit concern wtih monopolistic functions per se. Results of my national survey in 1982 indicate that only 13 percent of standing committees in state and metropolitan associations are concerned with self-regulation or monopoly.

plinary functions removed.[8] Other changes have been undertaken voluntarily, as in the case of professional advertising or as in the voluntary relinquishment of costly disciplinary activities. Moreover, when professionals are asked to state priorities for their collegial bodies, they do not rank traditional monopoly concerns above the variety of other functions professional associations are expected to perform.[9] Similar indications of a shift in priority can be found in the rapidly diminishing proportion of association budgets concerned with admission, unauthorized practice, discipline, fees, and ethics.[10] The most prestigious lawyers in major metropolitan and state bar associations do not make their commitments to the profession in areas germane to market control but are much more likely to be concerned with ongoing professional education, government, the courts, and legislation. Finally, neither bar association records such as annual reports, nor leadership minutes, nor transcripts, would support the view that monopolization remains the major priority of the organized profession. To the contrary, it appears indisputable that ostensible activity of collegial associations directed to market control represents a steadily diminishing component of associational actions whether measured in terms of the expenditure of time or effort, of frequency or proportion of supporting organizational structures, or in terms of the principal goals or expectations of association members or leaders.

As explicitly monopolistic foci have diminished in significance, the formative stage has given way to a more established phase. The concept of *established professionalism* can be defined both negatively and positively. It does not connote

8. An instance of voluntary relinquishment has been documented by Michael J. Powell, "Professional Divestiture: The Cession of Responsibility for Lawyer Discipline," *American Bar Foundation Research Journal* 1986 [Winter]: 31–56. Powell's subsequent research on the Association of the Bar of the City of New York provides an example of involuntary relinquishment. *From Upper Class to Professional Elite: The Transformation of a Patrician Legal Association* (New York: Russell Sage Foundation, forthcoming). It should be noted that several states, including Wisconsin and Michigan, have transferred disciplinary functions to commissions independent of the organized bar. These commissions may also have lay participants. Similar reforms have been proposed by the Law Reform Commission of New South Wales in Australia.

9. Compare the ratings on objectives of bar associations given by respondents in the cross-sectional survey of the Chicago bar (John P. Heinz et al., "Diversity, Representation, and Leadership in an Urban Bar," *American Bar Foundation Research Journal* 1976 [Summer]: 744–47). In that rating of objectives, e.g., discipline of lawyers and prevention of unauthorized practice are ranked sixth and tenth, respectively, whereas improving the quality of the judiciary, improving the efficiency of court procedures, and initiating legislaton are ranked second, third, and fifth, respectively. The 1982 survey of state and metropolitan associations also found that, of five factors emerging from a factor analysis of nine goals, the monopoly factor (disciplining lawyers, preventing unauthorized practice) rated third, after "upgrading legal system" and "efficiency of law" but ahead of "legislation" and "social and legal change."

10. The 1982 survey found that only 25 percent of budgets in all associations were committed to self-regulation. Broken down the respective figures were 37 percent for unified associations, 14 percent for voluntary state associations, and 17 percent for metropolitan associations (Halliday, "The Monopoly Motif").

completeness; nor does it imply full or ultimate organizational development. Both connotations are nonsensical when applied to social institutions. Professional associations are no exception. Further development, decline, or persistence of current patterns are all possible. Rather establishment designates a new phase of the professionalization movement. Thus it can be partially defined as that stage reached if or when a profession has successfully negotiated the formative challenges—the stage at which the primary goal is self-preservation. The established profession is less occupationally vulnerable, less reflexively self-protective and self-preoccupied, and less collectively narcissistic.

Defined positively, the established phase of professionalism is that point—or, more accurately, that succession of points—at which growth of resources allows a profession to take on a broader range of functions and action than market control. A larger, structurally differentiated, and highly coordinated professional body has the organizational capacities to render the profession less vulnerable. Public relations departments, political lobbyists, the facility to build political alliances, and the emergence of political mobilization infrastructures all provide some degree of structural insurance for a profession—an expanded ability to fend off incursions at any level. As a result, organizational size, stature, and tradition allow an established profession some putative independence from the statutory or judicial powers on which rest its legitimate domination of service domains. The profession can be more detached and more autonomous from the fiat of the original grantors of monopolistic authority. Privileges become rights. A complete reversal of institutionalized monopoly appears inconceivable. Thus the profession can largely take for granted what previously it had constantly to negotiate. With the energies and resources released from securing and maintaining monopolies, professions attain new capacities for the exercise of influence through assertive collective action.

The expanded capacities and functions of the established profession are reflected both internally and externally. Internally, associations have engaged in a wider spectrum of services to members: continuing education; licensing of specialists; channeling of work to practitioners through referral programs; advice on the economics and management of professional offices; and the like. The more fundamental mark of professional maturity, however, can be found externally, particularly in changes in relations between professions and the state. The *dependency relations* with the state in the formative period can be transformed into *contributory relations* in the established phase. Whereas in the former a vulnerable occupation is at the behest of an empowering state, in the latter a vulnerable state can rely on the expertise of empowered professions. The dependency relation casts professions on the state for the critical structural elements of professionalism itself; the contributory relation provides the profession with increased leverage on strains in the primary responsibilities of government itself.

Just as the reach of this thesis requires qualification, so too its contingency demands emphasis. The data of American lawyers are consistent with a historical transition from formative to established professionalism. Much of the same logic should in theory apply to other professions. If it can secure its occupational niche and protect its vital economic interests, then a profession's resources can be freed from market concerns for other causes. Nevertheless, it does not follow that all professions succeed in accomplishing the formative phase: their economic situation may remain unstable and demand high involvement in occupational deference. Indeed, this may be the fate of most occupations that aspire to professionalism. Many must settle for the equivocal status of semiprofessions. Success at establishing market control will also turn on historical milieus: in some periods, such as late nineteenth-century America, governments proved readier to grant occupational privileges than in others, such as the heyday of Jacksonian democracy.

Even if professions do successfully negotiate a formative stage, they can never take entirely for granted the persistence of monopoly. The possibility of reversal is illustrated by Starr's argument that a decline in medical sovereignty occurred in the 1970s when, "for the first time in a century, American physicians faced a serious challenge simultaneously to their political influence, their economic power, and their cultural authority."[11] Furthermore, if the assistance a profession renders the state proves to be flawed, inaccurate, blatantly self-serving, or unhelpful, it bears a greater chance of rejection on subsequent occasions; a resurgent populism, for instance, might strike at the secure access to power that many professions currently boast.

Nevertheless, the reverses confronted by the medical profession and similar developments among lawyers are far from persuasive evidence of widespread deprofessionalization and a "crisis of professions."[12] Most professions, including law, have confronted an increased public skepticism that has been translated into some modest judicial and legislative incursions on professions' perquisites. But the challenges—to advertising, fixed fee schedules, and other staples of monopoly, together with the routinization of some simpler professional tasks—represent at most a marginal erosion of professions' economic advantages and cultural authority. If there have been structural adjustments in the relations of professions with the state, most are better construed as reprofessionalization than as deprofessionalization; there is no evidence of widespread dismantling of the classic professions' apparatuses.[13] To the contrary, diminution of influence in some do-

11. Paul Starr, *The Social Transformation of American Medicine* (New York: Basic, 1982), 380.

12. Thomas L. Haskell, introduction to, *The Authority of Experts: Studies in History and Theory*, ed. Thomas L. Haskell (Bloomington: Indiana University Press, 1984), xiii.

13. On deprofessionalization and the concept of "reprofessionalization," see Michael Powell, "Developments in the Regulation of Lawyers: Competing Segments and Market, Client, and Government Controls," *Social Forces* 64 (December 1985): 281–305.

mains is vigorously counterbalanced by expansion in collective associations and resources. At the subnational level of government, the legal profession has if anything multiplied its political influence and cultural authority. In terms of collective attributes, the legal profession has never been more powerful than it is a century after the first wave of bar association foundings.

The characterization of changes in professions' occupational situations as a form of reprofessionalization points to a further aspect of the transitions over the last century. In the shift from a stage at which the market has priority to a phase at which the state itself commands more attention, the underlying supports of professionalism itself undergo some change. Earlier foundations of market control and professional competence are not ineluctable. It is entirely conceivable that they can be replaced, after a century of economic and political consolidation, by alternative structural supports that are more differentiated, sturdier, less state dependent, and cheaper.[14] The rise of a substantial government practice for lawyers and with the enormous growth of large law firms both point to alternative ways of controlling legal work and protecting lawyers' prerogatives. A more robust, economically entrenched, and bureaucratically structured profession, with powerful representative associations, may afford itself the luxury of dispensing with some of the expensive and elaborate scaffolding erected in formative years. The partial externalization of lawyer discipline from bar associations represents a case in point. The appearance of lay members of the public on previously restricted panels of lawyers for discipline, legal aid, and the delivery of legal services represents yet other instances. None, however, implies a complete dismantling of the profession's sinecures; at most, they indicate shifting bases or underpinnings of professionalism.

Whereas on the one side a new symbiosis requires a competent and authoritative profession inclined to mobilize its resources on behalf of the state, on the other side it demands a state that is disposed to appropriate a profession's capabilities. Professions can cement a contributory relation only at the state's behest—by cooperating with it rather than competing against it (although cooperation with one branch can precipitate resistance from another). That in turn is a function of the state's capacities: when it is ineffective, incapacitated, or under strain, then it is most likely to seek resolution of its difficulties in the private or quasi-private sector. Yet a constructive rapport does not necessarily require the abnormality of general state crisis or crippling ungovernabilty, although these might be precipitating factors in the onset of a new relation. Rueschemeyer and Evans rightly observe that in the normal course of events the modern state is confronted perpetually by questions of effectiveness. It cannot be assumed "that even a well-organized bureaucratic apparatus will have sufficient knowledge to intervene

---

14. I am indebted to Andrew Abbott for his observations along these lines.

effectively in the complex of inter-relations of socio-economic processes and patterns."[15] Insatiable for expertise, the contemporary state finds in professions the densest concentration of technical competence in civil society. In every-day governmental affairs, the need for adaptation and the development of new mechanisms persist in circumstances short of crisis. In short, the emergence of a symbiosis between an empowered profession and a weakened state is historically, nationally, and institutionally contingent. Neither inexorable nor irreversible, the conjunction between professions and the state is likely to obtain under a fairly restricted set of conditions. When the capacity of the state is low and the legitimacy and resources of a profession are high, then a contributory relation has a higher probability of emerging. When the legitimacy of a profession falls and the effectiveness of the state rises, then any contributory relation is more likely to be obviated or attenuated.

The contributory or constructive relations of the legal profession fall into two classes. The contribution of the legal profession to the definition of state powers represents a course of action distinctive to the legal profession through the relation of lawyers, as officers of the court, to the state. The contribution of lawyers to change in the legal system, on the other hand, indicates the scope of action a profession may aspire to in its primary institutional sphere and that may well be paralleled in their respective spheres by other professions. We may briefly consider aspects of each set of contributions in turn. In conclusion, both sets of contributions can be subsumed under a more generic argument.

Established Professionalism and Legal Change

Lawyers have a distinctive relation with the state because at once they stand astride the public-private boundary of the state and have a normative epistemology. Taken alone, each attribute offers considerable leverage; taken together, the mandate for influence is unparalleled among professions in scope if not intensity. Consequently, the argument presented here cannot simply be generalized from lawyers to other professions. But what of the macrosociological implications of the legal profession's actions in its primary institutional sphere? Although its partial insertion into a branch of government makes it somewhat exceptional, its patterns of collective action do have significance for the capacities of other professions to exert their authority in primary institutional spheres, especially those aspects of primary institutions that intersect with the state or are constitutive of it.

I have proposed that the sum of bar association efforts within the legal system can be interpreted holistically in terms of the profession's drive both to effect a

15. Dietrich Rueschemeyer and Peter B. Evans, "The State and Economic Transformation: Toward an Analysis of the Conditions Underlying Effective Interventions," *Bringing the State Back In*, ed. Peter B. Evans et al. (Cambridge, Mass. Harvard University Press, 1985), 52.

greater degree of autonomy for the legal system and at the same time to bring the system more fully under the control of the profession's collegial bodies. That argument, however, while consistent with theses on other professions, such as the professional dominance thesis applied by Freidson to the medical profession, can be placed in a different context.[16]

At the point of its greatest maturation, the legal profession finds itself at a significant juncture in the development of the American legal system. Nonet and Selznick have proposed a model of legal systems derived from "three modalities or basic 'states' of law-in-society," each corresponding to distinctive jurisprudential traditions. Their formulation, though contestable in several ways, nonetheless provides a most useful heuristic for situating the influence profile of bar associations in the historical matrix of general legal change.

According to Nonet and Selznick, a system of repressive law has two cardinal features—"close integration of law and politics in the form of direct subordination of legal institutions to public and private governing elites . . . and rampant official discretion."[17] Law is subordinated to the requirements of government, and the development of distinctive legal institutions is inhibited by a lack of differentiation of law-related institutions from political institutions. Thus there is constant intervention in legal processes by political authorities, court and legal officials are appointed and manipulated by rulers, rules are ultimately subservient to expediency and political purpose, and "*raison d'état*" or social defense is the basis of legal legitimacy. In short, " 'the separation of spheres' is alien to repressive law."[18]

Autonomous law on the other hand contrasts with its repressive precursor precisely because there is a "disjunction of political will and legal judgment."[19] The "master strategy" for the legitimation of the autonomous legal system is the separation of law and politics. Procedural fairness replaces political purpose as the foundation of law. Hence the legal system is bureaucratized, rules are elaborated and bind the rulers as well as the ruled, there are limits on official discretion, and the judiciary gains independence from political control. An autonomous legal system is one that therefore emphasizes the institutional integrity of the legal process, the independence of law from politics, and the primacy of the rule of law—a standard "born when legal institutions acquire enough independent authority to impose standards of restraint on the exercise of governmental power."[20] The chief characteristic of this system is "the formation of specialized, relatively au-

16. Eliot Freidson, *Professional Dominance: The Social Structure of Medical Care* (Chicago: Aldine, 1970).

17. Philippe Nonet and Philip Selznick, *Law and Society in Transition: Towards Responsive Law* (New York: Harper & Row, 1978), 51.

18. Ibid.

19. Ibid., 57.

20. Ibid., 53.

tonomous legal institutions that claim a qualified supremacy within defined spheres of competence." [21]

A third form of legal system, however, that of responsive law, one derived from the conception of legal systems outlined by sociological and realist jurisprudence, restores a sovereignty of purpose but this time by the integration of legal and political aspirations to the end that law will become more responsive to social needs. This "instrumentalist jurisprudence" calls for legal institutions to "become more dynamic instruments of social ordering and social change." [22]

Repressive, autonomous, and responsive systems are more than analytical types; they can have a dynamic relation to each other. [23] Within each system there are strains and instabilities that tend to dispose a prior state of "law in society" to give way to a subsequent stage. Thus autonomous legal systems will often, but not always, follow repressive systems. [24] In turn Nonet and Selznick maintain that responsive law is the end toward which autonomous systems may—and should— head.

Although no formulation is offered of the institutional or organizational motors of transition from one stage to another, it is clear that the legal profession stands in a particularly favorable position to shape legal development. The evidence considered here strongly suggests that the profession has committed its resources to imprint on the legal order a distinctively professional conception of its proper character. That formal legalistic image of the relation between law and society has led legal associations to press energetically for a transition from enduring residues of a repressive legal order in the United States to a more purely autonomous legal system. At the same time, the profession has steadfastly resisted any further transformation of law in the direction of responsive law.

To draw the typological lines over sharply, the major drive of American metropolitan and state associations has been to detach and uncouple especially party politics from the legal system. Indeed the model of law repeatedly expressed in

21. Ibid., and, on autonomous law generally, 53–72.

22. Ibid, 73–113.

23. It must be said that Nonet and Selznick are quite aware of the "vexing" nature of developmental schemes in sociology and the pitfalls for less cautious evolutionary theorists. They cast their own formulation in very cautious terms and with caveats as to the limits of the scope of the scheme they present (Nonet and Selznick, *Law and Society*, 15–27). Note, however, the criticism by Erhard Blankenburg, "The Poverty of Evolutionism: A Critique of Teubner's Case for 'Reflexive Law,'" *Law and Society Review* 18, no. 2 (1984): 273–90.

24. The concepts of repressive and autonomous law accord with distinctions by earlier theorists, including Max Rheinstein, *Max Weber on Law in Economy and Society* (Cambridge, Mass.: Harvard University Press, 1954), and Roberto Unger, *Law in Modern Society* (New York: Free Press, 1976), as Nonet and Selznick themselves acknowledge (*Law and Society*, 53–54). The principal attraction of the formulation by Nonet and Selznick is an analytical clarity that provides considerable theoretical leverage and precision in empirical research.

theoretical formulations and drafts of enabling legislation and constitutional amendments closely approximates the ideal type of the autonomous system. Subnational associations have consistently lobbied for unified and bureaucratized court systems, for the merit selection of judges (free from political sponsorship), for the formulation of statewide court rules by the supreme court rather than the legislature, and for the regulation of judicial behavior (especially that which concerns politics) by codes of ethics. The organized bar continues to assert the primacy of the rule of the law at the expense of political or substantive intrusions into the legal system. The dual drives toward structural differentiation of law from politics and the internal bureaucratization of the court system are organizational goals explicitly directed to what in effect is the completion of the shift from a repressive to an autonomous legal order in American society.

Nevertheless, at the same time as professional associations are championing legal autonomy, they have been equally resistant to any subsequent movement toward responsive law. The relations of formal and substantive justice in the programs of the organized bar have been the subject of an enduring debate within the profession, a theme constantly revisited with specific proposals from civil rights and other lawyers for a more responsive law. The general reaction of the organized bar is little different from that exemplified in the attitude of the Chicago association to the civil rights issues of the 1950s and 1960s. Mobilization on social policy issues, including those on education, housing, voting, and other rights, was consistently subordinated to legal formalism. In part this repudiation of substantive law is due as much to the exigencies and imperatives of organizational integration as to the motives of individual lawyers or even a culture of legal professionalism. Substantive justice on social policy questions is highly contentious, and the consequences of such decision making and mobilization for a heterogeneous profession could be more disintegrative than an inclusive professional body could tolerate. Whatever the motivation, however, the evidence I have adduced suggests that the profession has the will and the ability to advocate a general transformation of the legal system toward autonomous law while rejecting the inexorability of the developmental process toward the subordination of a relatively autonomous rule-governed system to one in which systematic ideological principles and policies are paramount.

Much of this typological representation of legal systems can be subsumed under Weber's more universal formulations of cultural and legal change. If the task of sociology is to identify the sociocultural conditions under which rationalization will advance in modern societies, the evidence presented on bar associations indicates both an institution in which the advance of rationalization has not been adequately comprehended and the profession that in good measure drives change. Advancing rationalization in the legal system has not been complete, rapid, or without its reverses.[25] At best it is partial and moderate; it has proceeded painstakingly over several decades; and it often as not has taken one step back for each two or three forward. These important provisos notwithstanding, American bar associations have committed enormous resources over the post-World War II era in a manner that can parsimoniously be interpreted as a net movement toward a more rational and formally autonomous legal order. To recapitulate the thesis of part 3, both in the administration of justice, which constitutes a primary sphere for lawyers, and in the form and substance of law, whether civil or criminal, bar associations have committed themselves to a *moderate* rational-legal conception of the legal system. In the judiciary, a national drive for the bureaucratization of the courts has accompanied an impetus toward differentiation of judicial structures and roles from party politics, local government, and state legislatures. In the substance of law, bar associations have joined with each other and national reform bodies to implement state uniform legislation and codify (albeit weakly by Continental standards) civil and criminal law.

In these respects, the dynamics of American legal change brings together two threads of Weberian theory seldom connected—his sociologies of professions and of law. It should be apparent that the political action of the legal profession directed toward control of an area of work through mechanisms of monopoly represents a comparatively trivial instance of guild activity; far more fundamental than control of one corner of the market is rationalization of one institution of the state, not to mention formalism of the very language of the state itself.[26] Here the macrosociology of professions becomes interwoven with the highest-order theoretical formulation of Western cultural and institutional change. Hence the significance of a profession such as law for modernity inheres not in its capacity to stand outside class conflict, as many social commentators hoped, or only in its championing of collegiality as a bulwark against bureaucracy but in its furtherance of a bounded rationality in the central regulatory structures of the modern state.

25. It is necessary to say again that this exploration of advances in various forms of rationalization does not commit one to either evolutionary or unidirectional conceptions of legal and institutional change. The debate over the evolutionary and directional commitments of Weber himself continues unabated. See, for instance, Wolfgang Schluchter, *The Rise of Western Rationalism: Max Weber's Developmental History* (Berkeley and Los Angeles: University of California Press, 1981); Friedrich H. Tenbruck, "The Problem of Thematic Unity in the Works of Max Weber," *British Journal of Sociology* 31 (1980): 313–51; Guenther Roth, "Sociological Typology and Historical Explanation," in *Scholarship and Partisan: Essays on Max Weber*, ed. Reinhard Bendix and Guenther Roth (Berkeley: University of California Press, 1971); Donald Levine, *The Flight from Ambiguity* (Chicago: University of Chicago Press, 1985).

26. I am indebted to Magali Larson for her discussion of John Austin's notion of law as the "language of the state" and discussions with her over its implications for lawyers' influence.

Professional Empowerment and State Adaptation

In definition of state powers, the legal profession has a putative influence unique among professions. I have argued that professions' empowerment has converged with a particular moment in the development of states. That moment, as we saw in chapter 1, finds some elements of some states in a condition of weakness. In response, the legal profession has been able to broach some of its own solutions through the idiom of expertise to many of the pressures confronted by government. Some proposals have been consequential; others have been relatively insignificant. Some were positive; others negated proposed courses of action. But beyond the specifics of given legislation, the most fundamental thrust of legal professional action has been—and can be—to the structure of government itself rather than to any particular output. The former, of course, will come to be a condition of the latter. The contributory relations of an influential profession to a weakened state, as they are exemplified by the organized bar, fall into three broad classes: the redefinition of state powers; the structural upgrading of state machinery; and devolution of state functions through depoliticization.

DEFINING STATE POWERS

In propitious circumstances, yet incompletely understood, an established legal profession can influence the parameters of state power in several respects. First, legal associations are critically placed to bring their monopolies of competence to the reform of constitutional controls over government. Inasmuch as the ability of the state to react to new and unanticipated demands on various of its organs depends on the powers delegated to it, the authority delegated by constitutions to each branch of government will have a determinative effect on the adaptive ability of the state. One thrust of professional collective action therefore can be directed to constitutional adaptation, that is, the modification of the constitution to facilitate the problem-solving ability of the state. The profession inserts its expertise into the structure of society and government by offering solutions to its highest-order, codified, and controlling principles.

Amendment of the form and content of state constitutions is manifest in a number of ways. In order that it does not completely inhibit change, a constitution must be amenable to amendment in pragmatic, political terms—that is, it must be reasonably possible (but not overly so) to carry out reform through a referendum without the latter having to meet conditions that are to all intents impossible to attain. Constitutional adaptation will be stillborn when amendatory procedures demand majorities or pluralities of certain kinds that are completely unrealistic. If a profession can facilitate the process whereby constitutional change becomes more practicable, through such measures as of a gateway amendment, then it will already have made a substantial contribution to the state. Having achieved a relaxation of requirements for constitutional revision, there are two further means by which that contributory relation can be extended. One concerns the extent to which an article will embody a degree of flexibility, the extent to which constitutional provisions will be "frozen" in statutory-like form so that any new requirements of government controlled by the constitution will in turn require the cumbersome process of further state-wide referendums. Constitutional articles can be written as limits to, or grants of, power. The respective form taken by an article will substantially alter the capabilities of government. As a result, a profession committing its expertise to constitutional amendment will be strategically placed both to shape the form and subsequent flexibility of an article and to mold the substantive provisions that it embodies.

In the second place, beyond a contribution to the redefinition of the constitutional parameters of state powers, the legal profession in its established form can contribute to the redistribution of powers among branches of government. The Illinois case, and the national evidence, have emphasized the reequilibration of powers as they are viewed from the vantage point of the judiciary. In the Illinois example, modifications in any specific instance were not always radical; they were not necessarily perceptible; and changes did not always go in the same direction. Some of the shifts in powers followed from constitutional revision per se; others resulted from codification; and yet others occurred in smaller increments from various less prominent statutory reforms. Whether explicit or not, however, bar associations can be integrally involved in modifying the distribution of powers and reciprocal controls vested in the various branches of government. In the postwar decades, a number of measures strengthened the Illinois judiciary at the expense of the legislature. On the other hand, various drafts of the revenue article would have removed much discretion in taxation matters from the courts and vested them in the legislature. Similarly, various provisions in revision of the Criminal Code would have constrained and limited certain executive and enforcement powers, as would also the rules of procedure advocated during the McCarthy period have restricted legislative and executive investigatory discretion.

If a profession can affect constitutional controls over the state and a redistribution of powers among the branches of government, so too—and third—it can influence the power of the state vis-à-vis the rights of the individual. In the civil rights issues, for example, the Chicago profession resisted encroachments by the government into individual affairs, whether from the left in pursuit of liberal goals, or from the right in pursuance of conservative political ends. On the one hand, it registered its opposition to state incursions on grounds of loyalty and law and order; it resisted excessive discretion and expanded powers of governmental agencies; it was exceedingly reluctant to approve wiretapping; and it recoiled from the invasion of government into the realm of beliefs. On the other hand, the organized bar was very reserved in its support—and in effect was nonsupportive—of government initiatives of a more liberal cast: it steadfastly refused to offer more than nominal assistance to the exercise of statutory compulsion in order to integrate housing, employment, and schooling. In this sense, associations of lawyers recapture aspects of the Tocquevillian vision of civil associations: private groups of citizens integrate individuals to counterbalance the state's penetration of the private realm. Depending on the ascendant political values of the moment, that countervailing power will have effects sometimes liberal and sometimes conservative. Concomitantly, the profession legitimates and thereby strengthens government as it counters and thereby bounds government.

ADAPTIVE UPGRADING

The redefinition of state powers and the transformations in forms of legal system contribute to the adaptive capacity of the state. The facility to induce adaptive upgrading, however, does not belong to the legal profession alone but may occur for other established professions in their primary institutional sphere.[27]

Adaptation by social organizations at any level can occur when forces, whether from within or without, place such strain on a social unit that its structure is no longer adequate for the functions demanded of it; as a result, pressure builds for the adaptive upgrading of social units or institutions. Upgrading occurs when "a wider range of resources is made available to social units, so that their functioning can be freed from some of the restrictions on its predecessors."[28] Resources can be defined widely indeed: they may include the emergence of altered values, the implementation of structural modifications, and the development of new bases of institutional legitimacy. Of course legitimacy will likely be strengthened if structural innovations result in higher performance. Structural differentiation is a dominant mode of adaptation—the process by which one structure is divided

27. The concept of adaptive upgrading can be applied either narrowly or broadly. It has been brought to the service of theoretical schemes that offer frameworks of societal evolution (cf. n. 28 below); and it has been used as a criterion against which societies with widely differing structures are rank ordered. The criticisms of this level of analysis are well taken (e.g., Mark Granovetter, "The Idea of 'Advancement' in Theories of Social Evolution and Development," *American Journal of Sociology* 85 [November 1979]: 489–515). They do not, however, obviate the application of this notion to more limited empirical phenomena, although they do indicate the care that must be taken in doing so. We can speak of adaptive upgrading when specific institutions undergo adaptation in order to increase their functional capacities in a particular historical situation without subscribing to any sweeping evolutionary, long-term theory of universal change.

28. Talcott Parsons, *The System of Modern Societies*, p. 27, and on adaptive upgrading more generally, pp. 4–28. For similar or related concepts, see Granovetter, "The Idea of 'Advancement.'" A powerful criticism of Parsons's general evolutionary theory has recently been advanced by Anthony Giddens, *The Constitution of Society: Outline of the Theory of Structuration* (Berkeley and Los Angeles: University of California Press, 1984), 263–80, but it is not telling, in my judgment, against the restrictive use of concepts like "adaptive capacity" under empirically observable circumstances.

into two or more units that have separate functions but that together perform the tasks of the structure from which they originally divided.[29] Because the differentiated structures are more specialized, it is assumed that they will also be more efficient and their capabilities enhanced. Consequently, in this logic, differentiation increases the ability of a social unit to deal with environmental factors, whether they are predictable or uncertain, thus ensuring a higher degree of adaptive capacity for the unit. Differentiation is not the only form of structural adjustment to changed circumstances; rationalization of internal organization, redistribution of jurisdictions and powers, and fusion of uncoordinated organizations all present structural alternatives relevant in particular situations. Indeed, the rationalization of the administration of justice by the organized bar combines elements of all these.

The legal profession has responded to the incapacities of the legal system and the threat to the legitimacy of the rule of law by endeavoring to effect structural differentiation of the system from politics, by bureaucratizing the organization of the judiciary so as to increase its efficiency, and by modernizing substantive and procedural law so as to streamline and simplify the legal process. The adaptational intents of the profession are even more manifest in its attempts to redefine state powers. Thus by attempting to alter at the highest levels of normative control the broad functions of government and the extent and limits of its powers, as did the bar in its mobilization for constitutional revision, the profession was in effect engaged in an exercise of constitutional and governmental upgrading—broadening the adaptive machinery of the latter through a revision of the former.

Adaptive upgrading of state apparatuses consequently occurs not through disembodied and reified social processes but through the exercise of power by highly organized groups of professionals in spheres in which expert and moral authority will be most efficacious. This alternative interpretation of empowered professionalism amplifies Crozier's contention that the resilience of the liberal democratic state results from "self-correcting mechanisms" that react and adapt to new exigencies.[30] The state-constitutive attributes of the legal profession entail responsibility for self-correction; the civil association features of the organized

29. Although structural differentiation has also been a central component in various functionalist evolutionary theories (cf. Talcott Parsons, *Societies: Evolutionary and Comparative Perspectives* [Englewood Cliffs, N.J.: 1963]; Niklas Luhmann, "Differentiation of Society," *Canadian Journal of Sociology* 2 [1977]: 29–53), and indeed Parsons links it explicitly with the four-stage process in which adaptive upgrading is a component, the concept can have explanatory power without carrying the freight of a universal socio historical evolutionism. An example of just such use—structural differentiation employed without commitment to evolutionary theory—is provided by Bertrand Badie and Pierre Birnbaum, *The Sociology of the State* (Chicago: University of Chicago Press, 1983), esp. 49–60. It is in the latter rather than the former sense that the concept is used here.

30. Michael Crozier, Samuel Huntington, and Joji Watanuki, *The Crisis of Democracy* (New York: New York University Press, 1975), chap. 5.

bar provide an extragovernmental site for adaptive alternatives to be formulated and implemented. Put in Janowitz's terms, the legal profession exercises its partially public responsibilities by deploying its private associations to engage in "institution building," [31] whether through institutional construction de novo, deconstruction of extant institutions, or reconstruction of renovated institutions. By exploiting the resources of a profession that straddles the public-private boundary, the state multiplies its mechanisms of self-correction and thereby increases its adaptive flexibility. The resilience and adaptability of the state therefore becomes a partial function of the quality of its rapprochement with a professionalism unprecedented in its resourcefulness.

DEVOLUTION AND DEPOLITICIZATION

Whereas adaptive upgrading and structural readjustment occur by changing the state, a third class of contributory actions proceeds by relieving the state. The former requires an enhancement of state capacities; the latter proceeds by devolution of functions. To appropriate Habermas's concept—and reverse his valuation—the legal profession invites a devolution of state functions and a depoliticization of state decision-making. [32] The Illinois instances—drafting of the Civil Practice Act, the Criminal Code, and the Code of Criminal Procedure— unveil a pattern of activity by which controversial, aging, or inadequate statutes are "withdrawn" from the public realm, drastically revised in a private "depoliticized" setting, and then reintroduced to public debate with most of the explosive provisions already substantially defused by "prepolitical" negotiation and compromise.

It is clear that bar associations aspire to, and frequently have accomplished, an extensive advisory role for government—a function that is likely to increase in proportion to the volume and complexity of demands on government; it will presumably grow also in times of fiscal conservatism when expenditure on government agencies will decline. I have maintained that the collegial organizations of professions concentrate expertise and provide organizational infrastructures for the deployment of competence on behalf of various causes. That expertise can in turn become a resource for governments. Very often, particularly in smaller states with limited governmental facilities or where governments are simply overloaded by legislative proposals, bar associations are available as highly spe-

31. Morris Janowitz, *The Last Half Century* (Chicago: University of Chicago Press, 1978), 399–406.
32. See Jurgen Habermas, "What Does a Crisis Mean Today? Legitimation Problems in Late Capitalism," *Social Research* 40 (1973): 642–67 and *Legitimation Crisis* (Boston: Beacon, 1975), 75–90; and Magali Sarfatti Larson, "The Production of Expertise and the Constitution of Expert Power," in *The Authority of Experts: Studies in History and Theory*, ed. Thomas L. Haskell (Bloomington: Indiana University Press, 1984), esp. 52–55.

cialized consultative bodies for tasks so comprehensive that they would not readily be undertaken by government. Consequently, essential tasks that are of less
than the highest priority but are nonetheless critical, such as codification of law
or modernization of statutes, can be devolved on private organizations, which
thereby take on themselves the form of a quasi-governmental advisory body. Advice subsumes a range of activities from the investigation of facts relevant to legislation to legal research and analysis. Bar associations, very often in concert
with university law schools, can draw on comparative and historical materials
and have access to codifying and uniform model legislation generated from reform bodies such as the American Law Institute and the National Conference of
Commissioners on Uniform State Laws. They can therefore set proposed courses
of action by a given state in a much broader context, ensuring that a state benefits
from the expertise and experience generated elsewhere, in addition to assuring a
degree of continuity in legislative enactments across state lines.

There are also negotiative and quasi-legislative features of the governmental
relation. Because bar associations occupy positions of structural centrality
among other major organizational centers of power, they are well situated to provide a forum in which can be negotiated the competing claims of interested parties to legislative or constitutional reform. Indeed it may be that a representative
bar association can function as a de facto legislature because it reproduces in
microcosm close to the full spectrum of political interests within a state. Proceeding informally, the professional association provides a setting in which ideas
are exchanged and differences among disputants partially resolved. The final
consensus may then be more readily achieved on the floor of the legislature or in
constitutional convention. Negotiative activities border on legislative functions.
In the formulation and drafting of codes, for instance, associations can proceed
outside the legislature, mediating statewide conflicts over particular provisions,
ultimately to bring to the state house an almost complete negotiated consensus
that can pass through the legislature without crippling deconstruction. Such a
procedure opens the door to a striking rapprochement between government and
the professions, one in which the latter take on ancillary functions considerably
in excess of legislative drafting in narrow and restricted areas of the law that has
long been a feature of profession—state relations.[33] Moreover, it is also clear that
the type of professional action envisaged here far exceeds that of an interest
group acting in public competition with a variety of other such groups.[34] Rather
the profession appropriates its partly state constitutive advantages to act under

33. Corinne Lathrop Gilb, *Hidden Hierarchies: The Professions and Government* (New York:
Harper & Row, 1966), chap. 6.
34. Albert Melone, *Lawyers, Public Policy and Interest Group Politics* (Washington, D.C.: University Press of America, 1977).

the umbrella of government itself, not quarreling outside government for relative advantage, but cooperating with government to supplement its aggregatory and legislative functions.

It does not follow, as has sometimes been supposed, that some degree of depolitization necessarily represents a decline in participation or democratic representation. There might be justification for that position if the volume and significance of issues being addressed by government have remained constant; any casting off of issues to extraparliamentary bodies would coincidentally reduce the issues remaining in the public domain. But the assumption that the volume of issues being brought to government has remained unchanged, and the further assumption that they vary not at all in consequence, cannot be sustained. Quite the contrary. One response is to enlarge the state at a pace correlative with the enlargement of issues brought to it. Although that has already occurred, particularly in the executive, untrammeled expansion of the state brings in its wake yet another set of problems. An alternative response is to redirect the treatment of some issues out of the public domain. Some may be returned to the private sector completely. Others may be delegated to private administration, under government oversight. Yet others of great consequence for society at large—and it is these on which I focus here—can be "depoliticized," but only under two strict conditions: first, when depoliticization is partial and applies to the beginning and intermediate stages of policy formation, statutory drafting, and constitutional revision and, second, when the policy formulation is reintroduced into the political forum for debate. This conception of depoliticization, already fairly advanced in some states, connotes not the loss of democratic participation but the redirection and concentration of its attention, not an abandonment of issues but the removal of lesser issues to make way for those of greater significance. It bears emphasis that this limited "privatization" of issues, which at once have substantial technical components and considerable conflictual implications, proceeds on the assumption that areas of law, negotiated and legislated outside government, will be reintroduced to it for debate and adoption. Depoliticization of this kind removes a *stage* of the political process from government. It devolves treatment of issues that *can* be delegated to ensure priority for those that must *not*. At once, depoliticization of some classes of issues proximate to professions' expertise can improve the quality of work on those issues and at the same time focus more thoroughly the strategic political functions of representative government.

It is my contention, therefore, that the established legal profession, standing in a position of close rapport with the state promises a constructive relation with it; in redefining state powers and supplementing state functions, it offers some relief to the weight of expectations impinging on government. That relation can have a twofold yield: one enables the state to reform itself so as better to cope with the "revolution of rising expectations"; the other presents the state with a supple-

mentary body able to contribute concentrated expertise at low cost and to perform quasi-legislative aggregatory functions in lieu of political parties and other
instrumentalities that are in default of their traditional roles.

Contributory relations with the state therefore can operate at three overlapping
levels in descending order of scope: readjustment of state powers and reequilibration of relations among branches of government; adaptation of state structures;
and private aid for public decision making, frequently through depoliticization.
All levels of action, whether through the governing articles of state constitutions
or the cycles of depoliticization and "repoliticization," are legitimated by the
mandate of technical authority and couched in the idiom of legalism. The legal
profession mobilizes its knowledge mandate to exercise moral authority in primary and secondary spheres while all the time clothing its actions in the neutral
guise of legalism and formalism. By extending the reach of its influence, it accomplishes a measure of state responsiveness to crises of demands and state recognition of limits to its knowledge.

Civic Professionalism: Some Normative Considerations

By casting the relations between professions and the state in these terms, the
ideal of professional service—a powerful value in many theories of professions—can be reconstructed. In American writings of the post war period, the
concept has been treated individualistically. In the microsociology of professional
role performance, relations of lawyer and client or doctor and patient were construed not only as economic, but, more vigorously, as service relations. The
argument here does not rest on this assumption but expresses a macrosociology
more consistent with the concept of collective service enunciated by Carr-
Saunders and Wilson and intimated by Durkheim. The established profession
can mobilize its concentration of expertise and bring its associational influence
not at the individual but at the *collective* level to the service of state power.[35]

To make this claim is not to displace an old heresy of unbridled monopolism
with a new orthodoxy of collective civic professionalism. To do so would merely
reflect in mirror image the tendentiousness of theories wed entirely to material
interests. It is rather to hold monopoly considerations in tension with considera-

35. I borrow the concept of "service" from the context set by A. M. Carr-Saunders and P. A.
Wilson (*The Professions* [Oxford: Oxford University Press, 1933]). It does not imply that professions
are merely the handmaidens of government, buttressing the status quo and legitimating the current
regime. It does imply that professions contribute to a liberal democratic conception of the state more
generally by proffering expertise to decision making and administration; in so doing, the professions
can be both critical and constructive, may press for legal change and or dislocation of the status quo,
and may indeed contribute to the replacement of a regime altogether. Compare Emile Durkheim,
preface to *The Division of Labor in Society*, 2d ed. (New York: Free Press, 1964); and Steven Lukes,
Emile Durkheim: His Life and Works (New York: Peregrine, 1973), 540–41.

tions of collective professional civility. Professions have monopolies of competence; they command specialized skills and advanced knowledge. Very often, as conditions of these, they have developed organizational infrastructures for mobilization as circumstances demand. But it is naive to suppose that professions will commit their distinctive resources to the state irrespective of the interests of the profession—as it were, to write a blank check for the state to cash in on professional expertise when the state finds it expedient without any expectation of a quid pro quo. The state must recognize that a profession bringing its competencies to the needs of institutional and societal adaptation is not without its interests.

Although the interests of professionals have not been systematically pursued in this book, for this argument they are of three general kinds. First, there are sectional interests, sometimes material and sometimes ideal, that segment and stratify the profession internally. The array of dimensions on which those interests can be expressed were reviewed in the description of diversity in the Chicago bar. Sometimes those interests are reflected in intraprofession "classes," as in Heinz and Laumann's two hemispheres thesis;[36] on occasion, the profession divides politically, as in the struggle between blocs loyal to the Chicago Democratic machine and those opposed to it; in other circumstances yet again, dissent arises between plaintiff's and defendant's lawyers, between corporate practitioners and civil litigators. Policy initiatives of the organized bar can be partly explained by the ascendancy of one or another set of interests in the bar association power structure. Where lawyers opposed to the Chicago machine controlled the ruling board, then a program in favor of merit selection, which would attack partisanship in the judiciary, could become official bar policy. When lawyers who were political conservatives faced the assertive liberal legislation of the civil rights era, then bar policy reflected that prevailing set of ideal interests.

Nevertheless, sectional interests help explain struggles within the profession, but they do not account for values intrinsic to the profession itself. If one set of those values are a diffuse commitment to an advantagous market situation, the profession also exemplifies collective interests in an efficient and effective legal system, in the legitimacy of law as an institution, and in the intrinsic merits of procedural justice and legalism. The often-expressed commitment to the rule of law represents not a cynical catch phrase for ideological manipulation but a sincere value commitment that bonds the profession as a distinctive community— and not infrequently pits it against contrary claims for a substantive justice unencumbered by procedural restraint, whatever its partisan label.

36. John P. Heinz and Edward O. Laumann, *Chicago Lawyers: The Social Structure of the Bar* (New York: Russell Sage; Chicago: American Bar Foundation, 1982).

Above both sectional and communal interests, however, rise interests beyond the profession—an orientation to a civic professionalism. Transcending the particularism of specialties, the pecuniary interests of employment, and even the community commitment to proceduralism, some segments of bar elites—practitioners, judges, or legal academics—pursue courses of action animated by a civic consciousness. One element of that consciousness may arise from a sense of individual responsibility as a citizen; another element arises from some sense of collective obligation. If an organization can be a fictive corporate individual, then an association of lawyers can be a collective citizen. As the individual has responsibilities as well as rights, the organization has duties as well as perquisites.

It is imperative to insist immediately that interests are frequently incompatible, and that, indeed, just as often as not, sectional claims prevail over communal values and personal advantages are espoused at the cost of civic responsibility. Instances of rapaciousness by individual lawyers can be matched by repeated examples of self-interested and even cynical mobilization by specialties. Recent drafts of professional codes of ethics have been at one moment construed as championing narrow professional interests and at another moment as aspiring to some deal of public service, even at the expense of those interests.[37] If an enduring struggle between self-interest and altruism underlies individual motivation, a never stable tension between civic and monopolistic values permeates the collective professionalism of lawyers.

In the nature of things, therefore, it is unlikely that professions will serve the state without any consideration of cost to themselves. But it is equally implausible to believe that the only driving motivation of professions is an unbridled bid for collective gain. Consequently, for the state to profit from professional resources it must sometimes recognize, sometimes guard against, and sometimes appropriate the interests of professions—indeed press them beyond monopoly. The consequence may be, and in some cases already has been, an implicit concordat between states and established professions: in exchange for the state's implicit guarantee that the traditional monopoly of the profession will be largely preserved, not withstanding occasional adjustments in response to public pressure or professional lapses, the profession will commit its monopoly of competence and its organizational resources to state service, so long as the substance of its service does not directly erode the general control of the market the profession has attained, although it may be prepared to roll back monopoly in certain areas. Indeed the actual service function of the profession provides one of the best forms of insurance that the state will not dismantle the traditional perquisites of

37. Terence J. Johnson, *Professions and Power* (London: Macmillan, 1972).

the profession. In effect, aspects of such a contract already exist. Because the statutory and judicial powers endowed on the legal profession have not been dramatically revised, the profession has not needed a massive diversion of resources to shore up its defenses against demonopolization.

The state therefore has moral claims on professions as well as economic leverage over them. The latter inheres in the grant to protect occupational turf. The former stems from the moral calling a state can make to civic professionalism. Should professions prove disinclined to contribute their technical expertise to a general public interest, even at the periodic expense of their sectional interests, and should they choose to honor a civic professionalism only in the breach, then moral claims must yield to economic constraint and regulatory adjustments. The state can alienate occupational territory from a profession if a constituency is too poorly—or too expensively—served by it. Nothing inherent in professionalism per se ultimately inhibits the transfer of self-regulation by a profession to other-regulation by the state, so long as the latter is adequately staffed by professionals familiar with practice yet primarily loyal to the public, rather than professional, interest. In short, given the moderate economic monopoly and autonomy granted professions by the state, a commitment to civic professionalism can be not only expected but enforced.

Such an implicit concordat has substantial consequences for the legitimacy of the state. The contributions of professions to social institutions or society at large offer more than the ideological gloss or a veneer of legitimation. It is true that professions generate and maintain an ideology or system of beliefs about the system that they serve; but it is a mistake to conclude that their principal function is little more than to polish and patch an ideology that bears little relation to empirical situations. If legitimacy for the state is to be broadened in advanced capitalist societies with the assistance of professions, it will be founded on structural and institutional changes that professions themselves have precipitated or supported. It will not occur only through the elaboration of a distracting ideology that bears only a tangential relation to class relations or social formations. Neither will it be sustained by skirting over the strains in society or the periodic crises faced by the state.

Greater legitimation for social institutions and the state in advanced capitalist societies will occur when professions take some responsibility for the relief of crises through the adaptation of those institutions in which they have authority and whose legitimacy is most at threat. Accordingly, legitimacy derives not merely from a more skillful and refined elaboration of a bourgeois ideology but from the practical utilization of professional competencies and the expertise from which their monopolies are derived. By not ignoring or dismantling professional monopolies but by critically appraising, periodically revising, and system-atically appropriating them for its own purposes the state gains an additional means of upgrading its capacity to meet new demands.

This does not connote an open license for professions' self-aggrandizement. Because professions have and do exploit their advantaged market position in ways that neither are in the public interest nor adequately deliver vital services, it is imperative that the shape of their autonomy must be subject to close recurrent scrutiny. Where monopoly is abused, or where structural alternatives represent better means of delivering services—even at the cost of redefining boundaries of professional work—there the state has a responsibility to weigh the contributions of the profession against the value of altering its occupational jurisdiction. In many instances, a constriction of the latter will outweigh the former. The peri-odic redrafting of occupational boundaries therefore represents nearly as crucial a function by the state in the market as reapportionment of electoral districts in the polity. Nonetheless, structural revision of market controls and the occasional movement of occupational frontiers (backward as well as forward) scarcely con-stitutes deprofessionalization. It does present the state, however, with the vexing problem of weighing costs to itself of redefining monopolies, even if marginally.

By harnessing the resources of established professions to its more pressing needs, not only does the state obtain an advantage from vestiges of the monopoly with which it originally invested professions, but, in preserving a core if not the totality of that monopoly, it can also better induce the profession to take on itself a more constructive relation that incorporates not only monopoly but much be-yond. The evidence suggests that the movement to this new symbiosis between professions and the state may already have begun for the legal profession at the subnational level in the United States.

Whether any new symbiosis can go beyond subnational elements of the state remains an open question. It was suggested in chapter one that there are good reasons to expect that in the United States the legal profession will have greater influence in state than federal government, not the least because state govern-ments are—or have become—constitutionally weaker. There are no data to sup-port the contrary. Despite the range of activity in which the American Bar Asso-ciation engages at the federal level, there are few indications of its ubiquitous efficacy or any significant symbiotic relationship except in limited areas such as the selection of federal judges.

Whether this argument confirms the exceptionalism of the legal profession also remains unresolved. I have consistently maintained that because lawyers have a broad knowledge mandate and because they are a partially state-constitutive pro-fession they have unusual access to state power. Yet as Terence Johnson has pointed out, most contemporary professions are variously entangled with the state and, if that interpenetration is neither so broadgauged nor so complete for most other professions as for lawyers, all professions do have expertise that is pertinent to state functions.[37] Consistent with my comparative analysis of professions in chapter 2, for example, it may well be the case that the profession of medicine can exert a more focused and powerful influence at the state level than even the profession of law. Accordingly, questions both of what is—the extent of medical, military, academic, or other symbiosis—and what ought to be—the obligations of civic professionalism—can be directed at other professions, although their configurations of relations with the state will have their own distinctive character. In cases other than law the issue remains the same: if an established professionalism has been attained by occupations, how far do—or how much can—those professions contribute their expertise towards the adaptive capacity of states facing stress, strain, and crisis? To what degree is professional self-defense and self-aggrandisement balanced by professional responsibility and collective citizenship?

Whether the convergence of empowered professions and weakened states extends beyond the United States also warrants careful scrutiny. The literatures on governability have had as much a European as American focus. And the classic formulations of professional civic consciousness long preceded the advent of American functionalist thought. In neither case, therefore, are the theories of empowered professions and weakened states exclusively American. Nevertheless the conjunction of a weak state and richer associational life in the United States may make its configurations of professional politics peculiarly its own—or perhaps place it at one extreme on a continuum. But the blurring of the private-public boundary can also be found in countries whose professions derive from the British model; and new modes of public-private negotiation have appeared in numerous Continental countries.[38] In every case, the changing permutations of knowledge and power should not remain immune from careful scrutiny.

The possible emergence of a new symbiosis resurrects the antinomy introduced at the outset of this book. Although the need for state adaptation to structural incapacity appears unexceptionable, a mode of adaptation that implies the removal of issues from a public to a private arena and that seeks a solution of governmental strains in the organizations of a privileged occupation counterposes the representative authority of the open polity with the expert authority of a restricted polity. For some observers, it is a short step from partial state reliance on occupational expertise to the label "antidemocratic."

38. See Rueschemeyer, "Comparing Legal Professions," and Terence C. Halliday, "Lawyers and Politics: Neo-Corporatist Variations on the Pluralist Theme of Liberal Democracies," *Lawyers in Society: A Comparative Approach,* Vol. 3, *Comparative and Theoretical Studies,* ed. Richard Abel & Philip Lewis (Berkeley: University of California Press, forthcoming).

Nevertheless, this rush to judgment warrants critical examination. Although the central civic significance of professionalism will be the responsible deployment of expertise in ways that neither enshrine economic exploitation nor subvert democratic politics, a conundrum does exist between the requirements of knowledge and the distribution of power. On the one hand, the state does require sophisticated expertise to maintain its effectiveness and legitimacy; on the other hand, the purchase of efficiency can be exacted at the expense of participation. But neither the theory of professions nor that of liberal democracy is served by simplistic labeling, at one extreme, or simplistic all-purpose panaceas, at another. While this most critical issue for liberal democracies cannot be resolved by a few quick strokes of the pen, the tension must be confronted, even if imperfectly.

If it does not work, the state serves none but those who seek its demise. Yet if it works too well, like a thoroughly oiled machine unencumbered by the vagaries of democratic decision making, it subverts the values of those in whose name it stands. If expertise is necessary for it to work, then that expertise cannot be denied it. Yet it can be as dangerous to liberal democratic values to have all expertise in a given domain lodged in a profession as it is to have a monopoly of knowledge vested in the state. The classic response to the concentration of power, from Locke through Publius at the foundation of the "first new nation," is its fragmentation and division. To a point, segmentation already pervades the professions, but only at one level of interests. The advantage in this segmentation for politics writ large stems from the microcosm of wider divisions as they are reproduced in the internal politics of professions. Insofar as the legal profession, for instance, has internalized a very broad spectrum of interests in its voluntary associations, through open and even compulsory recruitment, its most significant policies are already likely to be somewhat moderated and less than blatantly sectional.

But if inclusiveness does partially reflect the political diversity of the wider populace and a degree of internal professional segmentation results, two additional problems remain: those interests of the profession at large that transcend sectional disputes and that are not checked internally by one faction against another and those policies that are adopted by an oligarchic leadership despite internal dissent.

The latter case is partly mitigated for lawyers by those attributes of their professionalism that are resistant to entrenched oligarchy. Yet that does not hold for all legal or professional associations, and it consequently remains a fragile protection at best. The former case remains the more stubborn. When a reasonably unified profession presents a technically sophisticated solution to structural strain or state crisis, the state confronts two difficulties: it must be able to distinguish that which is authentically technical and completely legitimate from that which is an expression of moral preference and of less certain legitimacy; and the state, itself divided, must also be able to discern the interests embedded in the moral component of the scheme and thereby treat them on their own merits in the public sphere.

In short, expertise must be appraised by expertise. Without the latter, the idiom of legalism will enlarge the moral universe of lawyers' influence under the shield of technical virtuosity. It follows that the fracturing of expertise within the profession is not enough. The appropriation of expert professional knowledge for a liberal democracy therefore requires that not all expertise be concentrated in an autonomous profession and not all professional knowledge be centralized in a technocratic state. Accordingly, a state that aims to take advantage of the expert knowledge offered it by a profession will require its own staff that at once has professional technical skill as well as primary loyalty, not to the profession, but to the state or that part of it in which the position is located. When the state "contracts out" certain of its responsibilities, it needs its own capacity, independent of the profession, to evaluate the competence and moral values implicit in the product generated by the profession. In addition, the state can always check technical products with academic professionals, who usually enjoy a degree of autonomy from practitioners. In either case, the state requires access to countervailing expertise; it is likely to be assured of this only when it has its own staff of experts beholden to a public rather than a private interest. Those experts will marginally increase the size of some government machinery but decrease the need for the state to expand its own resources in order to generate knowledge and alternatives of the same quality it can find in the profession.

In the final instance expertise must be legitimated by public choice. Experts, by the very character of their common expertise, coexist in a community of interest, however minimal; and, we can assume, they share some basic assumptions—a *weltanschauung*—about what constitutes crucial issues and how they should be treated. Lawyers think in a distinctive way. Even when their institutional loyalties may be plain, they continue to share a mode of cognitive reasoning. Consequently, the employment of expert knowledge by a weakened state will compound its weakness as a representative body unless the clearly distilled moral content of "technical" contributions receives critical examination in its own right by representative nonexperts. Expertise and power can be articulated in contrasting ways. In one, professions circumvent representative institutions. This extraparliamentary route eschews not only elections and referenda but also legislative deliberation by properly constituted authorities. Government by regulation or decree represents a case in point. Alternatively, professions can mediate their contributions through channels where informed representative authority has a basis for moral evaluation as does expert authority for technical and moral consequences. This route does not necessarily imply statewide controversy or extended debate on a House floor. It does imply that representatives, briefed by experts who are substantially independent of the profession, provide a checkpoint through which the exercise of moral authority, garbed in technical terms, will be subject to rigorous scrutiny.

If that gatekeeping function is taken seriously, then expertise will be subject to informed evaluation within government itself, and, in turn, representative authority will check technical facility. In the latter alternative, the state can externalize undue conflict and temporarily devolve burdens without abdicating ultimate responsibility. Knowledge emerging from private professions is challenged technically and evaluated morally by instrumentalities of the state itself. The pluralism within a profession is used against it—expertise checks expertise, and both are subject to review through democratic institutions.

In sum, knowledge can authentically serve and check power without undemocratically seizing it. Yet if a symbiosis between empowered professions and a burdened state has commenced already, awareness of the processes that constitute it and debate over the terms that govern it have scarcely begun. Bringing their knowledge to the service of power, properly understood, is the civic responsibility of established professions. Bringing understanding to this tension of expert and representative authority is the mandate for the macrosociology of professions.

Index

ABA. *See* American Bar Association (ABA)
Abortion, 15, 46, 134, 249–50
Abrahamsson, B., 35, 43
Academic profession, 373; epistemological bases of, 34, 36, 37; institutional spheres of, 41–42, 44, 47; as state constitutive, 52. *See also* Universities
Acheson, Dean, 236
Adaptive capacity, upgrading: of legal profession, 115; of state, 23–24, 361–65, 367–68, 371–72
Administration of Justice, Special Committee on the (CBA), 94
Administrative rationalization, 25–26, 286; incidence of, 294–95, 300–304; measurement of, 288–89, 297–98
Admission: to CBA, 69, 87; to Illinois bar, 67, 76
Admissions Committee (CBA), 68
Adultery, 249
Affirmation, politics of, 151, 175–81, 201–18
Age, and political beliefs of Chicago bar, 135
Allegheny County Bar Association, 118
Allen, Francis A., 246–47, 257
Althusser, Louis, 21–22
Amendment of the Law Committee (CBA), 68, 74–75
American Assembly, 9
American Bar Association (ABA), xix, 43, 64, 198, 286, 290, 291, 372; and antisubversion legislation, 230; Canons of Professional Ethics of, 186, 198; and Civil Rights Act of 1964, 244; Code of Ethics of, 72; Committee on Professional Ethics of, 186; judicial ethics canons of, 161, 162
American Judicature Society 11–12, 80, 88, 206, 286, 287

American Judicature Society Journal, 80
American Law Institute, 39, 247, 366
American Legion, 254
American Medical Association (AMA), xiii, 43, 50, 311
American Revolution, 60–61
Anastaplo, George, 229, 236–37
Ancel, Louis, 275, 282–83
Anglican Consultative Counsel, 43
Antisubversion legislation, 227–37, 253–59; federal, 227–33; in Illinois, 233–37
Antitrust law, 131
Appellate courts, in Illinois, 78, 156, 158, 168
Approval of proposals, types of, 332–33
Aquinas, Thomas, 33–34
Arkansas, tax system in, 266
Arney, William Ray, 22
Association of the Bar of the City of New York, 64, 65, 78, 81, 118, 122; and antisubversion legislation, 229–33; and Civil Rights Act of 1964, 244; as elite association, 107–9; founding committees of, 68
Atlanta Bar Association, 118
Auerbach, Jerold S., xiv, 124–25
Austin, Richard B., 248
Authority, professional: and institutional spheres, 45–47; two forms of, 37–41. *See also* Knowledge; Moral authority; Technical authority
Autonomous law, 357–60
Autonomy: of CBA leadership, 60, 74–75, 94–99, 312, 322–34, 343; of courts and judiciary, xv, 150–51, 164–74, 216–18; of legal profession, 3, 110–15, 370–71; of legal system, 24–26, 356–60. *See also* Court System, in Illinois; Oligarchy

Bachrach v. Nelson, 265, 276
Banks, 336
Bar Association of Metropolitan St. Louis, 118
Bar Association of San Francisco, 118, 123
Bar associations. *See* Legal profession; Metropolitan bar associations; State bar associations
Bar integration movement, 79–84, 109, 113–15, 136
Bar of Greater Cleveland, 118
Bar polls, of CBA, 190, 193, 196
Bell, Daniel, 5–6, 13, 17, 20
Bell, Griffin, 12
Bench and the Bar, Committee on (CBA), 94
Berlant, Jeffrey L., xiv, 21, 140
Betts, R. K., 40
Birch, Anthony H., 13
Black, William, 65
Blacks, 106; and CBA, 132, 135, 314; civil rights of, 242, 243
Bloomfield, Maxwell, 61
Book of the States, The, 286
Boston Bar Association, 65, 118, 120, 122
Boundary work, 33
Bradwell, Myra, 67
British Medical Association, 42, 50
Brittan, Samuel, 14
Brownell, Herbert, 230
Brown v. Board of Education, 256
Broyles, Paul W., 233–35, 257–58
Buildings, as resources, 105
Bureaucratization, 216, 348–49, 364; concept of, 25–26, 165; in Illinois judicial system, 150–51, 164–65, 167–74; incidence of in U.S., 294–95; measurement of, 289, 297; Weber on, 25–26, 168–69
Burger, Warren, 9
Burnham Building, 97–98

Calhoun, Daniel, 61
California, bar associations in, 81, 116, 298
California State Bar Association, 116
Calvin, John, 33–34
Candidates, Committee on (CBA), 88, 96–97, 327
Canons of Judicial Ethics, 166–67, 172, 175, 185–87, 198, 204; implementation of, 161–64
Canons of Professional Ethics (ABA), 186, 198
Capitalism, 3; and legal rationalization, 24, 164; professions under, 21–22, 349, 371; and ungovernability, 8, 12–16

Cappell, Charles, xii, xix, 125–33, 146n, 174n, 312–26
Carlin, Jerome, 124
Carr-Saunders, A. M., 17–19, 22–23, 37–38, 368
Carter, Jimmy, 5, 6
Case study method, 284–85, xviii
Cawson, Alan, 53
CBA. *See* Chicago Bar Association (CBA)
CBA Annual Report, 77
Celler, Representative, 231
Certificate of readiness, 211–12
Chandler, Alfred D., 110
Character and Fitness, Committee on (CBA), 236–37
Chicago, 258, 369, 338; Code of Fair Conduct in, 235–36; court congestion in, 208–12; discrimination and civil rights in, 238–39; municipal court system in, 79, 148, 197, 209; political patronage in, 67, 185–87, 197–98, 217–18, 281, 340; survey of bar in, xvi–xix, 125, 312, 352n
Chicago Association of Commerce and Industry, 270, 271
Chicago Bar Association (CBA), xi–xx, 55, 101, 115; admission fees of, 69, 72–74, 87, 88; admission requirements of, 69, 87, 100; and bar integration movement, 81–84; by-laws amendment of, 74, 94–95, 99; class representation in, 124–27; direct democracy in, 60, 74–75, 84, 94–99; dues of, 72–74, 87, 88, 97–98, 325; elections in, 74, 94–95; as elite association, 59–60, 63–79; expenditures by, 72–73, 116, 118; and federal courts, 212–13; goals of, bar association members on, 135–36; history of, 59–100; and Illinois court system (*see* Court system, in Illinois); inclusiveness and representativeness of, 65–66, 120–33, 310–12; law school representation in, 127–29, 314–16, 319; legal practice representation in, 129, 316, 319; and legal rationalization, 284, 304; legislative program of, 219–60, 283, 342; membership growth in, 65, 81, 84–89, 116, 123; as open association, 84–99; and professional ethics, 72, 76–78, 99–100; and public relations, 89–93, 114; resource accumulation by, 116; resource portfolios of, 107, 112–13; and revenue article (*see* Revenue article of Illinois Constitution); salaries in, 73; Speakers Service of, 93; specialties in, 131–33, 138, 316–19; and unauthorized

legal practice, 62–63, 69–72, 77–78, 100
—committees of, xi–xii, 100; and Board, relationship between, 74–75, 95–97, 324–33,
343–44; development of, 63–73; judicial,
differentiation of, 93–94; and legislative
issues, 220–27; specialties represented in,
131–33, 138; substantive law, 89. *See also
specific committees*
—leadership of, 68, 69, 113, 125; autonomy
and accountability of, 94–99, 322–26; and
committees, relationship between, 74–75,
95–97, 324–33, 343–44; control of member
demands by, 328–34; homogeneity of,
312–19, 326; reduction of member demands
by, 326–28; turnover and tenure of, 322,
326, 343
Chicago Bar Association Communicator, 243
Chicago Bar Project, xvi–xix, 125, 312, 352n
Chicago Bar Record, 86, 95, 98; on antisub-
version legislation, 228–29, 236; on bar in-
tegration movement, 83; on Constitutional
Convention, 275; criticism of Illinois Su-
preme Court in, 205, on Public Relations
Committee, 91; reorientation of, 92–93
Chicago Civic Federation, 270, 271
Chicago Council of Lawyers (CCL), 200, 342
Chicago Daily News, 64
Chicago Law Bulletin, 243
Chicago Legal News, 64, 67
Chicago Real Estate Board, 271
Chicago school of sociology, xix
Chicago Women's Club, 78
Church of England, 40
Circuit Court Rules Committee (CBA), 327,
328, 331
Citizens' Committee, 340
Citizens of Greater Chicago, 215
City bar associations. *See* Metropolitan bar
associations
Civic professionalism, 368–76
Civil law: Continental, 25; division of criminal
law and, 164
Civil Practice Act, Illinois. *See* Illinois Civil
Practice Act of 1933
Civil Practice Committee, 327
Civil Procedure, Committee on (CBA), 212–13
Civil Rights Act of 1964, 241–45, 254, 256,
325
Civil Rights Committee (CBA), 222, 227–44,
252, 329, 331
Civil rights legislation, 219, 227, 237–45,
253–60, 280, 325, 331, 359; and adaptation

of legal profession, 115; attitudes of Chicago
bar toward, 134–35; consideration of, as
issue, 220–22; federal, 237–38, 241–45;
and Illinois legislature, 238–41, 256
Clark, Dean, 92
Class: and CBA membership, 124–27; and professional monopoly, 348–49
Clausewitz, C. von, 35
Clergy, 22, 111; epistemological base of,
29–30, 32–34, 36; institutional spheres of,
41–43, 46–47; organization for collective
action by, 47–49; professional authority of,
39, 40
Coalitions, formation of by professions, 48–49
Code of Ethics, ABA, 72
Code of Fair Conduct, 235–36
Code of Judicial Ethics, 183
Codification, 25, 360, 366; of criminal law in
Illinois, 227, 245–52, 256–57, 259; as in-
dicator of rationalization in U.S., 287, 292,
297, 298, 303; Weber on, 25
Cohn, Rubin, 158
Cold War, 227–37, 257, 259
Coleman, J. S., 311
Columbia University, 127–29, 246, 314–16
Commercial Club, 340
Common law, 256–57; and legal rationaliza-
tion, 25, 26; pleading at, 158–59
Communism. *See* Antisedition legislation
Communist Control Act of 1954, 253
Compensation: of judges in Illinois, 149, 157,
166, 173, 183, 201, 206–7, 338; of lawyers,
203, 206
Competition. *See* Monopoly, economic
Complete legitimacy, 46
Congress of Industrial Organizations (CIO),
337
Constitution, of Illinois. *See* Illinois
Constitution
Constitution, U.S., 255
Constitutional Convention, in Illinois: of
1921–22, 98; of 1969–70, 274–78, 310
Constitutional revision, 219–20, 222; attempts
at, as indicator of rationalization, 287–88,
292–94, 296–98, 300, 303; in redefinition
of state powers, 361, 364
Constitution Revision, Committee on (CBA),
152, 222, 267, 269, 275, 276, 279, 282–83,
329
Constitution Study Commission, 275–76
Consumer Credit Committee (CBA), 222
Contested legitimacy, 46

Contingent legitimacy, 46
Convertible resources, 103–5
Cook County, 78, 340; and Constitutional Convention of 1969–70, 275, 276; court congestion in, 208–9; court system in, 147–49; magistrate system in, 207; real estate classification in, 271, 272
Corporation Act of 1933, 240
Corporation Law Committee (CBA), 222
Corporations, 336; growth of, and legal profession, 62–63, 75, 76; legal practice by, 63, 78
Corps intermediaires, 17–18, 20, 23
Countability of resources, 103
Court Rules, Committee on (CBA), 93
Courts Commission, 199
Court system, federal: and CBA, 212–13, crisis of, 9–11, 345–46. *See also* U.S. Supreme Court
Court system, in Illinois, 78–79, 99–100, 362, 365; autonomy of, 145–75, 176, 216, 259, 340; clerks in, 158, 167; congestion in, 179, 201, 208–12; control of, 72, 157, 175–218; crisis of, 145–51, 345–46; rationalization of, 164–74; rules and procedures of, 201, 212–16; and tax policy, 266–67. *See also* Canons of Judicial Ethics; Illinois Civil Practice Act of 1933; Illinois Supreme Court; Judges, in Illinois; Judicial article of Illinois Constitution
Crime, 9, 10, 260
Criminal Committee (CBA), 222
Criminal law, 131, 134, 318; codification of, in Illinois, 227, 245–52, 256–57, 259, 292; division between civil law and, 164. *See also* Illinois Criminal Code
Crises, xv, 139; concept of, 12–16; fiscal, 261–83; of legitimacy, 14–15, 145–218; of postwar America, xv, 145; of professions, 354–56; of rights, 219–59; and ungovernability, 4–11, 139, 345–47, 370–76. *See also* Ungovernability
Crozier, Michael, 15, 364
Cushman, Robert, 270, 280–82

Dahrendorf, Ralf, 15
Daley, Richard J., 132–33, 155, 197–98, 238–39, 275, 282, 338, 341
Dallas Bar Association, 118
Dawson, Mitchell, 91–93
Defense Lawyers' Association, 251
Deficits, government, 8, 262

Democracy: in CBA, 60, 74–75, 84, 94–99; and civic professionalism, 373–76; and criminal law, 246; and depoliticization, 367; and integrated bar, 80; Jacksonian, 61–62, 67, 115, 354; knowledge-power relationship in, 19, 22–23, 54, 368–76; and professional associations, 114, 115, 310–12, 334, 343; ungovernability and crisis of, 3, 9, 13–15, 345–47, 368–76
Democratic Party, 5, 79, 267, 282, 369; affiliation of CBA membership with, 132–34; and Constitutional Convention of 1969–70, 275, 276; and Illinois judiciary, 149, 191, 196–97, 340, 341
Denver Bar Association, 118
De Paul University, 129
Depoliticization, 361, 365–68
Depression, Great, 85, 88, 264
Description, versus prescription, 30–32
Detroit Bar Association, 118
Development of Law Committee (CBA), 152
Dexter, Wirt, 65
Dickson, David L., 99
Differentiation. *See* Organizational differentiation; Role differentiation; Structural differentiation
Directory of Bar Activities (ABA), 286
Directory of Bar Associations (ABA), 286
Disbarments, 76–77
District of Columbia Bar, 230
Doctrine, military, 35–36
Downing, Richard, 153n
Durkheim, Emile, 17–20, 23, 368

Economic growth, 4, 8
Education, of bar members. *See* Law schools
Eighteenth Amendment, 98
Eisenhower, Dwight D., 230
Elite association(s), 47, 119, 137, 140, 289, 309, 343; CBA as, 59–60, 63–79, 220–22; concept of, 106–8; consensus in, 139; theoretical dynamics of, 110–15; transition from, 108–10, 119
Elites: autonomy and accountability of, 312, 322–26; homogeneity of, 312–19; turnover and tenure of, 312, 322. *See also* Chicago Bar Association (CBA), leadership of
Elliott, Sheldon D., 9
Emergency Committee on Crime (Chicago), 236
Enclave committees, 327
Engineering profession: epistemological base

of, 32; institutional spheres of, 41–42; organization for collective action by, 47–49
England. *See* Great Britain
Epistemological bases of knowledge, 29–37. *See also* Normative professions; Scientific professions; Syncretic professions
Established professionalism, 60, 100, 110–11, 347–56
Ethnicity, 191, 348; and CBA membership, 124–25, 132–34, 314, 319
Evaluation of Candidates, Committee on (CBA), 190–97
Evans, Peter B., 51n, 355–56
Exclusive associations, 50. *See also* Elite associations
Executive branches, and ungovernability, 6, 9
Expert authority. *See* Knowledge; Technical authority
Expertise: and democracy, xix, 19, 22–23, 27, 139, 259–60, 346–47, 373–76; and economic policy, 278–83; of professions, 36, 37–41, 103–8, 116, 136; and service to power, xvi, 18–19, 119, 139, 219, 365–76; and the state, 51, 310, 346–47, 355–56, 367–68. *See also* Technical authority; Knowledge
Expert witnesses, 211
Externalization of conflicts, 330, 332

Fair employment and housing. *See* Civil rights legislation
Federal Civil Procedure Act, 213
Federal court system. *See* Court system, federal
Federal government: and civic professionalism, 372; deficits of, 8, 262; legal professional organization at level of, 53–54. *See also* United States
Federal Judiciary Committee (CBA), 93
Federal legislation, 220; antisubversion, 227–33, 253–54; civil rights, 237–38, 241–45
Federal Legislation, Committee on (CBA), 232
Field, Marshall, 65
Finer, S. E., 43–44
Fisher, Glenn, 266
Flamm, Arnold, 282–83
Formative professionalism, 60, 100, 110–11, 347–54
Fornication, 249
Foucault, Michel, 22–23
Fourth Assembly of the World Council of Churches, 43

France: Durkheim on *corps intermediaires* in, 17–18; and ungovernability, 16
Frankfurter, Felix, 236
Friedman, Milton, 20–21
Friedson, Eliot, 38, 357
Fuller, Melville, 65
Fungibility of resources, 103
Fusion, in bureaucratization, 169–70

Gale, George, 63
Garceau, Oliver, 311, 322
Gatekeeper strategy, 331
Gateway Amendment, 268, 282
Gawalt, Gerald W., 60
Geography: density of professionals by, 104–5; and forms of professional organizations, 109–10
George, Henry, 76
Germany: legal rationalization in, 26, 286–87; and ungovernability, 16
Giddens, Anthony, 140
Gieryn, T. F., 33
Goldwater, Barry, 5
Goode, William, 30
Goudy, William, 65
Government practice, and CBA membership, 129, 316
Governments, spending by, 8. *See also* State; Ungovernability
Graduated income tax, 265, 266, 269, 272, 273, 277
Gramsci, Antonio, 21–22
Granfors, Mark W., 63n, 105
Great Britain, 36, 43–44; and Jacksonian democracy, 61–62; legal rationalization in, 26, 305; medical profession in, 17, 21; and ungovernability, 6, 7, 16
Gregory, Stephen, 65
Greylord, Operation, 200nn
Grievance Committee (CBA), 68–72, 76–78
Guilds, 17–18, 22, 26, 347

Habermas, Jurgen, 12, 14, 31, 304, 365
Halliday, Terence C., xiin, xixn, 3, 28n, 63n, 66n, 67n, 105, 133n, 146n, 174n, 227n, 312n, 319, 352n, 373n
Handbook of the National Conference of Commissioners on Uniform State Laws, 286
Handler, Philip, 40
Harley, Herbert, 79–80, 83, 84
Harvard University, 127–29, 314–16

Heinz, John P., xvi–xix, 125–36, 251–52,
  309, 352n, 369
Hennepin County Bar Association, 118
Heterogeneity. See Inclusiveness
Hiss, Alger, 227–28, 236
Holley, I. B., 36
Homogeneity of elites, 312–19, 326
Homosexuality, legalization of, 15, 134, 249,
  251
Horizontal organizational fusion, 169
House Un-American Activities Committee
  (HUAC), 227–28
Houston Bar Association, 118
Hoyne, Thomas, 65
Hughes, Everett C., 38
Humanities, 36
Hume, David, 30
Huntington, Samuel P., 13, 15

Illinois, 75, 337; admission to bar in, 76; and
  bar integration movement, 80–84; Constitutional Convention of 1921–22 in, 98;
  Constitutional Convention of 1969–70 in,
  274–78, 310; fiscal crisis in, 264–68, 278;
  general revenue fund in, 265, 273. See also
  Court system, in Illinois; Illinois legislation
Illinois Agricultural Association, 270
Illinois Association of Real Estate Boards, 271
Illinois Bankers Association, 271
Illinois Civil Practice Act of 1933, 92, 98, 166,
  168, 172, 213, 310, 330, 341, 365; enactment of, 158–60; 1955 revision of, 152,
  160–61, 175, 210
Illinois Code of Criminal Procedure, 240, 257,
  310, 330, 365; enactment of, 252–53
Illinois Commission on Revenue, 282
Illinois Committee for Constitutional Conven-
  tion, 275, 283
Illinois Constitution: of 1818, 149; of 1870,
  148–49, 155, 208, 265, 271, 274; of 1970,
  157–58, 167, 172, 173, 274–78. See also
  Judicial article of Illinois Constitution; Revenue article of Illinois Constitution
Illinois Courts Commission, 157, 172–73
Illinois Criminal Code, 225, 257, 259, 292,
  310, 330, 337, 339, 362; enactment of,
  245–53
Illinois General Assembly, 151–52, 229, 310,
  337; and antisubversion legislation, 233–37;
  and Civil Practice Act revision, 159; civil
  rights bills in, 238–41; and court congestion, 208–10; and Illinois Code of Criminal

Procedure, 252–53; and Illinois Criminal
  Code, 251–52; and judicial article amend-
  ment, 152–58; and legislative program of
  CBA, 220–25; and revenue article amend-
  ment, 265–66, 269–78, 280, 281
Illinois Institute of Technology at Chicago-
  Kent, 129
Illinois Judiciary Advisory Council, 248
Illinois legislation, 220; antisubversion,
  233–37, 253–54, 257–58; civil rights,
  238–41, 256; criminal code and procedure,
  247–53
Illinois Manufacturers Association, 271
Illinois Retail Merchants' Association, 271
Illinois State Bar Association (ISBA), 124,
  206, 208, 304; and Canons of Judicial Ethics, 162–63; conflict between CBA and, 81;
  and Criminal Code revision, 248–52; honors
  system of, 205–6; and Illinois Civil Practice
  Act, 92, 98, 159–61, 213; and judicial article, 276; legislative program of CBA and,
  224–27
Illinois State Board of Charities, 78
Illinois State Chamber of Commerce, 271
Illinois Supreme Court, 69, 98, 193, 198, 199,
  217, 248, 267, 325; and admission to bar,
  76; and Bachrach v. Nelson, 265, 276; and
  Civil Practice Act, 159–61, 166; and court
  congestion, 209–11; criticism of, in Bar
  Record, 205; and judicial article, 152–58;
  and judicial crisis in Illinois, 148–49; professional ethics cases of, 77; and rationalization of court system, 166–73; and Thorp v.
  Mahin, 276
Immunity of witnesses, 230–33, 253, 255, 257
Impeachment of judges, 149, 170, 184, 198
Incentives: selective, 84–85, 326–28; solidary,
  84n, 138, 327
Inclusiveness, 119–39, 282, 309–44, 374; of
  CBA, 65–66, 120–33; concept of, 50, 136;
  cost of, 49–51, 119, 133–39; and elite, at-
  tributes of, 312–26; and organizational
  management, 326–34; and organizational
  networks, 334–42, 344; and represen-
  tativeness, 120–24; as resource, 104, 116.
  See also Elite associations; Open associa-
  tions; Universal associations
Income tax, 262, 264, 266; enactment of, in
  Illinois, 276–78; graduated, 265, 266, 269,
  272, 273, 277
Individualism, 17–18
Inquiry, Committee on (CBA), 72

Insider approach, 339–42, 344
Institutional spheres. *See* Primary institutional spheres; Secondary institutional spheres
Institution building, 365
Insurgency, 101–2
Intangible resources, 103–5
Interdependency, 334–36
Interests: in CBA elite, 312–21; and divisions in CBA, xvi–xviii, 133–36, 146n, 309–10; and interest groups, 5, 7, 17, 34, 53, 174, 259, 263, 281–82, 336–42, 345, 365–67; of lawyers, 69, 369–70; of professions and professionals, xiv, 3, 368–76; and structural differentiation, 174. *See also* Civic professionalism; Monopoly
Internal Security Act of 1950, 253
International Typographers Union, 311
Interpenetration, 334–36
Iron Law of Emulation, 6
Iron law of oligarchy, 310–11, 343–44
Italy, and ungovernability, 16

Jacksonian democracy, 61–62, 67, 115, 354
Janowitz, Morris, 365
John Marshall School of Law, 129
Johnson, Terence, 372–73
Joint Chiefs of Staff, 40
Joint Committee on Judicial Salaries, Pensions, and Retirement Benefits, 206–7
Joint Committee on the Revenue Article, 271–73, 281
Judges, in Illinois: compensation of, 149–50, 157, 166, 173, 183, 201, 206–7, 338; conditions of service for, 179, 201–8, 216; demeanor and ethics of, 161–62, 179, 181–90, 192–93, 198, 204–5, 216; impeachments of, 149, 170, 184, 198; merit selection of, 152–58, 170–72, 310, 325, 341; retention of, 195–97, 338; retirements of, 157, 166; tenure of, 149, 152–53, 170–71, 183, 201. *See also* Judicial elections, in Illinois
Judges' Committee on Circuit Court Rules, 214
Judicial Advisory Council, 206–7
Judicial article of Illinois Constitution, 166–72, 175, 185, 217, 268–69, 273, 276, 310, 325, 332, 336–37, 340–42; chronology of amendment to, 152–58; consideration of issues involving, 179; judicial elections under, 156, 158, 185–87, 207; judicial tenure under, 207; legal power of bar under, 189
Judicial Conference of Illinois, 163, 185

Judicial Conference of the United States, 213
Judicial elections, in Illinois, 152, 175, 325, 338; consideration of issues involving, 179; evaluation of candidates in, 190–201, 216; under judicial article, 156, 158, 185–87, 207; and judicial ethics, 183, 185, 204; political control of, 149, 166, 185, 197–98
Judicial Inquiry Board, 173, 199
Judiciary, 112, 135, 140; and balance of powers, 256–57, 263–64; in bar associations, 290–91; and criminal law, 246; and legal rationalization, 25–26; legitimacy crisis of, 145–47; nonlawyer positions in, abolition of, 297, 303–4; normative economy of control of, 175–77, 215–18; reciprocal relationship between bar associations and, 338–39, 342; and ungovernability, 6, 9–12, 16. *See also* Court system, federal; Court system, in Illinois; Judges, in Illinois
Judiciary Committee (CBA), 68, 93, 182, 182–83, 195–96, 199
Juries: sentencing by, 250, 251; trials by, 210–11
Justices of the peace, 289; in Illinois, 78, 79, 149–50, 154, 167, 172, 209
Juvenile Court Act of 1965, 213–14
Juvenile Courts, 78, 213–14
Juvenile Courts Committee (CBA), 93, 213–14
Juvenile Delinquents Committee (CBA), 331

Kalberg, Stephen, 24
Katz, Harold, 273
Katzenbach, Nicholas deB., 244
Keating, Representative, 230
Kerner, Otto, 265, 267, 273
King, A., 4
Knowledge: epistemological bases of, 29–37; mandates of, 29, 31, 101; and power, 18–27; as resource, 104. *See also* Authority, professional
Kogan, Herman, xx
Kristol, Irving, 13

Labour Party (Great Britain), 6
Larson, Magali Sarfatti, xiv, 21, 23, 30, 140
Laumann, Edward O., xvi–xix, 125–36, 369
Law Association of Philadelphia, 62
Law Club of Chicago, 75–76
Law firm lawyers, 120; in CBA, 129, 315
Law professors, in bar associations, 290–91
Law schools, 366; representation of, in CBA membership, 127–29, 314–16, 319

Law Society of Upper Canada, 79
Lawyer Reference Plan, 326–27
Lawyers: compensation of, 203, 206; as judges,
    185; judges' treatment of, 181–82. *See also*
    Legal profession
Lee, Noble W., 272–73
Legal Education Committee (CBA), 68, 76
Legalism, idiom of, 253–60, 368, 375
Legal practice, representation of, in CBA, 129,
    316, 319
Legal profession, xiii, xvi, 22; adaptation of
    state by, 361–68; admission to bar, 67, 76;
    and advance of legal rationalization, 23–27,
    284–305; and bar integration movement,
    79–84; and civic professionalism, 368–76;
    epistemological base of, 29–30, 32–34; for-
    mative and established phases of, 60, 100,
    110–11, 347–56; institutional spheres of,
    41–47; and legal system evolution, 356–60;
    negative image of, 90–91; organization for
    collective action by, 47–49; professional au-
    thority of, 38–41; resource portfolios of (*see*
    Resources, of professional associations); and
    the state, 23–27, 42–43, 51–54, 345–76;
    unlicensed practitioners in, 62–63, 69–72,
    77–78. *See also* Metropolitan bar associa-
    tions; State bar associations
Legal rationalization, 11, 23, 284–305,
    359–60; of Illinois judicial system, 164–74;
    incidence and advance of, 291–95, 298,
    305; measurement of, 284–91, 295–98; and
    resources of bar associations, 298–303;
    Weber's theory of, 24–27. *See also* Adminis-
    trative rationalization; Procedural rational-
    ization; Substantive rationalization
Legislative Committee (CBA), 220–27,
    235–36, 238, 239, 327–32
Legislative Planning Conference, 227
Legislatures: and criminal law, 246; and taxa-
    tion, 263–64; transfer of power from
    judiciary to, 256–57; and ungovernability,
    6, 9
Legitimacy, types of, 46–47. *See also* Au-
    thority, professional
Legitimation crisis, Habermas on, 14–15
Liaison members, 324–25, 329
Liberal economists, on ungovernability, 13–14
Libraries, 84–85, 105
Licensing, 16, 50, 52, 348, 350
Lincoln, Robert Todd, 65
Lipset, S. M., 311
Lloyd, Henry Demerest, 76

Lobbying, 4–5, 53, 290, 300
Los Angeles County Bar Association, 118, 123
Louisiana, criminal law in, 247
Loyola University, 129
Lyons, Thomas, 275

McCarthy, Eugene, 5
McCarthy, Joseph R., 227–28
McCarthyism, 135, 145, 227–37, 253, 362
McGovern, George, 5
McKay, David H., 5
Maine, bar associations in, 61
Maitland, F. W., 39
Managing Committee (CBA), 88
Marcuse, Herbert, 31
Marginal legitimacy, 46–47
Marijuana, 134
Martin, David, 40
Martin, Edward M., 190
Marx, Karl, 20
Marxism, 31; neo-, 8, 13, 21–23, 347–50
Massachusetts, early bar association in, 60–61
Matrimonial Committee (CBA), 210, 222
Matrimonial law, 131, 318
Media, and judiciary, 92, 94, 202–3, 205
Medical profession, xiii, 17, 21, 22, 322; epis-
    temological base of, 29, 30, 32–34, 36;
    institutional spheres of, 41–43, 46, 51; orga-
    nization for collective action by, 47–49;
    professional authority of, 38, 39
Membership size: and bar activism, 290, 300;
    of CBA, 65, 81, 85–86, 116; and in-
    clusiveness, 136; as resource, 105
Mental states, and criminal code, 248, 250
Meritocracy, 21
Merit selection of judges, 359, 369; campaigns
    for, as indicator of rationalization, 289, 294,
    297, 300; CBA advocacy of, 152–58,
    170–72, 310, 325, 341
Metaethics, 31
Metropolitan bar associations, 63n, 346; and
    bar integration movement, 81–83; growth of,
    67; and legal rationalization, 291, 298–304;
    resource portfolios of, 109–10, 116
Michels, Robert, 311, 343–44
Miliband, Ralph, 51n
Military profession, 373; epistemological base
    of, 34–37; institutional spheres of, 41–44;
    organization for collective action by, 48;
    professional authority of, 39, 40; as state
    constitutive, 52
Miller, Arthur H., 9

Missouri Plan, 152, 153n, 155
Mobilization, political, 60, 174; problem of, 48–51, 136–39; and professional influence, 29; and resources of professional associations, 101–2
Model Penal Code, 247, 249
Monetarism, 8
Money, as resource, 105, 107–8
Monopoly, economic, 41, 47–48, 54, 59, 69, 101, 119–20, 139; civic professionalism versus, 371–72; and professional association development, 99–100, 110, 140, 349–54; theory of, xiv–xvi, 3, 16–24, 347–51
Moral authority, 140–41, 147, 174, 216–17, 259–60, 283, 309, 331, 375–76; concept of, 37–41; and institutional spheres, 45–47
Moynihan, Daniel P., 6
Municipal Court, in Chicago, 79, 148, 197, 209
Municipal Court Committee (CBA), 332
Myrdal, Gunnar, 31

Nassau County Bar Association, 118
National Conference of Commissioners on Uniform State Laws (NCCUSL), 39, 286, 287, 291, 366
National Council of Churches, 43
National Lawyers Guild, 233
National Rifle Association, 251
Negativism, politics of, 151, 175–202, 215–18
Neoconservatism, 8, 13
Neo-Marxism, 8, 13, 21–23, 347–50
Netsch, Dawn Clark, 275–76
Networks, organizational: as resources, 104, 107; transcendence of inclusiveness through, 334–42
Neutralization of dissent, 330, 332
New Deal, 242
New Hampshire, bar associations in, 61
New Membership, Special Committee on (CBA), 86
New York City, judiciary in, 67
New York Code of Civil Procedure, 159
New York County Lawyers' Association, 81, 118, 120
New York State, 247, 262; bar associations in, 67, 116
Nielsen, Kai, 31
Nisbet, Robert, 44
Nominating Committee (CBA), 74, 95, 99, 324
Nonconvertible resources, 103–5

Nonet, Philippe, 165, 357–58
Non-state constitutive professions, 52
Normative economy of judicial control, 175–77, 215–18
Normative professions: epistemological bases of, 32–34; institutional spheres of, 41–47, 51, 52; organization for collective action by, 48–51; professional authority of, 39–41
Northwestern University, 127–29, 315, 337

Occupational groups, and CBA membership, 312–14, 319
Occupation and franchise taxes, 262, 266
O'Connor, James, 14
Offe, Claus, 14
Oligarchy, 310–12, 343–44
Open association(s), 48–49, 140; CBA as, 84–99; concept of, 106–8; growth of, 61; inclusiveness and (*see* Inclusiveness); and legal rationalization, 289, 291, 298–300; resource accumulations by, 116; specialties in, 138; theoretical dynamics of, 110–15; transition to, 108–10, 119
Organizational differentiation, 166
Otis, James, 275, 283
Outsider approach, 340–42, 344

Pandectists, 25
Parkin, Frank, 140
Parry, Jose, 140
Parry, Noel, 140
Parsons, Talcott, 17–20
Partee, Cecil, 245
Partial horizontal fusion, 169
Partially state-constitutive professions, 52, 372–73
Patent Law Committee (CBA), 222, 331–32
Pennsylvania Bar Association, 230
Personal injury, 131
Persons Assuming to Practice Law without a License, Committee on (CBA), 69
Philadelphia Bar Association, 81, 118, 120,122
Phillips, Harry, 10
Plea bargaining, 12
Police, 150, 257
Police magistrates, in Illinois, 148–50, 154, 157–58, 167, 185, 207
Political parties, 34, 216, 345; Chicago bar affiliations with, 132–39; decline in organization of, 5–7, 13; and Illinois judiciary, 146–51, 162–63, 187, 190–97. *See also* Democratic Party; Republican Party

Popper, Karl, 32
Post industrial society, 20
Pound, Roscoe, 61, 80
Powell, Michael J., 63n, 105, 111n, 133n,
    351–52
Power, and knowledge, relationship between,
    18–27. See also Authority, professional
Prescription, versus description, 30–32
Presidential elections, 5
Prestige: of legal specialties, 131; and organiza-
    tion type, 107; as resource, 104, 105
Primary institutional spheres, 219, 261, 283,
    305, 344, 356; concept of, 41–47
Probate Committee (CBA), 222
Probate Court, 78, 209
Procedural rationalization, 25, 291–94,
    298–300, 303
Professional associations, xiii–xix; in-
    clusiveness of (see Inclusiveness); member-
    ship expansion by, 84–85; national peak, 48,
    53; as precondition for professional influ-
    ence, 47–48; and ungovernability, 16, 18.
    See also Elite associations; Open associa-
    tions; Resources, of professional associa-
    tions; Universal associations
Professional Ethics, Committee on (CBA), 72
Professions: authority of, 37–41; and civic pro-
    fessionalism, 368–76; contributory relations
    to state, 353–56, 367–68; dependency rela-
    tions on state, 353–56; deprofessionalization
    of, 354–55, 372; and economic monopoly,
    xiv–xvi, 3, 16–24, 347–49; epistemological
    bases of, 29–37; formative and established
    phases of, 60, 100, 110–11, 347–56; in-
    stitutional spheres of, 41–47; macro-
    sociology of, xvi, 3, 100, 119–20, 309–10,
    346, 360, 368–76; microsociology of, 3,
    26–27; organization for collective action by,
    47–51; and the state, 28–29, 51–54, 139,
    345–47, 352–56, 368n, 368–76. See also
    Normative professions; Professional asso-
    ciations; Scientific professions; Syncretic
    professions
Progressivism, 114, 155
Property tax, 262–64; in Illinois, 265, 266,
    269, 271–73, 276, 277. See also Revenue
    article of Illinois Constitution
Publicity and Public Relations, Special Com-
    mittee on (CBA), 90
Public relations, 89–93, 114, 290, 300
Public Relations Committee (CBA), 87,
    89–92, 114

Public Service, Committee on (CBA), 72
Punishment, 247, 250

Rationalization. See Legal rationalization
Rawls, John, 31
Referendums, 361–62; use of by CBA leader-
    ship, 325
Relation of the Press to Judicial Proceedings,
    Special Committee on (CBA), 92, 94
Religion, 19–20, 43; and CBA membership,
    124, 132, 134. See also Clergy
Religious groups, and CBA, 314
Repertoires of contention, 106
Representativeness. See Inclusiveness
Repressive law, 357–59
Republican Party, 5, 79, 340, 341; affiliation of
    CBA membership with, 132–34; and Consti-
    tutional Convention of 1969–70, 275, 276;
    and judicial elections, 191, 193, 196–97
Reserve infrastructures, 105
Resources, of professional associations,
    101–18; accumulation of, 115–16; and cate-
    gories of professional organization, 105–8;
    concept of, 102–3; consonance of, 112–13;
    historical transitions in portfolios of, 108–
    10; and legal rationalization, 289–90,
    298–303; theoretical dynamics of portfolios
    of, 110–15; two dimensions of, 103–5. See
    also Elite associations; Open associations;
    Universal associations
Responsive law, 358–60
Revenue article of Illinois Constitution, 310,
    325, 335, 337, 339, 342, 362; under Consti-
    tution of 1870, 265–68; chronology of
    amendment to, 261–83
Revised Cities and Villages Act, 238
Revision of Circuit Court Rules, Committee on
    (CBA), 214
Role differentiation, 166–67, 289
Roman Catholic Church, 251, 339
Royko, Mike, 200n
Rueschemeyer, Dietrich, 51n, 174, 355–56

Sacks, Howard, 282–83
Sales tax, 262, 264; in Illinois, 264, 266
San Diego Bar Association, 118
Sandquist, Elroy, 275
Schluchter, Wolfgang, 164–65
School desegregation, 242, 244
Schumpeter, Joseph A., 14, 15, 44, 261–62
Science, 19, 20, 44; as cognitive foundation of
    professions, 29–30, 32–37; normative dis-

course versus, 30–32. *See also* Scientific professions; Technical authority
Scientific professions: epistemological bases of, 32–34; institutional spheres of, 41–47; organization for collective action by, 48–51; professional authority of, 39–41
Seattle-King County Bar Association, 118
Secondary institutional spheres, 146, 219, 260, 283, 305, 344; concept of, 41–47
Securities law, 131
Sedition. *See* Antisedition legislation
Selection of Judges Committee (CBA), 93
Selznick, Philip, 165, 357–58
Sentencing, 250–51, 253, 257
Separation of powers, 6, 42–43, 165, 246, 256–57, 263–64, 362
Settlements, out-of-court, 211–12
Sex offences, 249–50
Shils, Edward, 32
Skogan, Wesley G., 167n
Smelser, Neil, 165
Socialism, 18
Social movement theory, 101
Social sciences, 36, 44
Solicitation of Business by Attorneys, Special Committee on (CBA), 69–70
Solo practitioners, 120; in CBA, 129, 135, 316
Sommers, Lawrence E., 75
Specialties, in CBA, 131–33, 138, 316–19
Standard formula of resistance, 254–56
Starr, Paul, 354
State, 3; and academic profession, 44; adaptive upgrading of mechanism of, 363–65; and civic professionalism, 368–76; concept of, 51n; devolution of, and depoliticization, 365–68; and legal profession, 23–27, 42–43, 51–54, 345–76; legal system evolution in, 356–61; neo-Marxism on legitimation of, 14–15, 21–22; redefinition of powers of, 361–63; Schumpeter on fiscal pressure of, 261. *See also* Ungovernability
State and Municipal Taxation, Committee on (CBA), 267, 272, 279, 282, 329–33
State bar associations, 53–54, 63n, 346; and bar integration movement, 79–84; growth of, 67; inclusiveness of, 120–24; and legal rationalization, 291, 298–304; resource portfolios of, 109–10, 116
State Board of Examiners (Illinois), 76
State constitutive professions, 23, 52
States, 51n; and civic professionalism, 372; court system crisis in, 11–12; fiscal crisis in,

13, 54, 262–64; legal rationalization incidence by, 298, 303–4; legitimacy crisis in, 345–46; professional organization in, 48, 53–54. *See also* State bar associations; United States
Stevenson, Adlai, 267
Stinchcombe, Arthur, 114
Structural differentiation, 25–26, 216, 363–64; concept of, 25–26, 165; of Illinois judicial system, 150–51, 164–67, 169–74; measurement of, 288–89, 299. *See also* Organizational differentiation; Role differentiation
Structural segmentation, in legal profession, 328–29, 343, 374
Substantive rationalization, 25, 286; incidence of, 291–94, 298–300, 303; measurement of, 287–88
Suffolk County Bar Association, 60
Sullivan's Law Directory, 77
Sunderland, Edson R., 160
Supreme Court of Illinois. *See* Illinois Supreme Court
Supreme Court of Kings County, New York, 9
Supreme Court of United States. *See* U.S. Supreme Court
Survey method, 285–86, 304
Syncretic professions: epistemological bases of, 34–36; institutional spheres of, 48–51; professional authority of, 40–41

Tangible resources, 103–5
Taxation, 43, 45, 145, 261–83. *See also* Revenue article of Illinois Constitution
Tax law, 131, 318
Taxpayers Federation of Illinois, 271
Technical authority, 140–41, 147, 174, 216–17, 259–60, 283, 309, 331; and civic professionalism, 374–76; concept of, 37–41; and institutional spheres, 45–47. *See also* Expertise
Technocracy, 21
Tenure: of CBA leadership, 322; of judges, 149, 152–53, 170–71, 183, 201
Thorp v. Mahin, 276
Tillich, Paul, 33–34
Tomei, Peter, 276, 283
Toulmin, Stephen, 31
Trial law, 318
Trow, M., 311
Trumbull, Lyman, 65
Trumbull, William, 147, 236

Turnover, in elites, 312, 322, 326, 343
Tydings Committee, 236

Unauthorized Practice Committee (CBA), 69
Unauthorized practice of law, 62–63, 69–72, 77–78
Ungovernability, 3–27, 28, 54, 119, 139, 345–47, 373; consequences of, 4–13; and professions, 16–22; theories of, 13–16
Uniform Commercial Code, 240, 283, 342
Uniform legislation, 337, 360, 366; efforts at implementation of, as indicator of rationalization, 287, 291–92, 298, 303. *See also* Codification
Uniform Probate Code, 291
Union League Club, 340
Unions, Chicago bar attitudes toward, 134
United States: academic profession in, 44; civic professionalism in, 372–73; crises of postwar, 145; forms of bar associations in, 109–12; legal order evolution in, 358–60; legal profession emergence in, 59–63; legal rationalization in, 25, 26, 284–305; medical profession in, 17, 21; military profession in, 43–44; national professional organizations in, 48, 53–54; normative professions in, 36; and ungovernability, 5–12, 16, 345–46. *See also* States
Universal associations, 140; concept of, 106–8; inclusiveness of (*see* Inclusiveness); and legal rationalization, 289, 291, 298–303; resource accumulations by, 116; specialties in, 138; theoretical dynamics of, 110–15; transition to, 108–10, 119
Universities: legal education beginnings in, 62; and legal profession, 337; political involvement of, 44; professional legitimation by, 21–22. *See also* Academic profession; Law schools
University of Chicago, 127–29, 148, 314–16
University of Illinois, 127–29, 235
University of Michigan, 127–29

University of Wisconsin, 127–29
U.S. Congress, 9, 10, 61, 240–41; and antisubversion legislation, 227–33, 255; and civil rights acts, 241, 249
U.S. Court of Appeals, 10
U.S. Supreme Court, 78, 80, 236, 255, 256, 338; Anastaplo case of, 236–37; public confidence in, 9

Valukas, Anton, 200n
Veblen, Thorstein, 76
Vertical organization fusion, 169
Vertical role fusion, 169
Voluntary associations. *See* Open associations
Voting rights, 242, 254

Watanuki, Joji, 15
Watson, Richard, 147n, 153n
Weber, Max, 15; legal rationalization theory of, 23–26, 164–71, 286–87, 290–91, 295–96, 359–60; professional monopoly theory of, 20–21, 347–49, 360; on sociology of professions and law, 23–26, 360; on the state, 51n
Wechsler, Herbert, 246, 257
Weisberg, Bernard, 276
Western civilization, and legal rationalization, 24, 164–65
Wham, Benjamin, 236
Wigmore, John, 80
Wildavsky, Aaron, 4–5, 8
Wilson, P. A., 17–19, 22–23, 37–38, 368
Wiretapping, 230–33, 253, 255, 362
Wisconsin, criminal law in, 247
Witwer, Samuel, 275–76, 282–83
Women, 106, 348; in CBA, 314
World War I, 69, 80, 86, 87, 261
World War II, 85–86, 99, 109, 264, 265

Yale University, 127–29, 314–16
Younger Members Committee (CBA), 88–89, 97, 195